RETURN TO PERDITION

VERTIGO CRIME

WRITER
MAX ALLAN COLLINS

ART
TERRY BEATTY

LETTERS
CLEM ROBINS

RETURN TO PERDITION

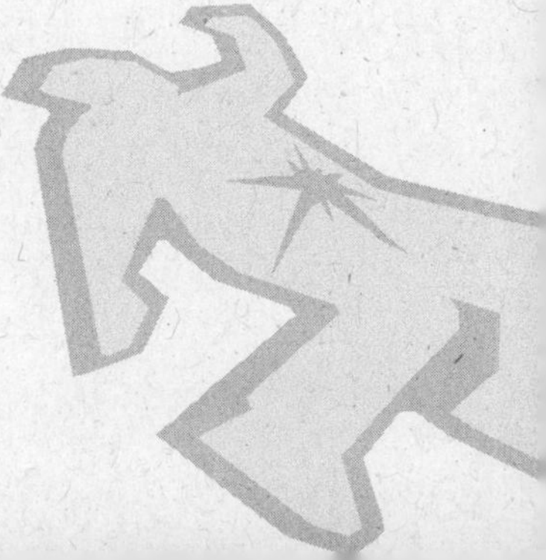

Will Dennis Editor
Ian Sattler Director Editorial, Special Projects and Archival Editions
Robbin Brosterman Design Director - Books

Karen Berger Senior VP - Executive Editor, Vertigo
Bob Harras VP - Editor in Chief

Diane Nelson President
Dan DiDio and Jim Lee Co-Publishers
Geoff Johns Chief Creative Officer
John Rood Executive VP - Sales, Marketing and Business Development
Amy Genkins Senior VP - Business and Legal Affairs
Nairi Gardiner Senior VP - Finance
Jeff Boison VP - Publishing Operations
Mark Chiarello VP - Art Direction and Design
John Cunningham VP - Marketing
Terri Cunningham VP - Talent Relations and Services
Alison Gill Senior VP - Manufacturing and Operations
David Hyde VP - Publicity
Hank Kanalz Senior VP - Digital
Jay Kogan VP - Business and Legal Affairs, Publishing
Jack Mahan VP - Business Affairs, Talent
Nick Napolitano VP - Manufacturing Administration
Sue Pohja VP - Book Sales
Courtney Simmons Senior VP - Publicity
Bob Wayne Senior VP - Sales

Special thanks to Christopher Jones and Bart King.

RETURN TO PERDITION
VERTIGO CRIME

Published by DC Comics, 1700 Broadway, New York, NY 10019.
Printed in USA. First Printing. DC Comics, a Warner Bros. Entertainment Company.
HC ISBN: 978-1-4012-2383-0 SC ISBN: 978-1-4012-2384-7

SUSTAINABLE FORESTRY INITIATIVE
Certified Sourcing
www.sfiprogram.org
This label applies to the text stock.

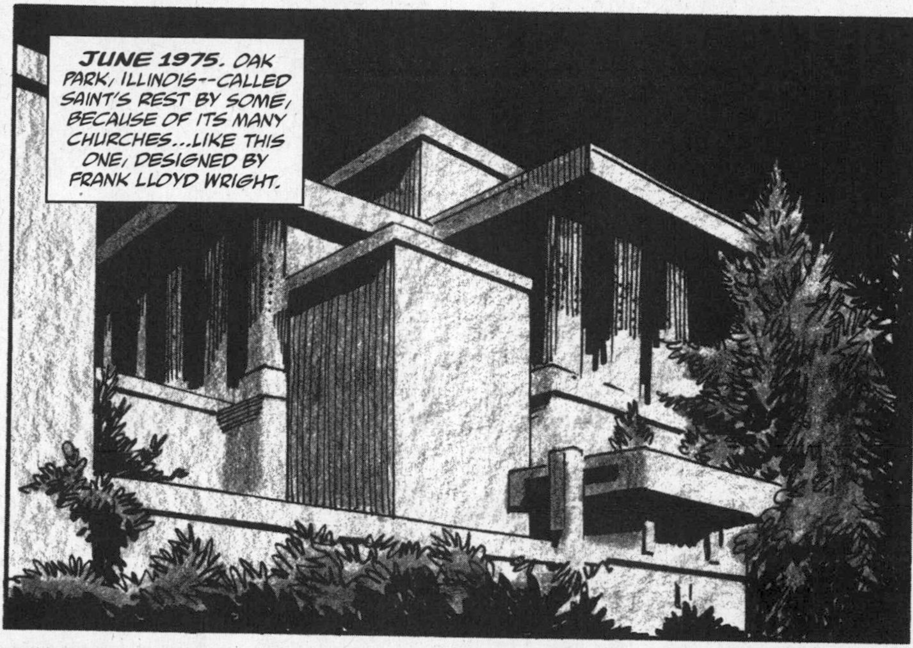
JUNE 1975. OAK PARK, ILLINOIS--CALLED SAINT'S REST BY SOME, BECAUSE OF ITS MANY CHURCHES...LIKE THIS ONE, DESIGNED BY FRANK LLOYD WRIGHT.

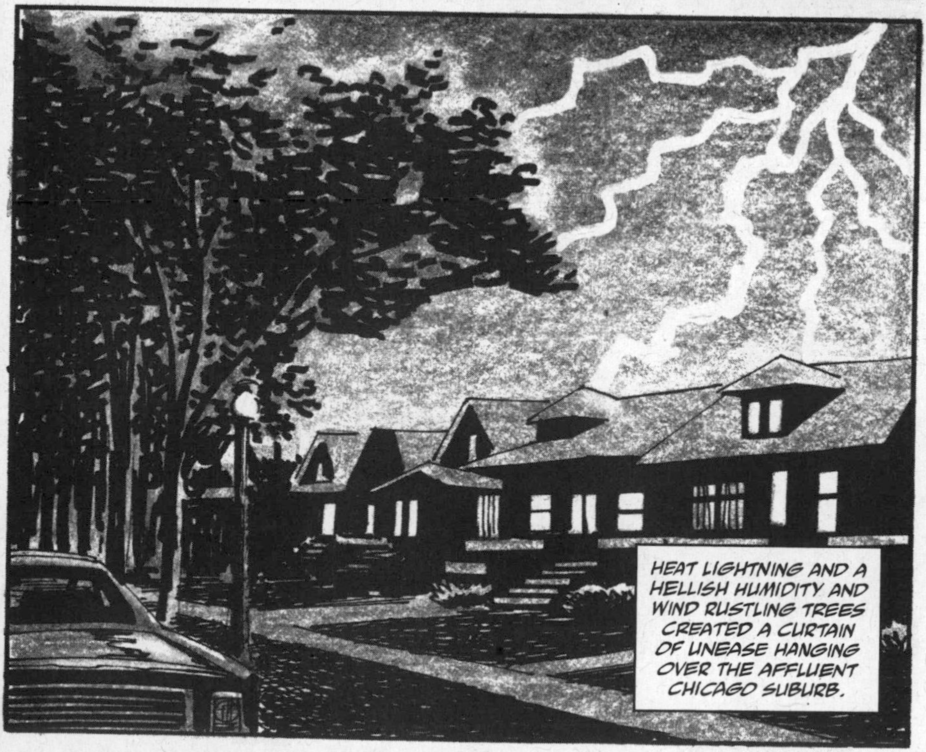
HEAT LIGHTNING AND A HELLISH HUMIDITY AND WIND RUSTLING TREES CREATED A CURTAIN OF UNEASE HANGING OVER THE AFFLUENT CHICAGO SUBURB.

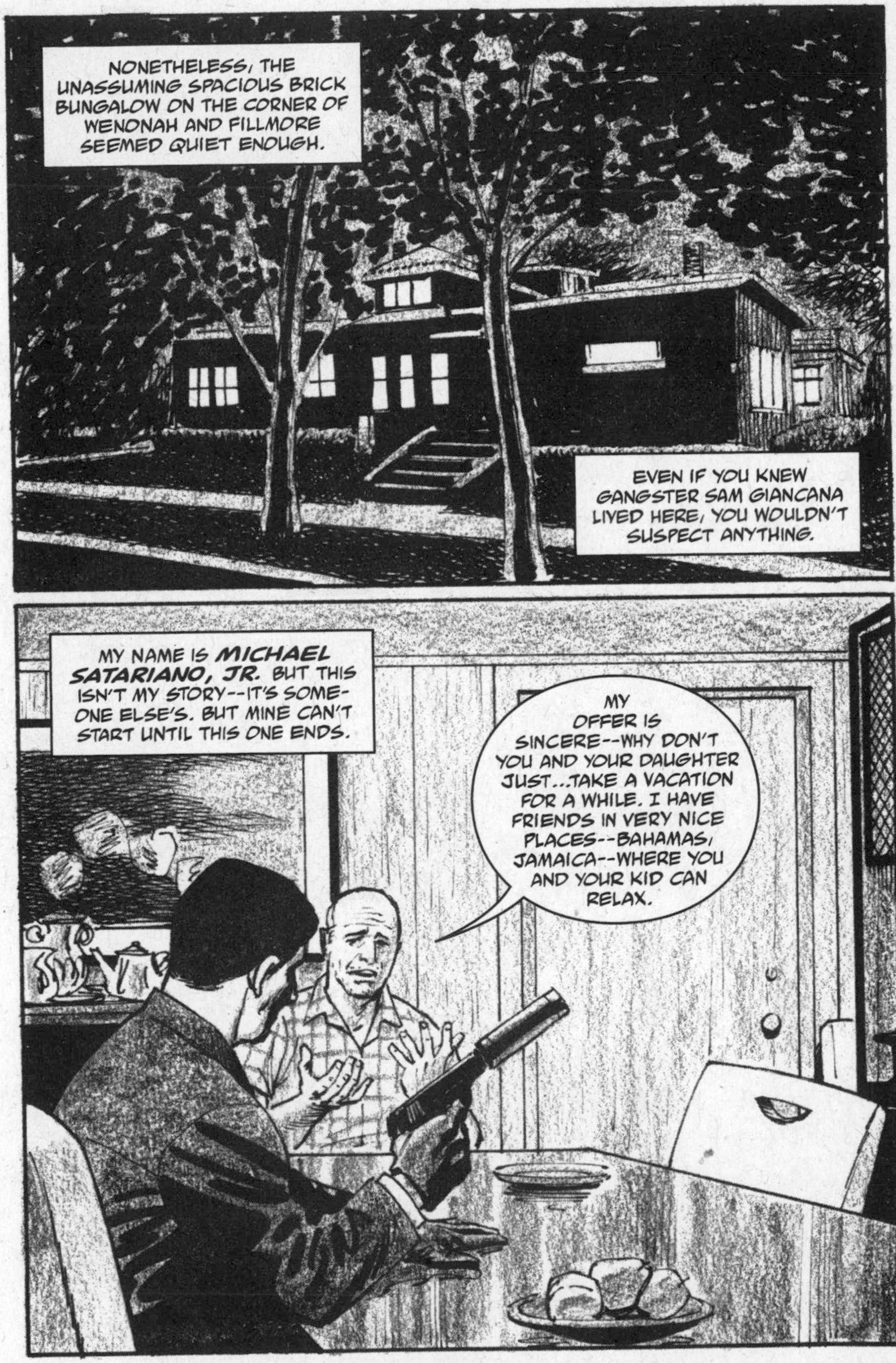
NONETHELESS, THE UNASSUMING SPACIOUS BRICK BUNGALOW ON THE CORNER OF WENONAH AND FILLMORE SEEMED QUIET ENOUGH.
EVEN IF YOU KNEW GANGSTER SAM GIANCANA LIVED HERE, YOU WOULDN'T SUSPECT ANYTHING.
MY NAME IS MICHAEL SATARIANO, JR. BUT THIS ISN'T MY STORY--IT'S SOME-ONE ELSE'S. BUT MINE CAN'T START UNTIL THIS ONE ENDS.
MY OFFER IS SINCERE--WHY DON'T YOU AND YOUR DAUGHTER JUST...TAKE A VACATION FOR A WHILE. I HAVE FRIENDS IN VERY NICE PLACES--BAHAMAS, JAMAICA--WHERE YOU AND YOUR KID CAN RELAX.

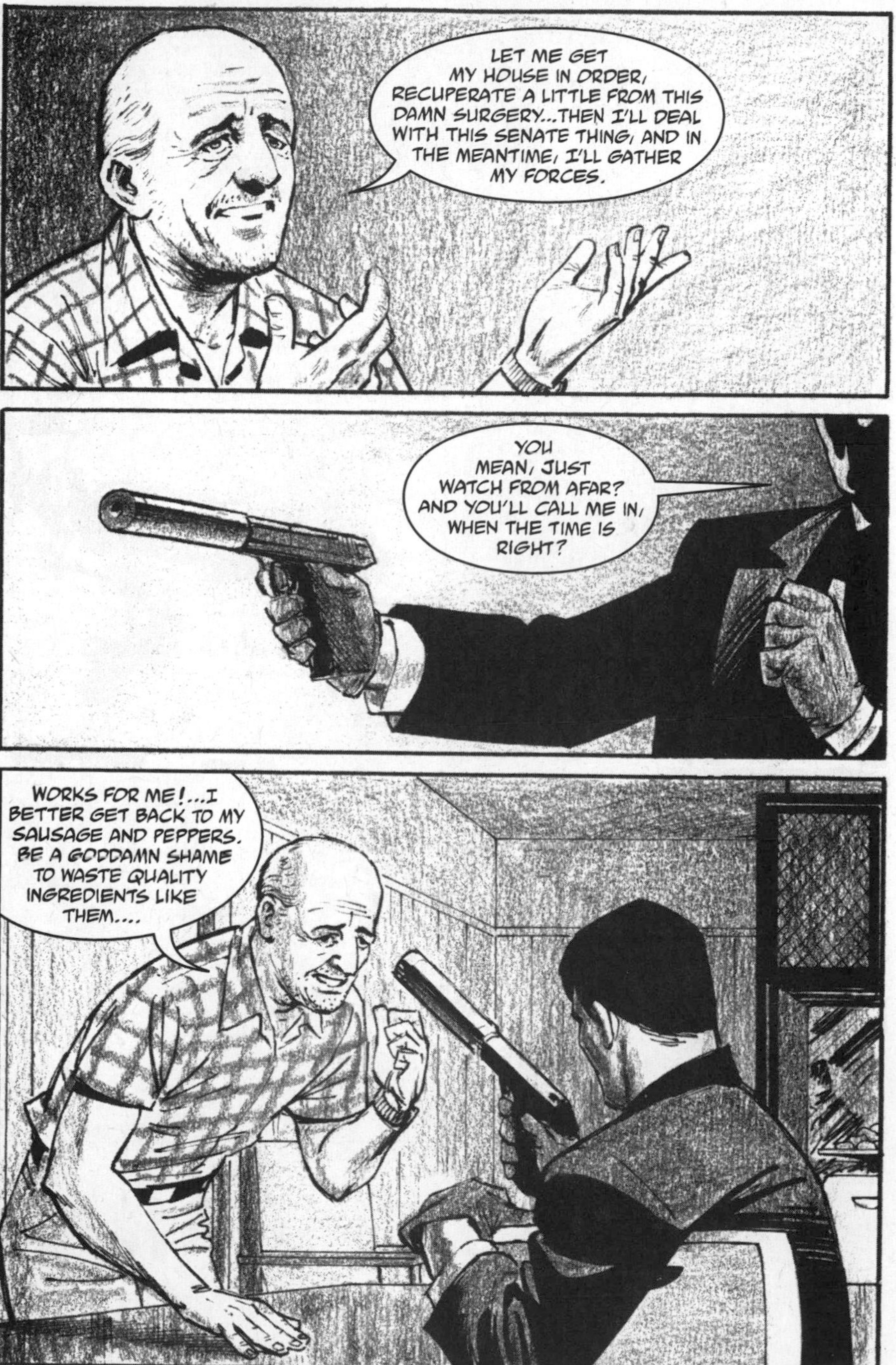
LET ME GET MY HOUSE IN ORDER, RECUPERATE A LITTLE FROM THIS DAMN SURGERY...THEN I'LL DEAL WITH THIS SENATE THING, AND IN THE MEANTIME, I'LL GATHER MY FORCES.
YOU MEAN, JUST WATCH FROM AFAR? AND YOU'LL CALL ME IN, WHEN THE TIME IS RIGHT?
WORKS FOR ME!...I BETTER GET BACK TO MY SAUSAGE AND PEPPERS. BE A GODDAMN SHAME TO WASTE QUALITY INGREDIENTS LIKE THEM....

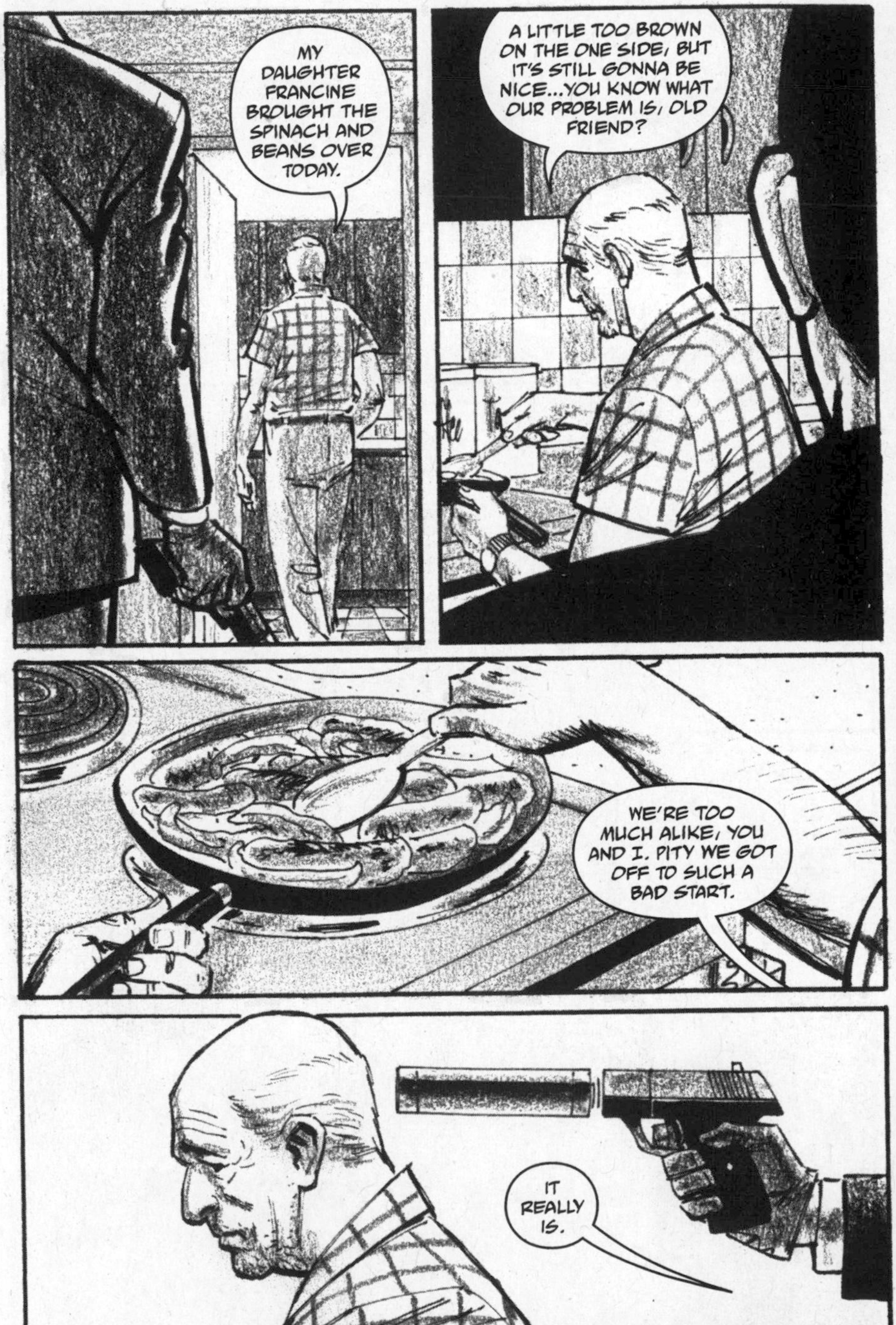
MY DAUGHTER FRANCINE BROUGHT THE SPINACH AND BEANS OVER TODAY.
A LITTLE TOO BROWN ON THE ONE SIDE, BUT IT'S STILL GONNA BE NICE...YOU KNOW WHAT OUR PROBLEM IS, OLD FRIEND?
WE'RE TOO MUCH ALIKE, YOU AND I. PITY WE GOT OFF TO SUCH A BAD START.
IT REALLY IS.

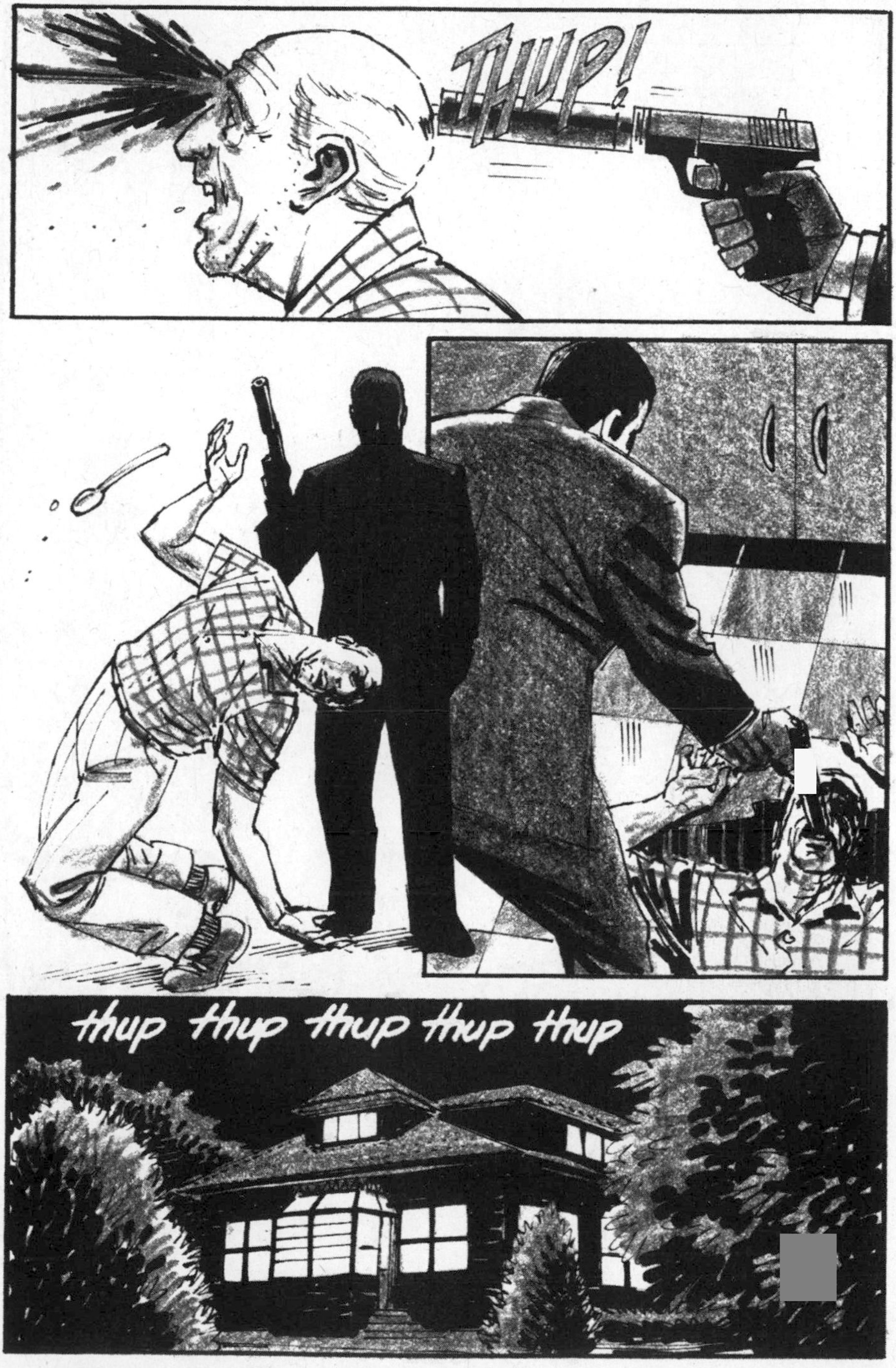
THUP!
thup thup thup thup thup

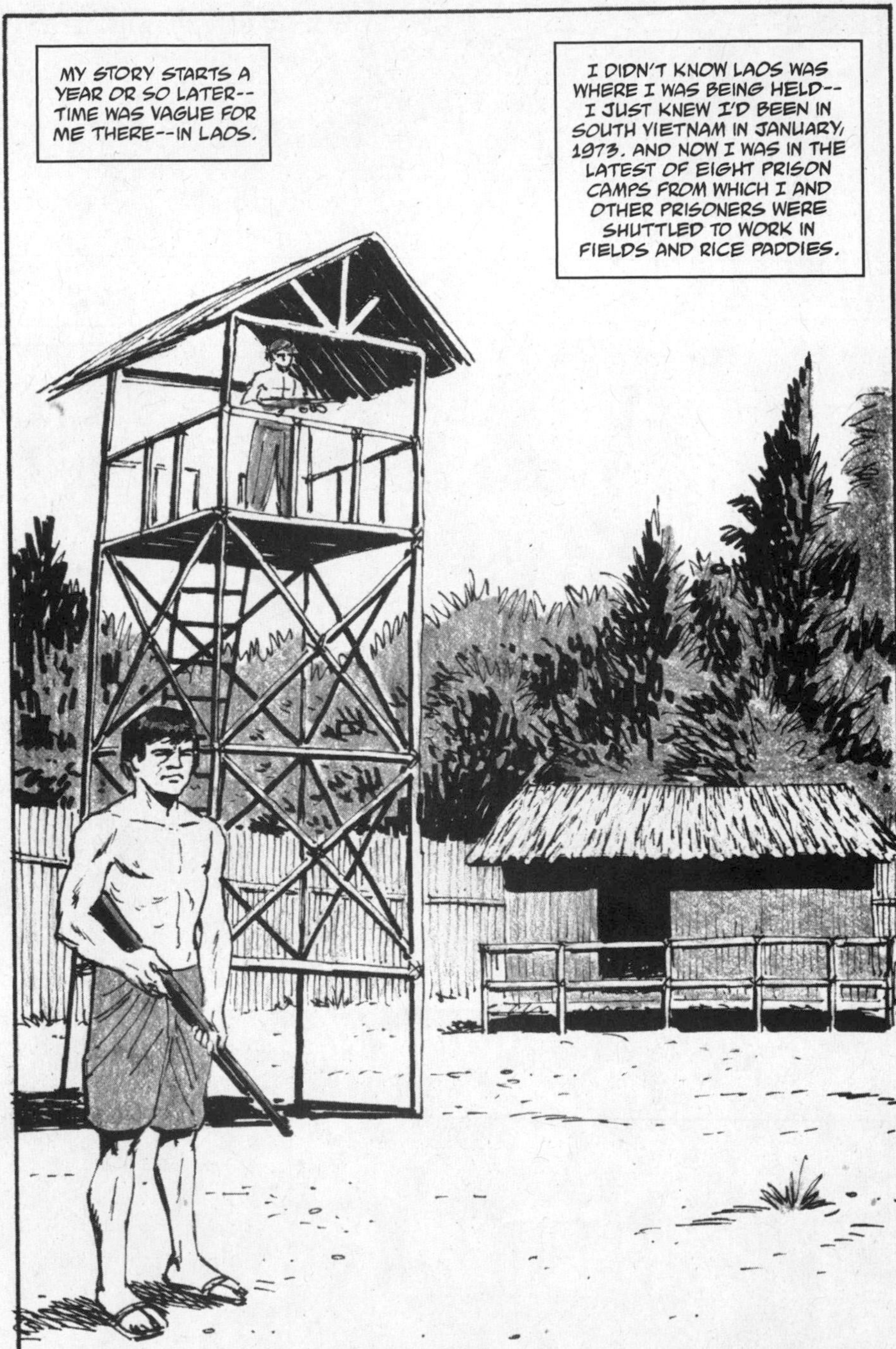
MY STORY STARTS A YEAR OR SO LATER--TIME WAS VAGUE FOR ME THERE--IN LAOS.
I DIDN'T KNOW LAOS WAS WHERE I WAS BEING HELD--I JUST KNEW I'D BEEN IN SOUTH VIETNAM IN JANUARY, 1973. AND NOW I WAS IN THE LATEST OF EIGHT PRISON CAMPS FROM WHICH I AND OTHER PRISONERS WERE SHUTTLED TO WORK IN FIELDS AND RICE PADDIES.

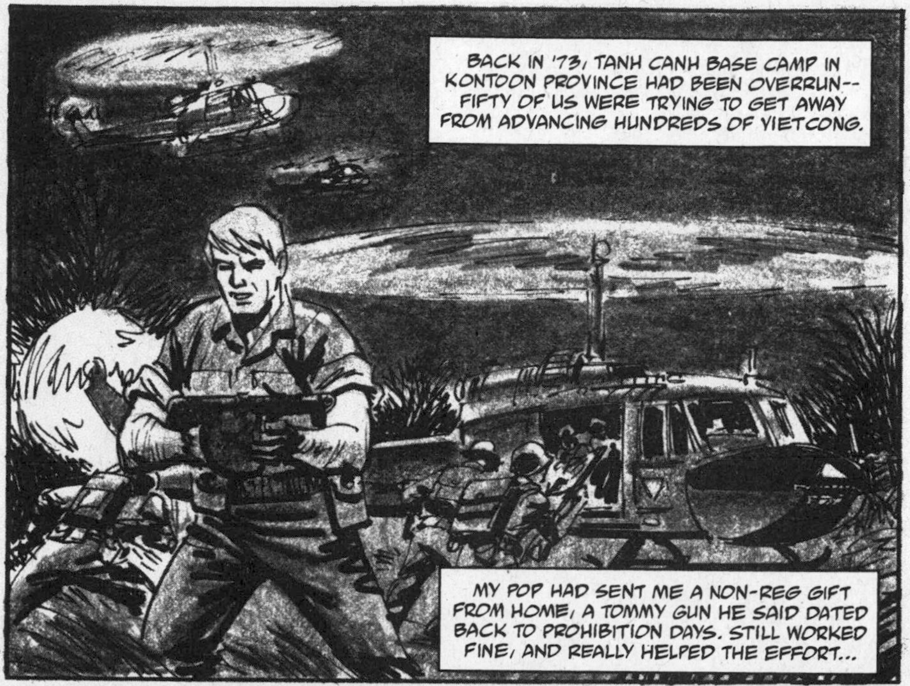
BACK IN '73, TANH CANH BASE CAMP IN KONTOON PROVINCE HAD BEEN OVERRUN-- FIFTY OF US WERE TRYING TO GET AWAY FROM ADVANCING HUNDREDS OF VIETCONG.
MY POP HAD SENT ME A NON-REG GIFT FROM HOME, A TOMMY GUN HE SAID DATED BACK TO PROHIBITION DAYS. STILL WORKED FINE, AND REALLY HELPED THE EFFORT...
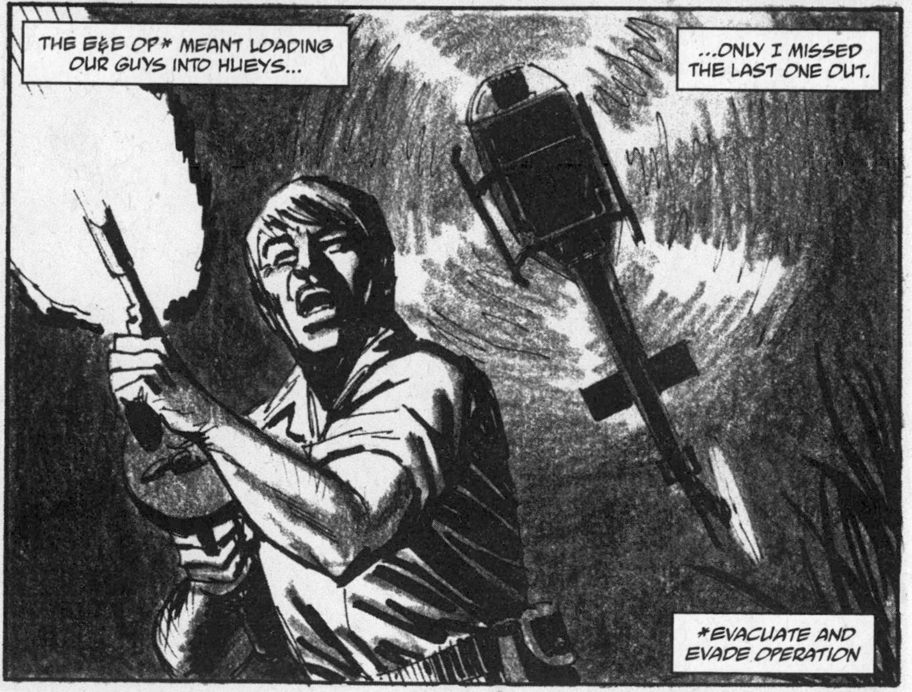
THE E&E OP* MEANT LOADING OUR GUYS INTO HUEYS...
...ONLY I MISSED THE LAST ONE OUT.
*EVACUATE AND EVADE OPERATION

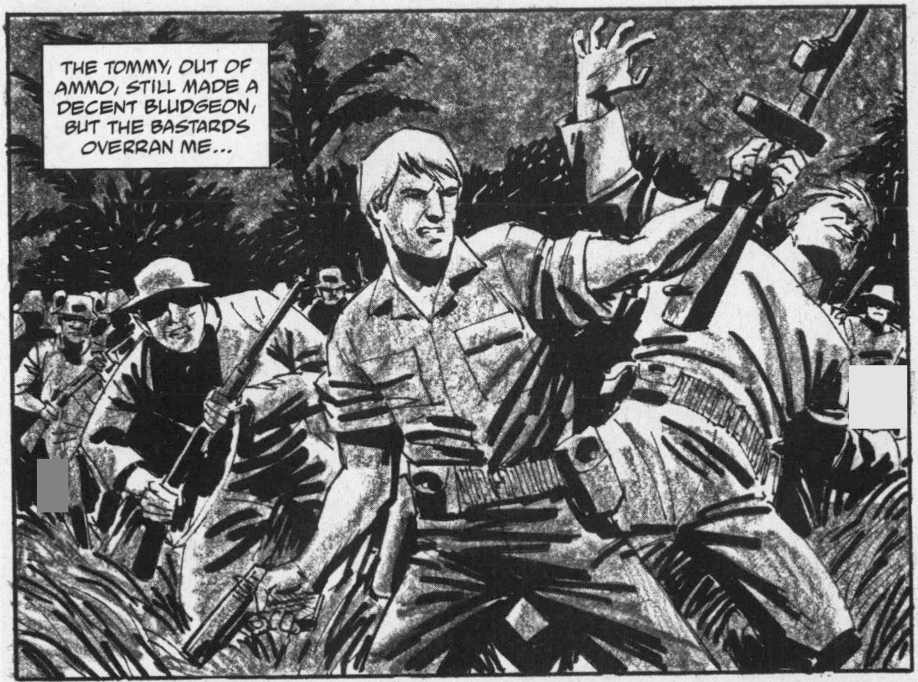
THE TOMMY, OUT OF AMMO, STILL MADE A DECENT BLUDGEON, BUT THE BASTARDS OVERRAN ME...

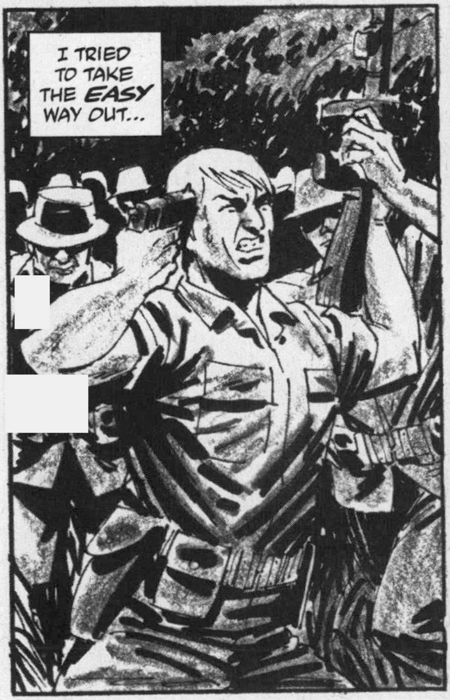
I TRIED TO TAKE THE *EASY* WAY OUT...

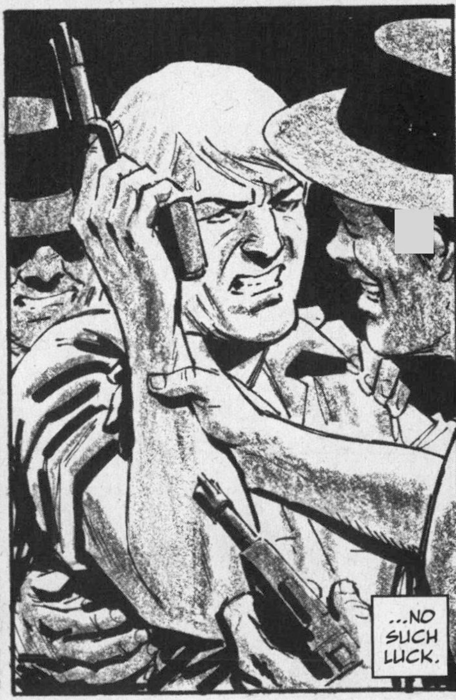
...NO SUCH LUCK.

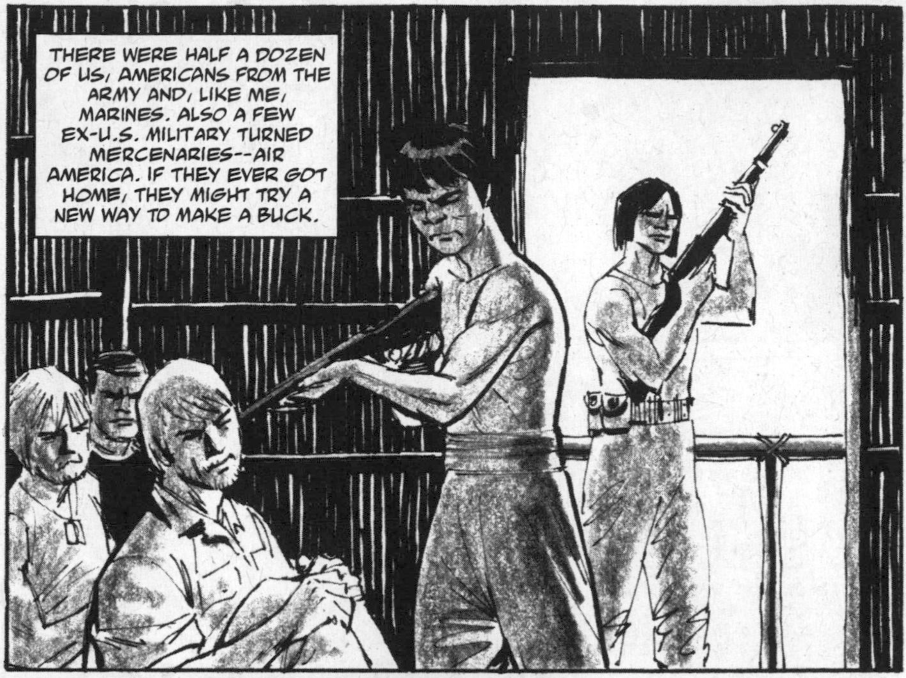
THERE WERE HALF A DOZEN OF US, AMERICANS FROM THE ARMY AND, LIKE ME, MARINES. ALSO A FEW EX-U.S. MILITARY TURNED MERCENARIES--AIR AMERICA. IF THEY EVER GOT HOME, THEY MIGHT TRY A NEW WAY TO MAKE A BUCK.

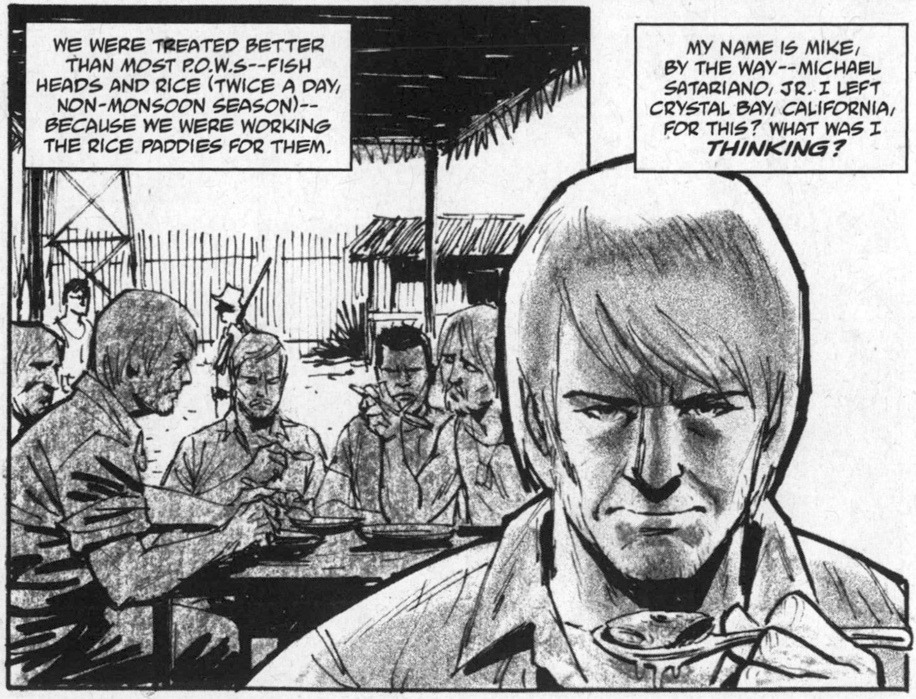
WE WERE TREATED BETTER THAN MOST P.O.W.S--FISH HEADS AND RICE (TWICE A DAY, NON-MONSOON SEASON)--BECAUSE WE WERE WORKING THE RICE PADDIES FOR THEM.
MY NAME IS MIKE, BY THE WAY--MICHAEL SATARIANO, JR. I LEFT CRYSTAL BAY, CALIFORNIA, FOR THIS? WHAT WAS I THINKING?

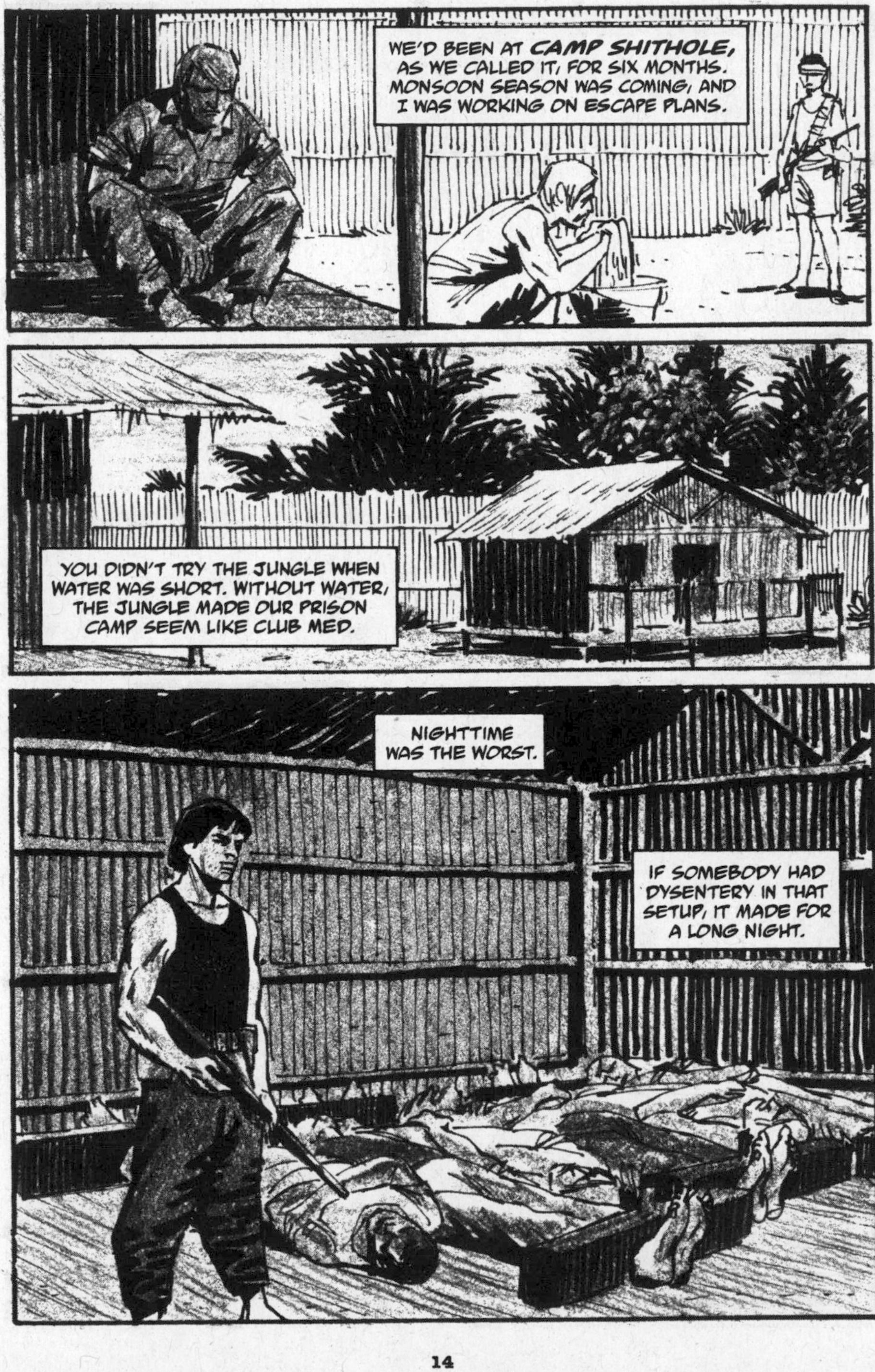
WE'D BEEN AT CAMP SHITHOLE, AS WE CALLED IT, FOR SIX MONTHS. MONSOON SEASON WAS COMING, AND I WAS WORKING ON ESCAPE PLANS.
YOU DIDN'T TRY THE JUNGLE WHEN WATER WAS SHORT. WITHOUT WATER, THE JUNGLE MADE OUR PRISON CAMP SEEM LIKE CLUB MED.
NIGHTTIME WAS THE WORST.
IF SOMEBODY HAD DYSENTERY IN THAT SETUP, IT MADE FOR A LONG NIGHT.

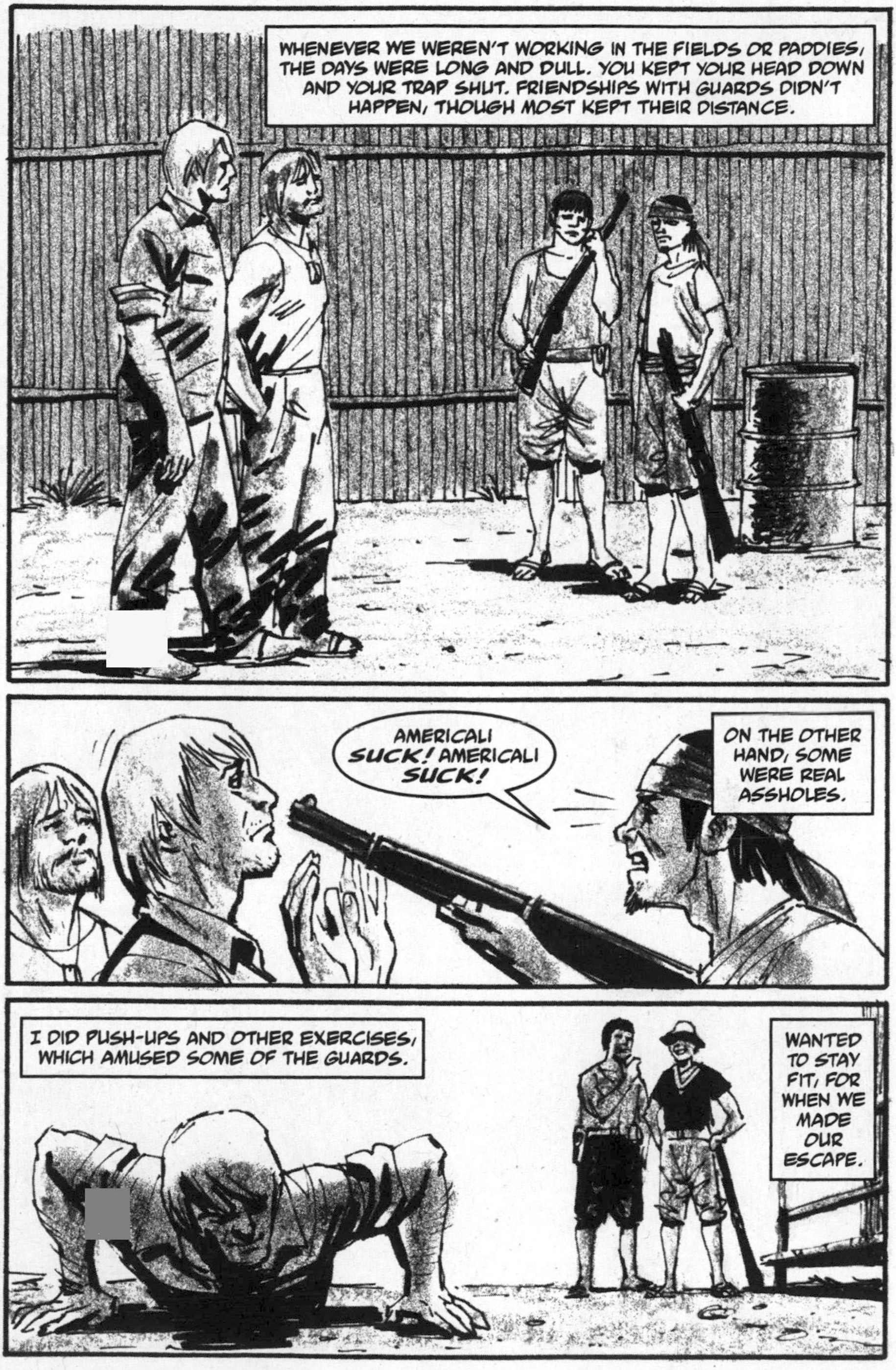
WHENEVER WE WEREN'T WORKING IN THE FIELDS OR PADDIES, THE DAYS WERE LONG AND DULL. YOU KEPT YOUR HEAD DOWN AND YOUR TRAP SHUT. FRIENDSHIPS WITH GUARDS DIDN'T HAPPEN, THOUGH MOST KEPT THEIR DISTANCE.
AMERICALI SUCK! AMERICALI SUCK!
ON THE OTHER HAND, SOME WERE REAL ASSHOLES.
I DID PUSH-UPS AND OTHER EXERCISES, WHICH AMUSED SOME OF THE GUARDS.
WANTED TO STAY FIT, FOR WHEN WE MADE OUR ESCAPE.

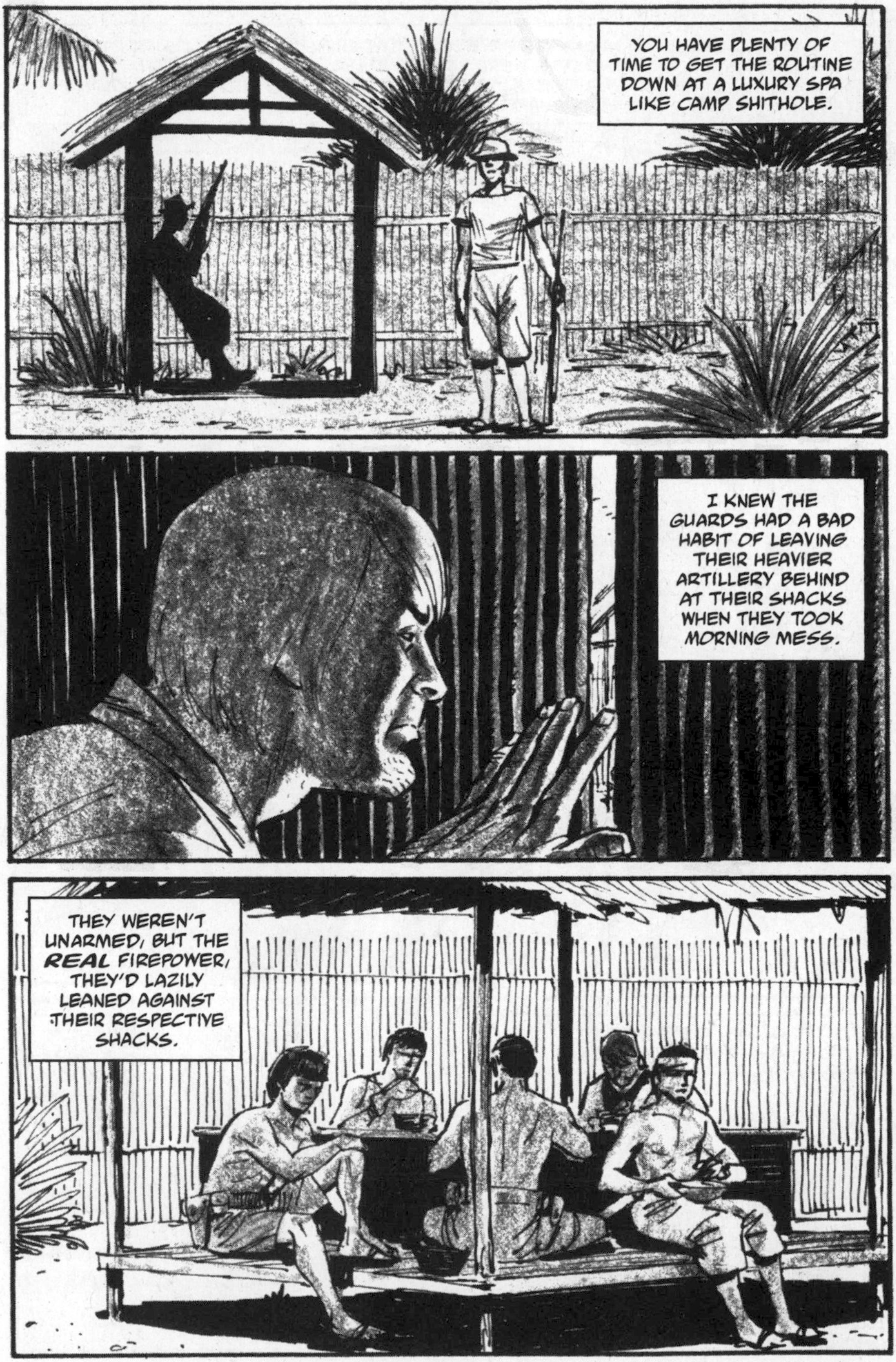
YOU HAVE PLENTY OF TIME TO GET THE ROUTINE DOWN AT A LUXURY SPA LIKE CAMP SHITHOLE.
I KNEW THE GUARDS HAD A BAD HABIT OF LEAVING THEIR HEAVIER ARTILLERY BEHIND AT THEIR SHACKS WHEN THEY TOOK MORNING MESS.
THEY WEREN'T UNARMED, BUT THE REAL FIREPOWER, THEY'D LAZILY LEANED AGAINST THEIR RESPECTIVE SHACKS.

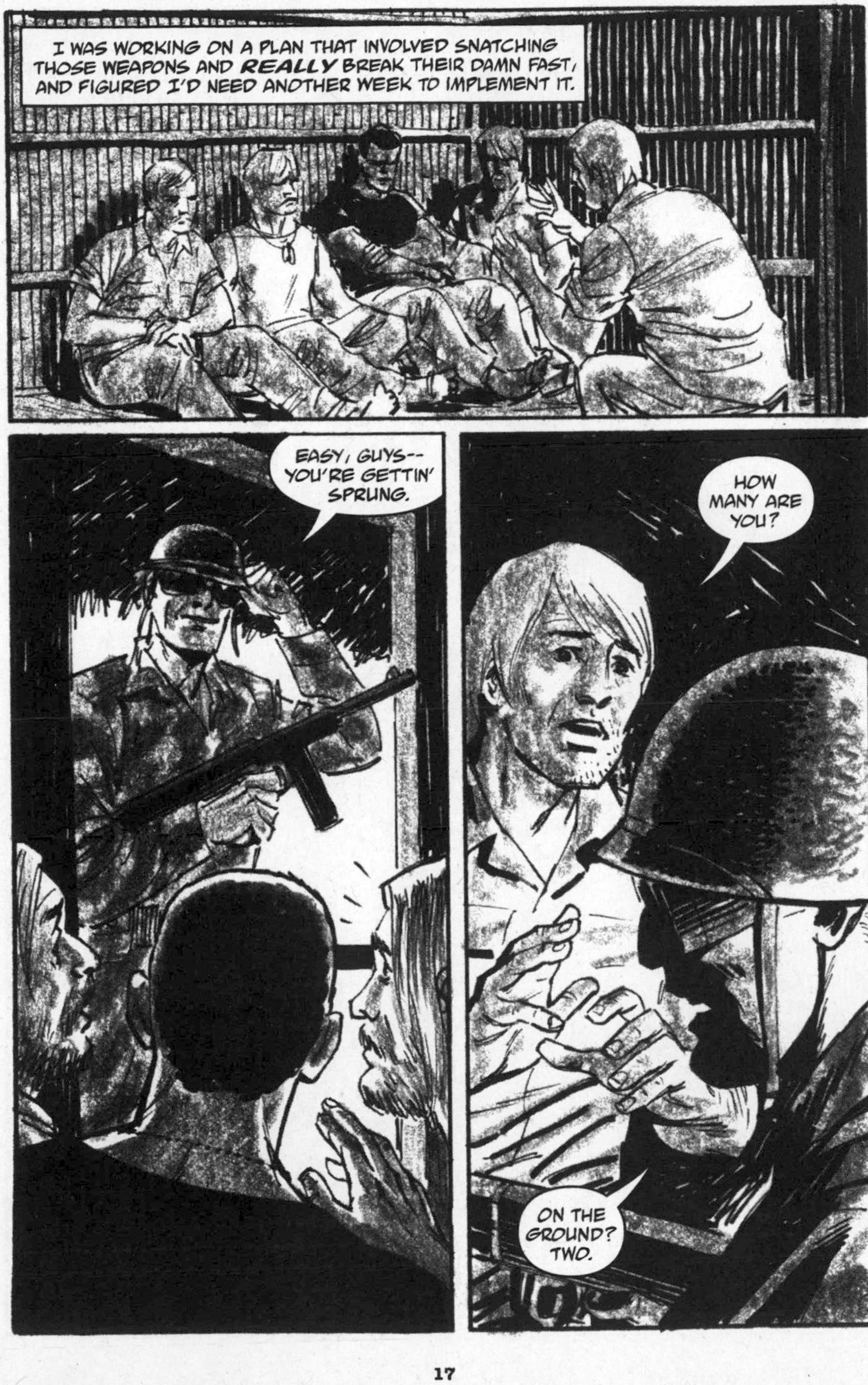
I WAS WORKING ON A PLAN THAT INVOLVED SNATCHING THOSE WEAPONS AND REALLY BREAK THEIR DAMN FAST, AND FIGURED I'D NEED ANOTHER WEEK TO IMPLEMENT IT.
EASY, GUYS-- YOU'RE GETTIN' SPRUNG.
HOW MANY ARE YOU?
ON THE GROUND? TWO.

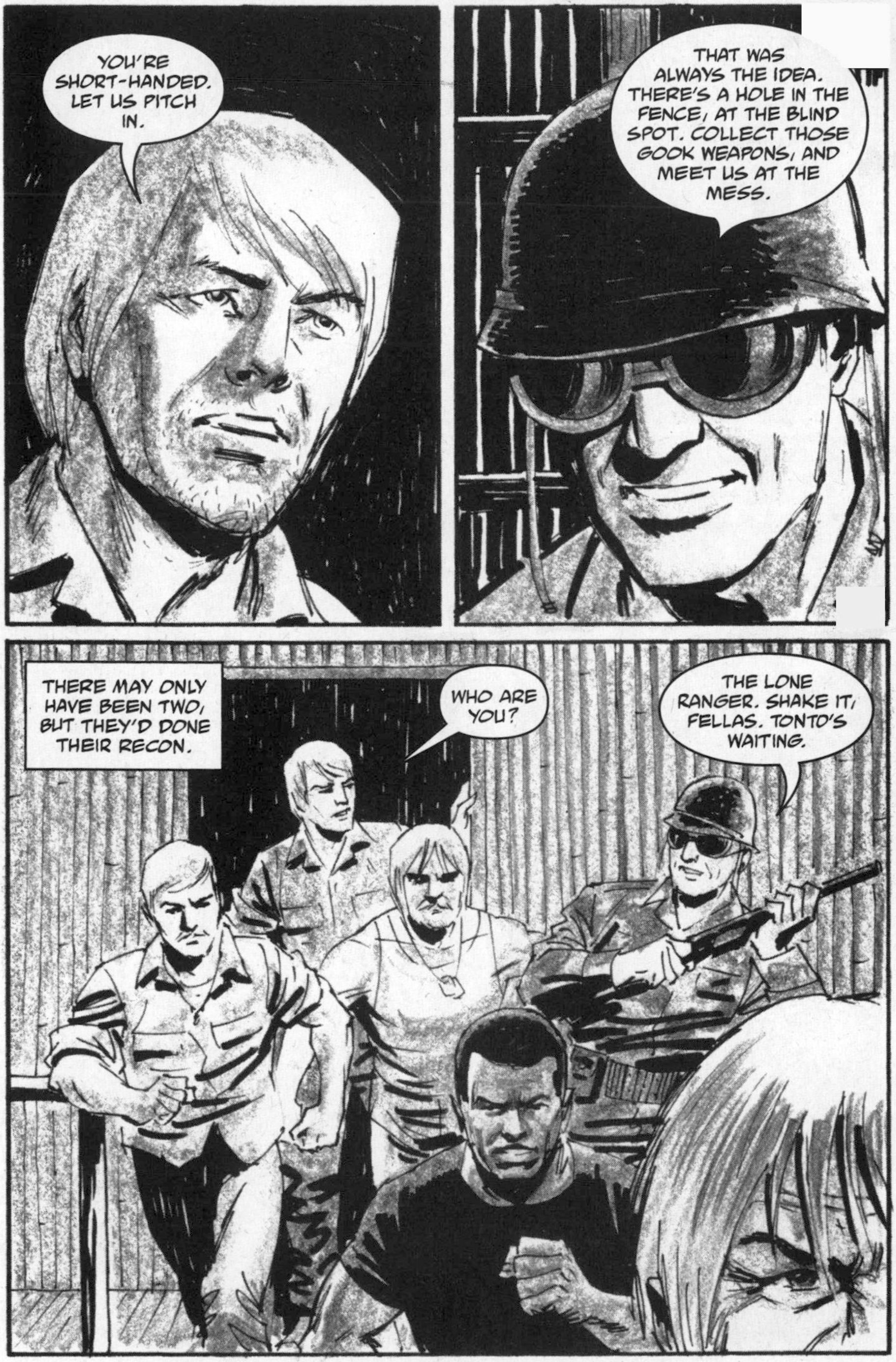
YOU'RE SHORT-HANDED. LET US PITCH IN.
THAT WAS ALWAYS THE IDEA. THERE'S A HOLE IN THE FENCE, AT THE BLIND SPOT. COLLECT THOSE GOOK WEAPONS, AND MEET US AT THE MESS.
THERE MAY ONLY HAVE BEEN TWO, BUT THEY'D DONE THEIR RECON.
WHO ARE YOU?
THE LONE RANGER. SHAKE IT, FELLAS. TONTO'S WAITING.

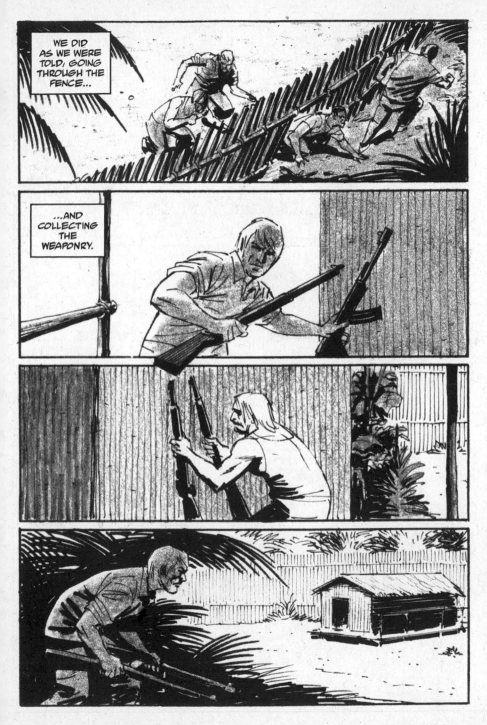

WE DID AS WE WERE TOLD, GOING THROUGH THE FENCE...

...AND COLLECTING THE WEAPONRY.

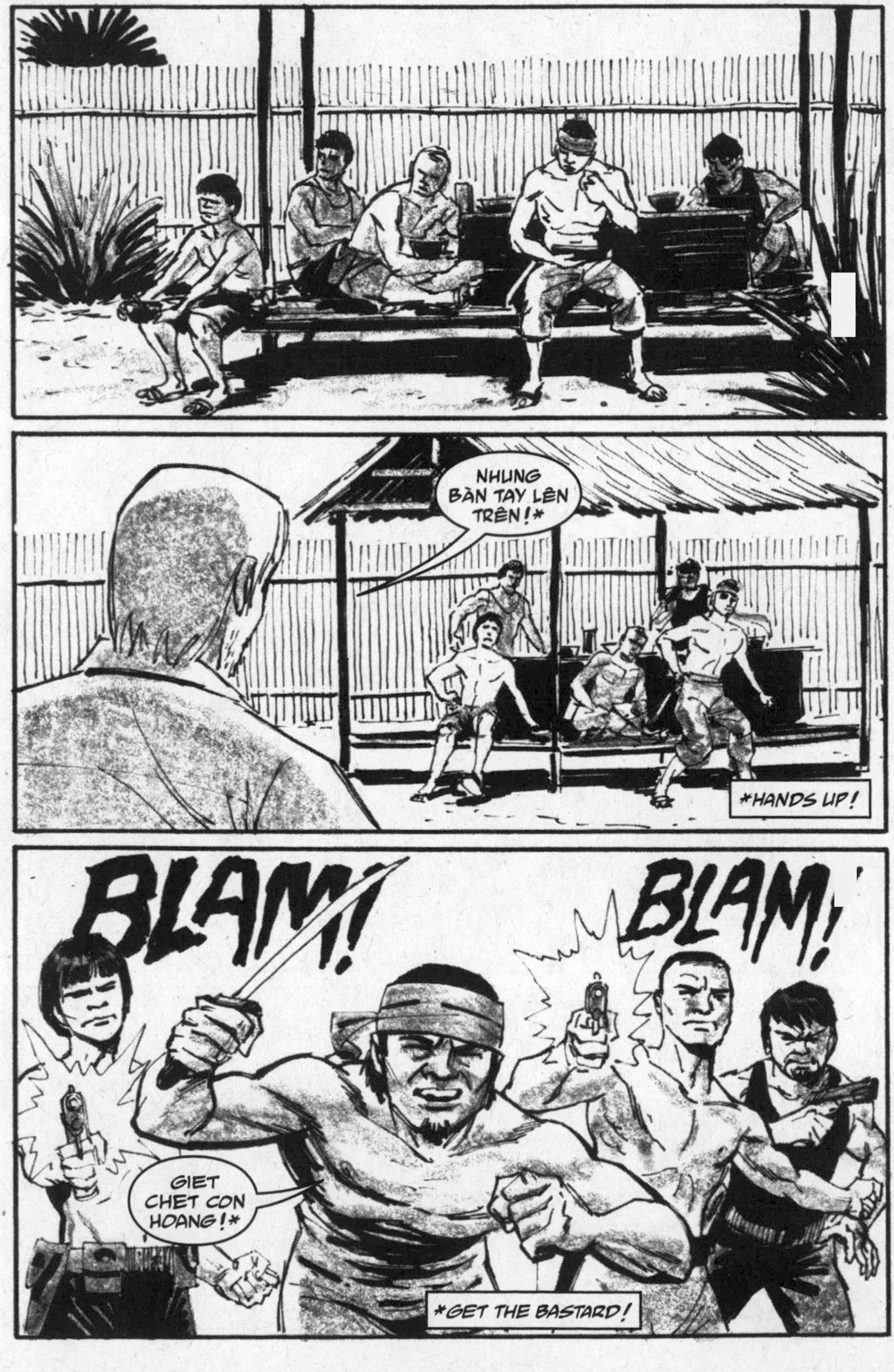
NHUNG BÀN TAY LÊN TRÊN!*
*HANDS UP!
BLAM!
BLAM!
GIET CHET CON HOANG!*
*GET THE BASTARD!

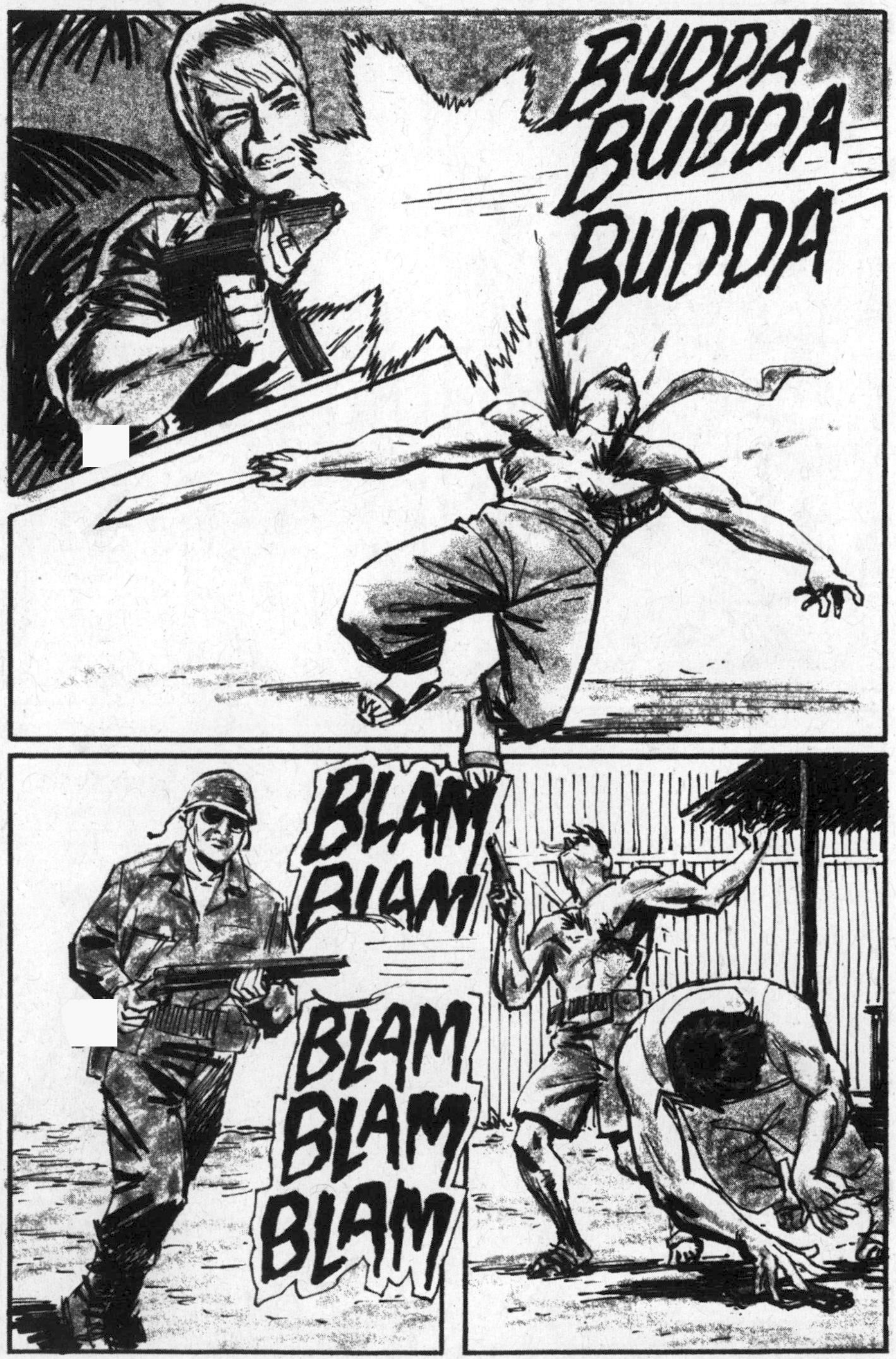
BUDDA
BUDDA
BUDDA
BLAM
BLAM
BLAM
BLAM
BLAM
BLAM

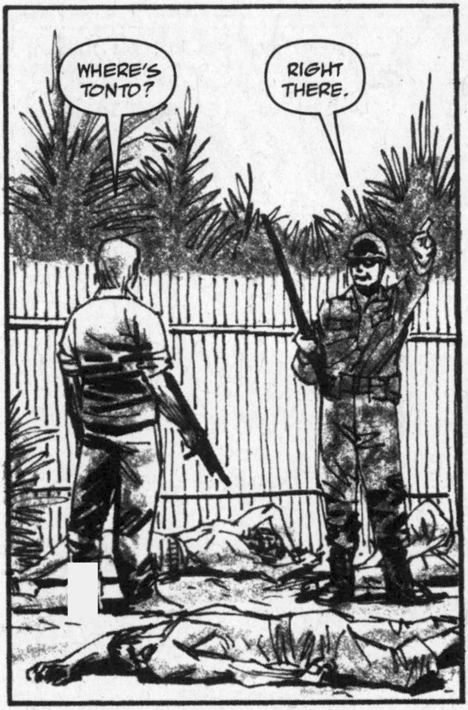
WHERE'S TONTO?
RIGHT THERE.

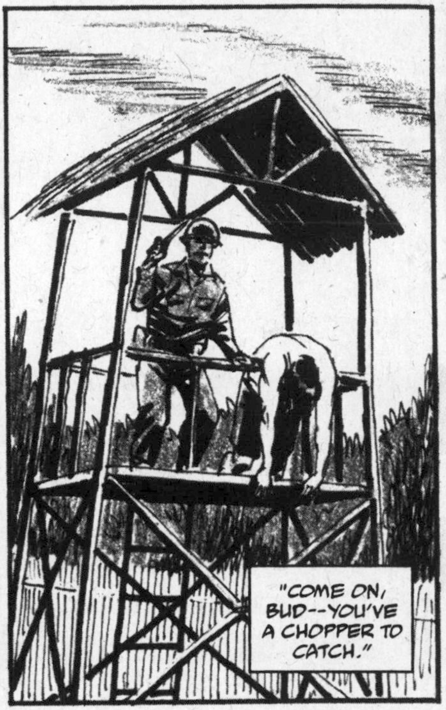
"COME ON, BUD--YOU'VE A CHOPPER TO CATCH."

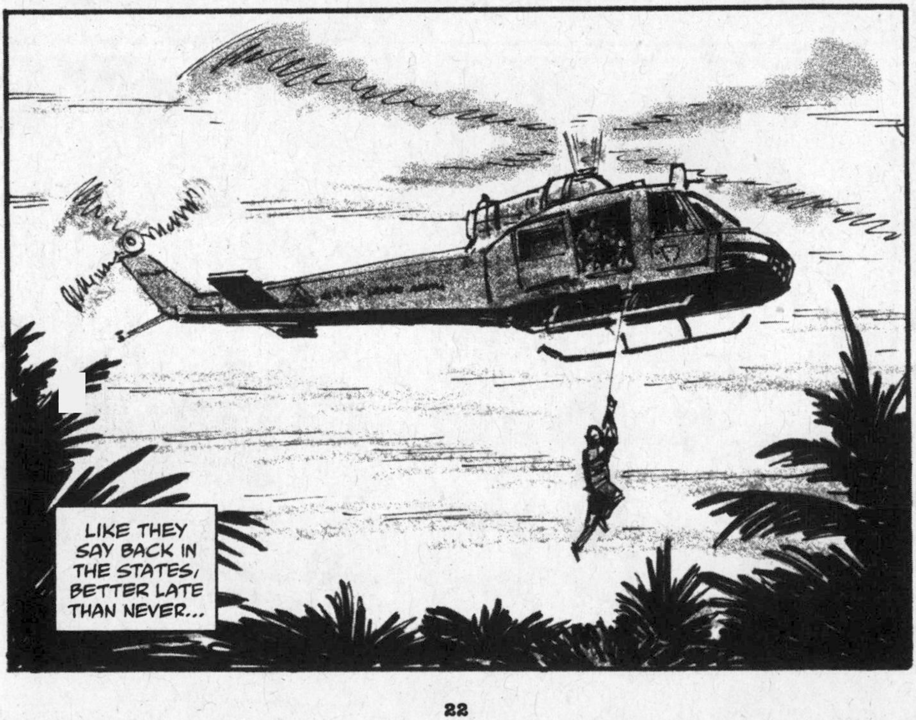
LIKE THEY SAY BACK IN THE STATES, BETTER LATE THAN NEVER...

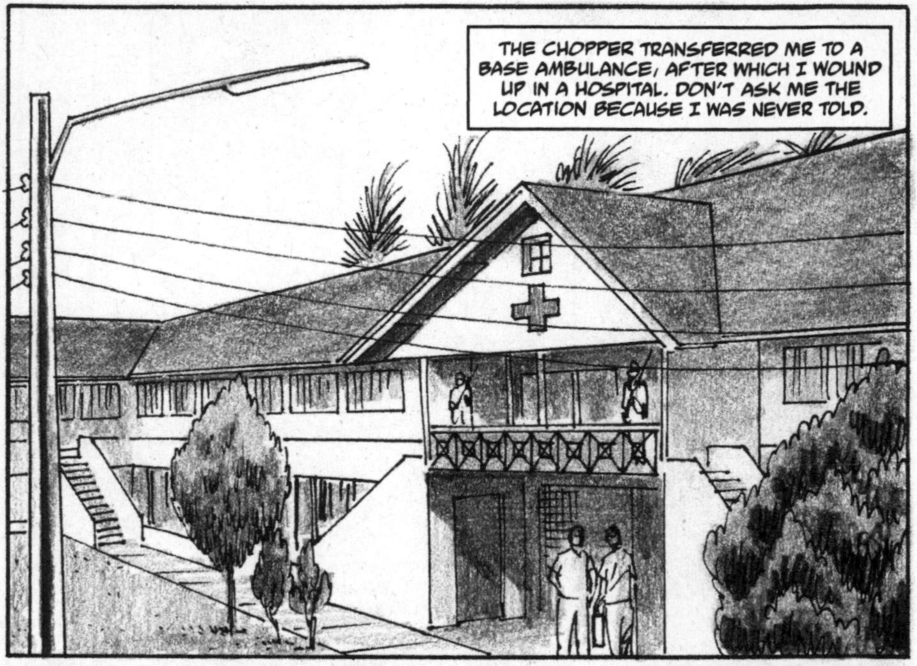
THE CHOPPER TRANSFERRED ME TO A BASE AMBULANCE, AFTER WHICH I WOUND UP IN A HOSPITAL. DON'T ASK ME THE LOCATION BECAUSE I WAS NEVER TOLD.

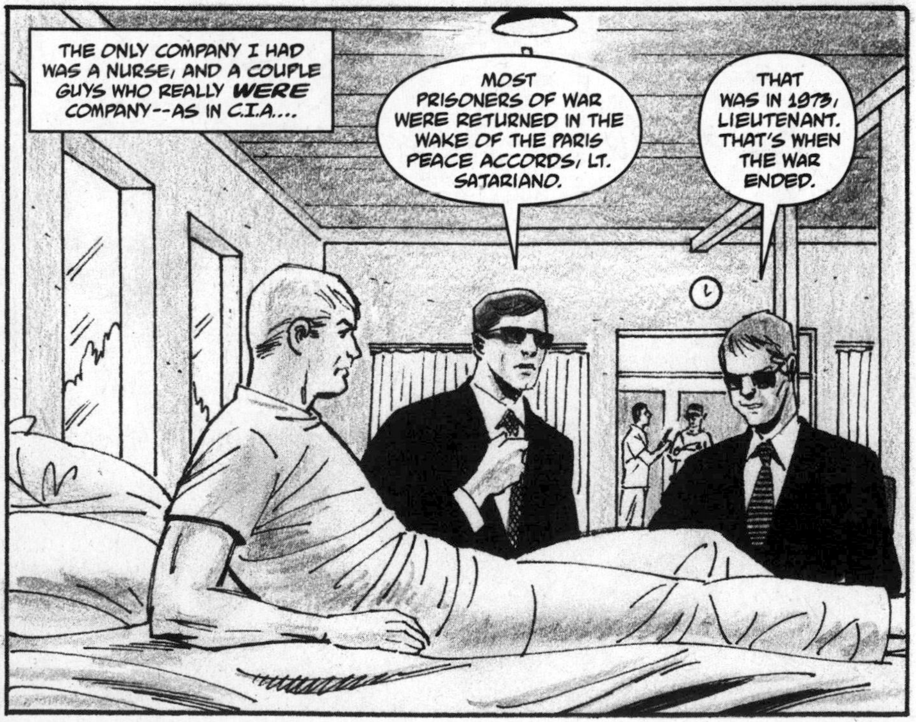
THE ONLY COMPANY I HAD WAS A NURSE, AND A COUPLE GUYS WHO REALLY **WERE** COMPANY--AS IN C.I.A....
MOST PRISONERS OF WAR WERE RETURNED IN THE WAKE OF THE PARIS PEACE ACCORDS, LT. SATARIANO.
THAT WAS IN 1973, LIEUTENANT. THAT'S WHEN THE WAR ENDED.

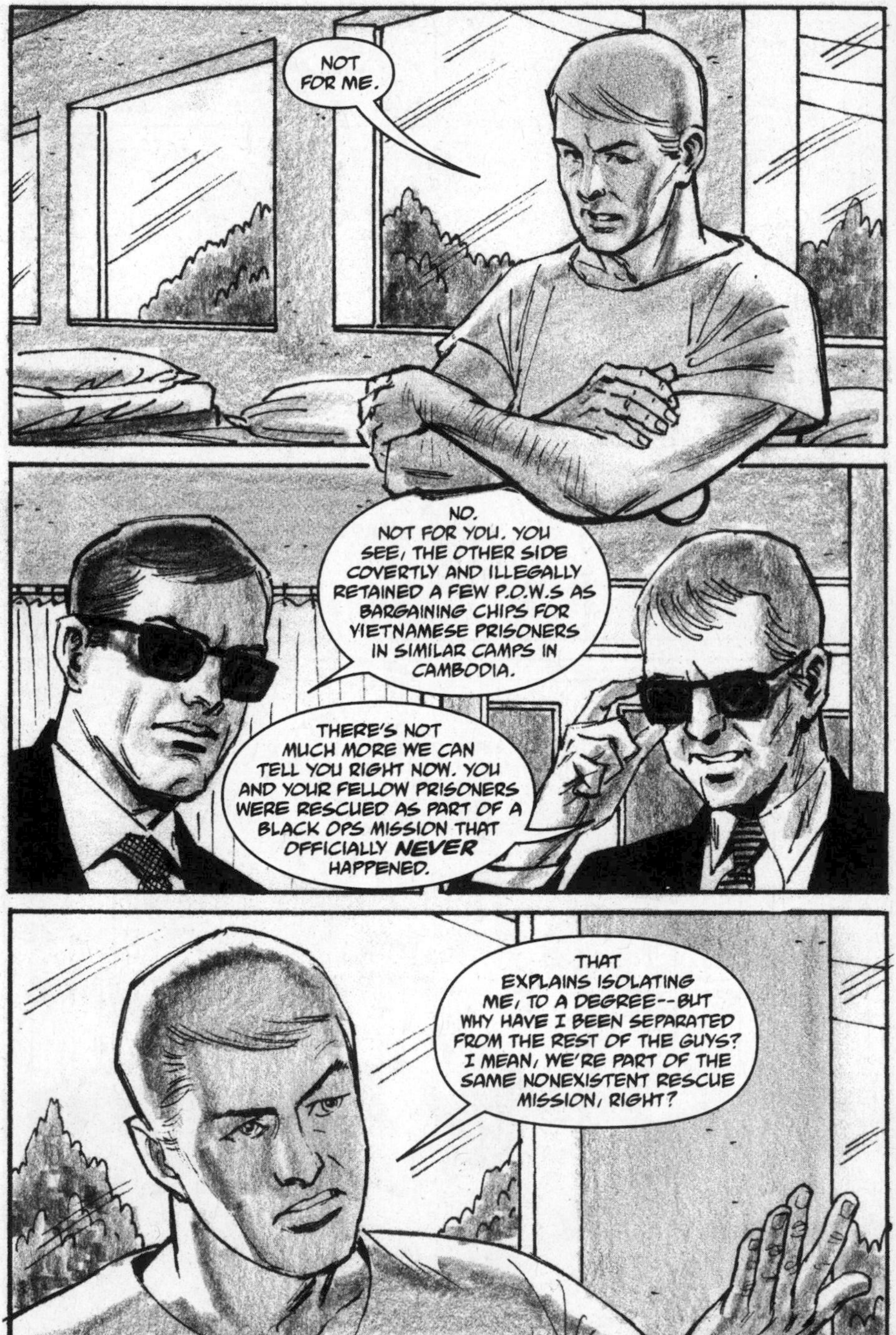
NOT FOR ME.
NO. NOT FOR YOU. YOU SEE, THE OTHER SIDE COVERTLY AND ILLEGALLY RETAINED A FEW P.O.W.S AS BARGAINING CHIPS FOR VIETNAMESE PRISONERS IN SIMILAR CAMPS IN CAMBODIA.
THERE'S NOT MUCH MORE WE CAN TELL YOU RIGHT NOW. YOU AND YOUR FELLOW PRISONERS WERE RESCUED AS PART OF A BLACK OPS MISSION THAT OFFICIALLY **NEVER** HAPPENED.
THAT EXPLAINS ISOLATING ME, TO A DEGREE--BUT WHY HAVE I BEEN SEPARATED FROM THE REST OF THE GUYS? I MEAN, WE'RE PART OF THE SAME NONEXISTENT RESCUE MISSION, RIGHT?

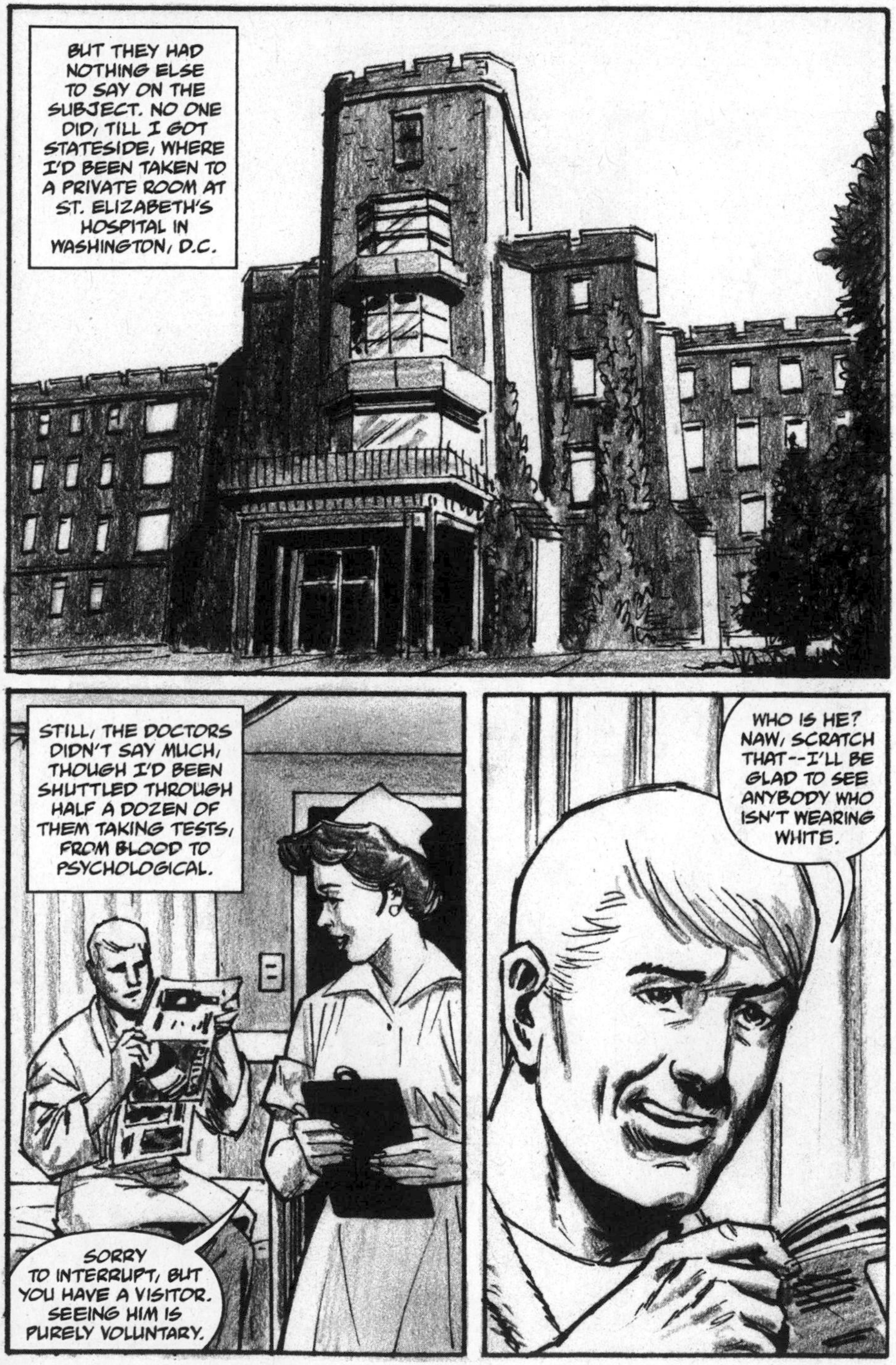
BUT THEY HAD NOTHING ELSE TO SAY ON THE SUBJECT. NO ONE DID, TILL I GOT STATESIDE, WHERE I'D BEEN TAKEN TO A PRIVATE ROOM AT ST. ELIZABETH'S HOSPITAL IN WASHINGTON, D.C.
STILL, THE DOCTORS DIDN'T SAY MUCH, THOUGH I'D BEEN SHUTTLED THROUGH HALF A DOZEN OF THEM TAKING TESTS, FROM BLOOD TO PSYCHOLOGICAL.
SORRY TO INTERRUPT, BUT YOU HAVE A VISITOR. SEEING HIM IS PURELY VOLUNTARY.
WHO IS HE? NAW, SCRATCH THAT--I'LL BE GLAD TO SEE ANYBODY WHO ISN'T WEARING WHITE.

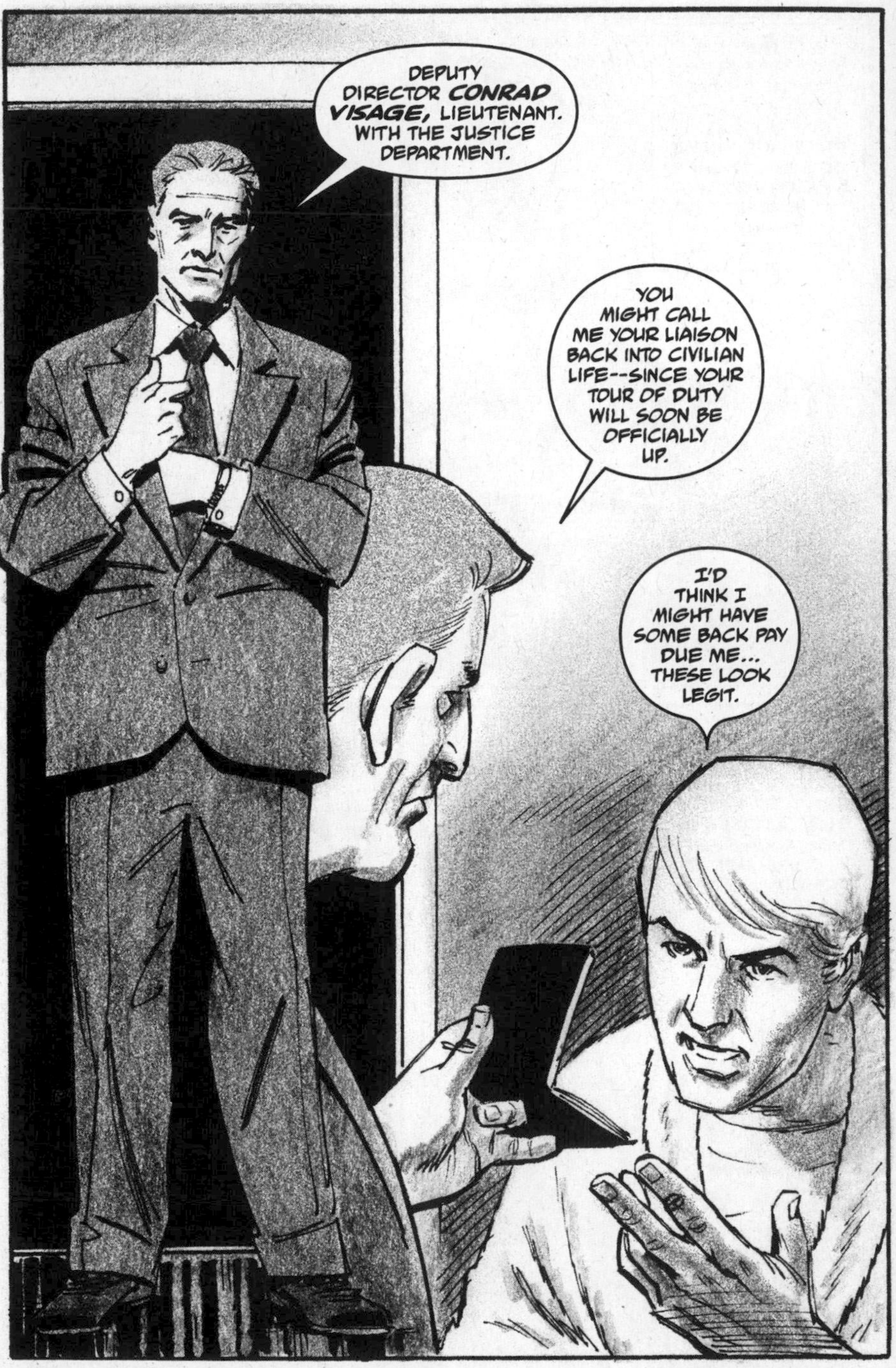
DEPUTY DIRECTOR CONRAD VISAGE, LIEUTENANT. WITH THE JUSTICE DEPARTMENT.
YOU MIGHT CALL ME YOUR LIAISON BACK INTO CIVILIAN LIFE--SINCE YOUR TOUR OF DUTY WILL SOON BE OFFICIALLY UP.
I'D THINK I MIGHT HAVE SOME BACK PAY DUE ME... THESE LOOK LEGIT.

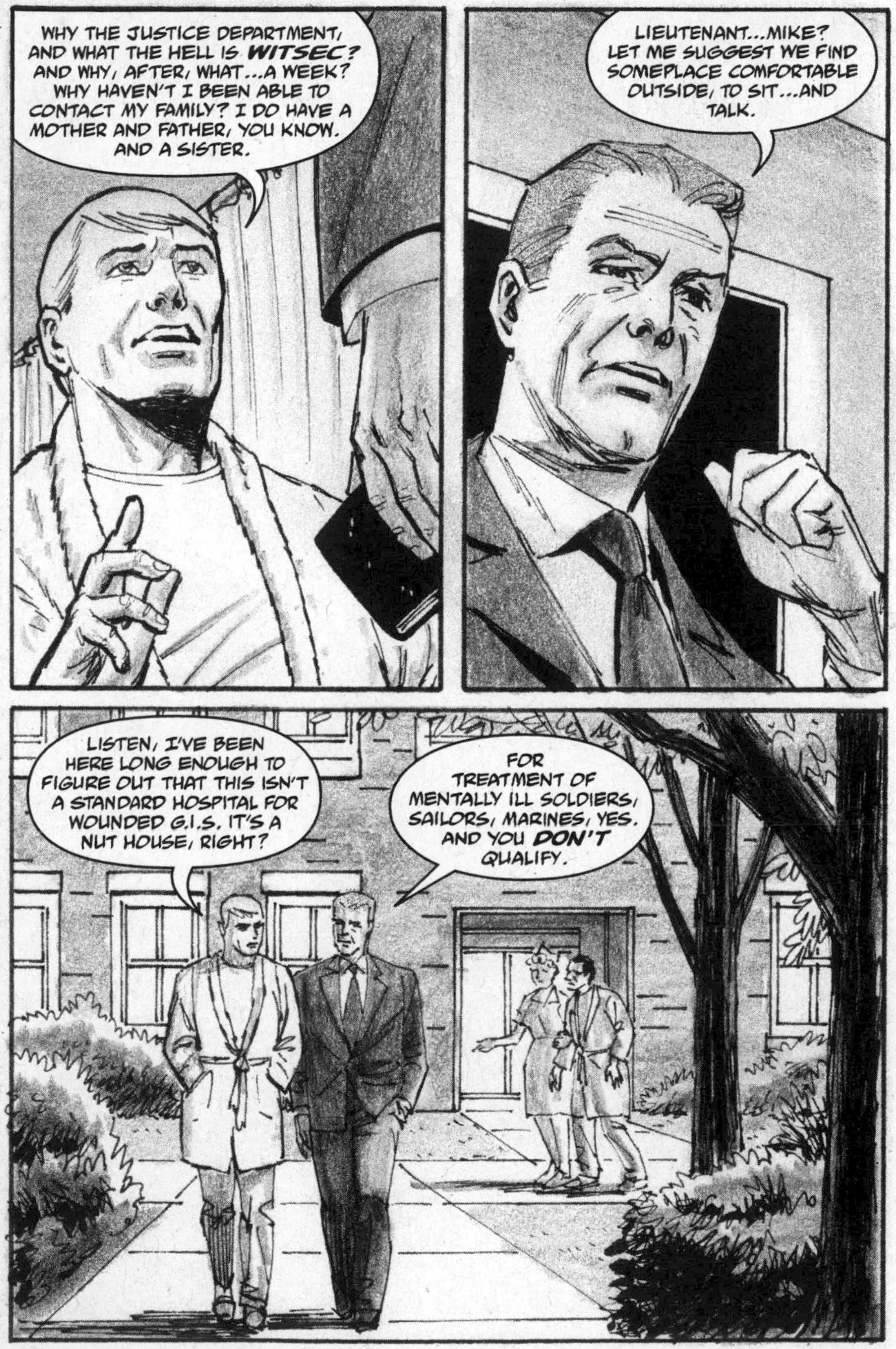
WHY THE JUSTICE DEPARTMENT, AND WHAT THE HELL IS **WITSEC**? AND WHY, AFTER, WHAT...A WEEK? WHY HAVEN'T I BEEN ABLE TO CONTACT MY FAMILY? I DO HAVE A MOTHER AND FATHER, YOU KNOW. AND A SISTER.
LIEUTENANT...MIKE? LET ME SUGGEST WE FIND SOMEPLACE COMFORTABLE OUTSIDE, TO SIT...AND TALK.
LISTEN, I'VE BEEN HERE LONG ENOUGH TO FIGURE OUT THAT THIS ISN'T A STANDARD HOSPITAL FOR WOUNDED G.I.S. IT'S A NUT HOUSE, RIGHT?
FOR TREATMENT OF MENTALLY ILL SOLDIERS, SAILORS, MARINES, YES. AND YOU **DON'T** QUALIFY.

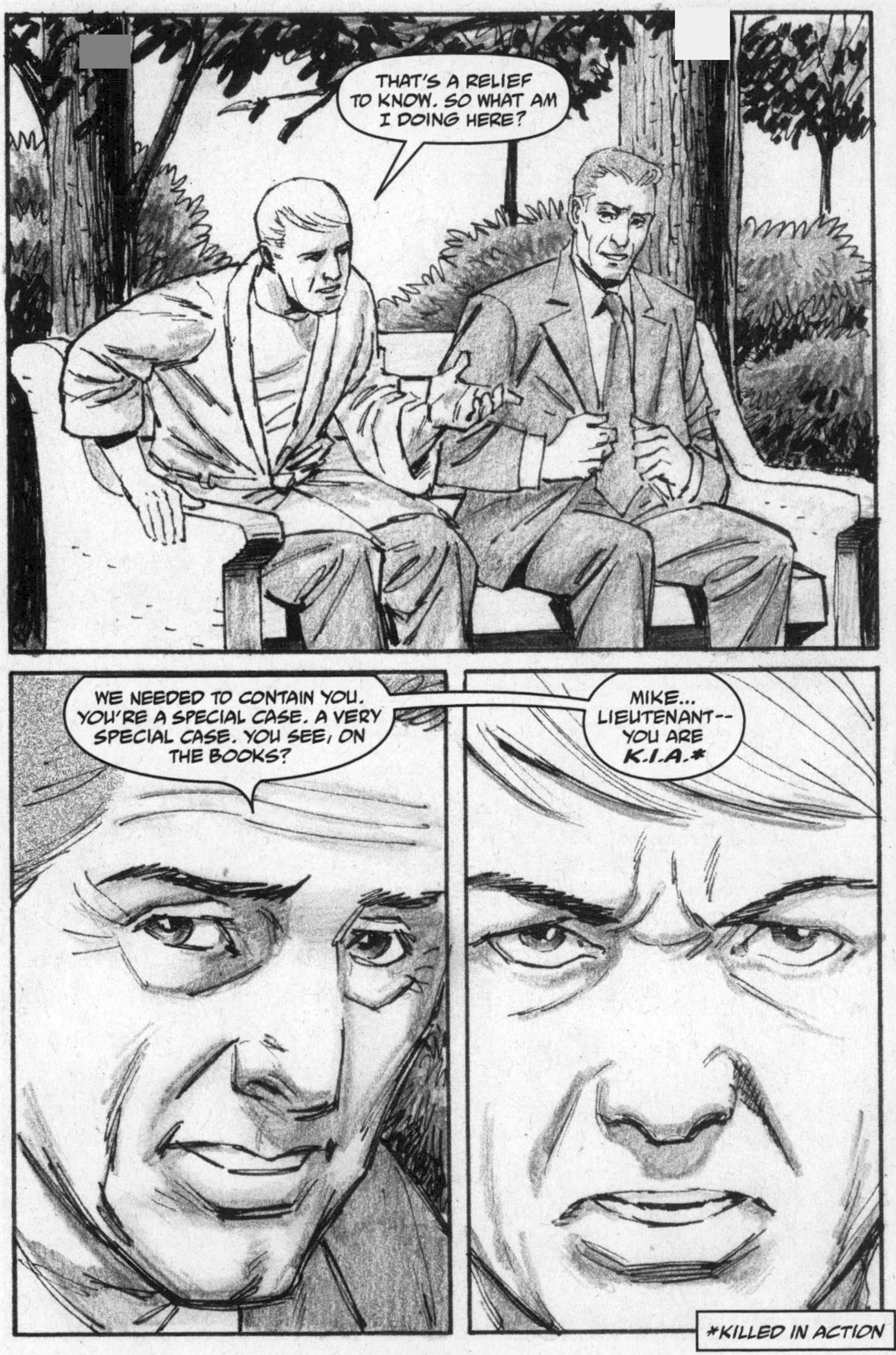
THAT'S A RELIEF TO KNOW. SO WHAT AM I DOING HERE?
WE NEEDED TO CONTAIN YOU. YOU'RE A SPECIAL CASE. A VERY SPECIAL CASE. YOU SEE, ON THE BOOKS?
MIKE... LIEUTENANT-- YOU ARE *K.I.A.**
*KILLED IN ACTION

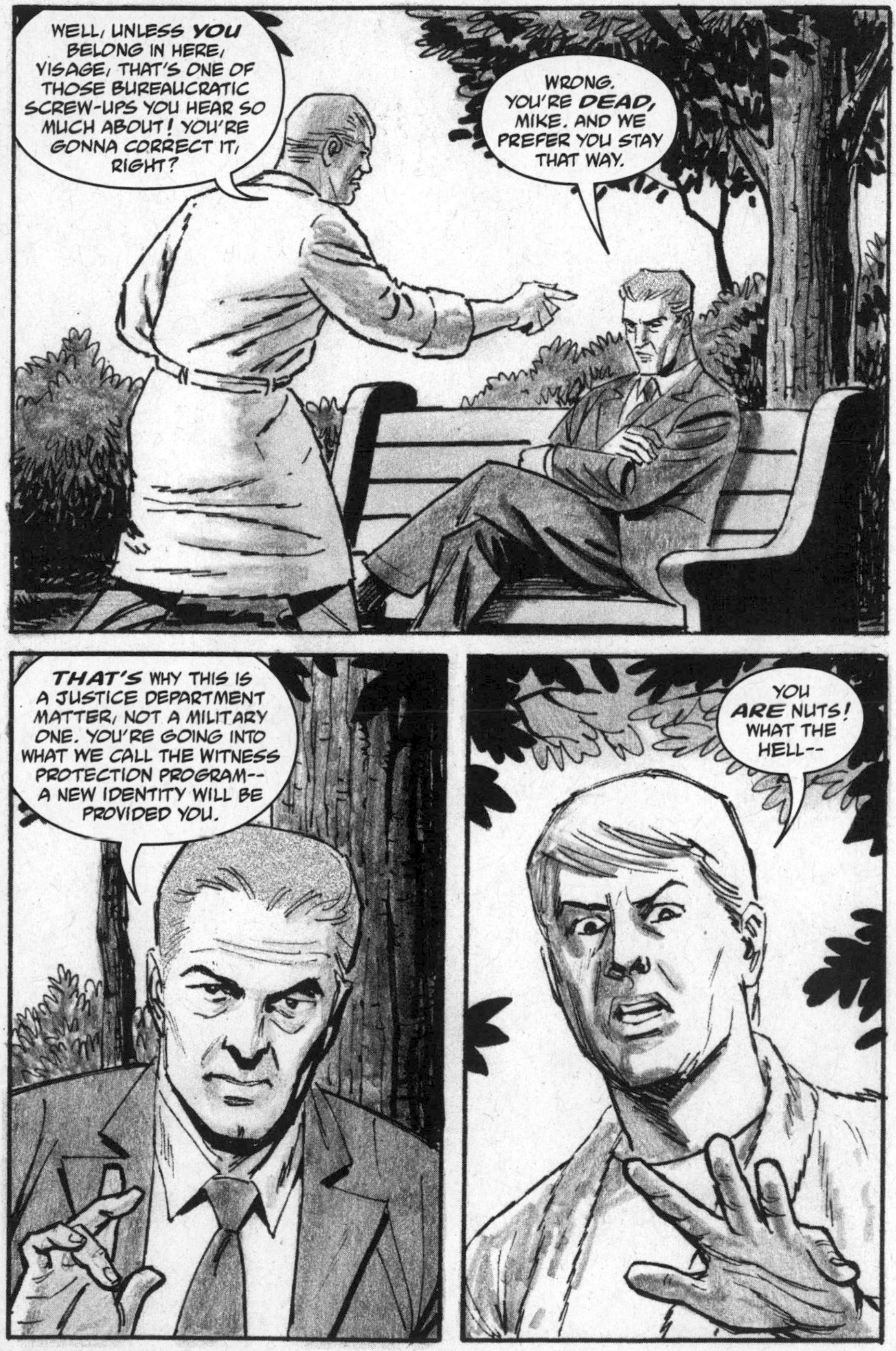
WELL, UNLESS YOU BELONG IN HERE, VISAGE, THAT'S ONE OF THOSE BUREAUCRATIC SCREW-UPS YOU HEAR SO MUCH ABOUT! YOU'RE GONNA CORRECT IT, RIGHT?
WRONG. YOU'RE DEAD, MIKE. AND WE PREFER YOU STAY THAT WAY.
THAT'S WHY THIS IS A JUSTICE DEPARTMENT MATTER, NOT A MILITARY ONE. YOU'RE GOING INTO WHAT WE CALL THE WITNESS PROTECTION PROGRAM-- A NEW IDENTITY WILL BE PROVIDED YOU.
YOU ARE NUTS! WHAT THE HELL--

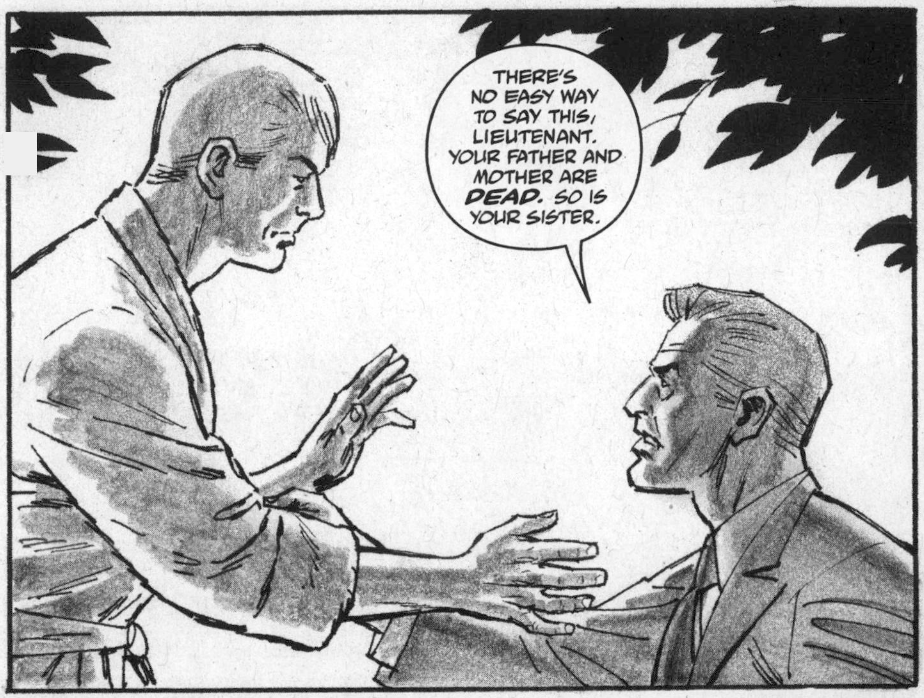
THERE'S NO EASY WAY TO SAY THIS, LIEUTENANT. YOUR FATHER AND MOTHER ARE **DEAD.** SO IS YOUR SISTER.

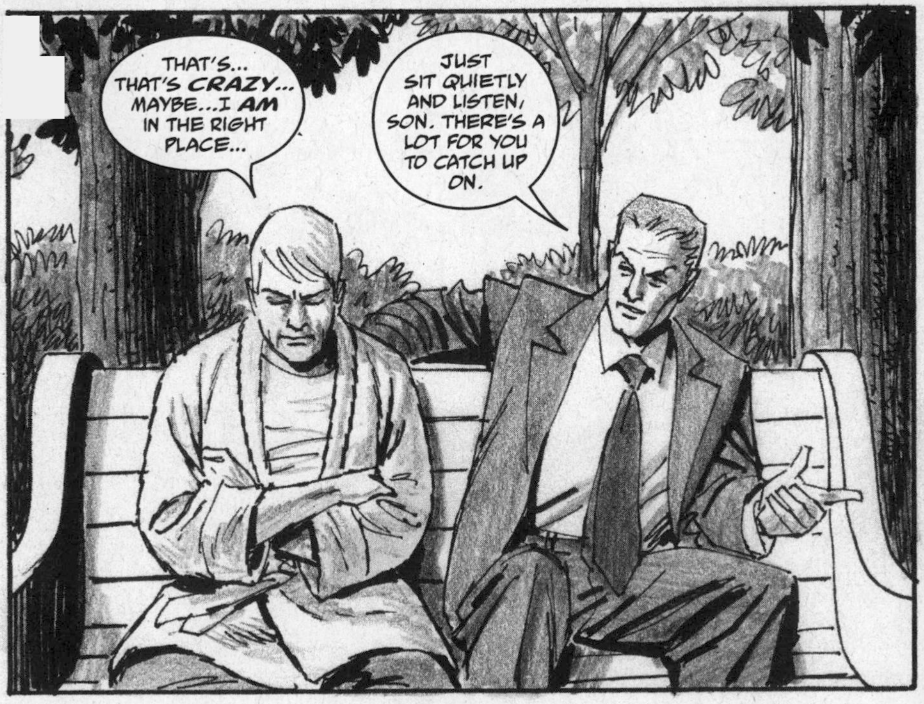
THAT'S... THAT'S ***CRAZY...*** MAYBE...I ***AM*** IN THE RIGHT PLACE...
JUST SIT QUIETLY AND LISTEN, SON. THERE'S A LOT FOR YOU TO CATCH UP ON.

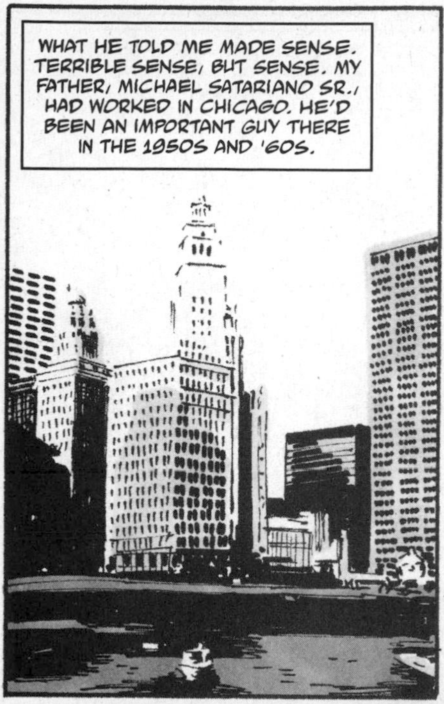
WHAT HE TOLD ME MADE SENSE. TERRIBLE SENSE, BUT SENSE. MY FATHER, MICHAEL SATARIANO SR., HAD WORKED IN CHICAGO. HE'D BEEN AN IMPORTANT GUY THERE IN THE 1950S AND '60S.

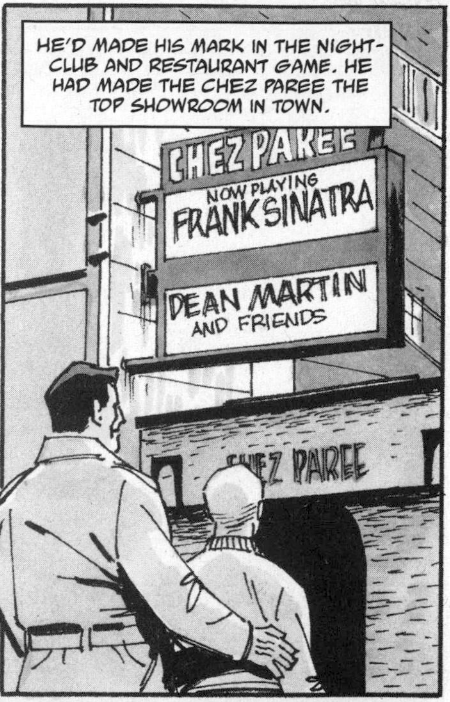
HE'D MADE HIS MARK IN THE NIGHT-CLUB AND RESTAURANT GAME. HE HAD MADE THE CHEZ PAREE THE TOP SHOWROOM IN TOWN.
CHEZ PAREE
NOW PLAYING
FRANK SINATRA
DEAN MARTIN
AND FRIENDS

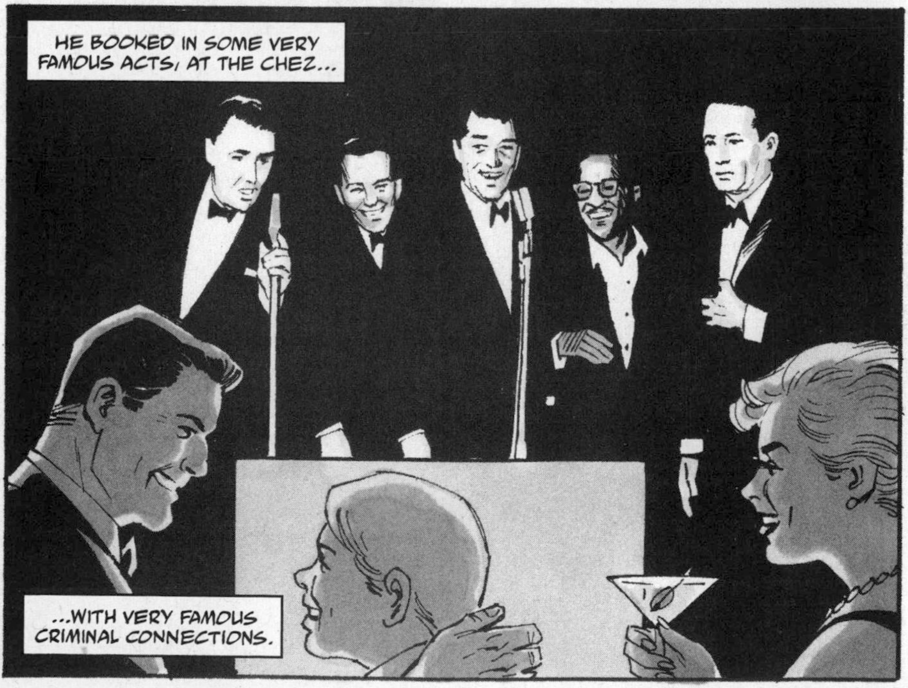
HE BOOKED IN SOME VERY FAMOUS ACTS, AT THE CHEZ...
...WITH VERY FAMOUS CRIMINAL CONNECTIONS.

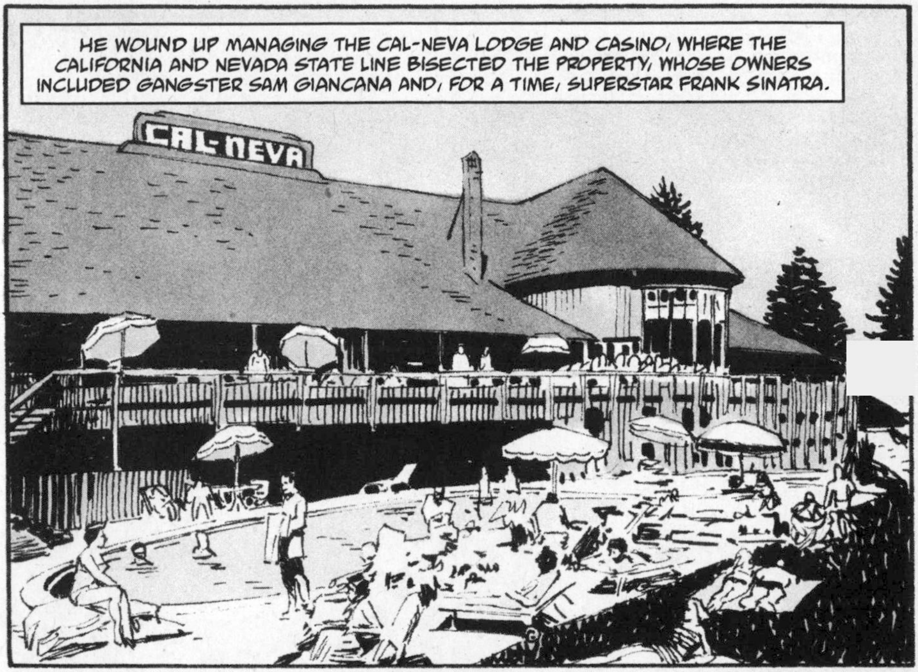
HE WOUND UP MANAGING THE CAL-NEVA LODGE AND CASINO, WHERE THE CALIFORNIA AND NEVADA STATE LINE BISECTED THE PROPERTY, WHOSE OWNERS INCLUDED GANGSTER SAM GIANCANA AND, FOR A TIME, SUPERSTAR FRANK SINATRA.
CAL-NEVA

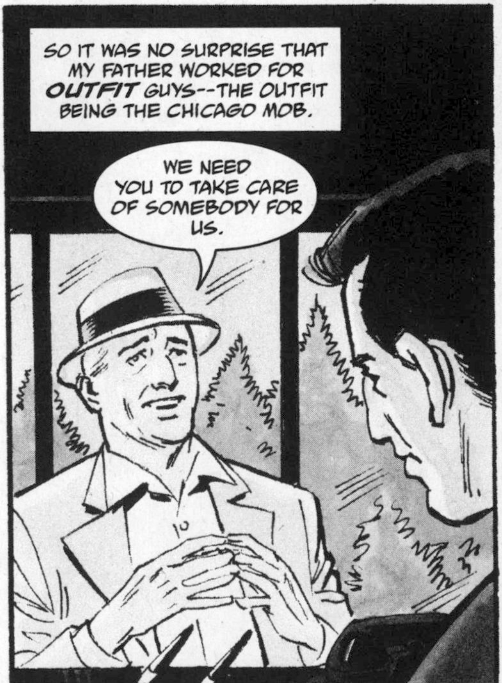
SO IT WAS NO SURPRISE THAT MY FATHER WORKED FOR OUTFIT GUYS--THE OUTFIT BEING THE CHICAGO MOB.
WE NEED YOU TO TAKE CARE OF SOMEBODY FOR US.

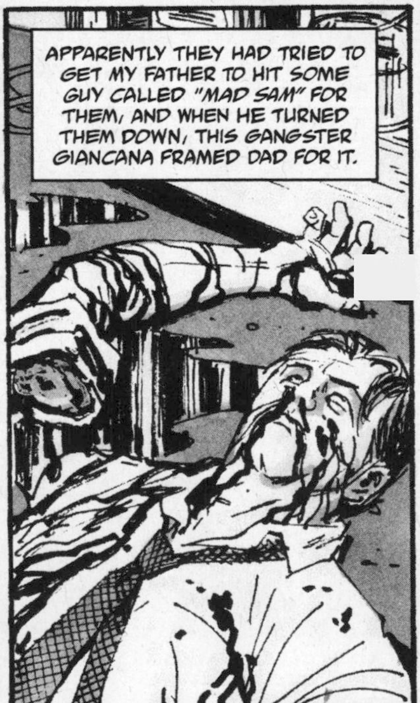
APPARENTLY THEY HAD TRIED TO GET MY FATHER TO HIT SOME GUY CALLED "MAD SAM" FOR THEM, AND WHEN HE TURNED THEM DOWN, THIS GANGSTER GIANCANA FRAMED DAD FOR IT.

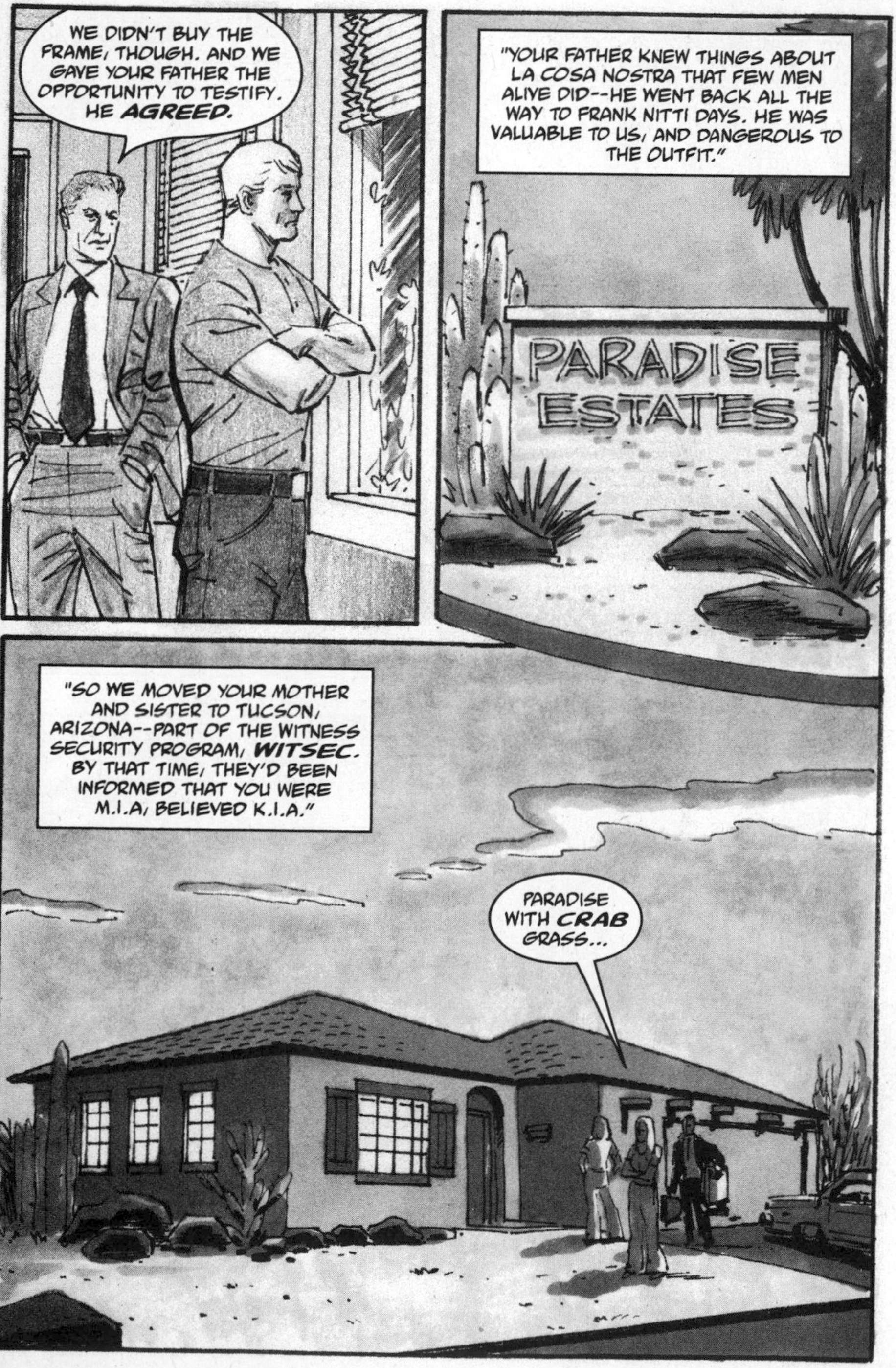
WE DIDN'T BUY THE FRAME, THOUGH. AND WE GAVE YOUR FATHER THE OPPORTUNITY TO TESTIFY. HE AGREED.
"YOUR FATHER KNEW THINGS ABOUT LA COSA NOSTRA THAT FEW MEN ALIVE DID--HE WENT BACK ALL THE WAY TO FRANK NITTI DAYS. HE WAS VALUABLE TO US, AND DANGEROUS TO THE OUTFIT."
PARADISE ESTATES
"SO WE MOVED YOUR MOTHER AND SISTER TO TUCSON, ARIZONA--PART OF THE WITNESS SECURITY PROGRAM, WITSEC. BY THAT TIME, THEY'D BEEN INFORMED THAT YOU WERE M.I.A, BELIEVED K.I.A."
PARADISE WITH CRAB GRASS...

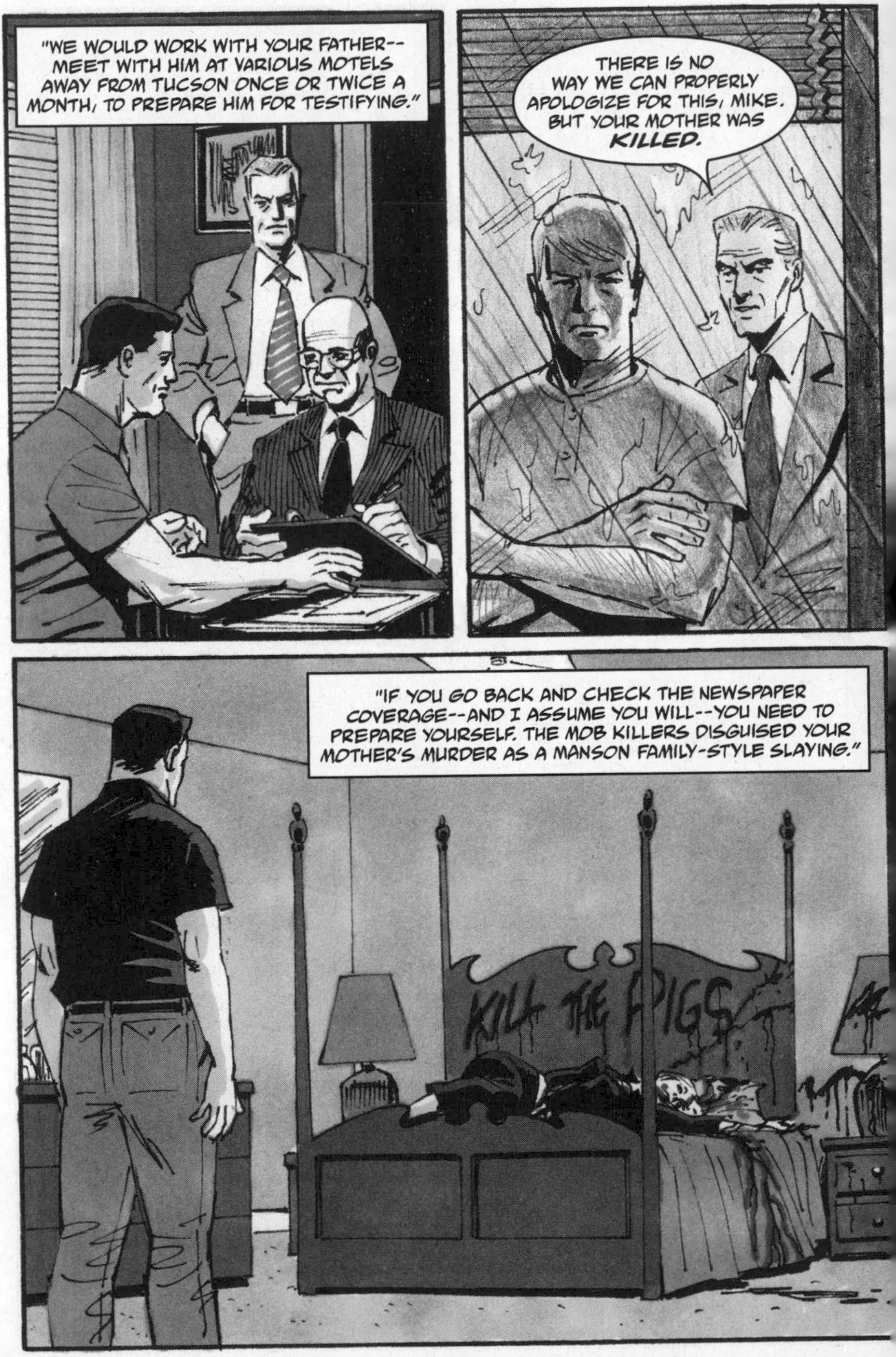
"WE WOULD WORK WITH YOUR FATHER--MEET WITH HIM AT VARIOUS MOTELS AWAY FROM TUCSON ONCE OR TWICE A MONTH, TO PREPARE HIM FOR TESTIFYING."
THERE IS NO WAY WE CAN PROPERLY APOLOGIZE FOR THIS, MIKE. BUT YOUR MOTHER WAS **KILLED.**
"IF YOU GO BACK AND CHECK THE NEWSPAPER COVERAGE--AND I ASSUME YOU WILL--YOU NEED TO PREPARE YOURSELF. THE MOB KILLERS DISGUISED YOUR MOTHER'S MURDER AS A MANSON FAMILY-STYLE SLAYING."

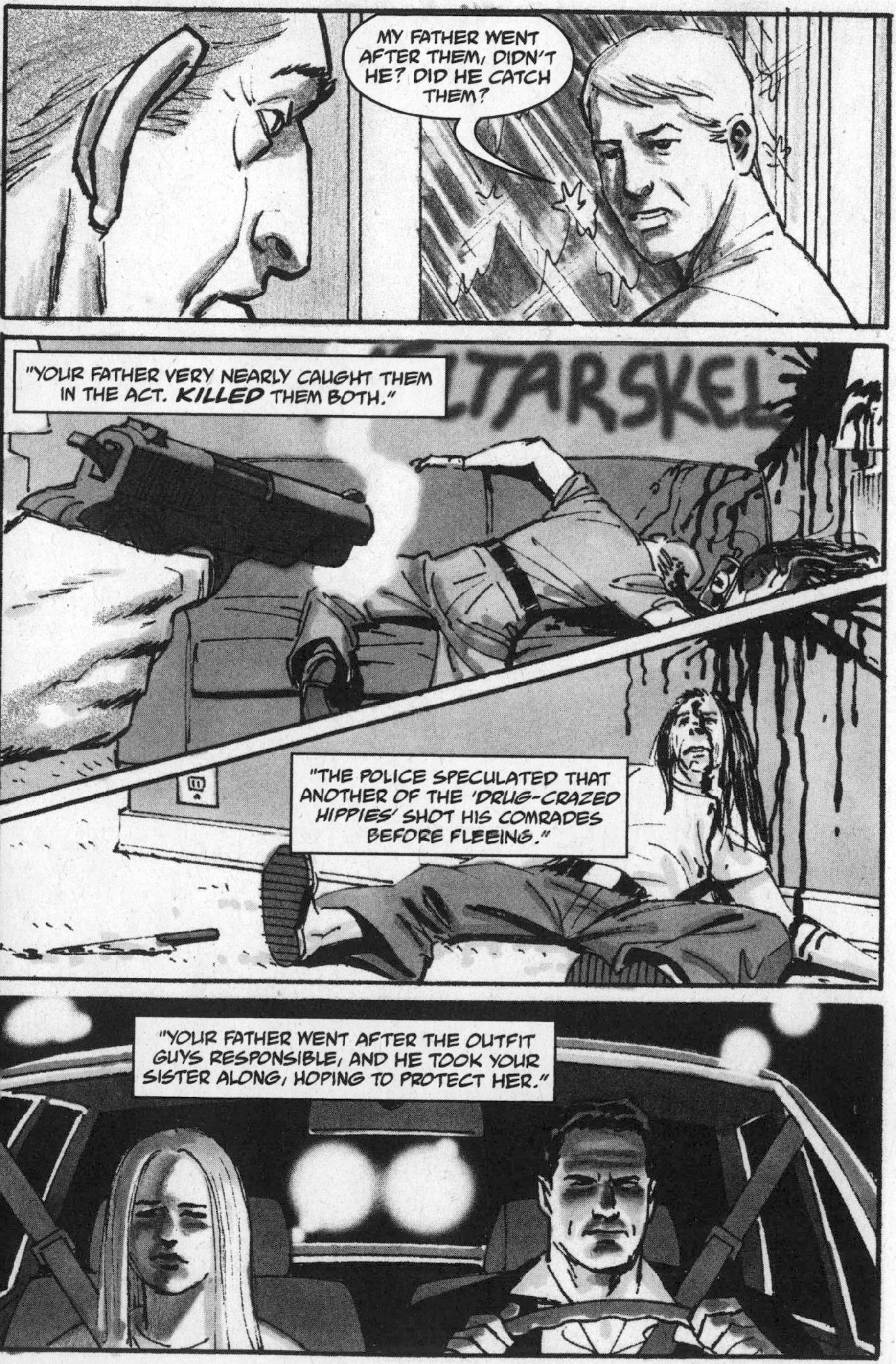
MY FATHER WENT AFTER THEM, DIDN'T HE? DID HE CATCH THEM?
"YOUR FATHER VERY NEARLY CAUGHT THEM IN THE ACT. KILLED THEM BOTH."
"THE POLICE SPECULATED THAT ANOTHER OF THE 'DRUG-CRAZED HIPPIES' SHOT HIS COMRADES BEFORE FLEEING."
"YOUR FATHER WENT AFTER THE OUTFIT GUYS RESPONSIBLE, AND HE TOOK YOUR SISTER ALONG, HOPING TO PROTECT HER."

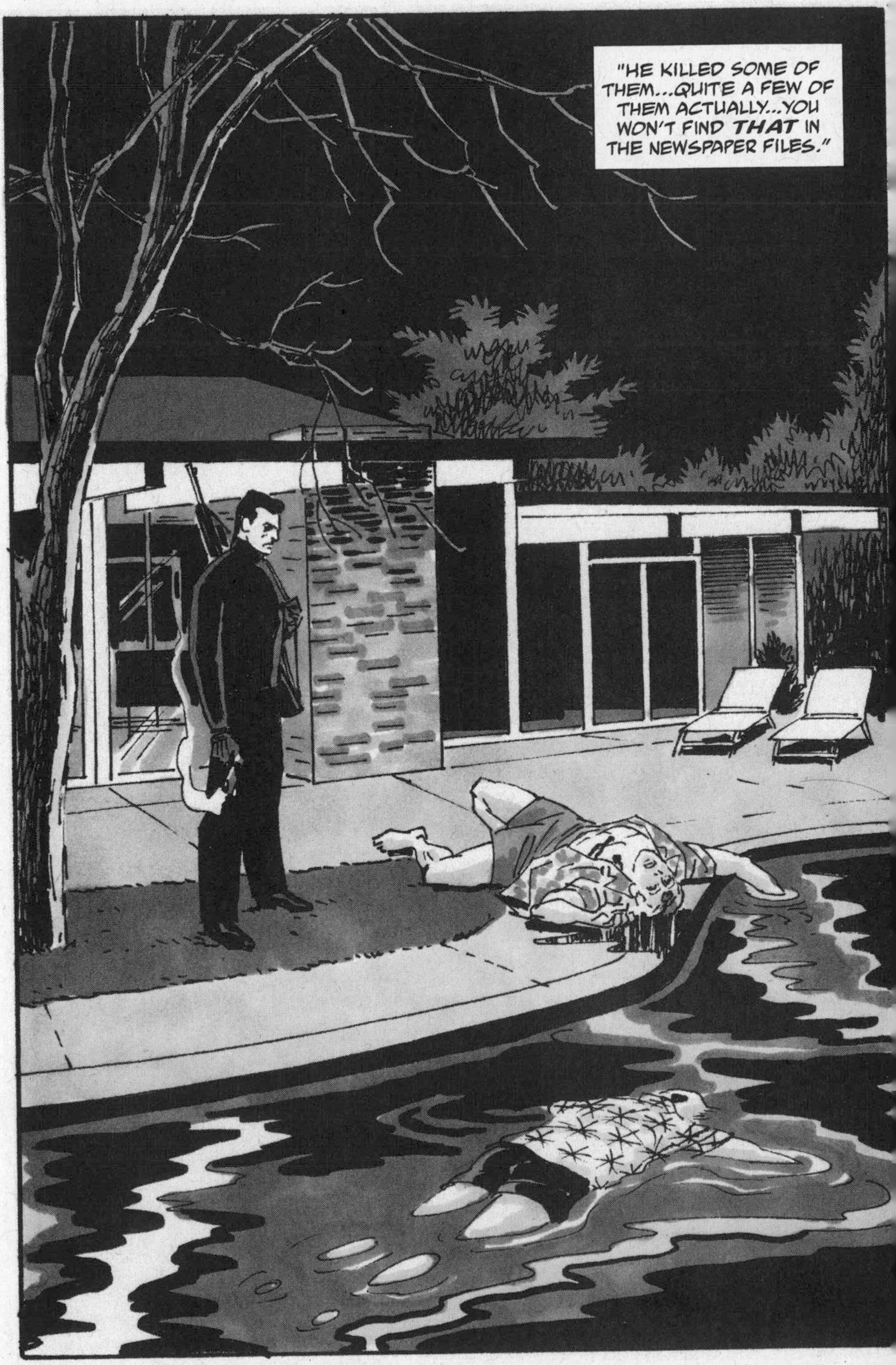
"HE KILLED SOME OF THEM...QUITE A FEW OF THEM ACTUALLY...YOU WON'T FIND THAT IN THE NEWSPAPER FILES."

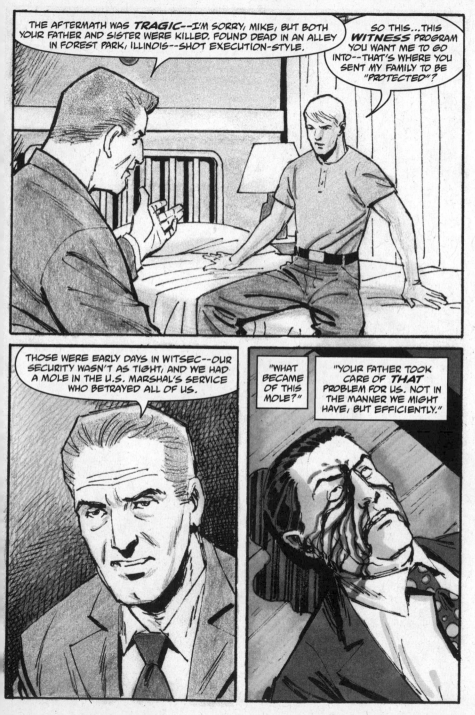

THE AFTERMATH WAS *TRAGIC*--I'M SORRY, MIKE, BUT BOTH YOUR FATHER AND SISTER WERE KILLED. FOUND DEAD IN AN ALLEY IN FOREST PARK, ILLINOIS--SHOT EXECUTION-STYLE.

SO THIS...THIS *WITNESS* PROGRAM YOU WANT ME TO GO INTO--THAT'S WHERE YOU SENT MY FAMILY TO BE "PROTECTED"?

THOSE WERE EARLY DAYS IN WITSEC--OUR SECURITY WASN'T AS TIGHT, AND WE HAD A MOLE IN THE U.S. MARSHAL'S SERVICE WHO BETRAYED ALL OF US.

"WHAT BECAME OF THIS MOLE?"

"YOUR FATHER TOOK CARE OF *THAT* PROBLEM FOR US. NOT IN THE MANNER WE MIGHT HAVE, BUT EFFICIENTLY."

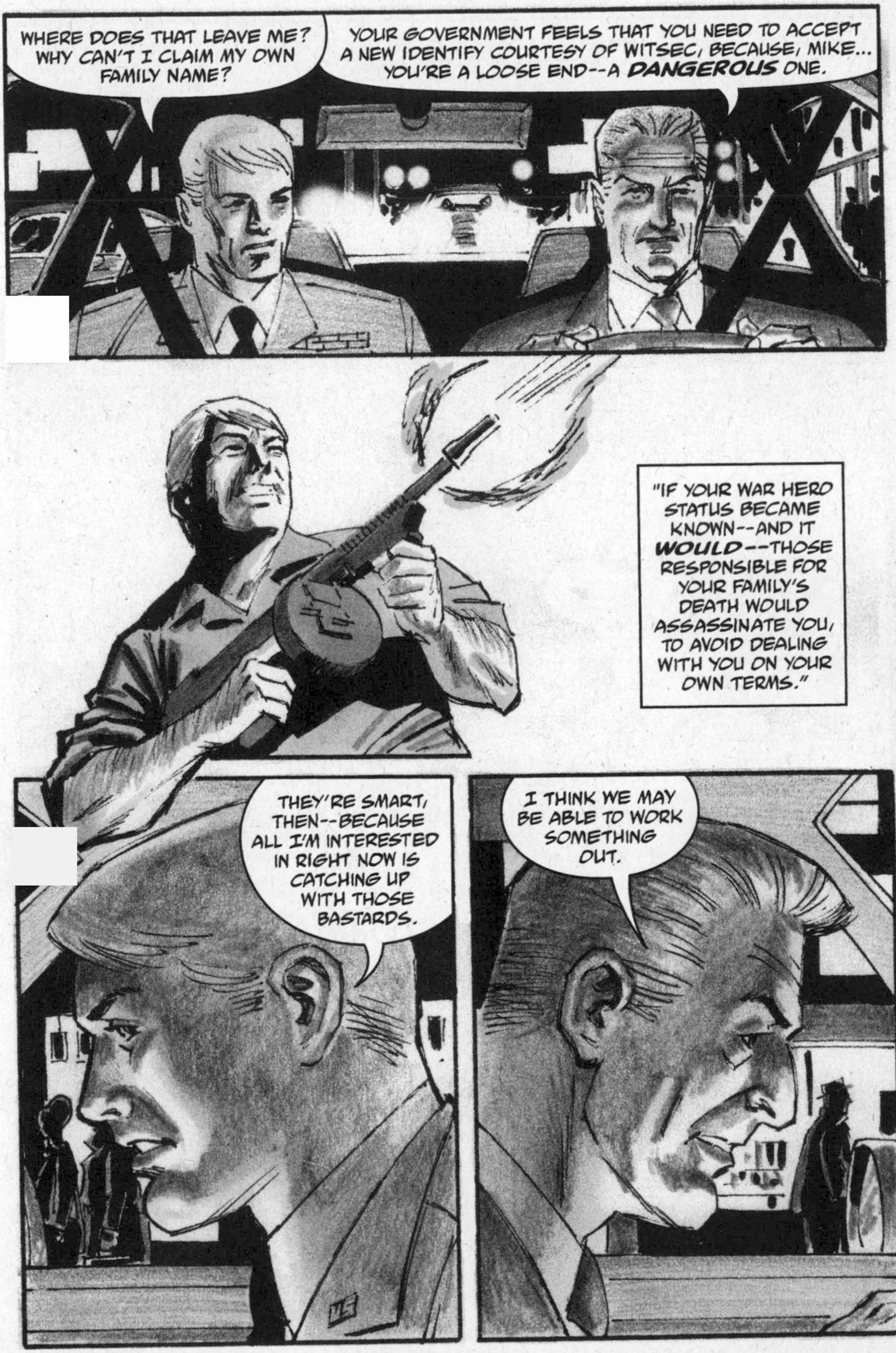
WHERE DOES THAT LEAVE ME? WHY CAN'T I CLAIM MY OWN FAMILY NAME?
YOUR GOVERNMENT FEELS THAT YOU NEED TO ACCEPT A NEW IDENTIFY COURTESY OF WITSEC, BECAUSE, MIKE... YOU'RE A LOOSE END--A DANGEROUS ONE.
"IF YOUR WAR HERO STATUS BECAME KNOWN--AND IT WOULD--THOSE RESPONSIBLE FOR YOUR FAMILY'S DEATH WOULD ASSASSINATE YOU, TO AVOID DEALING WITH YOU ON YOUR OWN TERMS."
THEY'RE SMART, THEN--BECAUSE ALL I'M INTERESTED IN RIGHT NOW IS CATCHING UP WITH THOSE BASTARDS.
I THINK WE MAY BE ABLE TO WORK SOMETHING OUT.

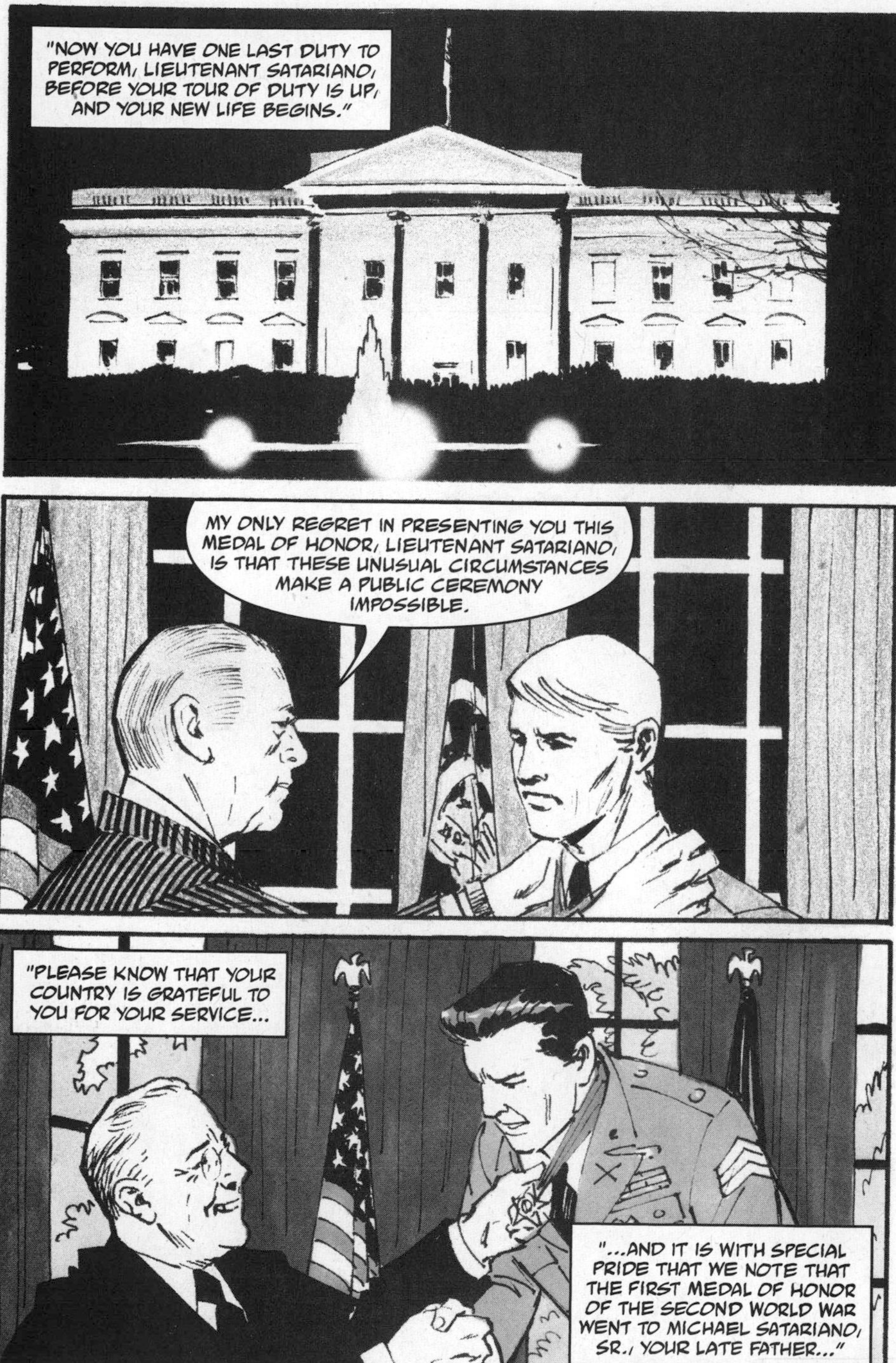
"NOW YOU HAVE ONE LAST DUTY TO PERFORM, LIEUTENANT SATARIANO, BEFORE YOUR TOUR OF DUTY IS UP, AND YOUR NEW LIFE BEGINS."
MY ONLY REGRET IN PRESENTING YOU THIS MEDAL OF HONOR, LIEUTENANT SATARIANO, IS THAT THESE UNUSUAL CIRCUMSTANCES MAKE A PUBLIC CEREMONY IMPOSSIBLE.
"PLEASE KNOW THAT YOUR COUNTRY IS GRATEFUL TO YOU FOR YOUR SERVICE...
"...AND IT IS WITH SPECIAL PRIDE THAT WE NOTE THAT THE FIRST MEDAL OF HONOR OF THE SECOND WORLD WAR WENT TO MICHAEL SATARIANO, SR., YOUR LATE FATHER..."

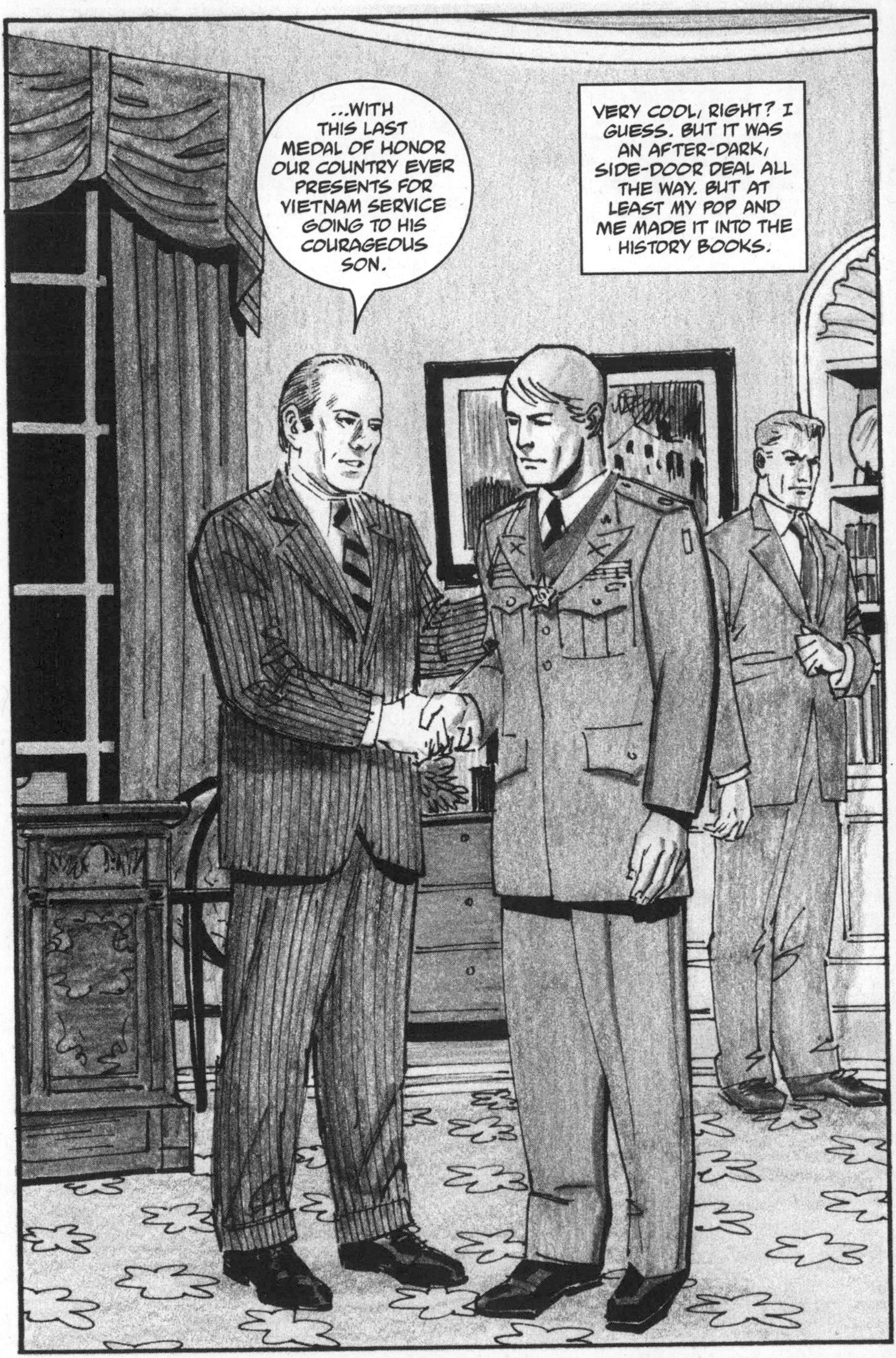
...WITH THIS LAST MEDAL OF HONOR OUR COUNTRY EVER PRESENTS FOR VIETNAM SERVICE GOING TO HIS COURAGEOUS SON.
VERY COOL, RIGHT? I GUESS. BUT IT WAS AN AFTER-DARK, SIDE-DOOR DEAL ALL THE WAY. BUT AT LEAST MY POP AND ME MADE IT INTO THE HISTORY BOOKS.

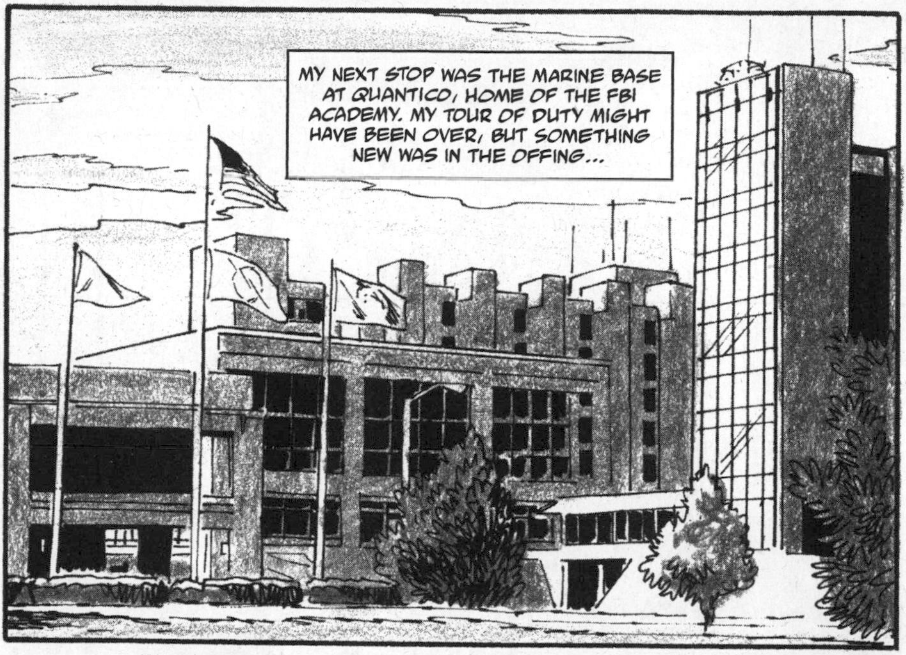
MY NEXT STOP WAS THE MARINE BASE AT QUANTICO, HOME OF THE FBI ACADEMY. MY TOUR OF DUTY MIGHT HAVE BEEN OVER, BUT SOMETHING NEW WAS IN THE OFFING...

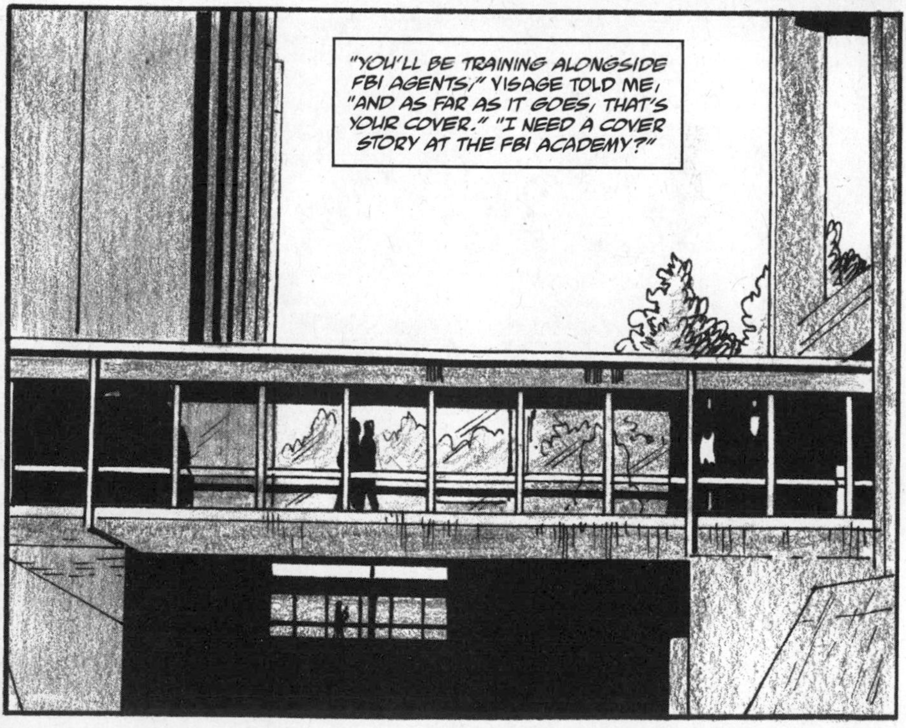
"YOU'LL BE TRAINING ALONGSIDE FBI AGENTS," VISAGE TOLD ME, "AND AS FAR AS IT GOES, THAT'S YOUR COVER." "I NEED A COVER STORY AT THE FBI ACADEMY?"

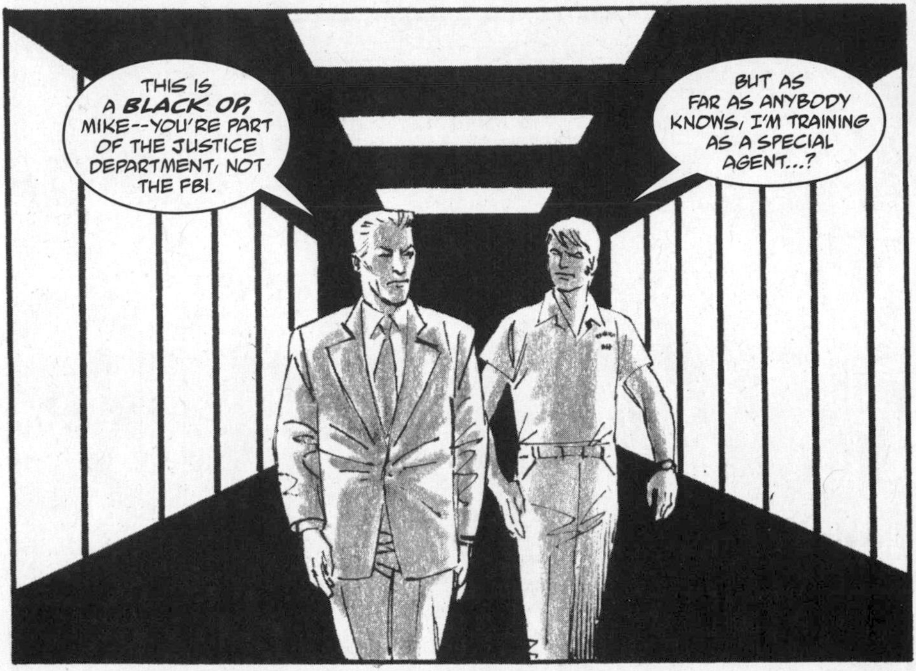
THIS IS A BLACK OP, MIKE--YOU'RE PART OF THE JUSTICE DEPARTMENT, NOT THE FBI.
BUT AS FAR AS ANYBODY KNOWS, I'M TRAINING AS A SPECIAL AGENT...?

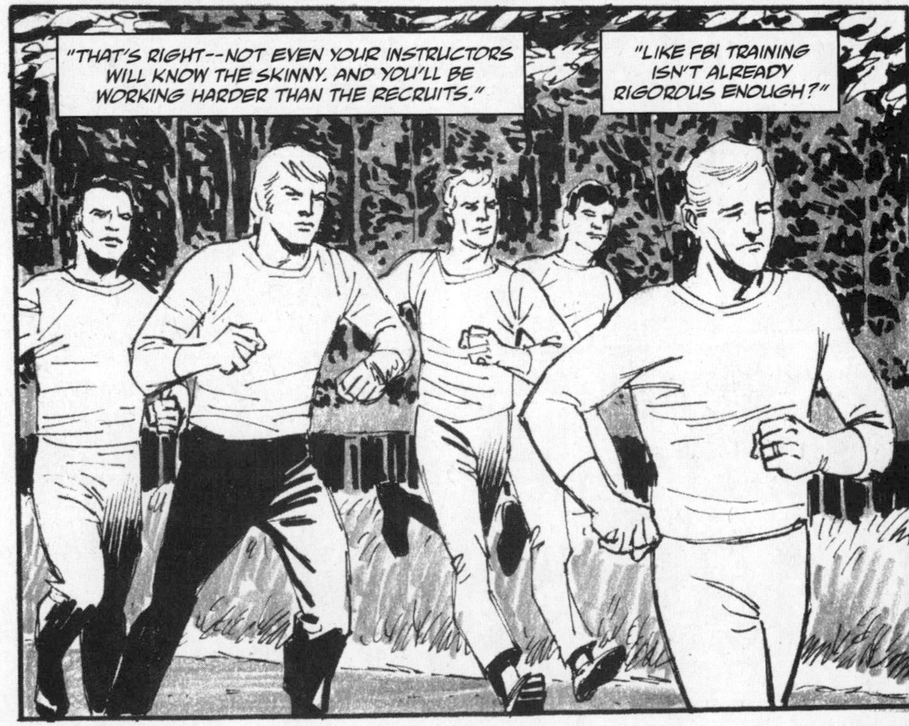
"THAT'S RIGHT--NOT EVEN YOUR INSTRUCTORS WILL KNOW THE SKINNY. AND YOU'LL BE WORKING HARDER THAN THE RECRUITS."
"LIKE FBI TRAINING ISN'T ALREADY RIGOROUS ENOUGH?"

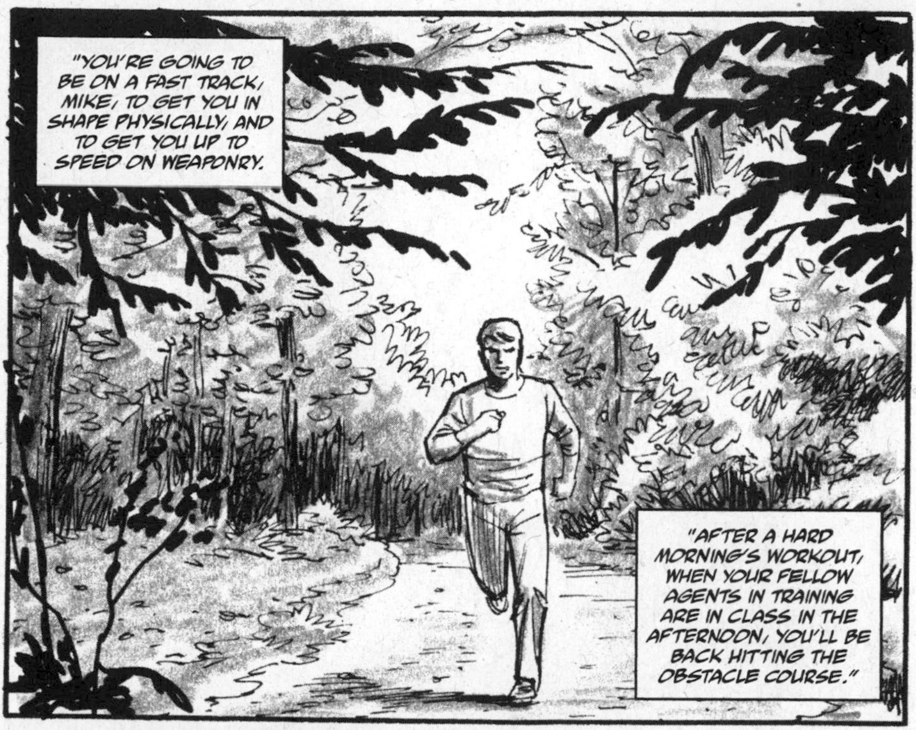
"YOU'RE GOING TO BE ON A FAST TRACK, MIKE, TO GET YOU IN SHAPE PHYSICALLY, AND TO GET YOU UP TO SPEED ON WEAPONRY.
"AFTER A HARD MORNING'S WORKOUT, WHEN YOUR FELLOW AGENTS IN TRAINING ARE IN CLASS IN THE AFTERNOON, YOU'LL BE BACK HITTING THE OBSTACLE COURSE."

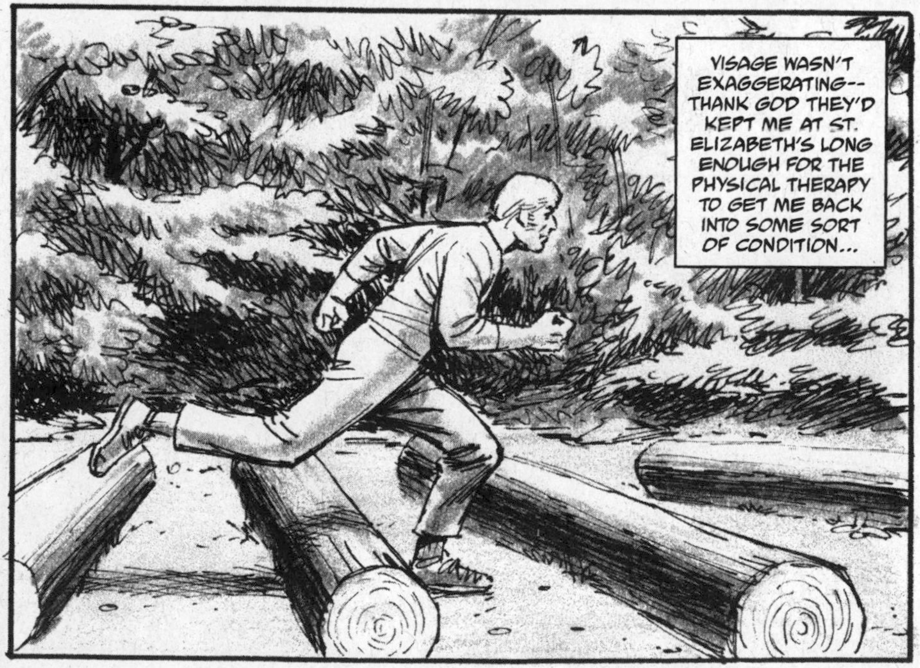
VISAGE WASN'T EXAGGERATING--THANK GOD THEY'D KEPT ME AT ST. ELIZABETH'S LONG ENOUGH FOR THE PHYSICAL THERAPY TO GET ME BACK INTO SOME SORT OF CONDITION...

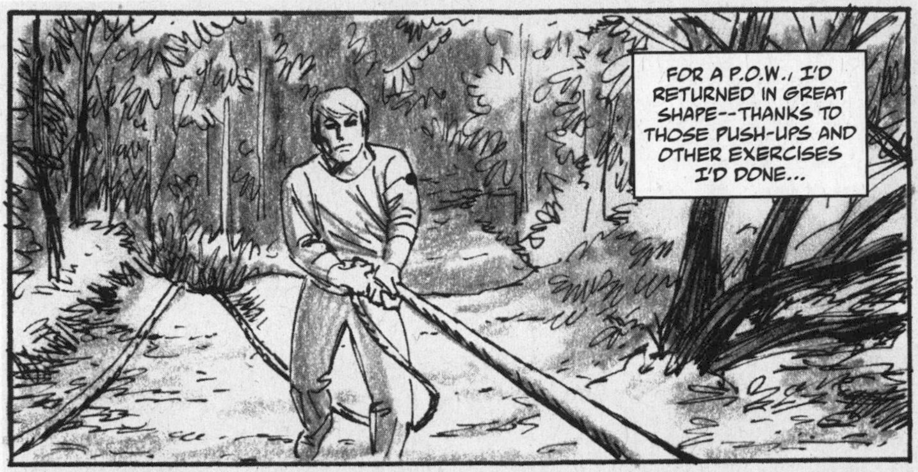
FOR A P.O.W., I'D RETURNED IN GREAT SHAPE--THANKS TO THOSE PUSH-UPS AND OTHER EXERCISES I'D DONE...

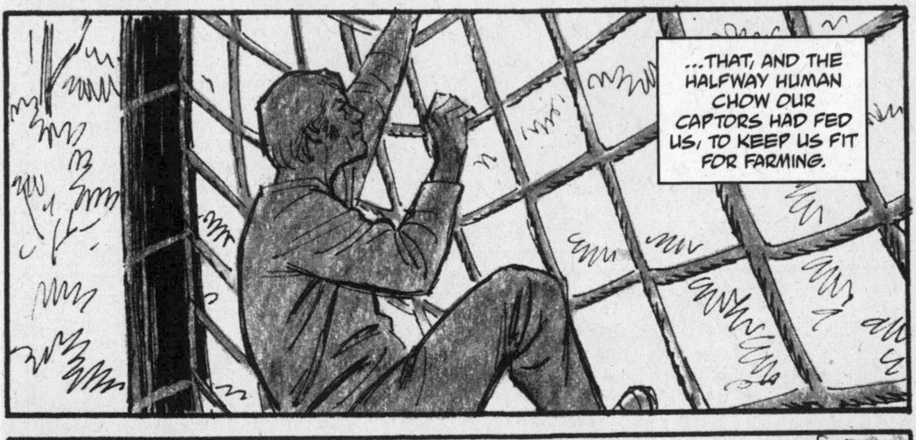
...THAT, AND THE HALFWAY HUMAN CHOW OUR CAPTORS HAD FED US, TO KEEP US FIT FOR FARMING.

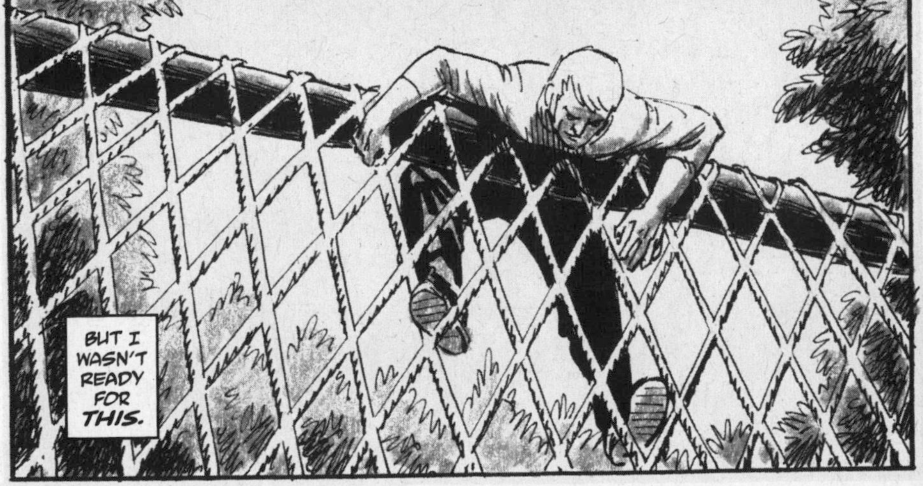
BUT I WASN'T READY FOR *THIS.*

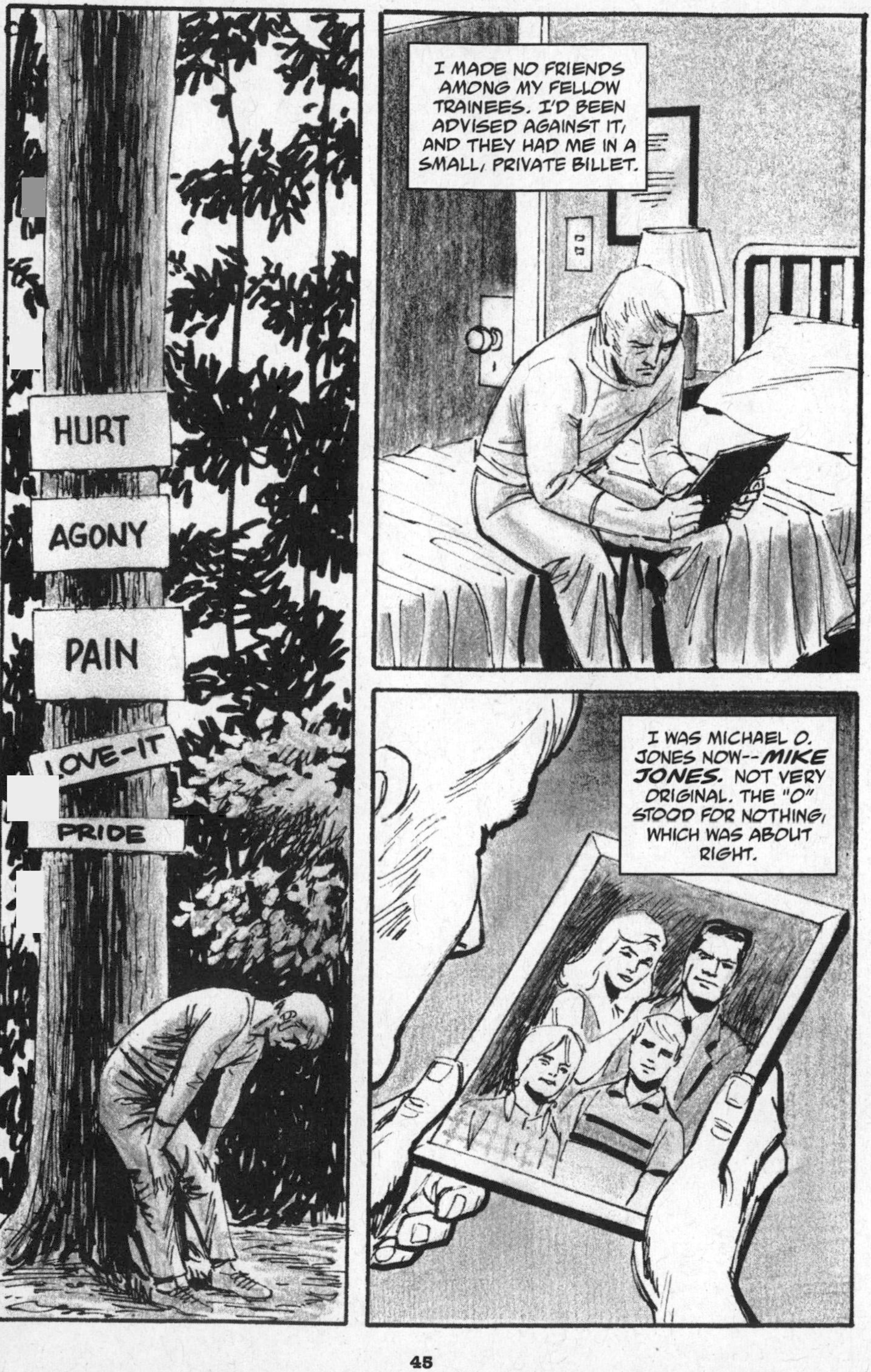
HURT
AGONY
PAIN
LOVE-IT
PRIDE
I MADE NO FRIENDS AMONG MY FELLOW TRAINEES. I'D BEEN ADVISED AGAINST IT, AND THEY HAD ME IN A SMALL, PRIVATE BILLET.
I WAS MICHAEL O. JONES NOW--*MIKE JONES.* NOT VERY ORIGINAL. THE "O" STOOD FOR NOTHING, WHICH WAS ABOUT RIGHT.

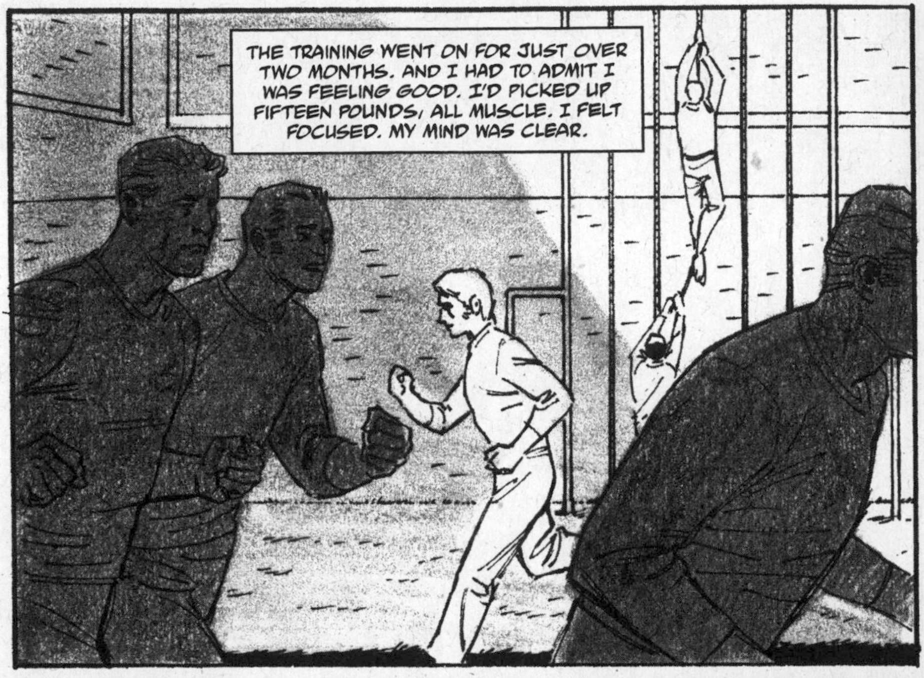
THE TRAINING WENT ON FOR JUST OVER TWO MONTHS. AND I HAD TO ADMIT I WAS FEELING GOOD. I'D PICKED UP FIFTEEN POUNDS, ALL MUSCLE. I FELT FOCUSED. MY MIND WAS CLEAR.
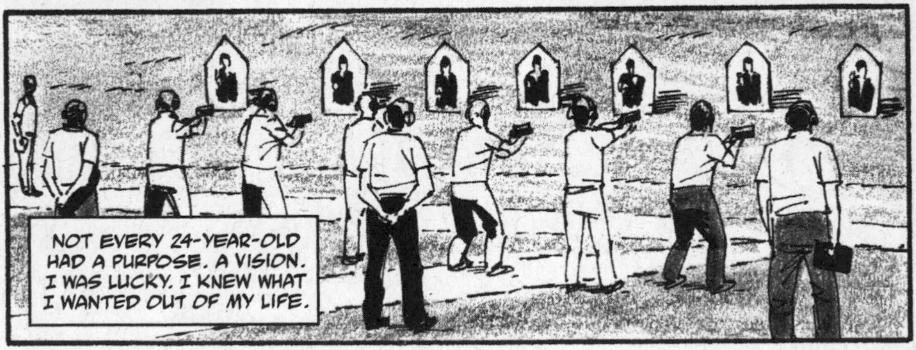
NOT EVERY 24-YEAR-OLD HAD A PURPOSE. A VISION. I WAS LUCKY. I KNEW WHAT I WANTED OUT OF MY LIFE.
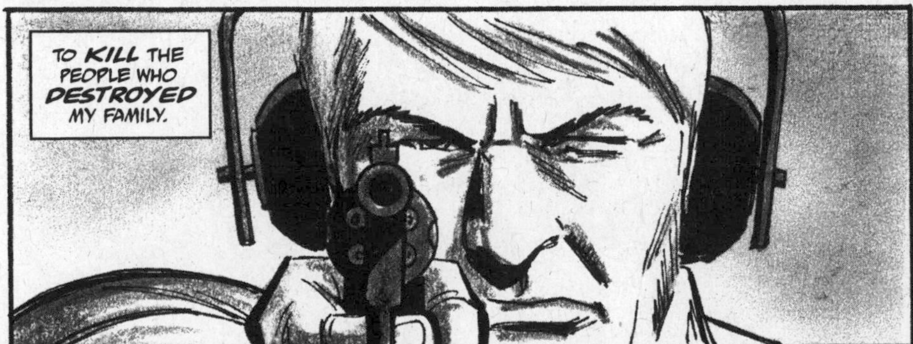
TO KILL THE PEOPLE WHO DESTROYED MY FAMILY.

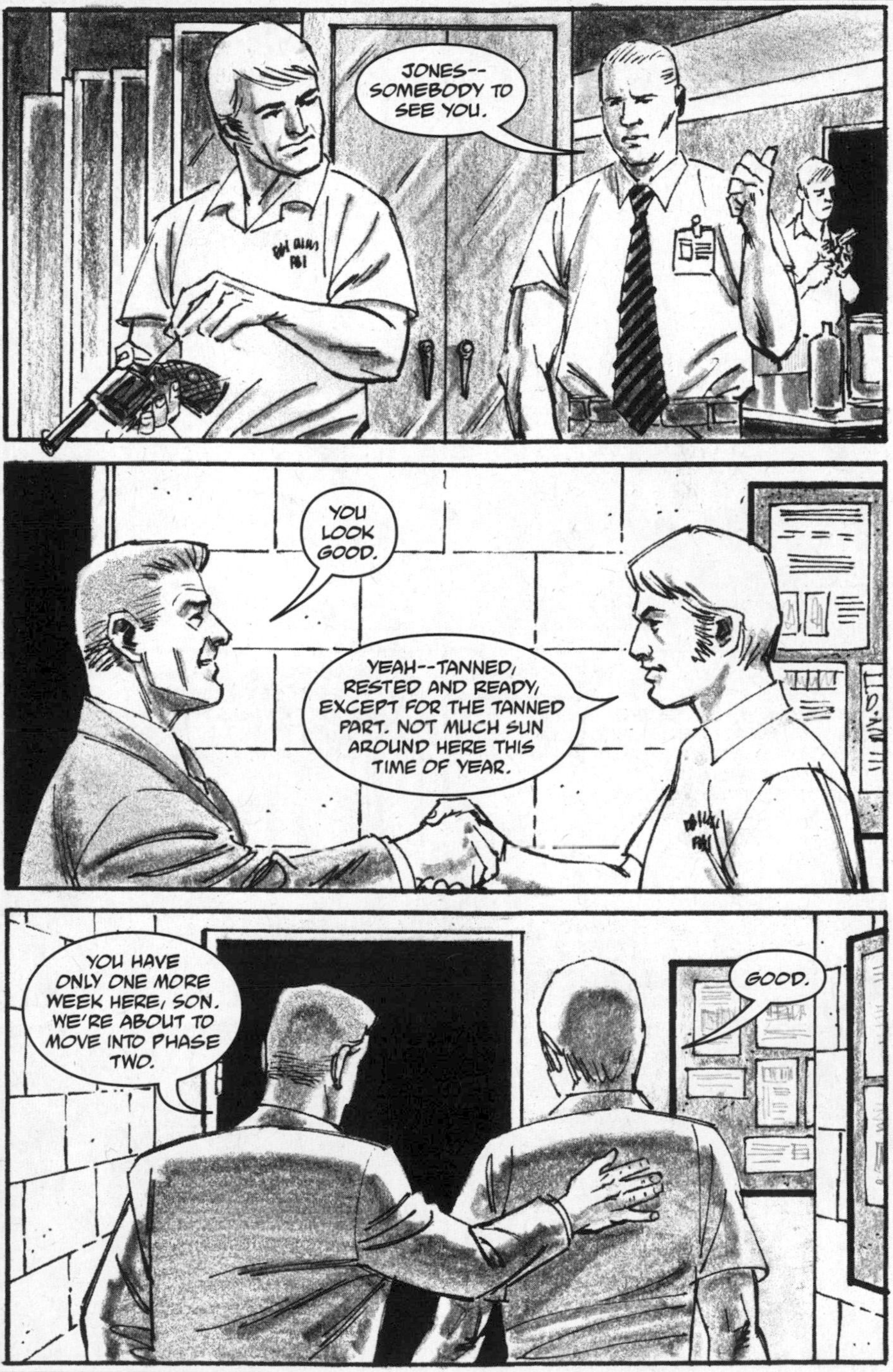

JONES--
SOMEBODY TO
SEE YOU.
YOU
LOOK
GOOD.
YEAH--TANNED, RESTED AND READY, EXCEPT FOR THE TANNED PART. NOT MUCH SUN AROUND HERE THIS TIME OF YEAR.
YOU HAVE ONLY ONE MORE WEEK HERE, SON. WE'RE ABOUT TO MOVE INTO PHASE TWO.
GOOD.

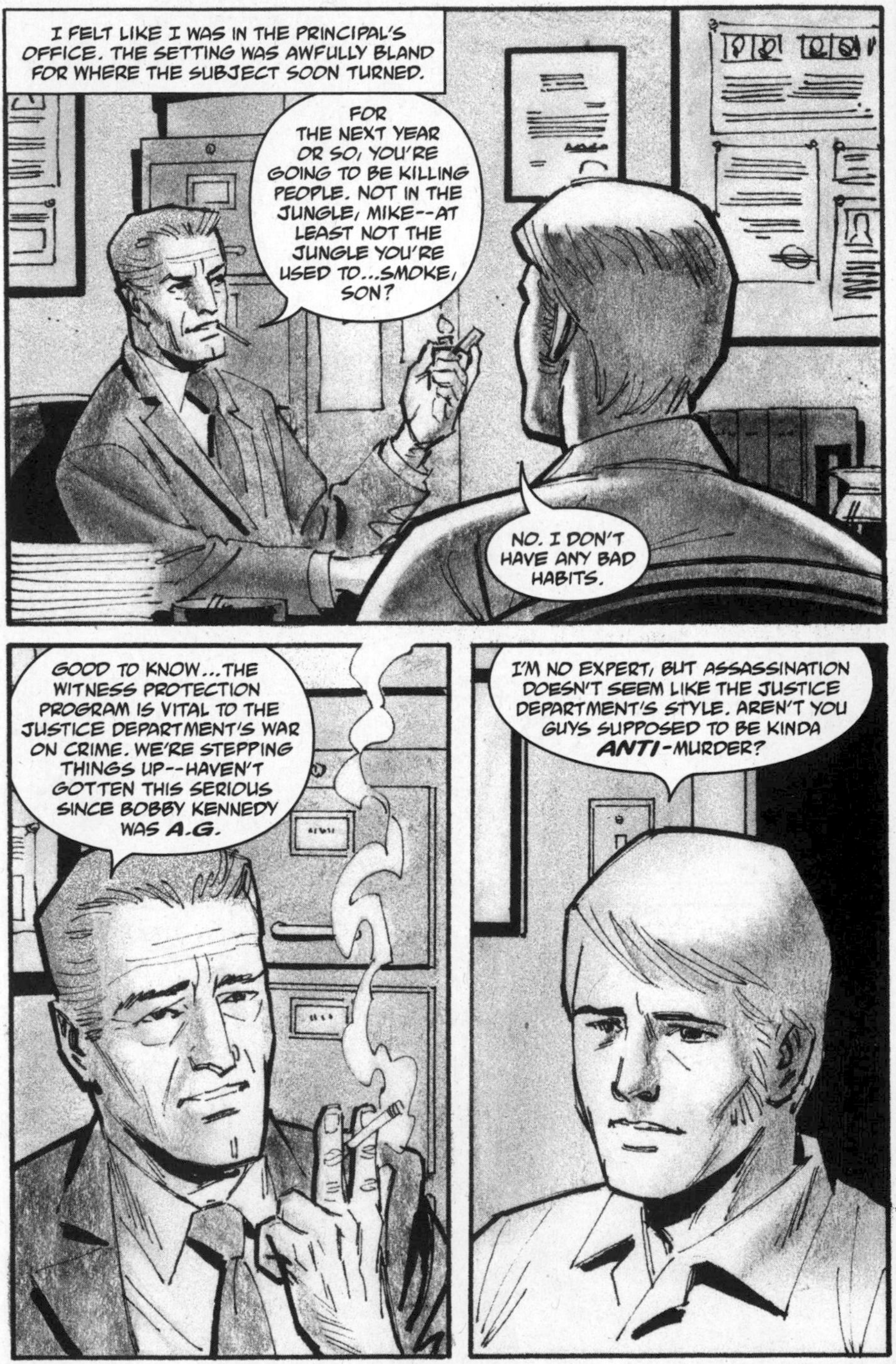
I FELT LIKE I WAS IN THE PRINCIPAL'S OFFICE. THE SETTING WAS AWFULLY BLAND FOR WHERE THE SUBJECT SOON TURNED.
FOR THE NEXT YEAR OR SO, YOU'RE GOING TO BE KILLING PEOPLE. NOT IN THE JUNGLE, MIKE--AT LEAST NOT THE JUNGLE YOU'RE USED TO...SMOKE, SON?
NO. I DON'T HAVE ANY BAD HABITS.
GOOD TO KNOW...THE WITNESS PROTECTION PROGRAM IS VITAL TO THE JUSTICE DEPARTMENT'S WAR ON CRIME. WE'RE STEPPING THINGS UP--HAVEN'T GOTTEN THIS SERIOUS SINCE BOBBY KENNEDY WAS A.G.
I'M NO EXPERT, BUT ASSASSINATION DOESN'T SEEM LIKE THE JUSTICE DEPARTMENT'S STYLE. AREN'T YOU GUYS SUPPOSED TO BE KINDA ANTI-MURDER?

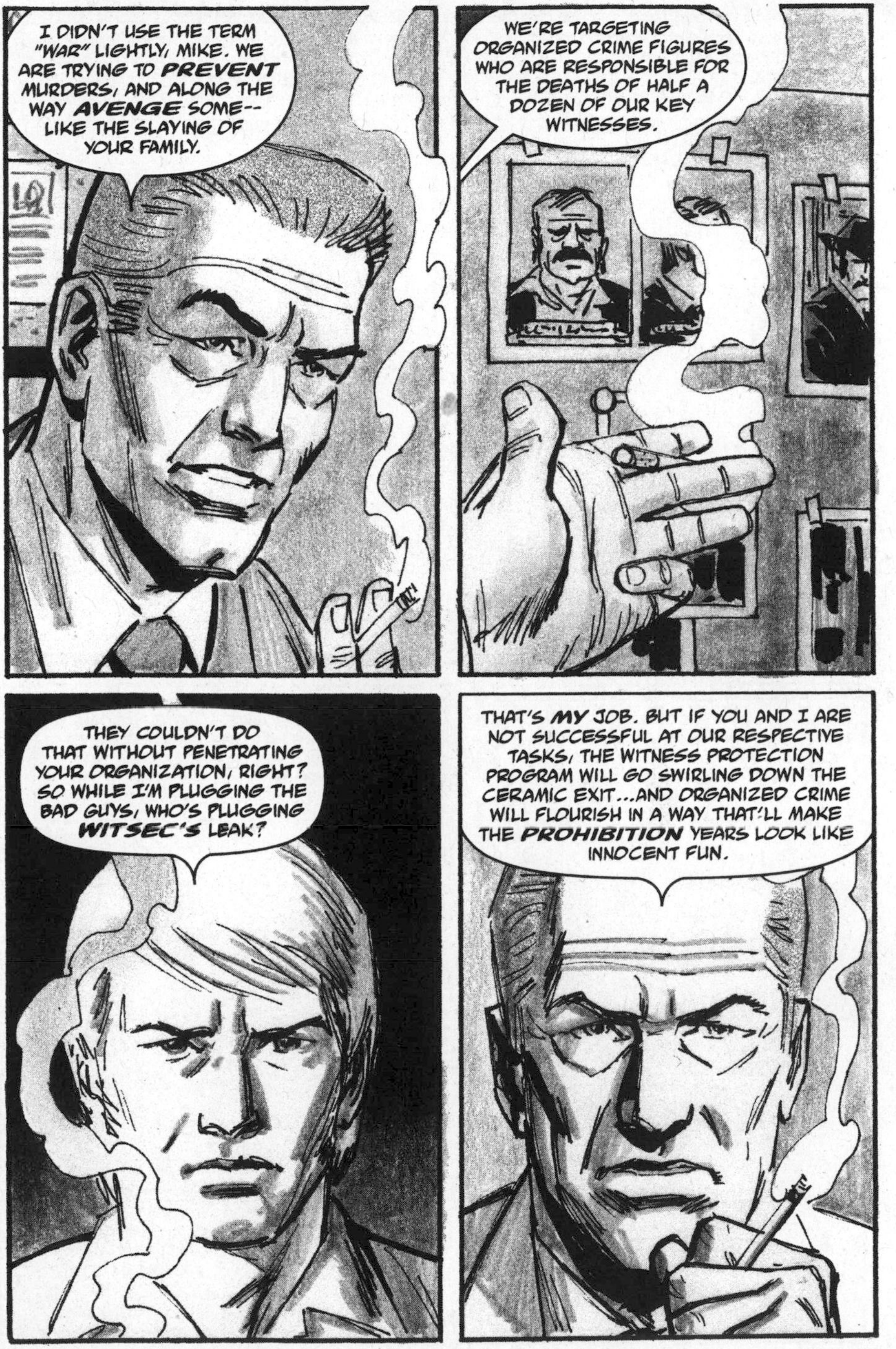
I DIDN'T USE THE TERM "WAR" LIGHTLY, MIKE. WE ARE TRYING TO PREVENT MURDERS, AND ALONG THE WAY AVENGE SOME-- LIKE THE SLAYING OF YOUR FAMILY.
WE'RE TARGETING ORGANIZED CRIME FIGURES WHO ARE RESPONSIBLE FOR THE DEATHS OF HALF A DOZEN OF OUR KEY WITNESSES.
THEY COULDN'T DO THAT WITHOUT PENETRATING YOUR ORGANIZATION, RIGHT? SO WHILE I'M PLUGGING THE BAD GUYS, WHO'S PLUGGING WITSEC'S LEAK?
THAT'S MY JOB. BUT IF YOU AND I ARE NOT SUCCESSFUL AT OUR RESPECTIVE TASKS, THE WITNESS PROTECTION PROGRAM WILL GO SWIRLING DOWN THE CERAMIC EXIT...AND ORGANIZED CRIME WILL FLOURISH IN A WAY THAT'LL MAKE THE PROHIBITION YEARS LOOK LIKE INNOCENT FUN.

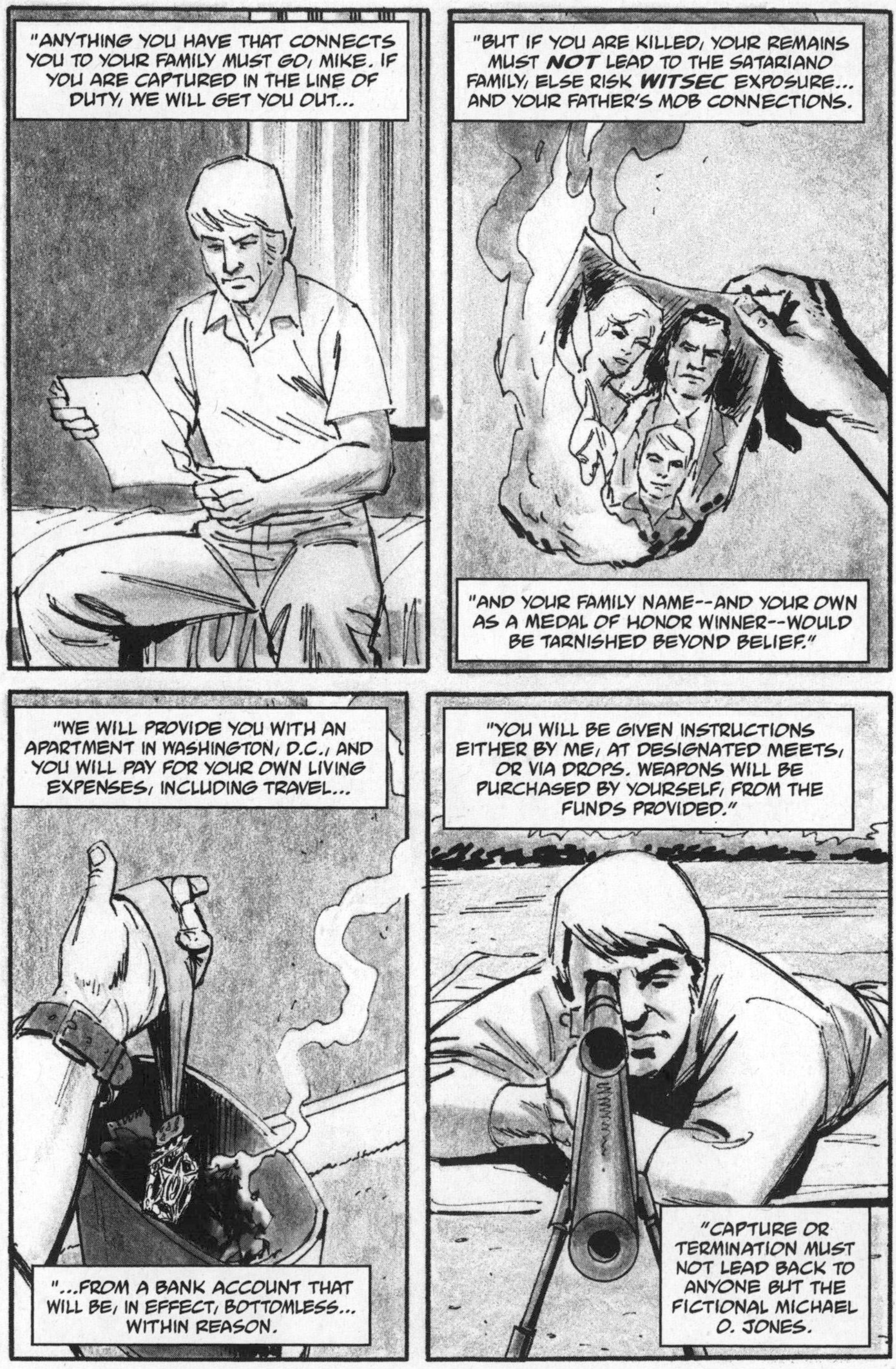
"ANYTHING YOU HAVE THAT CONNECTS YOU TO YOUR FAMILY MUST GO, MIKE. IF YOU ARE CAPTURED IN THE LINE OF DUTY, WE WILL GET YOU OUT...
"BUT IF YOU ARE KILLED, YOUR REMAINS MUST **NOT** LEAD TO THE SATARIANO FAMILY, ELSE RISK **WITSEC** EXPOSURE... AND YOUR FATHER'S MOB CONNECTIONS.
"AND YOUR FAMILY NAME--AND YOUR OWN AS A MEDAL OF HONOR WINNER--WOULD BE TARNISHED BEYOND BELIEF."
"WE WILL PROVIDE YOU WITH AN APARTMENT IN WASHINGTON, D.C., AND YOU WILL PAY FOR YOUR OWN LIVING EXPENSES, INCLUDING TRAVEL...
"...FROM A BANK ACCOUNT THAT WILL BE, IN EFFECT, BOTTOMLESS... WITHIN REASON.
"YOU WILL BE GIVEN INSTRUCTIONS EITHER BY ME, AT DESIGNATED MEETS, OR VIA DROPS. WEAPONS WILL BE PURCHASED BY YOURSELF, FROM THE FUNDS PROVIDED."
"CAPTURE OR TERMINATION MUST NOT LEAD BACK TO ANYONE BUT THE FICTIONAL MICHAEL O. JONES.

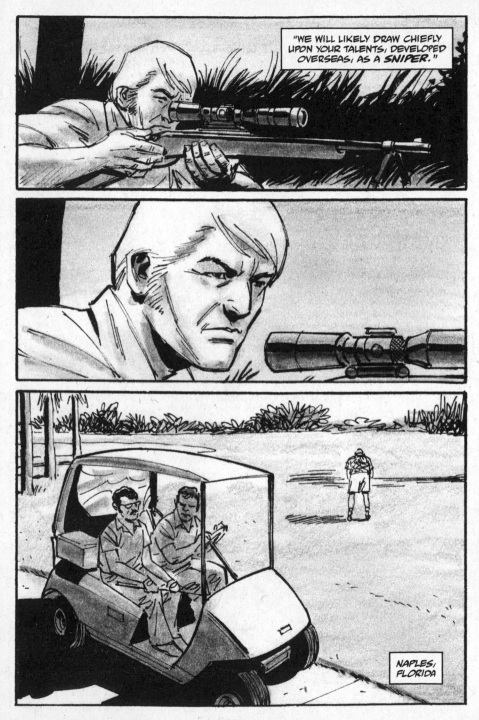

"WE WILL LIKELY DRAW CHIEFLY UPON YOUR TALENTS, DEVELOPED OVERSEAS, AS A *SNIPER.*"

NAPLES, FLORIDA

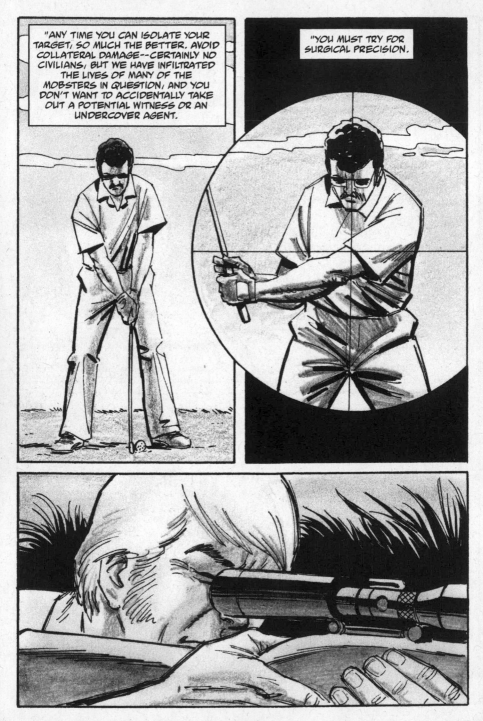

"ANY TIME YOU CAN ISOLATE YOUR TARGET, SO MUCH THE BETTER. AVOID COLLATERAL DAMAGE--CERTAINLY NO CIVILIANS, BUT WE HAVE INFILTRATED THE LIVES OF MANY OF THE MOBSTERS IN QUESTION, AND YOU DON'T WANT TO ACCIDENTALLY TAKE OUT A POTENTIAL WITNESS OR AN UNDERCOVER AGENT.

"YOU MUST TRY FOR SURGICAL PRECISION.

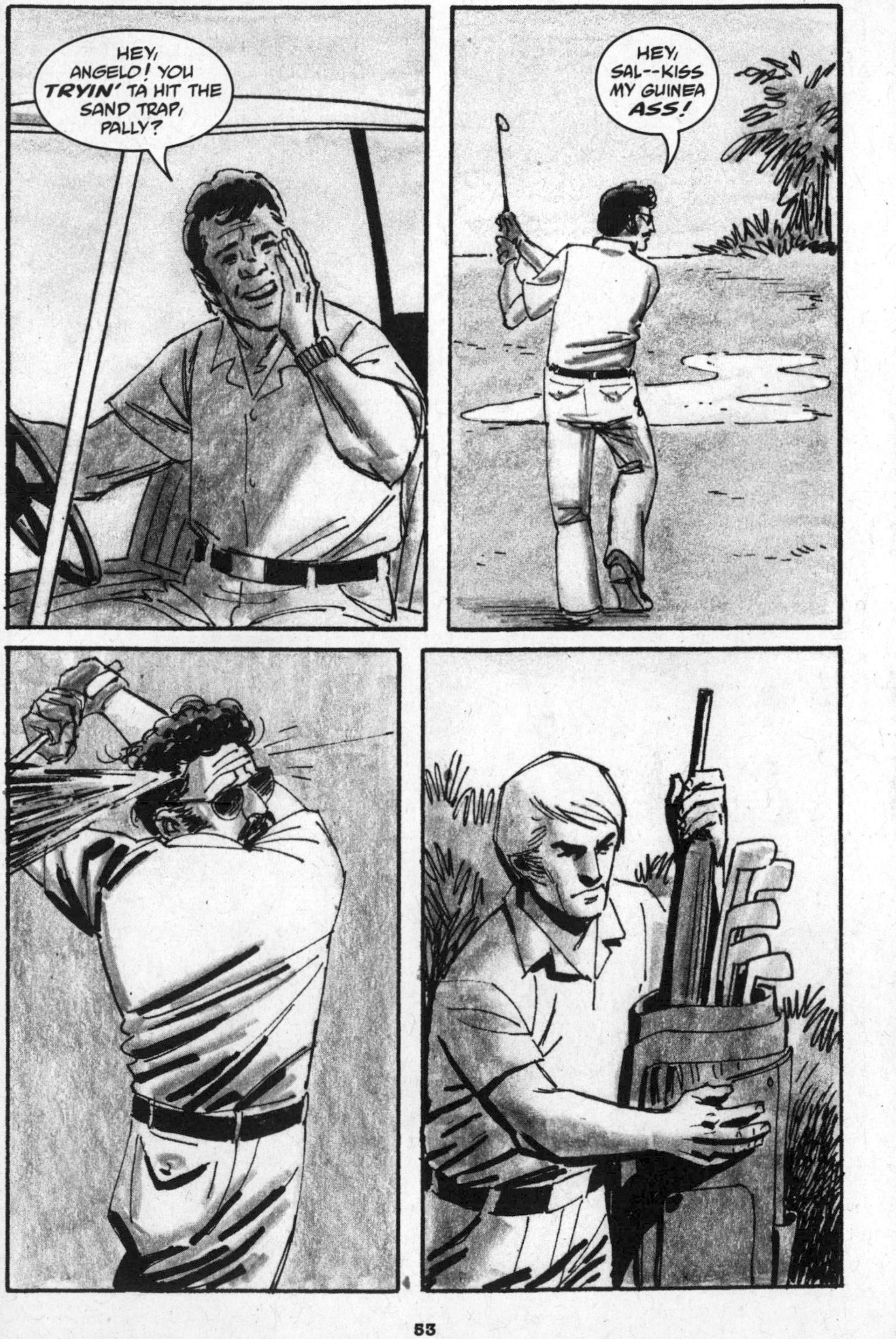
HEY, ANGELO! YOU TRYIN' TA HIT THE SAND TRAP, PALLY?
HEY, SAL--KISS MY GUINEA ASS!

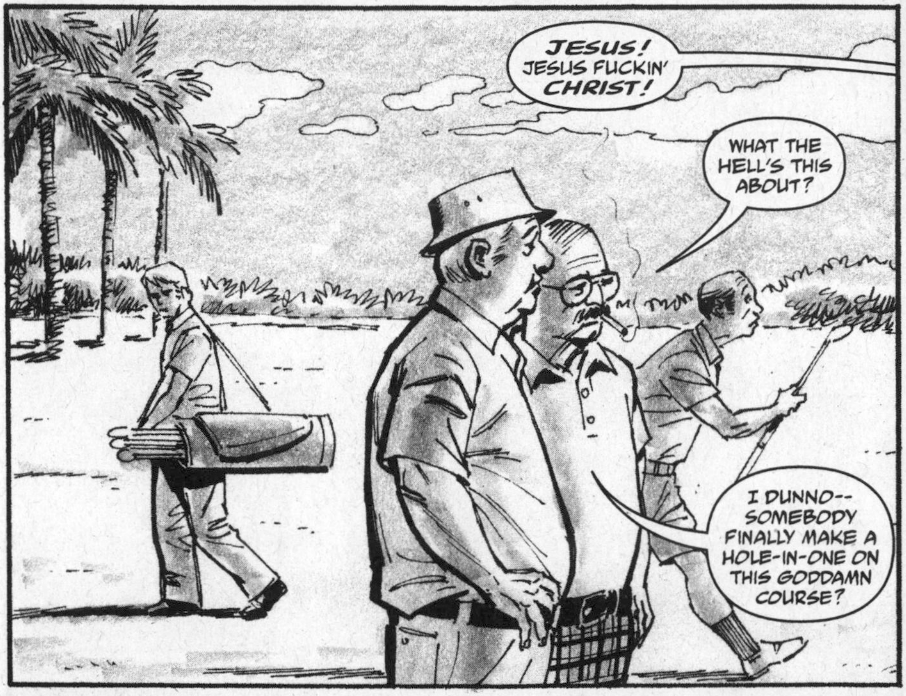
JESUS! JESUS FUCKIN' CHRIST!
WHAT THE HELL'S THIS ABOUT?
I DUNNO-- SOMEBODY FINALLY MAKE A HOLE-IN-ONE ON THIS GODDAMN COURSE?

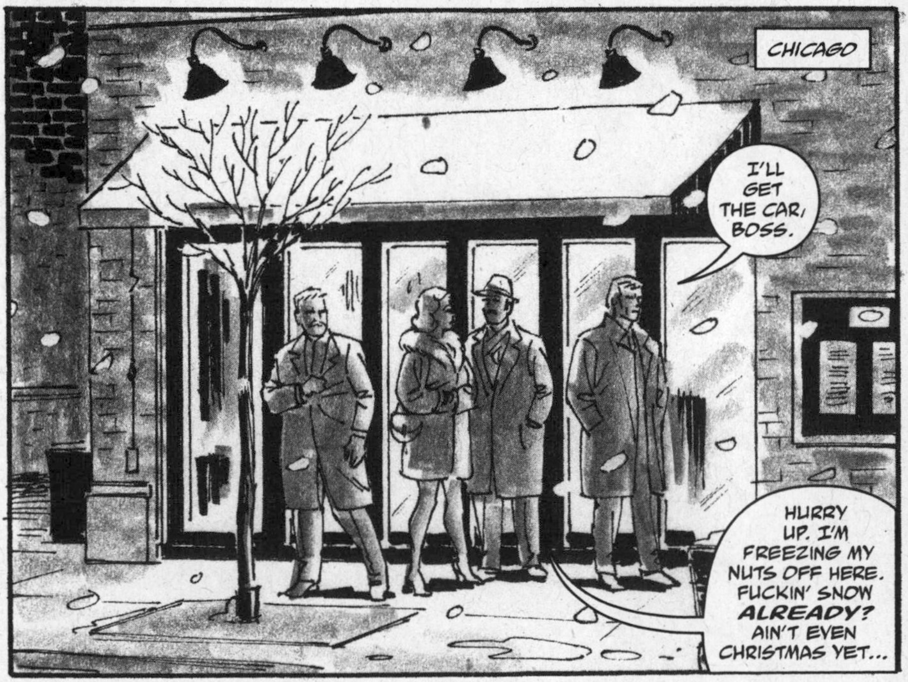
CHICAGO
I'LL GET THE CAR, BOSS.
HURRY UP. I'M FREEZING MY NUTS OFF HERE. FUCKIN' SNOW ALREADY? AIN'T EVEN CHRISTMAS YET...

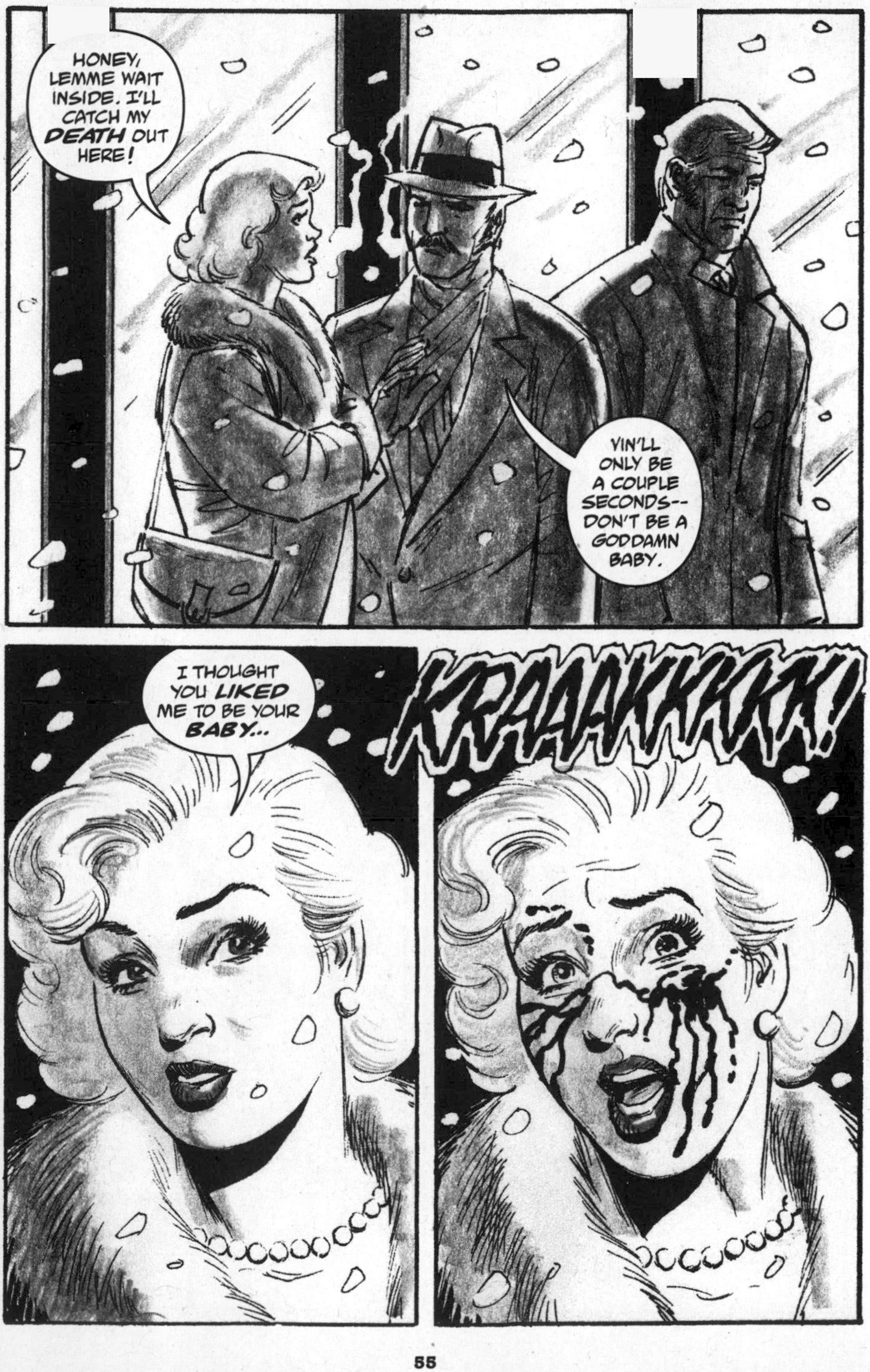
HONEY, LEMME WAIT INSIDE. I'LL CATCH MY DEATH OUT HERE!
VIN'LL ONLY BE A COUPLE SECONDS-- DON'T BE A GODDAMN BABY.
I THOUGHT YOU LIKED ME TO BE YOUR BABY...
KRAAAKKKKKK!

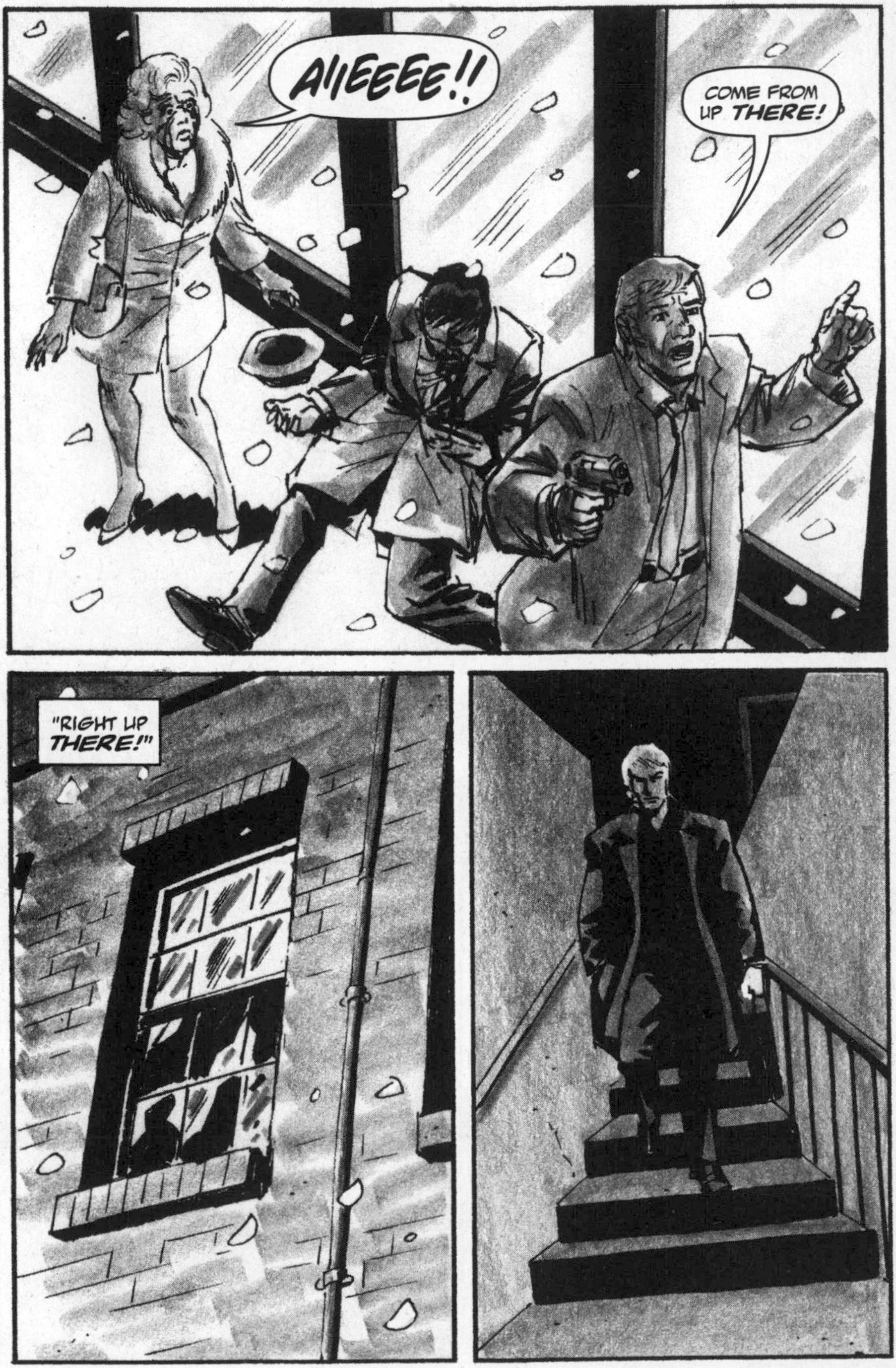
AIIEEEE!!
COME FROM UP THERE!
"RIGHT UP THERE!"

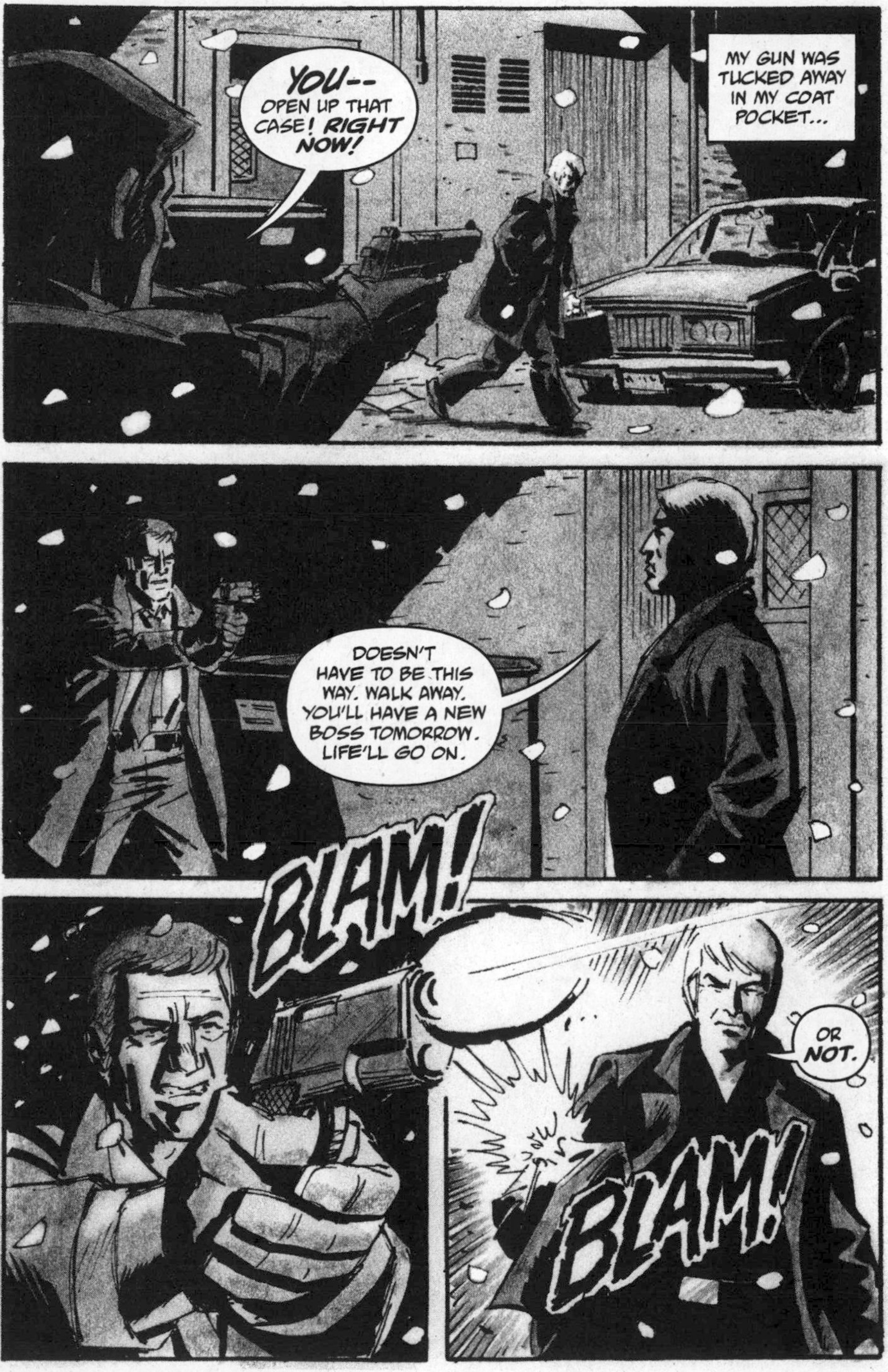
YOU-- OPEN UP THAT CASE! RIGHT NOW!
MY GUN WAS TUCKED AWAY IN MY COAT POCKET...
DOESN'T HAVE TO BE THIS WAY. WALK AWAY. YOU'LL HAVE A NEW BOSS TOMORROW. LIFE'LL GO ON.
BLAM!
OR NOT.
BLAM!

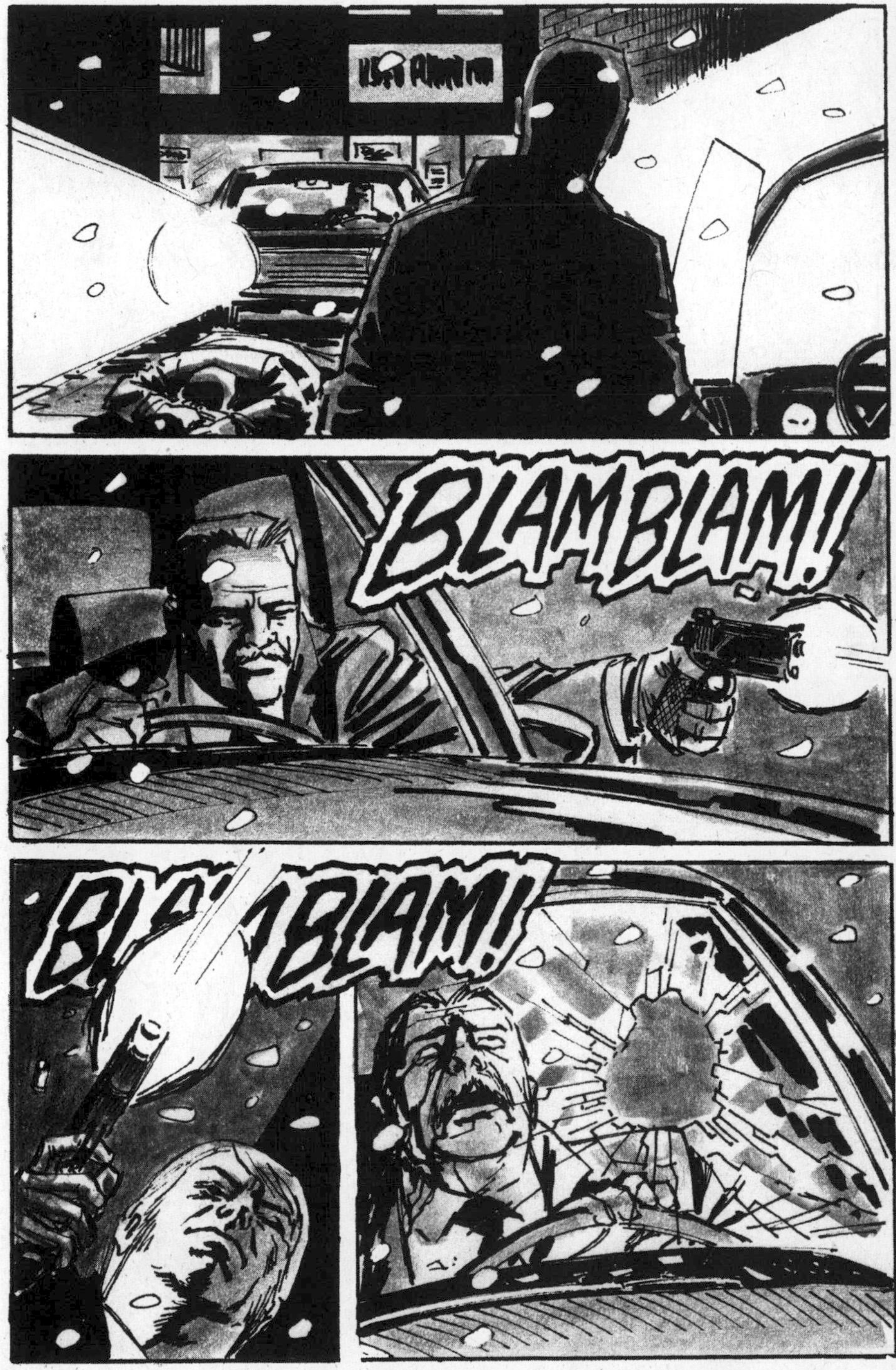
BLAMBLAM!
ABLAM!

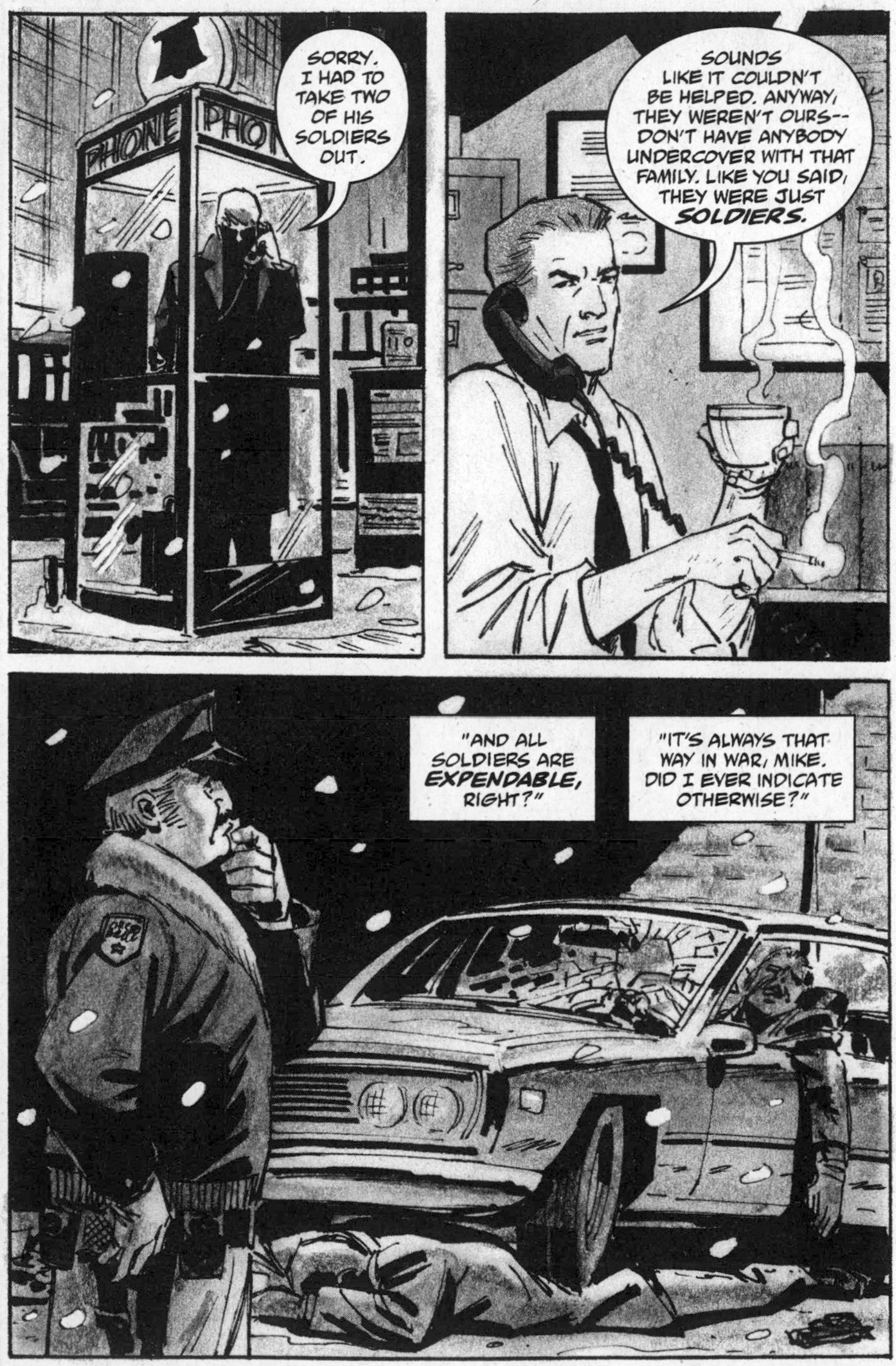
SORRY. I HAD TO TAKE TWO OF HIS SOLDIERS OUT.
PHONE
SOUNDS LIKE IT COULDN'T BE HELPED. ANYWAY, THEY WEREN'T OURS-- DON'T HAVE ANYBODY UNDERCOVER WITH THAT FAMILY. LIKE YOU SAID, THEY WERE JUST **SOLDIERS.**
"AND ALL SOLDIERS ARE **EXPENDABLE,** RIGHT?"
"IT'S ALWAYS THAT WAY IN WAR, MIKE. DID I EVER INDICATE OTHERWISE?"

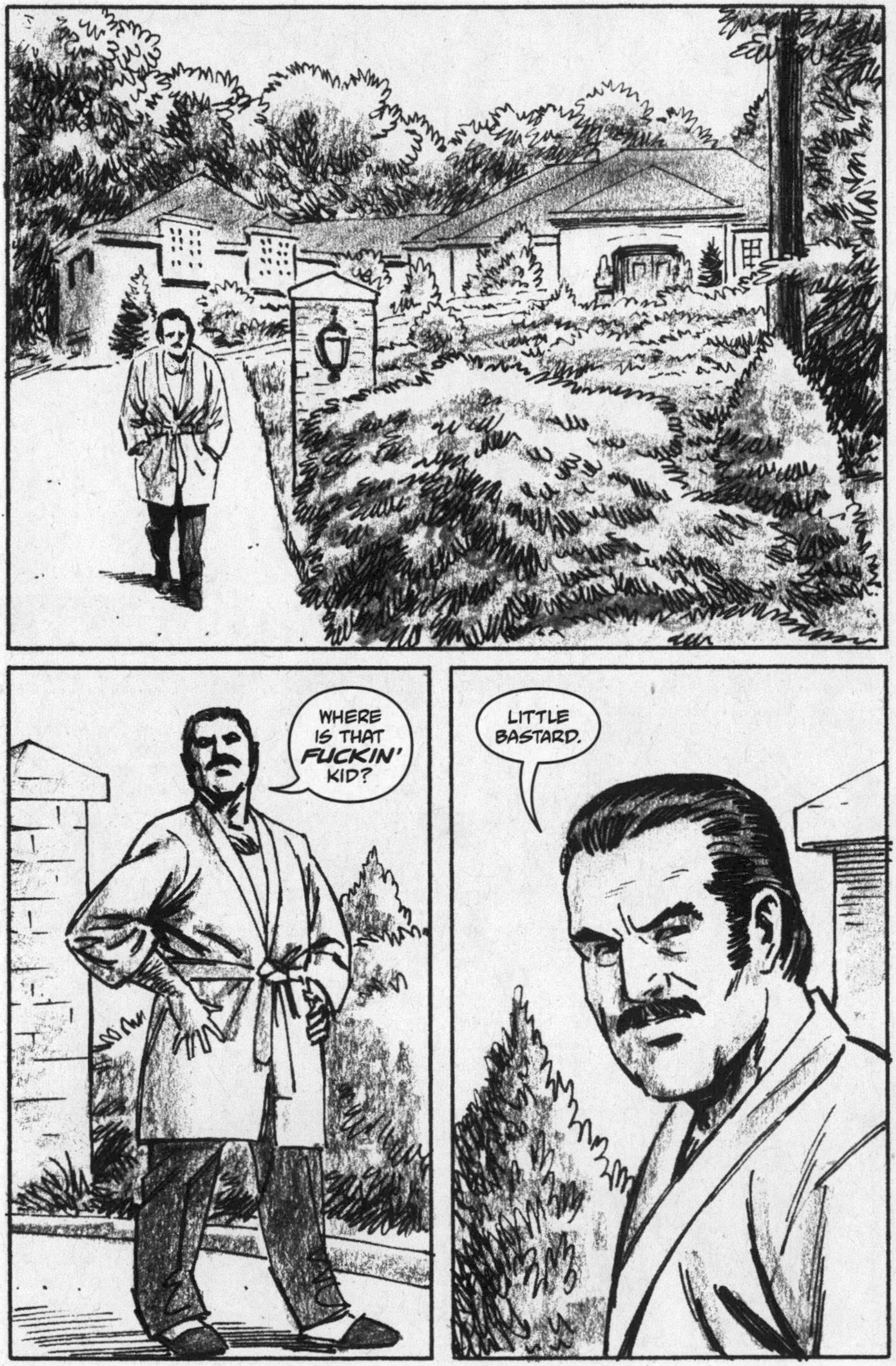
WHERE IS THAT FUCKIN' KID?
LITTLE BASTARD.

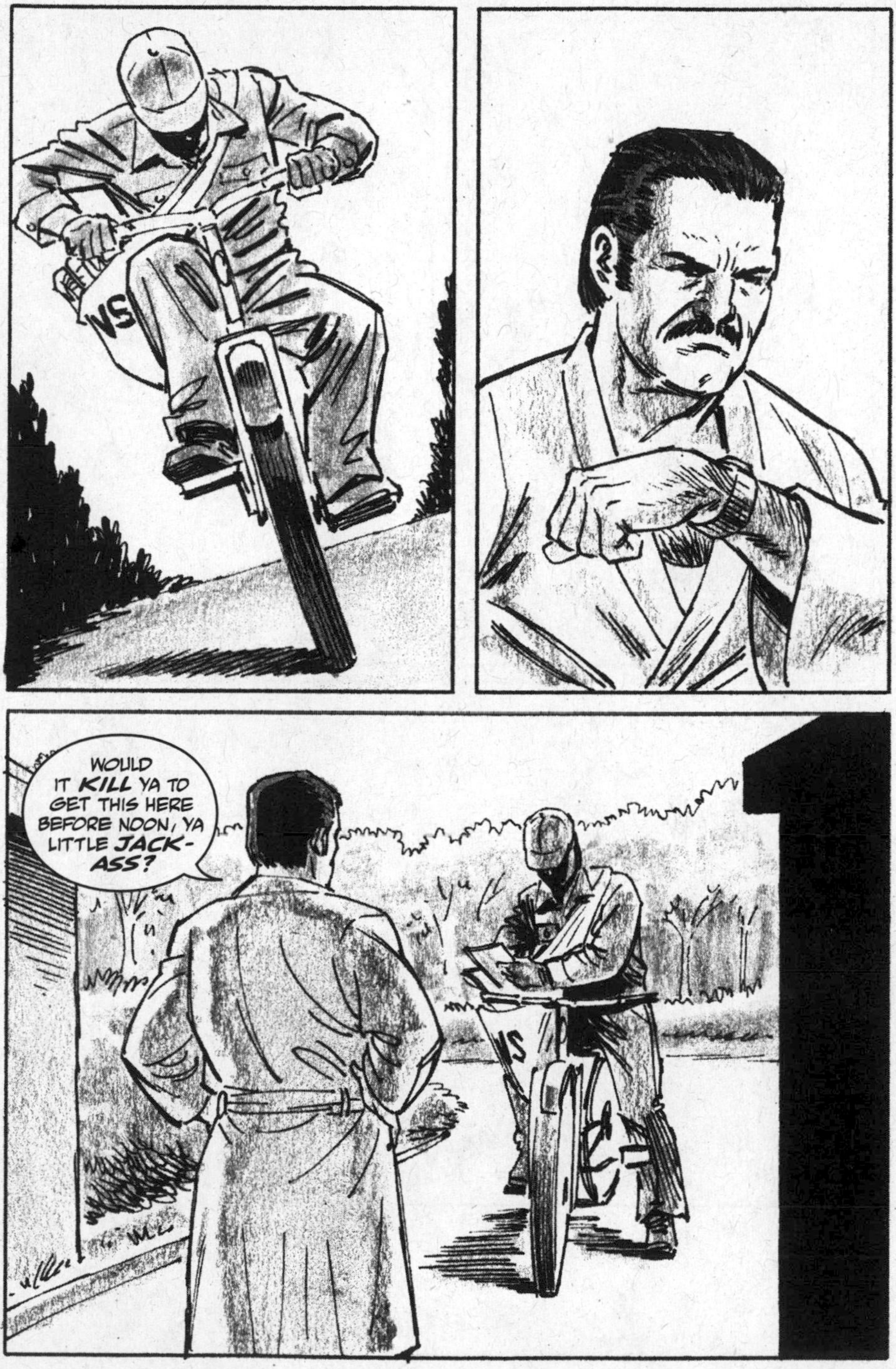
WOULD IT KILL YA TO GET THIS HERE BEFORE NOON, YA LITTLE JACK-ASS?

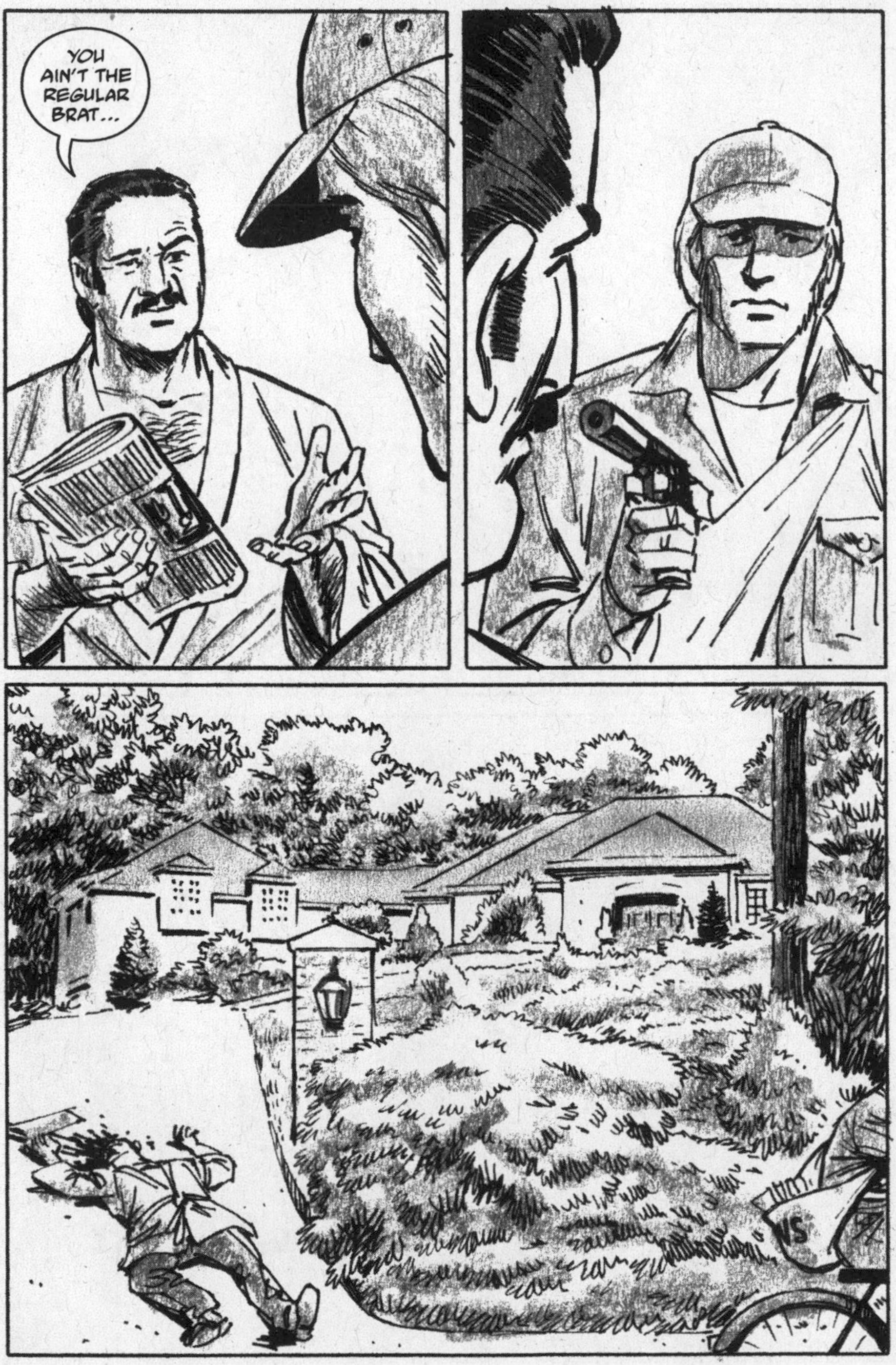
YOU AIN'T THE REGULAR BRAT...

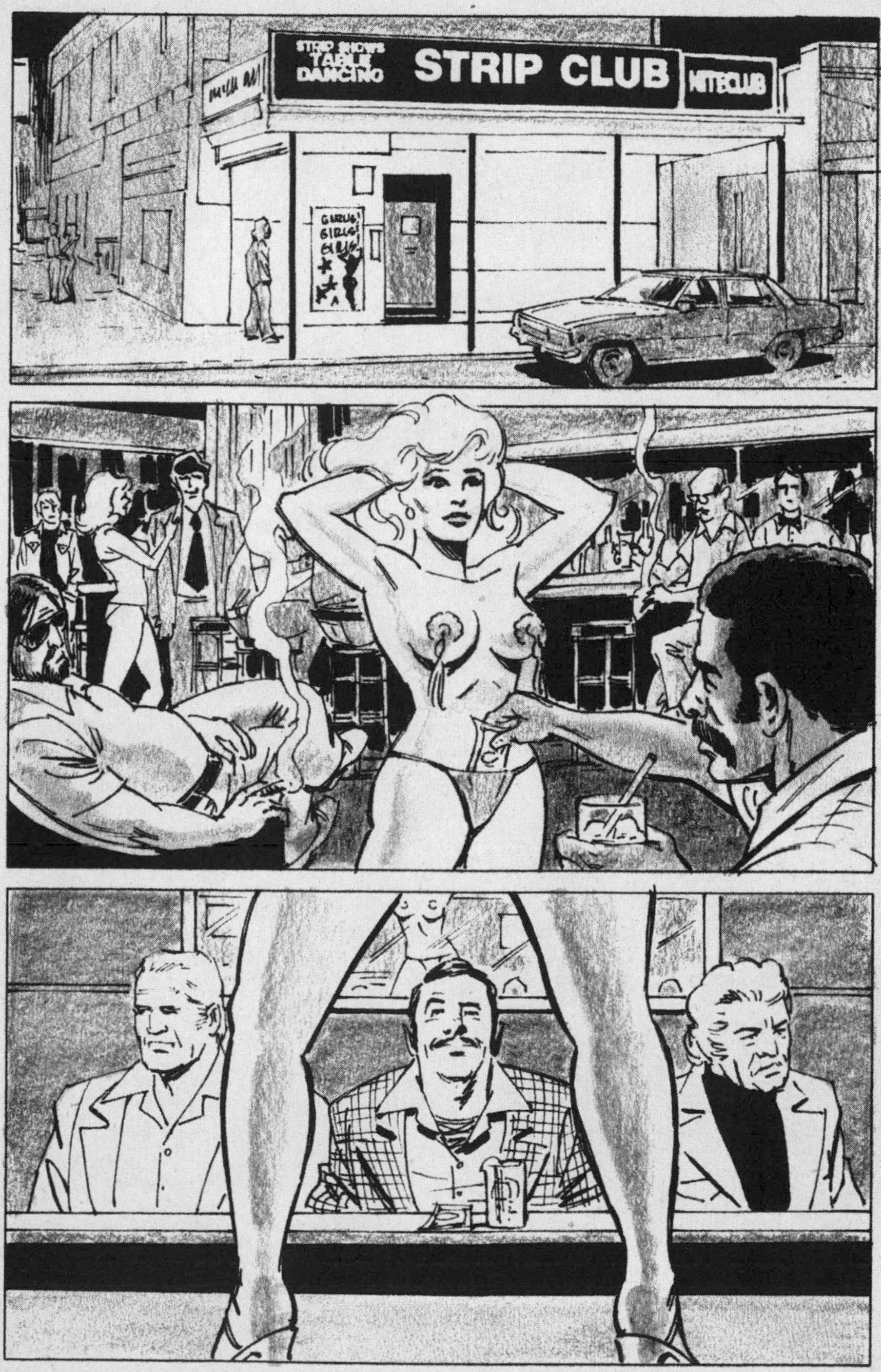
STRIP CLUB
NITECLUB

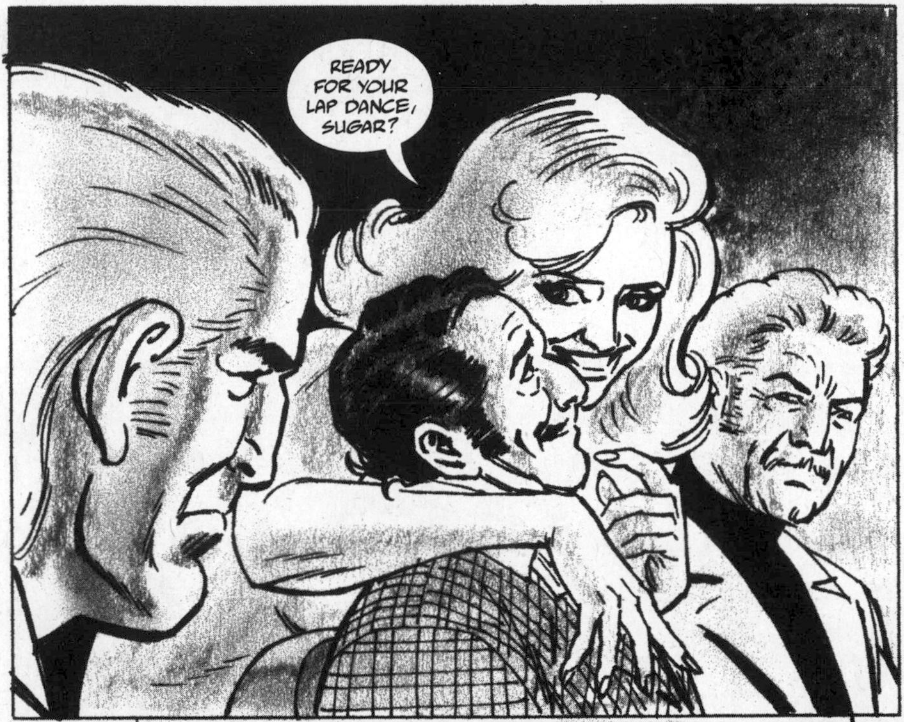
READY FOR YOUR LAP DANCE, SUGAR?

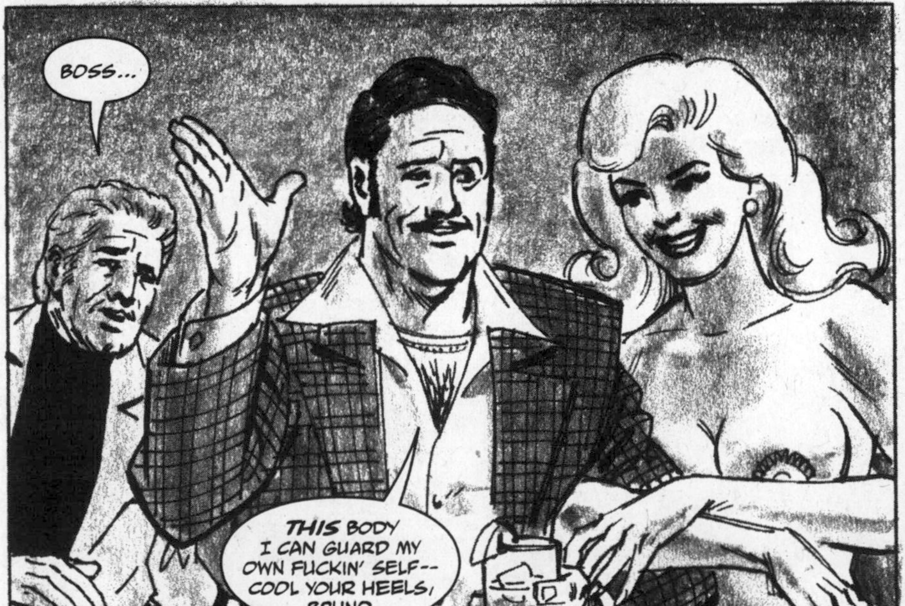
BOSS...
THIS BODY I CAN GUARD MY OWN FUCKIN' SELF-- COOL YOUR HEELS, BRUNO.

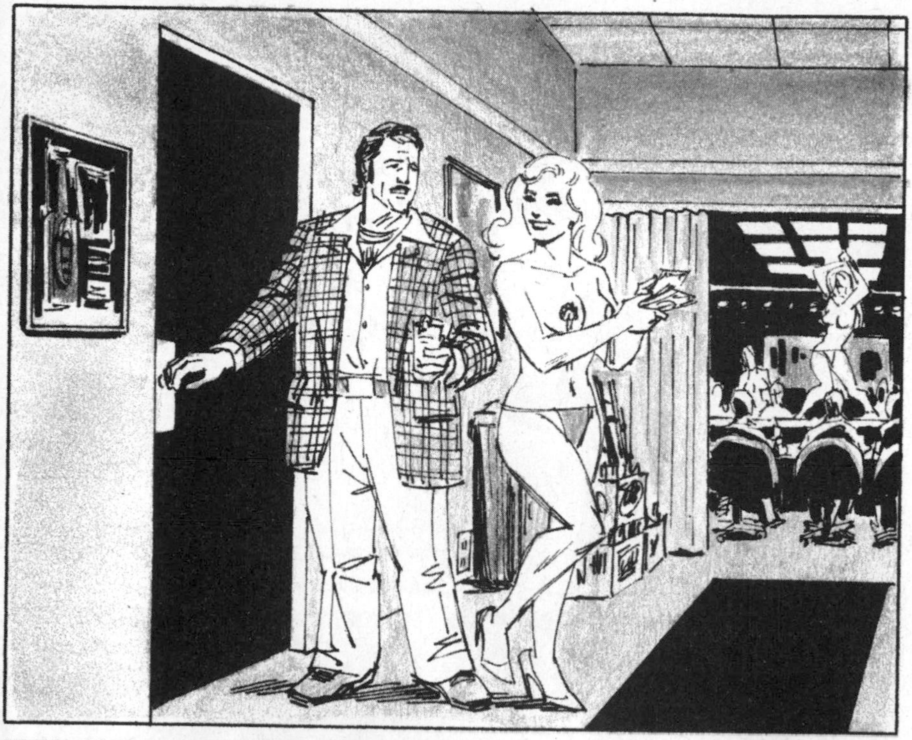

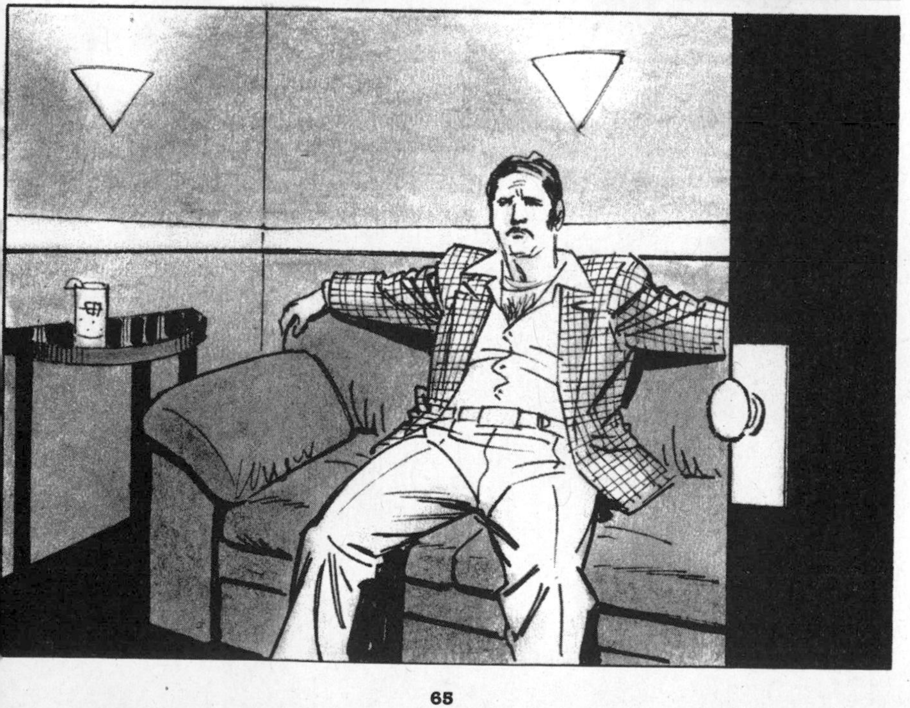

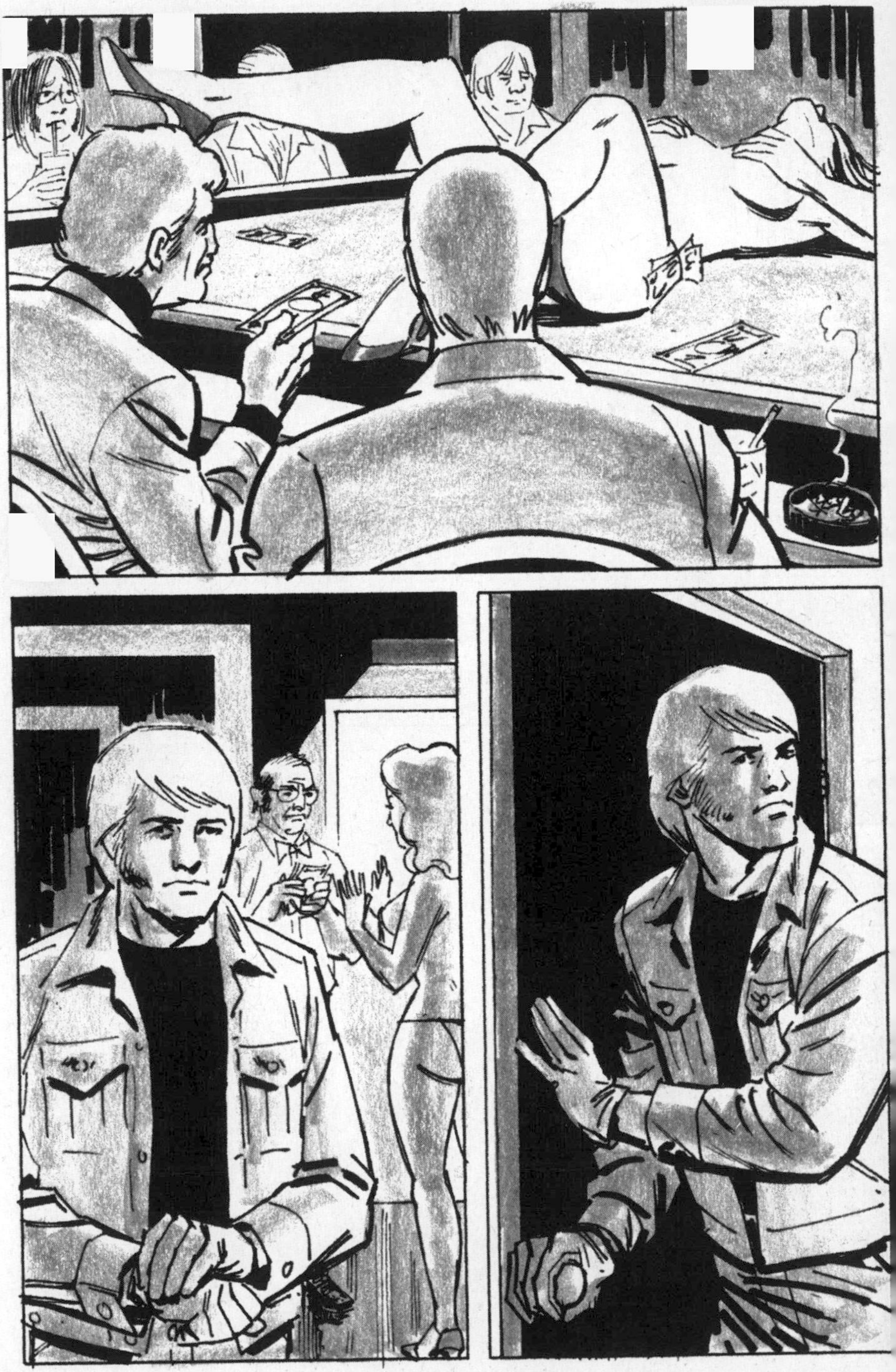

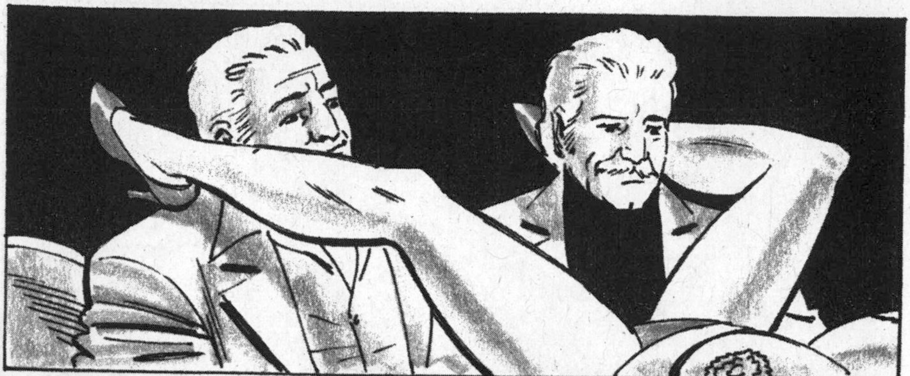

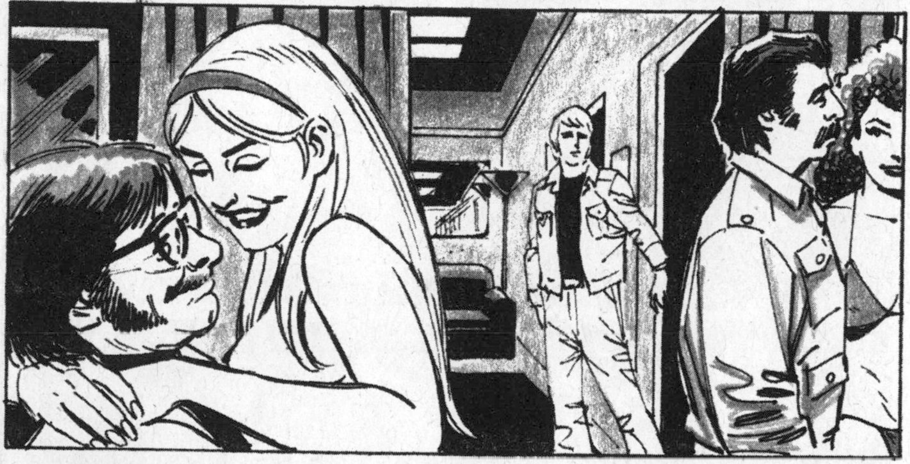

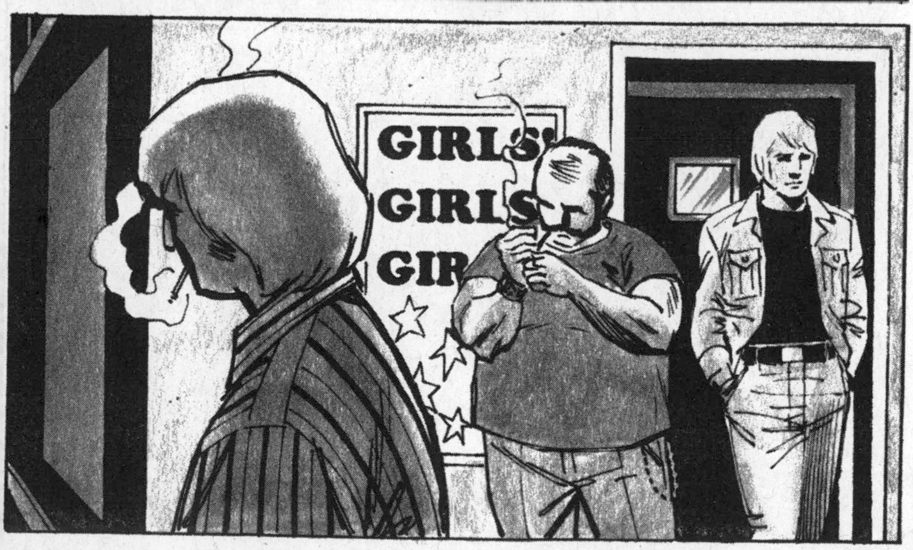
GIRLS
GIRLS
GIR

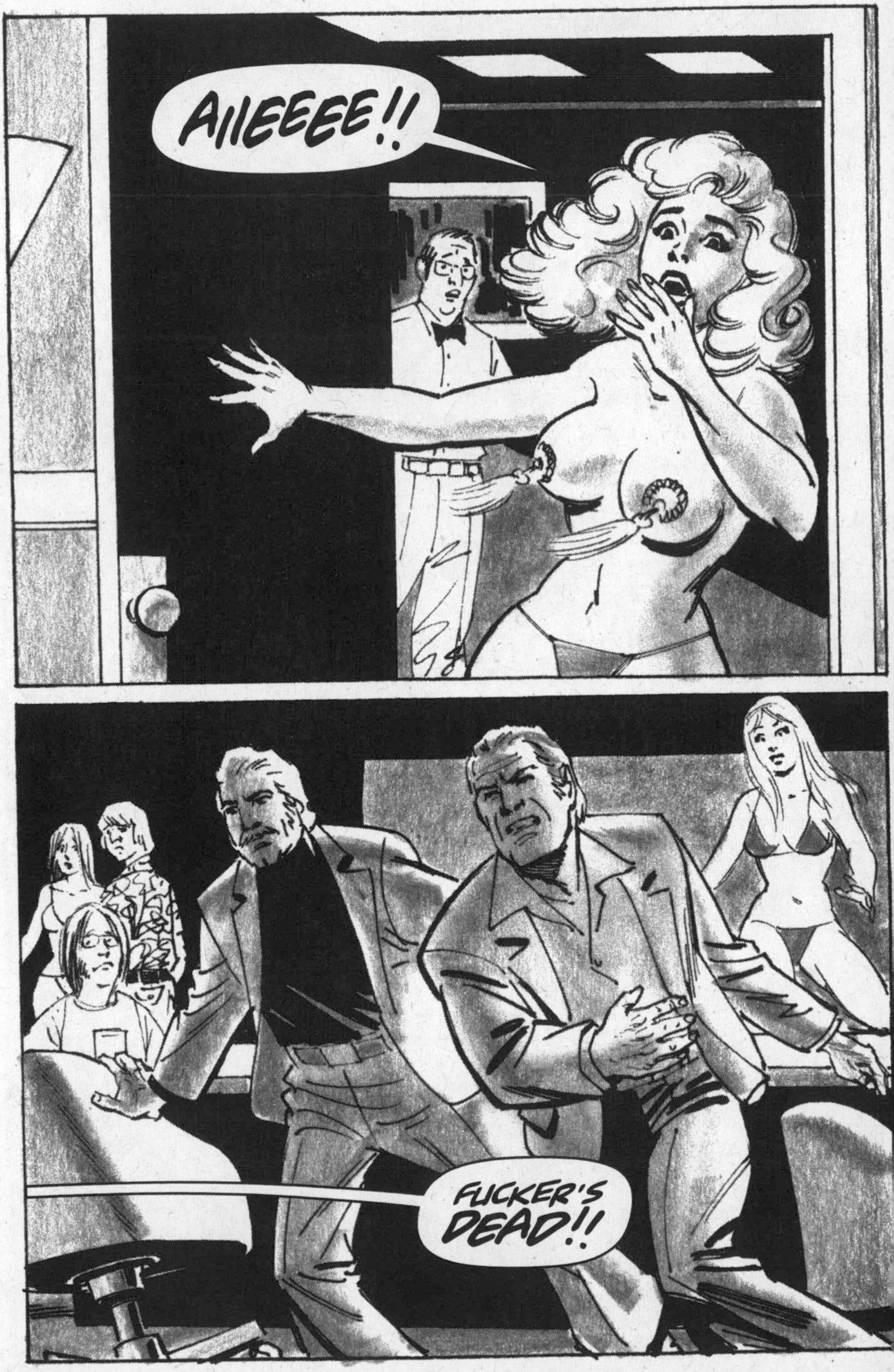
AIIEEEE!!
FUCKER'S DEAD!!

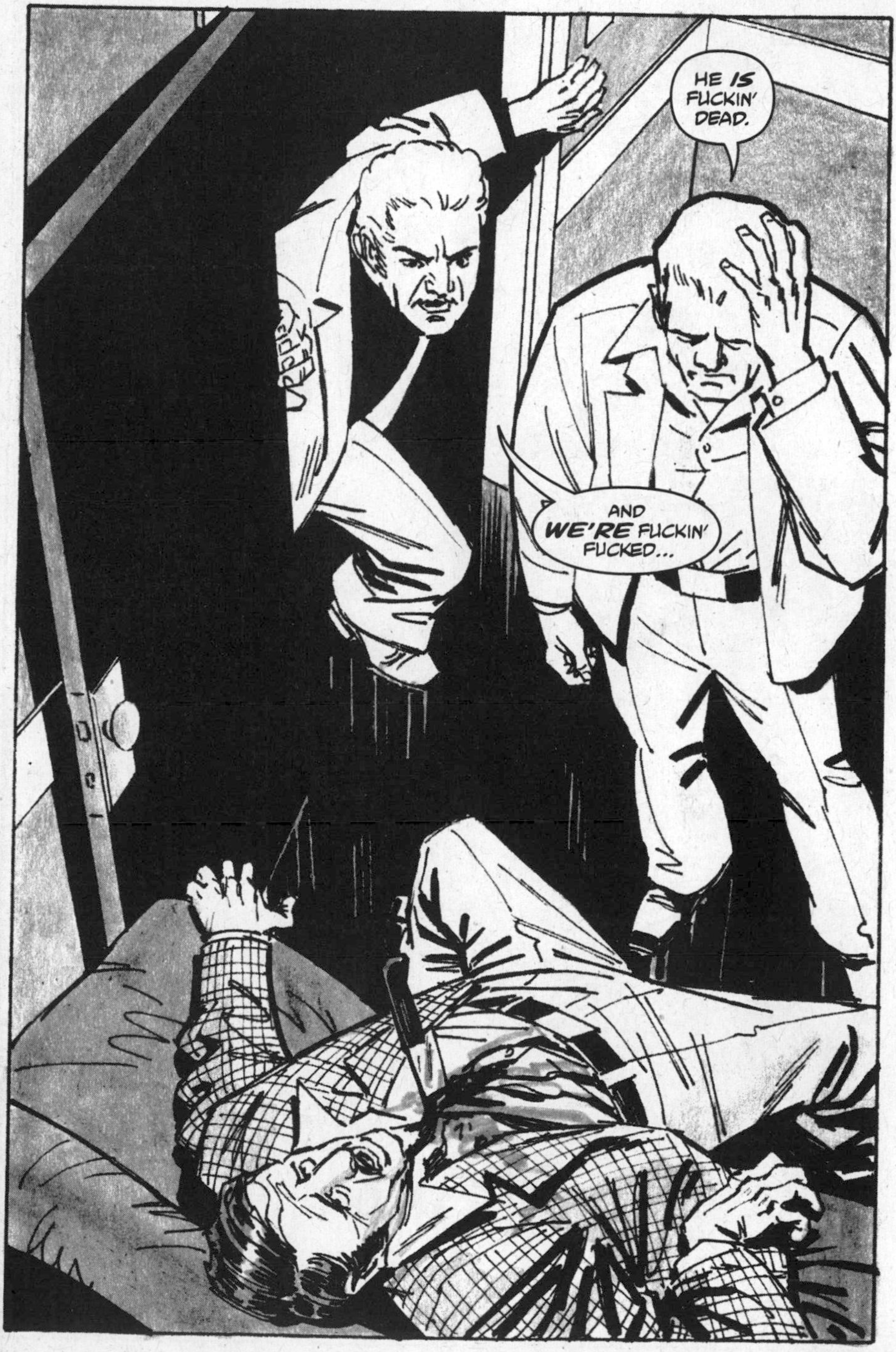
HE IS FUCKIN' DEAD.
AND WE'RE FUCKIN' FUCKED...

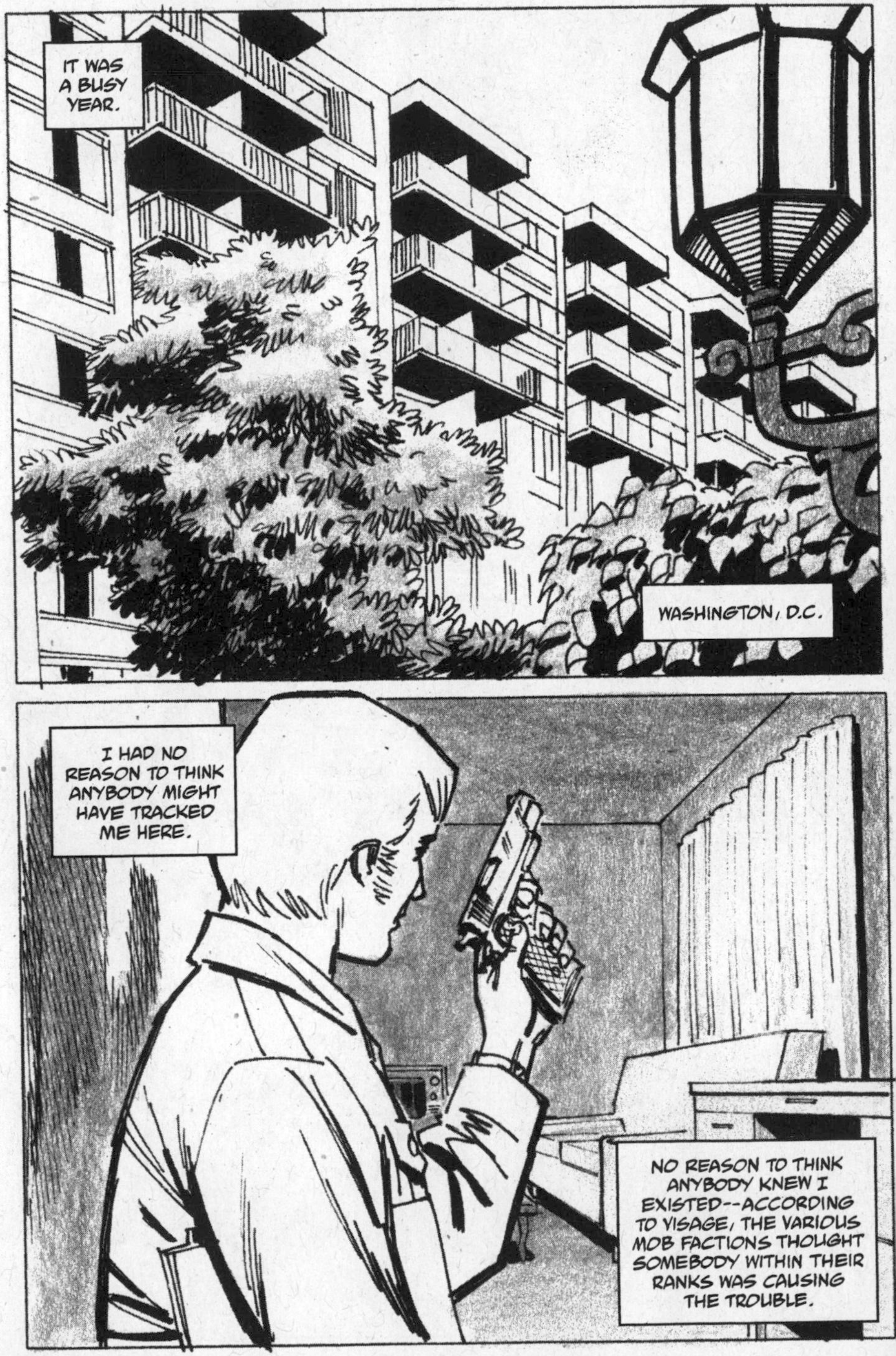
IT WAS A BUSY YEAR.
WASHINGTON, D.C.
I HAD NO REASON TO THINK ANYBODY MIGHT HAVE TRACKED ME HERE.
NO REASON TO THINK ANYBODY KNEW I EXISTED--ACCORDING TO VISAGE, THE VARIOUS MOB FACTIONS THOUGHT SOMEBODY WITHIN THEIR RANKS WAS CAUSING THE TROUBLE.

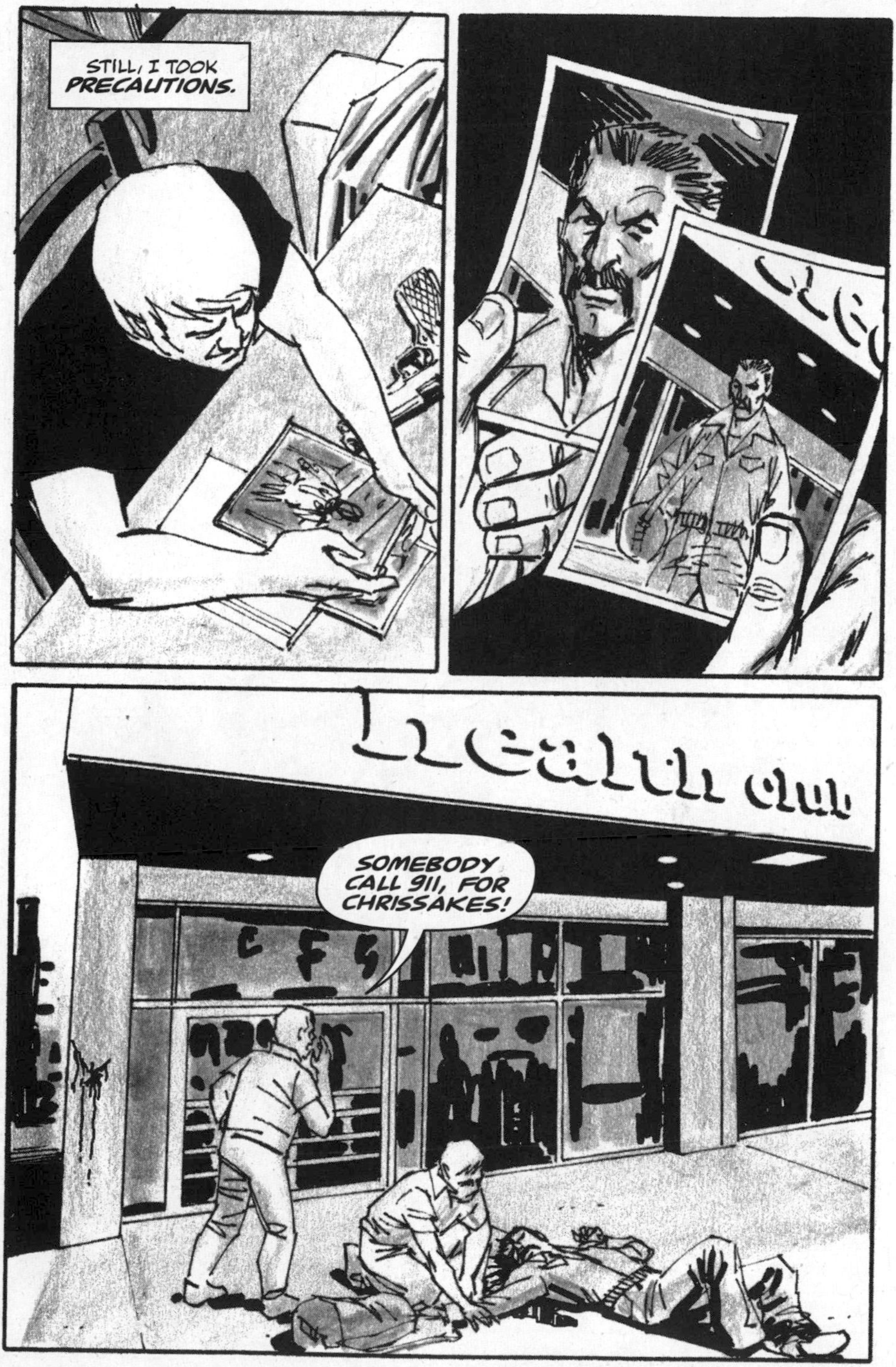

STILL, I TOOK PRECAUTIONS.
Health club
SOMEBODY CALL 911, FOR CHRISSAKES!

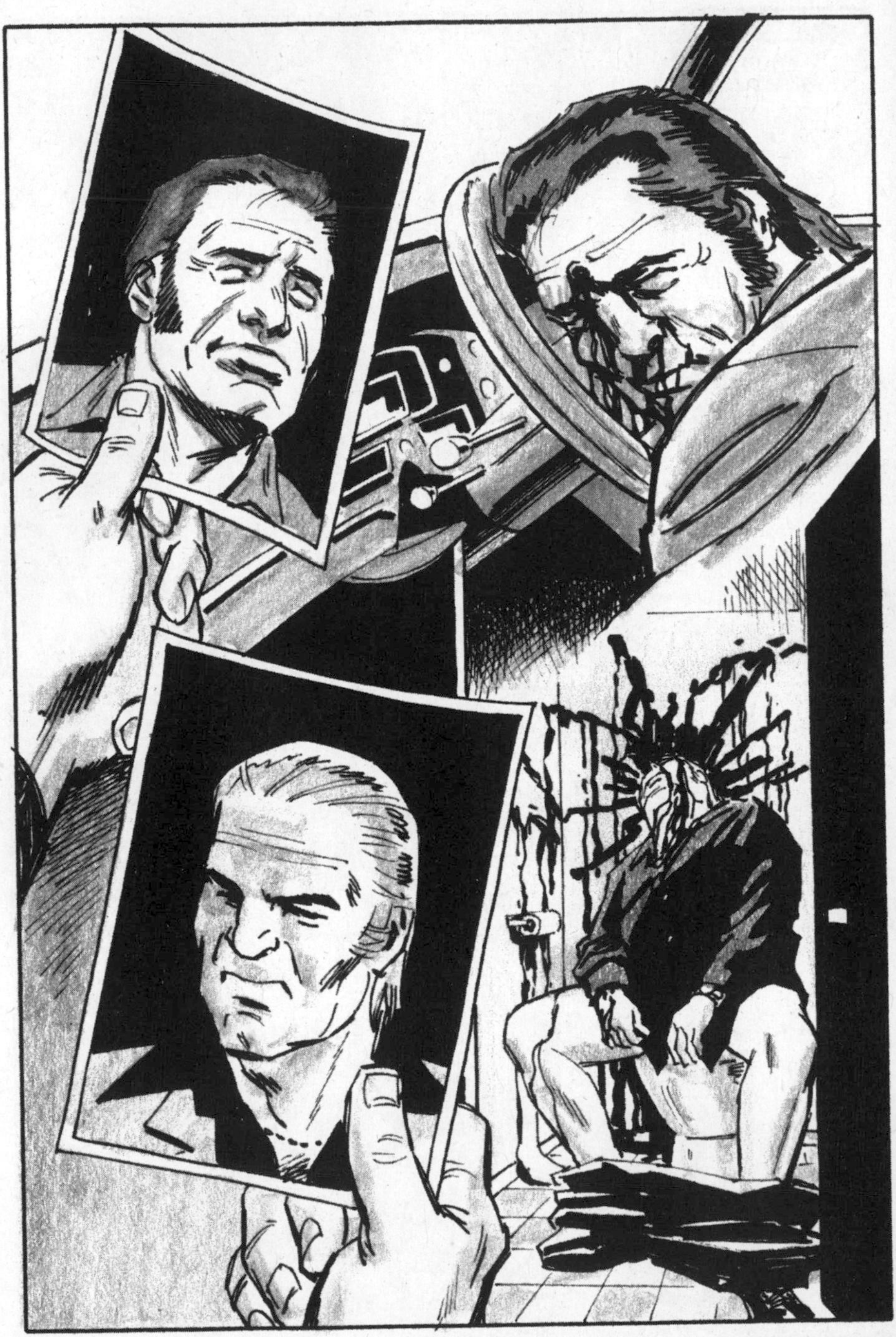

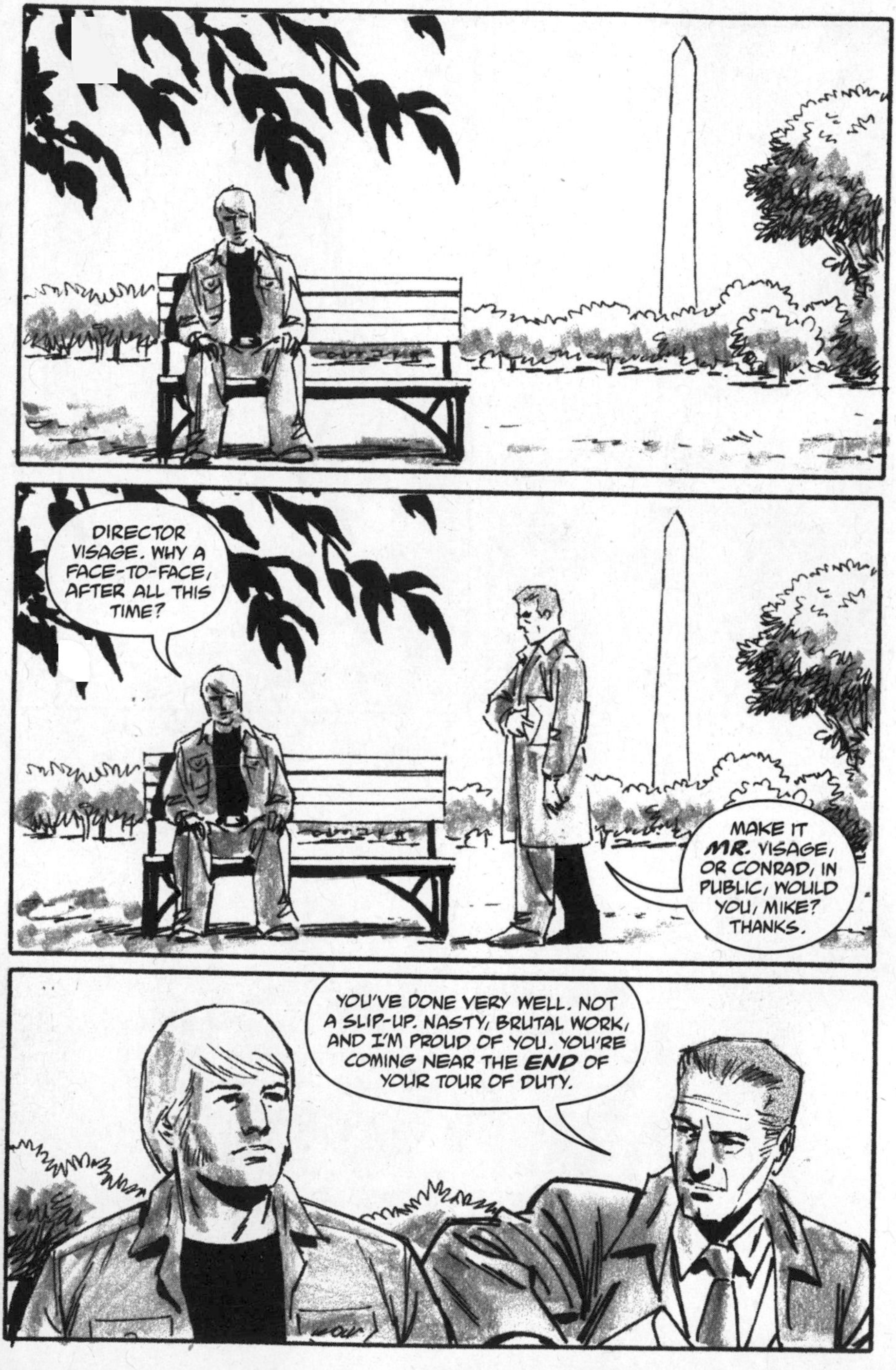
DIRECTOR VISAGE. WHY A FACE-TO-FACE, AFTER ALL THIS TIME?
MAKE IT MR. VISAGE, OR CONRAD, IN PUBLIC, WOULD YOU, MIKE? THANKS.
YOU'VE DONE VERY WELL. NOT A SLIP-UP. NASTY, BRUTAL WORK, AND I'M PROUD OF YOU. YOU'RE COMING NEAR THE END OF YOUR TOUR OF DUTY.

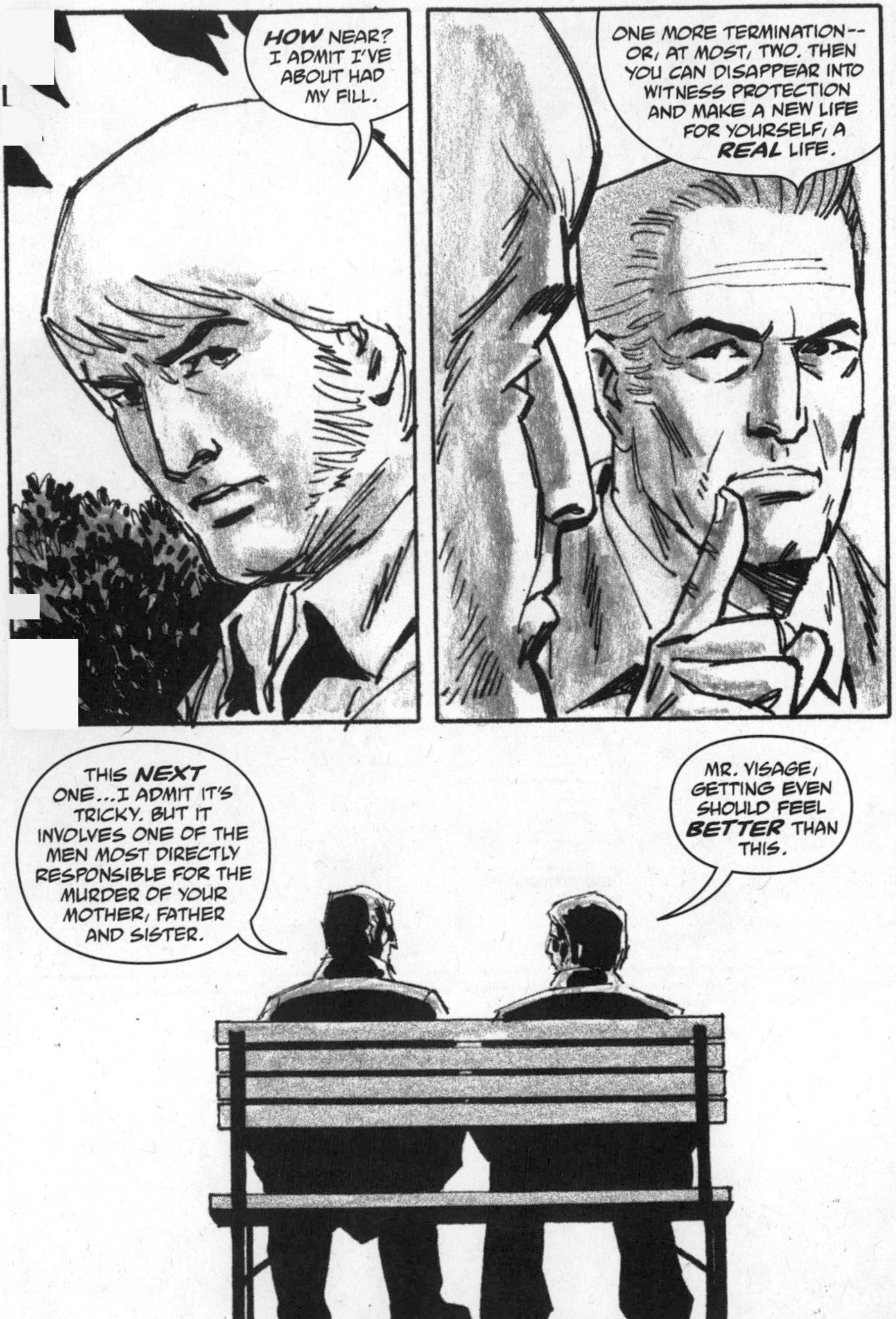
HOW NEAR? I ADMIT I'VE ABOUT HAD MY FILL.
ONE MORE TERMINATION-- OR, AT MOST, TWO. THEN YOU CAN DISAPPEAR INTO WITNESS PROTECTION AND MAKE A NEW LIFE FOR YOURSELF, A REAL LIFE.
THIS NEXT ONE...I ADMIT IT'S TRICKY. BUT IT INVOLVES ONE OF THE MEN MOST DIRECTLY RESPONSIBLE FOR THE MURDER OF YOUR MOTHER, FATHER AND SISTER.
MR. VISAGE, GETTING EVEN SHOULD FEEL BETTER THAN THIS.

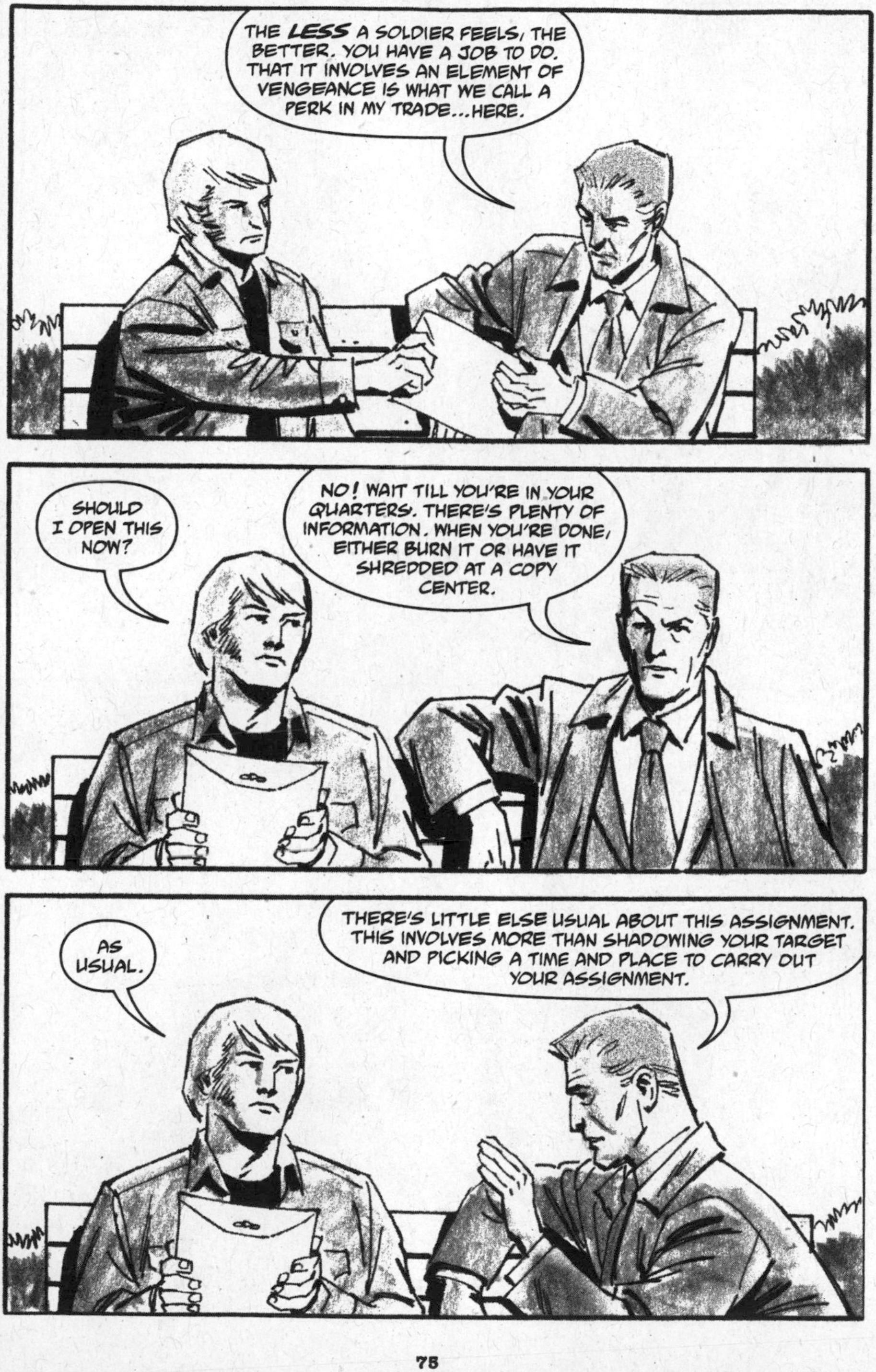
THE LESS A SOLDIER FEELS, THE BETTER. YOU HAVE A JOB TO DO. THAT IT INVOLVES AN ELEMENT OF VENGEANCE IS WHAT WE CALL A PERK IN MY TRADE...HERE.
SHOULD I OPEN THIS NOW?
NO! WAIT TILL YOU'RE IN YOUR QUARTERS. THERE'S PLENTY OF INFORMATION. WHEN YOU'RE DONE, EITHER BURN IT OR HAVE IT SHREDDED AT A COPY CENTER.
AS USUAL.
THERE'S LITTLE ELSE USUAL ABOUT THIS ASSIGNMENT. THIS INVOLVES MORE THAN SHADOWING YOUR TARGET AND PICKING A TIME AND PLACE TO CARRY OUT YOUR ASSIGNMENT.

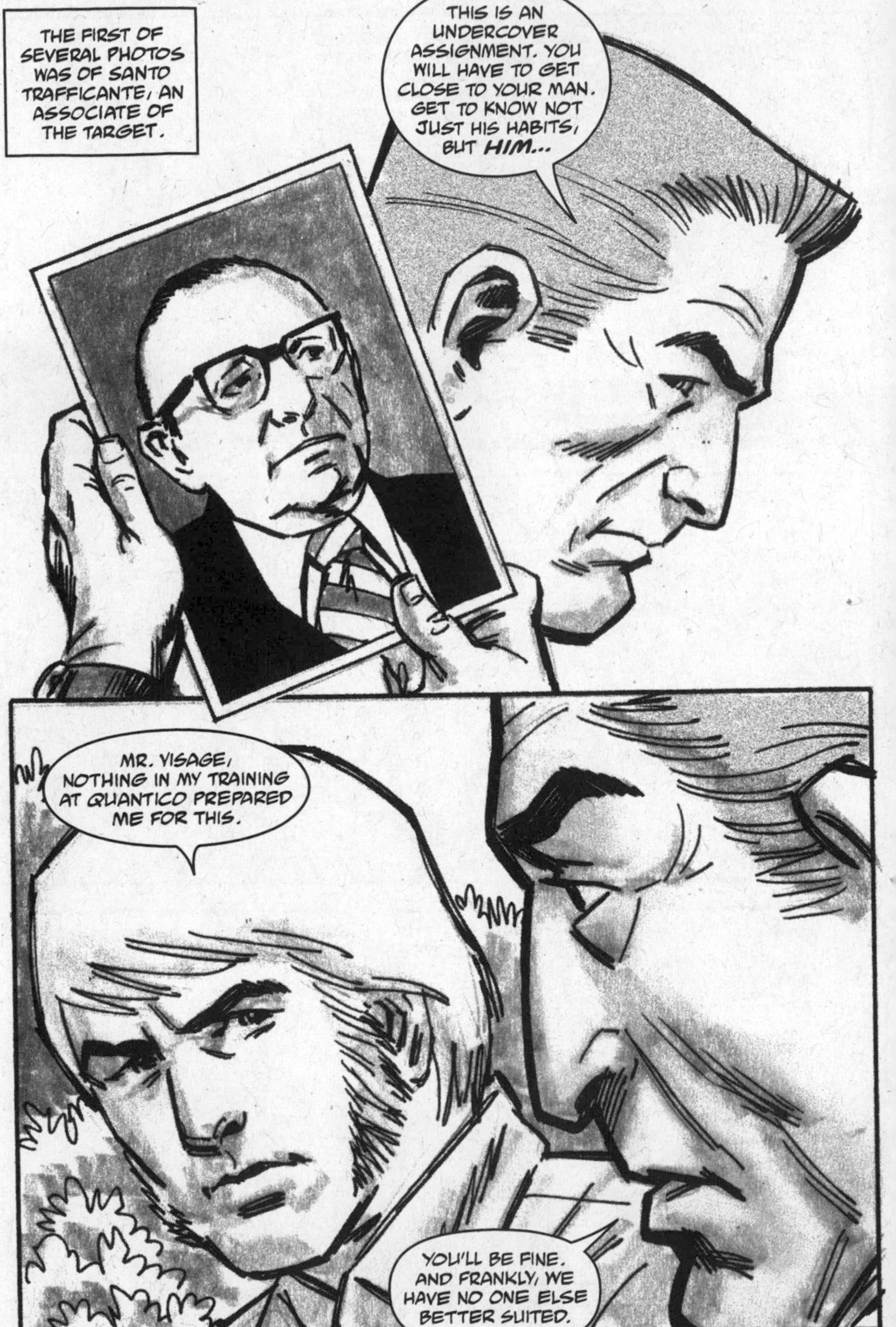
THE FIRST OF SEVERAL PHOTOS WAS OF SANTO TRAFFICANTE, AN ASSOCIATE OF THE TARGET.
THIS IS AN UNDERCOVER ASSIGNMENT. YOU WILL HAVE TO GET CLOSE TO YOUR MAN. GET TO KNOW NOT JUST HIS HABITS, BUT HIM...
MR. VISAGE, NOTHING IN MY TRAINING AT QUANTICO PREPARED ME FOR THIS.
YOU'LL BE FINE. AND FRANKLY, WE HAVE NO ONE ELSE BETTER SUITED.

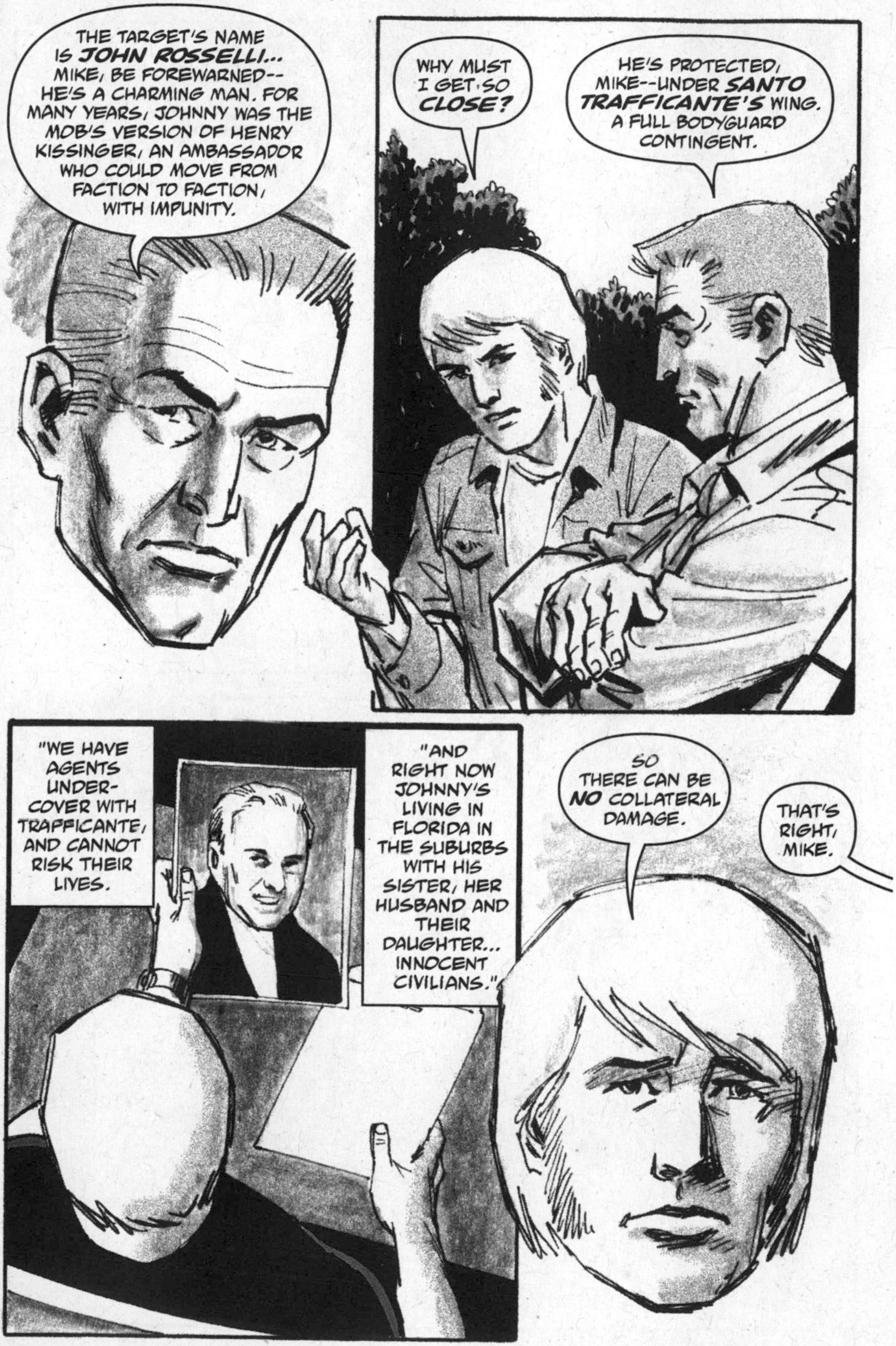
THE TARGET'S NAME IS JOHN ROSSELLI... MIKE, BE FOREWARNED-- HE'S A CHARMING MAN. FOR MANY YEARS, JOHNNY WAS THE MOB'S VERSION OF HENRY KISSINGER, AN AMBASSADOR WHO COULD MOVE FROM FACTION TO FACTION, WITH IMPUNITY.
WHY MUST I GET SO CLOSE?
HE'S PROTECTED, MIKE--UNDER SANTO TRAFFICANTE'S WING. A FULL BODYGUARD CONTINGENT.
"WE HAVE AGENTS UNDER-COVER WITH TRAFFICANTE, AND CANNOT RISK THEIR LIVES.
"AND RIGHT NOW JOHNNY'S LIVING IN FLORIDA IN THE SUBURBS WITH HIS SISTER, HER HUSBAND AND THEIR DAUGHTER... INNOCENT CIVILIANS."
SO THERE CAN BE NO COLLATERAL DAMAGE.
THAT'S RIGHT, MIKE.

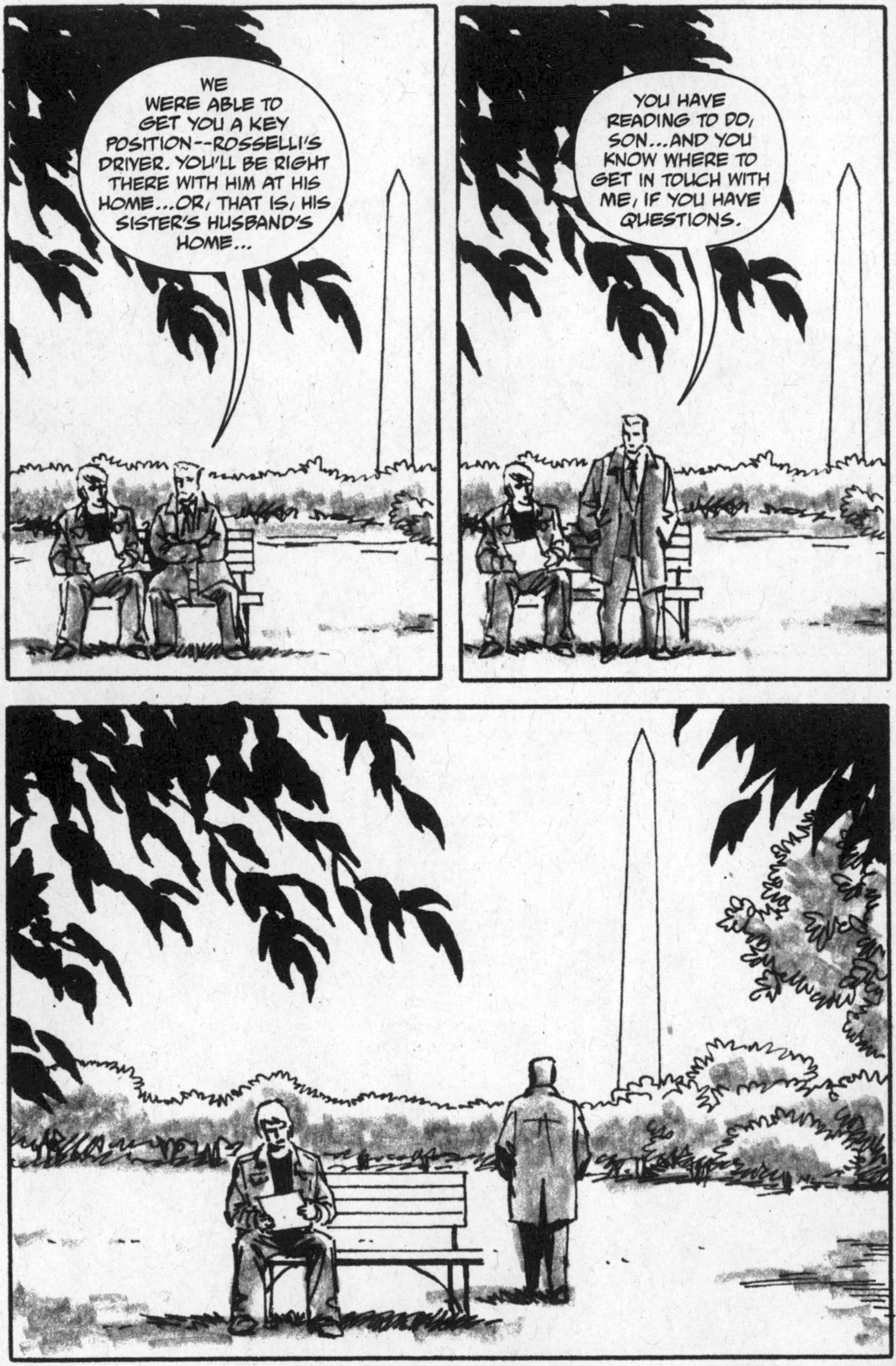
WE WERE ABLE TO GET YOU A KEY POSITION--ROSSELLI'S DRIVER. YOU'LL BE RIGHT THERE WITH HIM AT HIS HOME...OR, THAT IS, HIS SISTER'S HUSBAND'S HOME...
YOU HAVE READING TO DO, SON...AND YOU KNOW WHERE TO GET IN TOUCH WITH ME, IF YOU HAVE QUESTIONS.

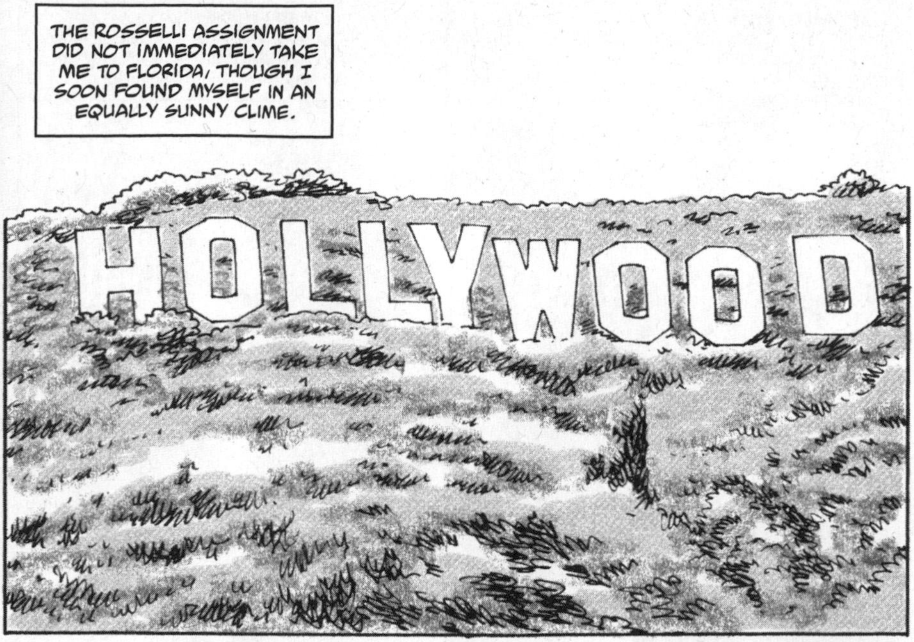
THE ROSSELLI ASSIGNMENT DID NOT IMMEDIATELY TAKE ME TO FLORIDA, THOUGH I SOON FOUND MYSELF IN AN EQUALLY SUNNY CLIME.
HOLLYWOOD

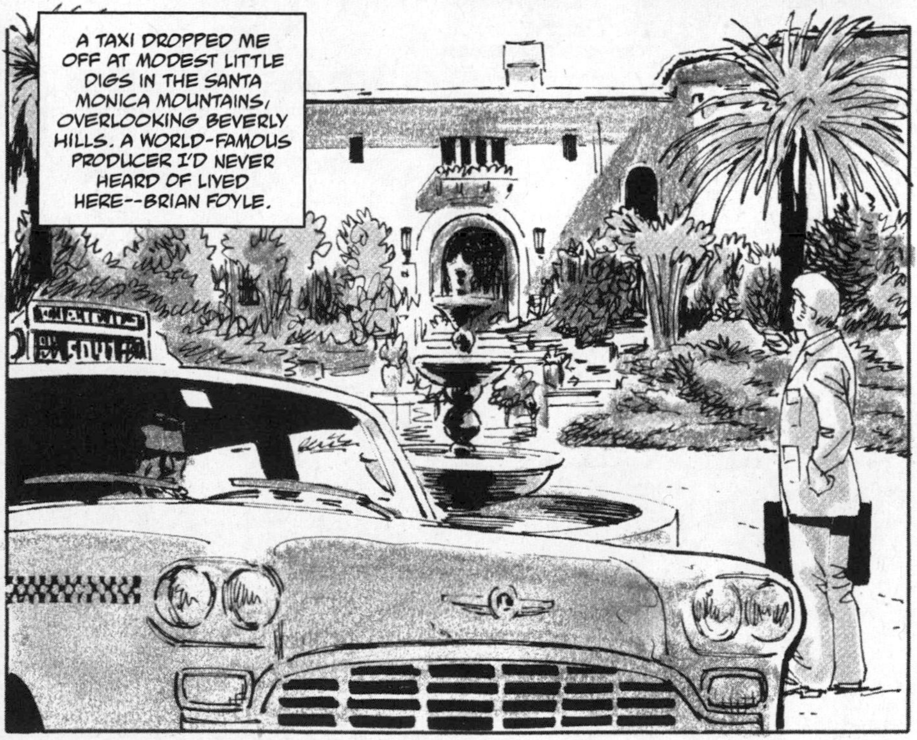
A TAXI DROPPED ME OFF AT MODEST LITTLE DIGS IN THE SANTA MONICA MOUNTAINS, OVERLOOKING BEVERLY HILLS. A WORLD-FAMOUS PRODUCER I'D NEVER HEARD OF LIVED HERE--BRIAN FOYLE.

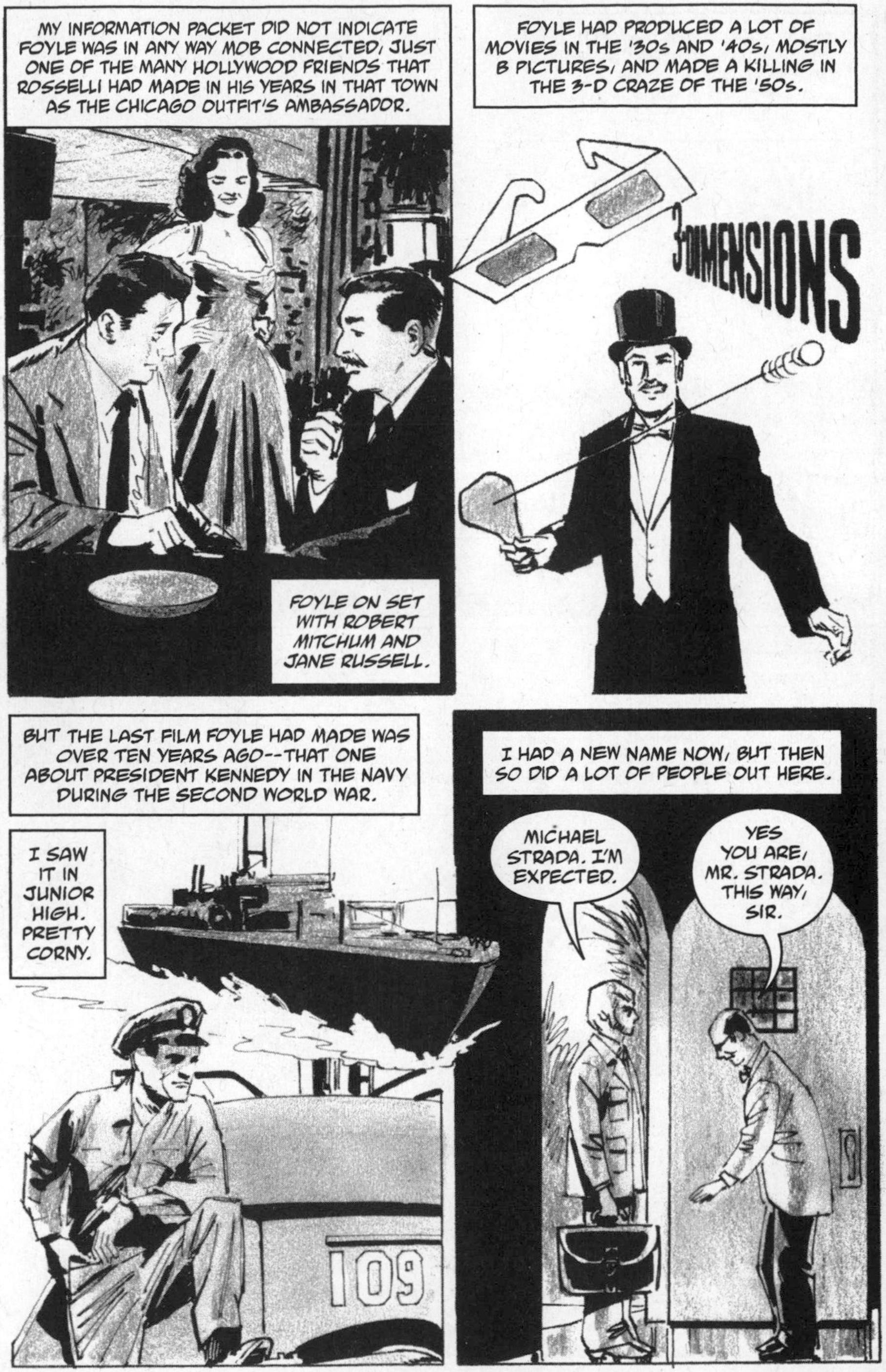
MY INFORMATION PACKET DID NOT INDICATE FOYLE WAS IN ANY WAY MOB CONNECTED, JUST ONE OF THE MANY HOLLYWOOD FRIENDS THAT ROSSELLI HAD MADE IN HIS YEARS IN THAT TOWN AS THE CHICAGO OUTFIT'S AMBASSADOR.
FOYLE ON SET WITH ROBERT MITCHUM AND JANE RUSSELL.
FOYLE HAD PRODUCED A LOT OF MOVIES IN THE '30s AND '40s, MOSTLY B PICTURES, AND MADE A KILLING IN THE 3-D CRAZE OF THE '50s.
3-DIMENSIONS
BUT THE LAST FILM FOYLE HAD MADE WAS OVER TEN YEARS AGO--THAT ONE ABOUT PRESIDENT KENNEDY IN THE NAVY DURING THE SECOND WORLD WAR.
I SAW IT IN JUNIOR HIGH. PRETTY CORNY.
109
I HAD A NEW NAME NOW, BUT THEN SO DID A LOT OF PEOPLE OUT HERE.
MICHAEL STRADA. I'M EXPECTED.
YES YOU ARE, MR. STRADA. THIS WAY, SIR.

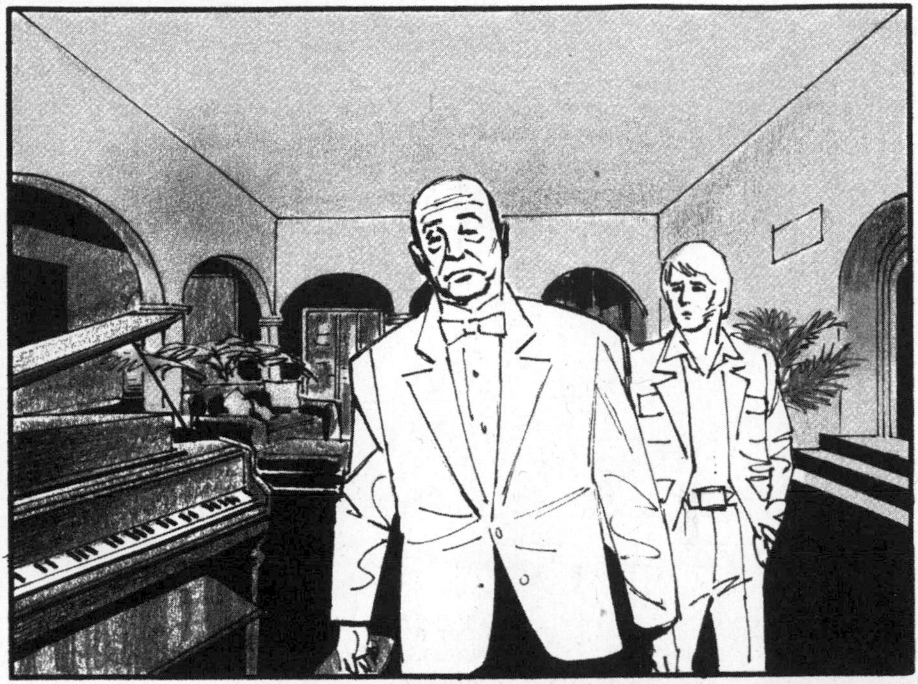

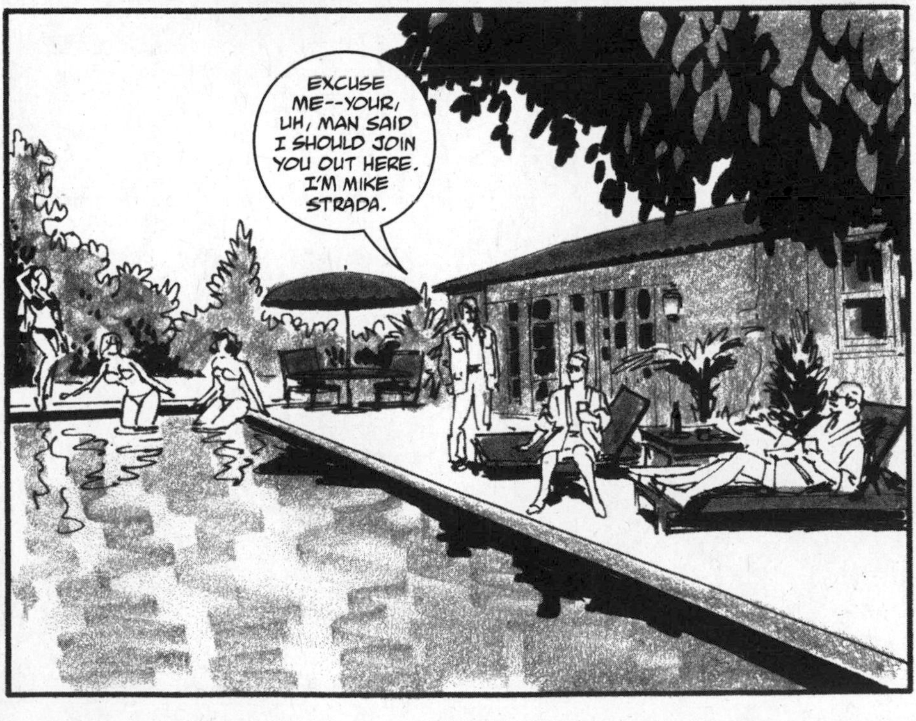
EXCUSE ME--YOUR, UH, MAN SAID I SHOULD JOIN YOU OUT HERE. I'M MIKE STRADA.

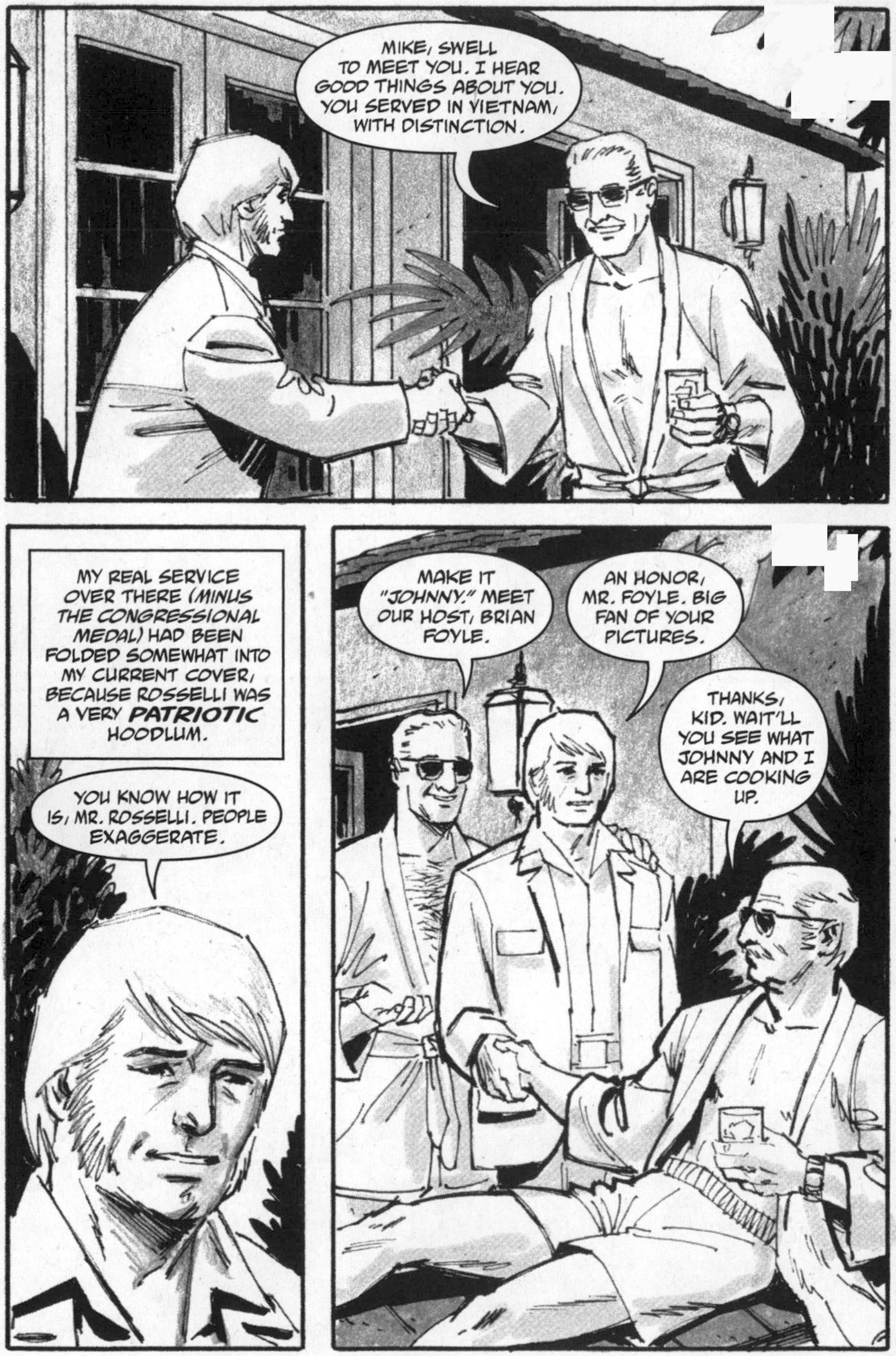
MIKE, SWELL TO MEET YOU. I HEAR GOOD THINGS ABOUT YOU. YOU SERVED IN VIETNAM, WITH DISTINCTION.
MY REAL SERVICE OVER THERE (MINUS THE CONGRESSIONAL MEDAL) HAD BEEN FOLDED SOMEWHAT INTO MY CURRENT COVER, BECAUSE ROSSELLI WAS A VERY PATRIOTIC HOODLUM.
YOU KNOW HOW IT IS, MR. ROSSELLI. PEOPLE EXAGGERATE.
MAKE IT "JOHNNY." MEET OUR HOST, BRIAN FOYLE.
AN HONOR, MR. FOYLE. BIG FAN OF YOUR PICTURES.
THANKS, KID. WAIT'LL YOU SEE WHAT JOHNNY AND I ARE COOKING UP.

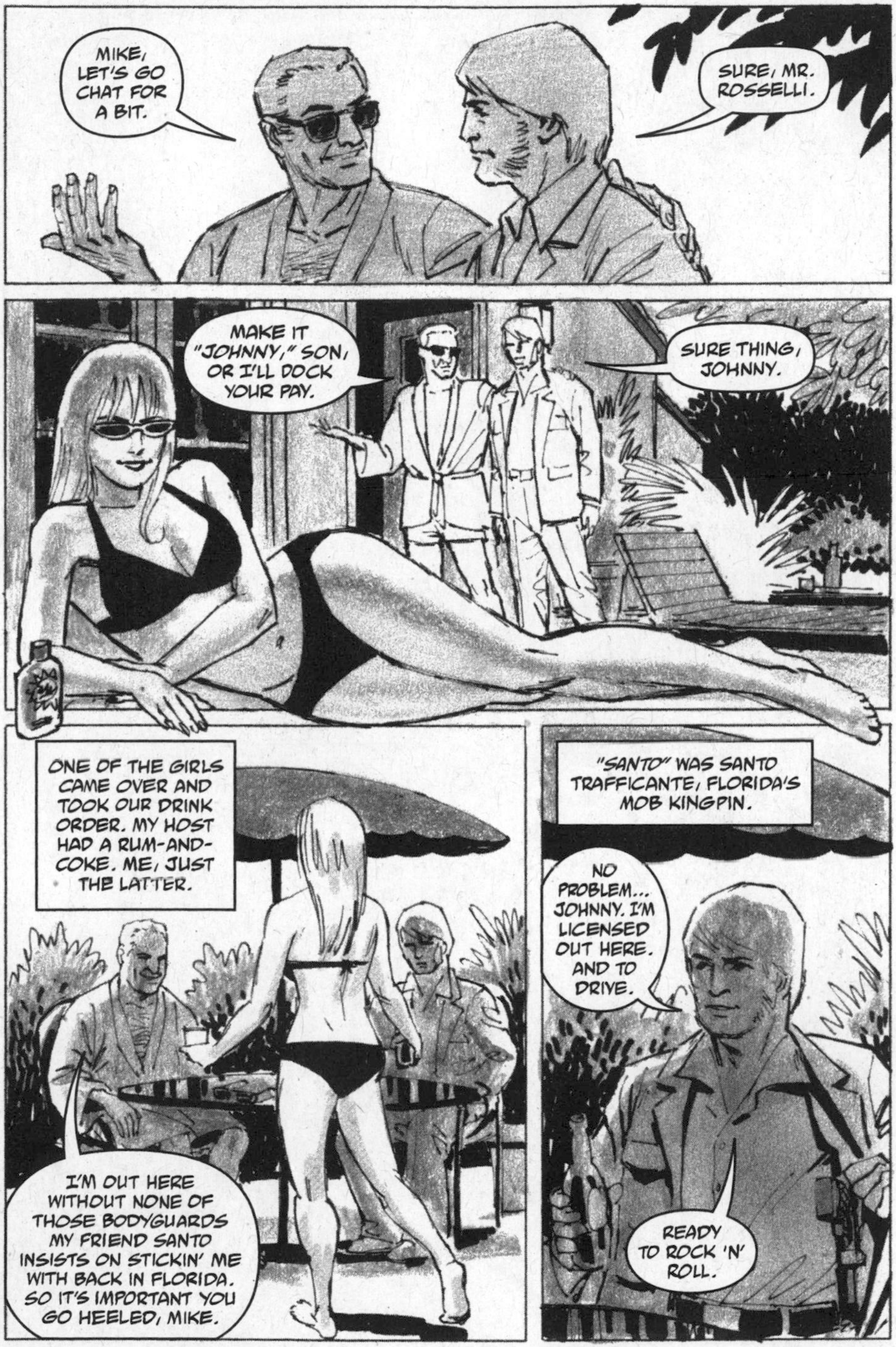
MIKE, LET'S GO CHAT FOR A BIT.
SURE, MR. ROSSELLI.
MAKE IT "JOHNNY," SON, OR I'LL DOCK YOUR PAY.
SURE THING, JOHNNY.
ONE OF THE GIRLS CAME OVER AND TOOK OUR DRINK ORDER. MY HOST HAD A RUM-AND-COKE. ME, JUST THE LATTER.
I'M OUT HERE WITHOUT NONE OF THOSE BODYGUARDS MY FRIEND SANTO INSISTS ON STICKIN' ME WITH BACK IN FLORIDA. SO IT'S IMPORTANT YOU GO HEELED, MIKE.
"SANTO" WAS SANTO TRAFFICANTE, FLORIDA'S MOB KINGPIN.
NO PROBLEM... JOHNNY. I'M LICENSED OUT HERE. AND TO DRIVE.
READY TO ROCK 'N' ROLL.

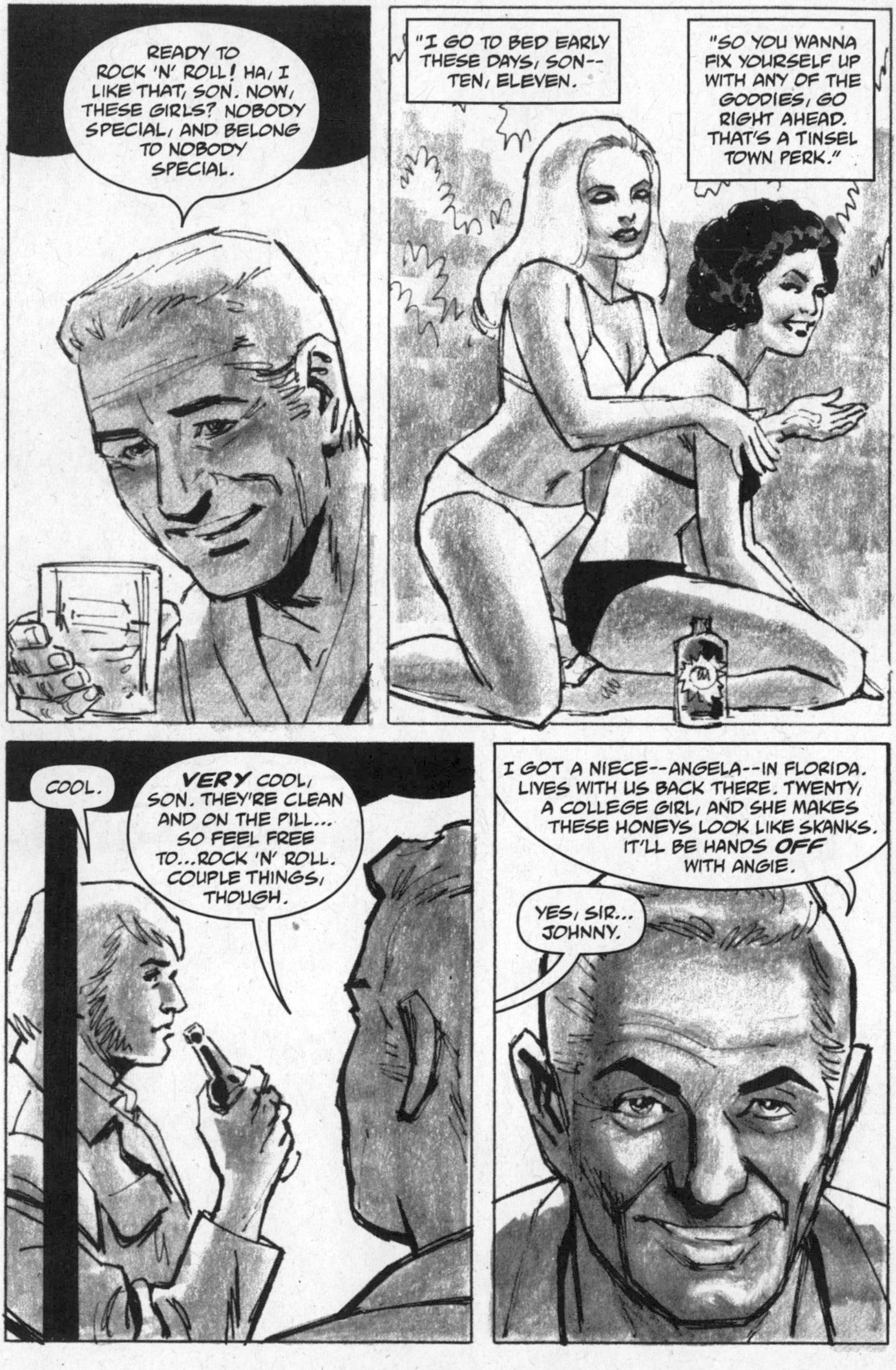
READY TO ROCK 'N' ROLL! HA, I LIKE THAT, SON. NOW, THESE GIRLS? NOBODY SPECIAL, AND BELONG TO NOBODY SPECIAL.
"I GO TO BED EARLY THESE DAYS, SON-- TEN, ELEVEN.
"SO YOU WANNA FIX YOURSELF UP WITH ANY OF THE GOODIES, GO RIGHT AHEAD. THAT'S A TINSEL TOWN PERK."
COOL.
VERY COOL, SON. THEY'RE CLEAN AND ON THE PILL... SO FEEL FREE TO...ROCK 'N' ROLL. COUPLE THINGS, THOUGH.
I GOT A NIECE--ANGELA--IN FLORIDA. LIVES WITH US BACK THERE. TWENTY, A COLLEGE GIRL, AND SHE MAKES THESE HONEYS LOOK LIKE SKANKS. IT'LL BE HANDS OFF WITH ANGIE.
YES, SIR... JOHNNY.

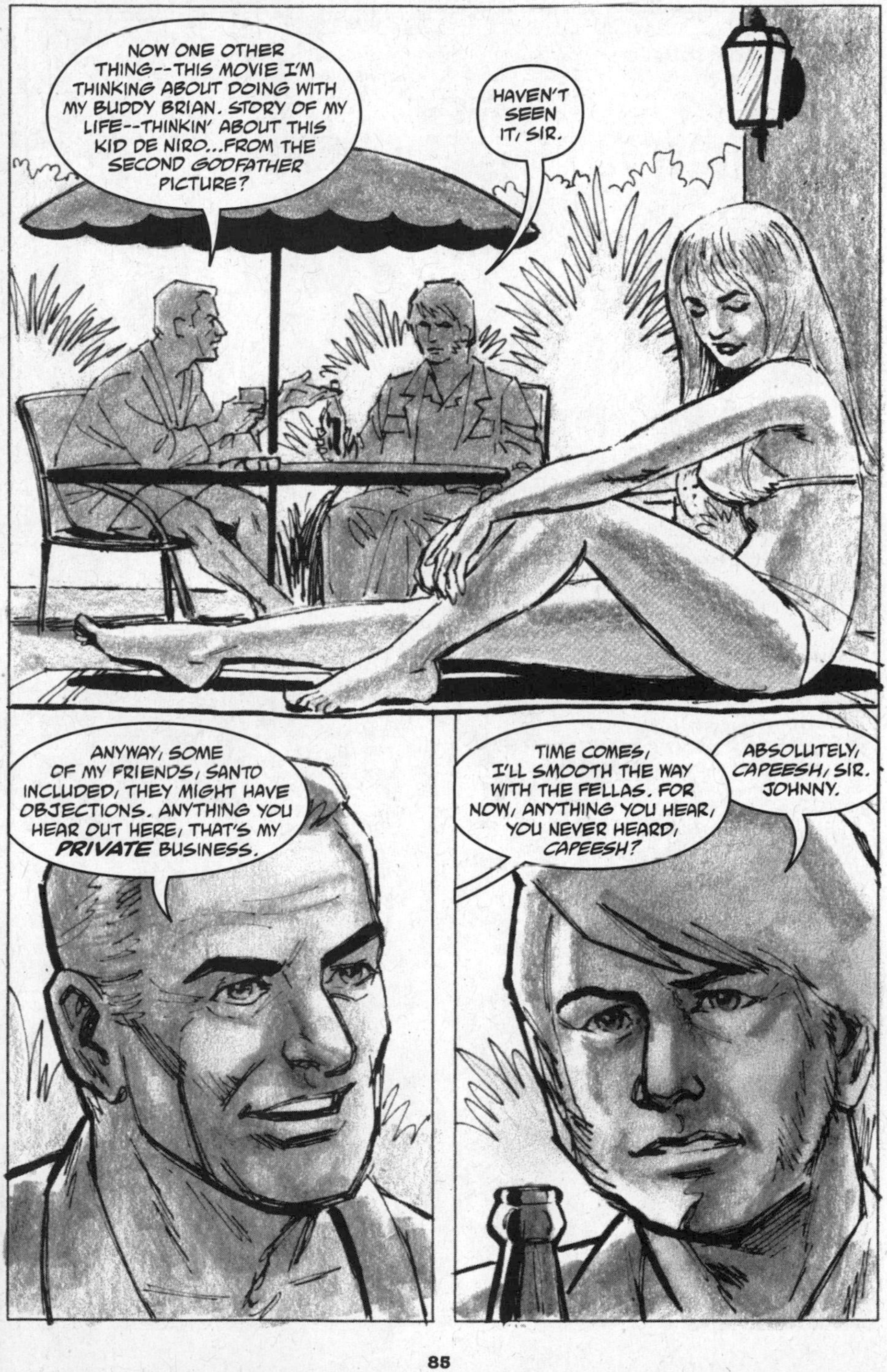
NOW ONE OTHER THING--THIS MOVIE I'M THINKING ABOUT DOING WITH MY BUDDY BRIAN. STORY OF MY LIFE--THINKIN' ABOUT THIS KID DE NIRO...FROM THE SECOND *GODFATHER* PICTURE?
HAVEN'T SEEN IT, SIR.
ANYWAY, SOME OF MY FRIENDS, SANTO INCLUDED, THEY MIGHT HAVE OBJECTIONS. ANYTHING YOU HEAR OUT HERE, THAT'S MY ***PRIVATE*** BUSINESS.
TIME COMES, I'LL SMOOTH THE WAY WITH THE FELLAS. FOR NOW, ANYTHING YOU HEAR, YOU NEVER HEARD, *CAPEESH?*
ABSOLUTELY, *CAPEESH*, SIR. JOHNNY.

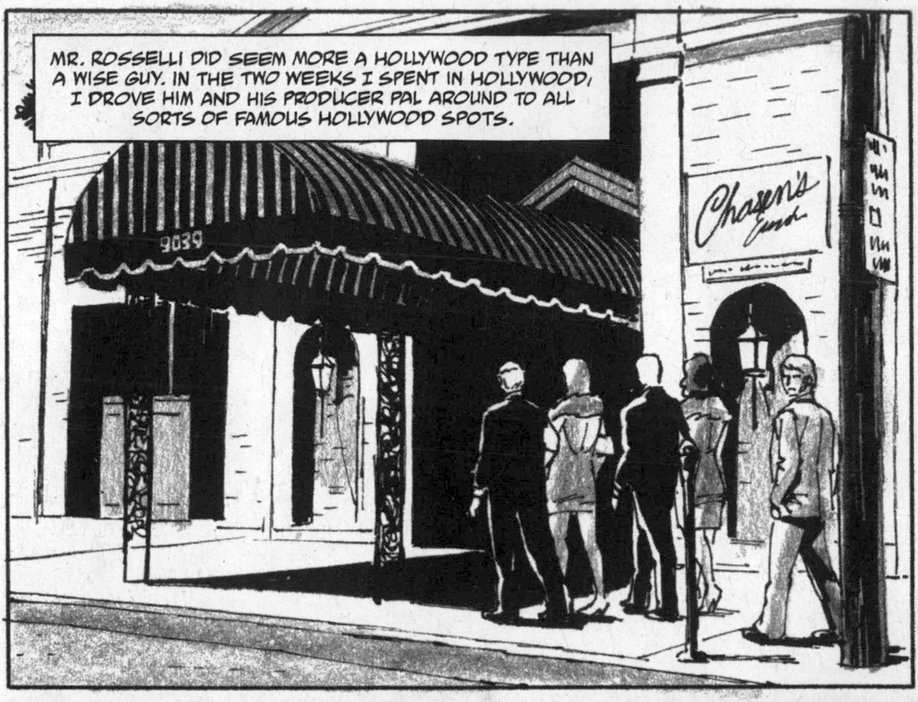
MR. ROSSELLI DID SEEM MORE A HOLLYWOOD TYPE THAN A WISE GUY. IN THE TWO WEEKS I SPENT IN HOLLYWOOD, I DROVE HIM AND HIS PRODUCER PAL AROUND TO ALL SORTS OF FAMOUS HOLLYWOOD SPOTS.
9039
Chasen's

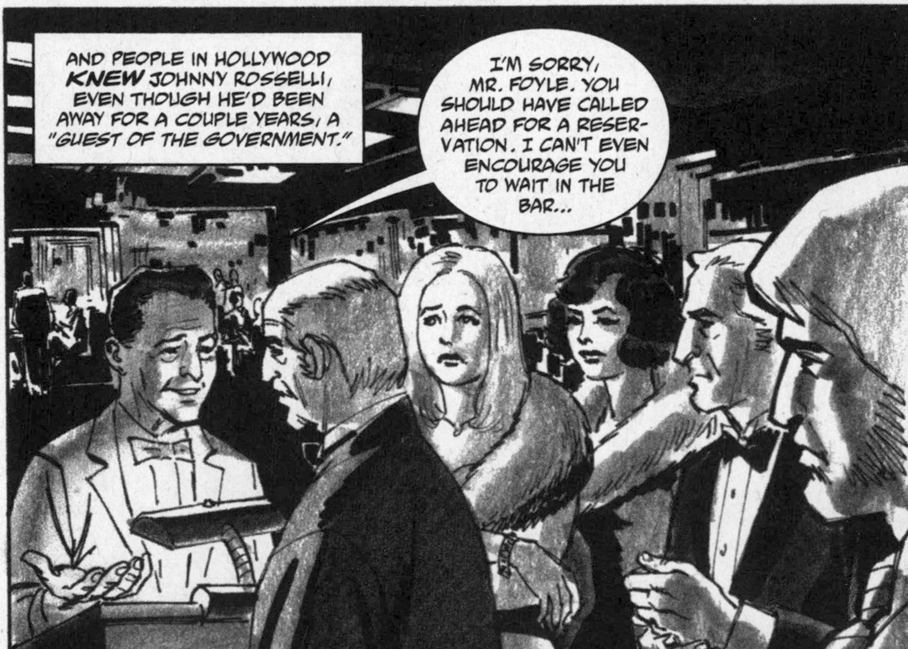
AND PEOPLE IN HOLLYWOOD ***KNEW*** JOHNNY ROSSELLI, EVEN THOUGH HE'D BEEN AWAY FOR A COUPLE YEARS, A "GUEST OF THE GOVERNMENT."
I'M SORRY, MR. FOYLE. YOU SHOULD HAVE CALLED AHEAD FOR A RESERVATION. I CAN'T EVEN ENCOURAGE YOU TO WAIT IN THE BAR...

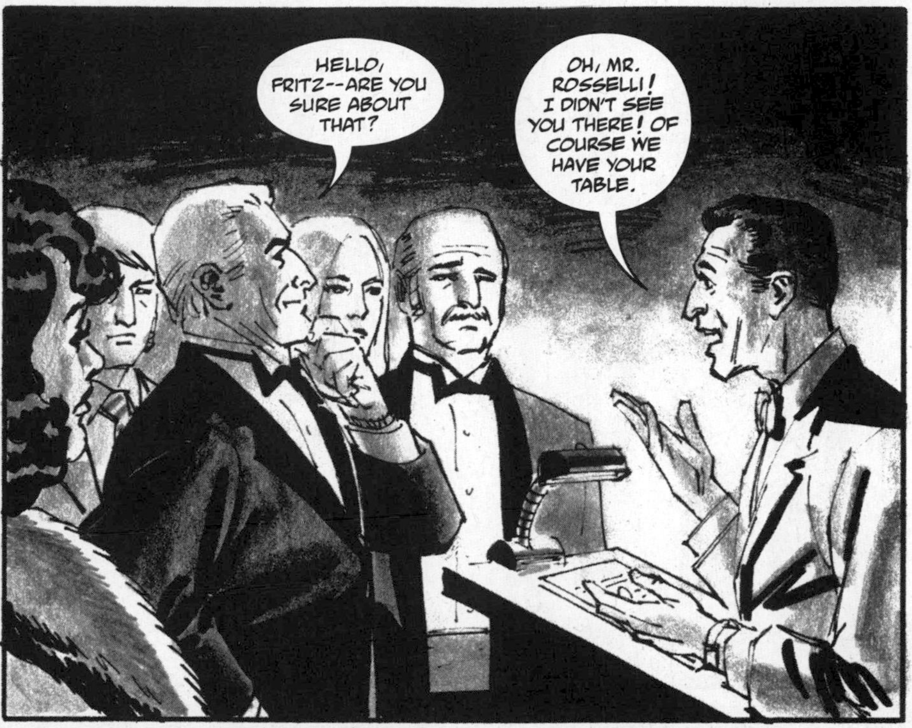
HELLO, FRITZ--ARE YOU SURE ABOUT THAT?
OH, MR. ROSSELLI! I DIDN'T SEE YOU THERE! OF COURSE WE HAVE YOUR TABLE.

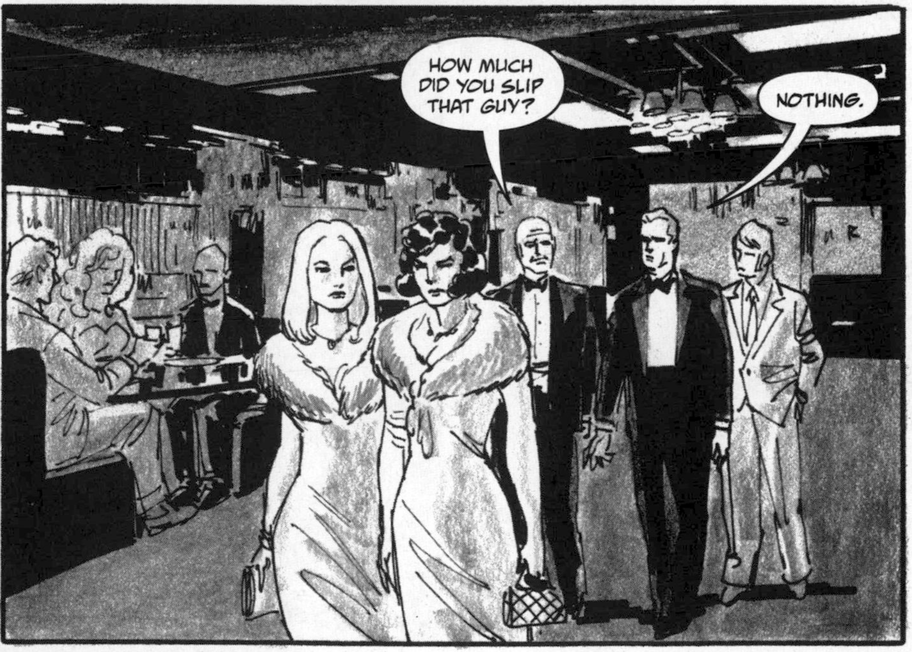
HOW MUCH DID YOU SLIP THAT GUY?
NOTHING.

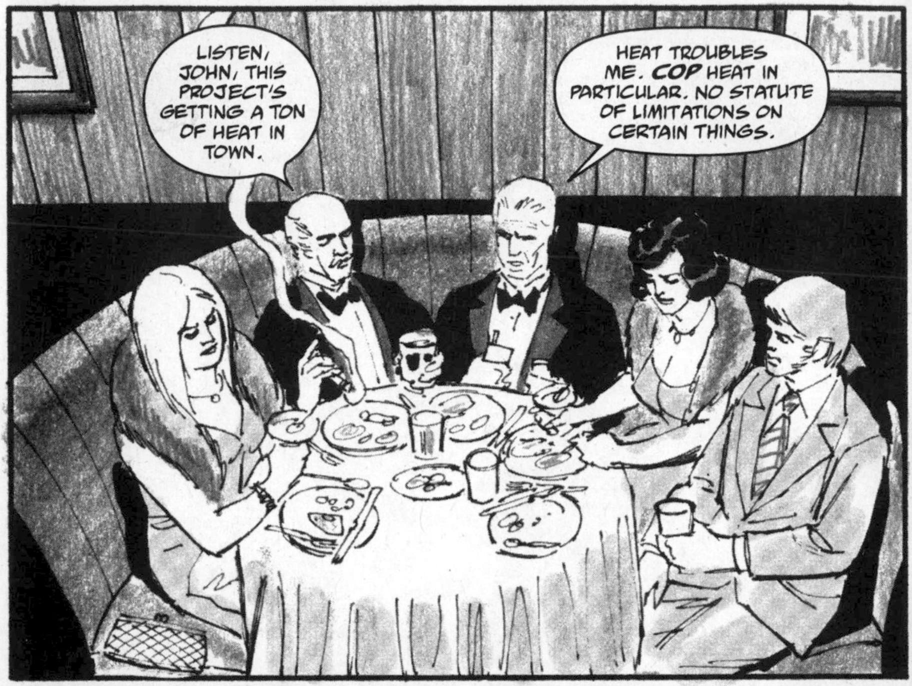
LISTEN, JOHN, THIS PROJECT'S GETTING A TON OF HEAT IN TOWN.
HEAT TROUBLES ME. COP HEAT IN PARTICULAR. NO STATUTE OF LIMITATIONS ON CERTAIN THINGS.

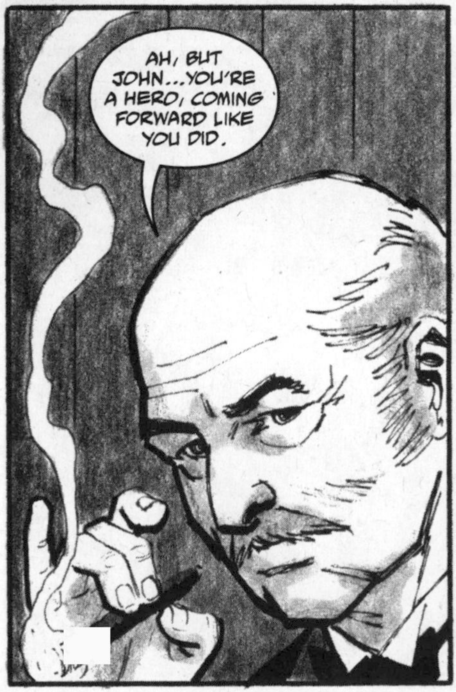
AH, BUT JOHN...YOU'RE A HERO, COMING FORWARD LIKE YOU DID.

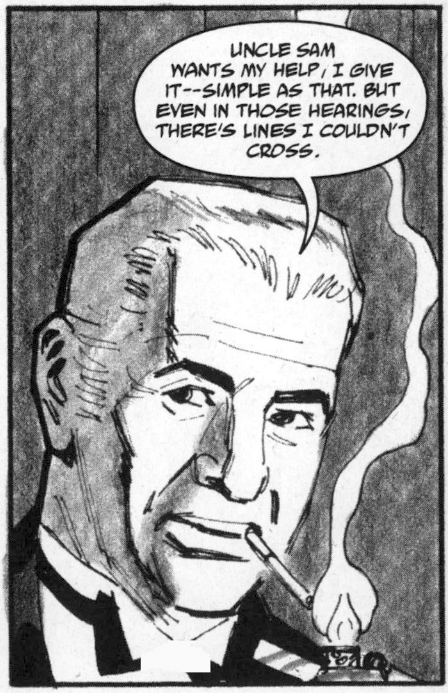
UNCLE SAM WANTS MY HELP, I GIVE IT--SIMPLE AS THAT. BUT EVEN IN THOSE HEARINGS, THERE'S LINES I COULDN'T CROSS.

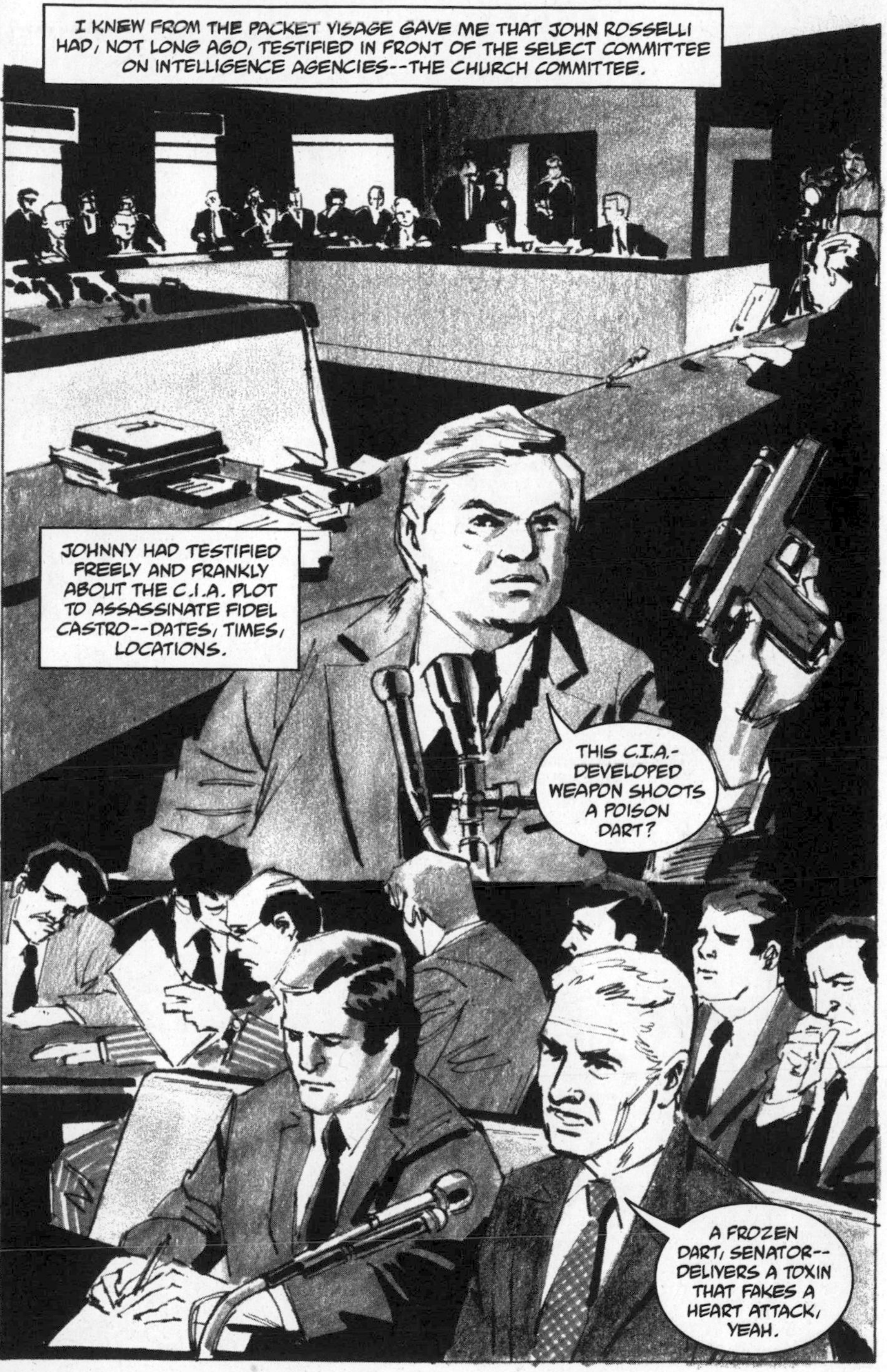
I KNEW FROM THE PACKET VISAGE GAVE ME THAT JOHN ROSSELLI HAD, NOT LONG AGO, TESTIFIED IN FRONT OF THE SELECT COMMITTEE ON INTELLIGENCE AGENCIES--THE CHURCH COMMITTEE.
JOHNNY HAD TESTIFIED FREELY AND FRANKLY ABOUT THE C.I.A. PLOT TO ASSASSINATE FIDEL CASTRO--DATES, TIMES, LOCATIONS.
THIS C.I.A.-DEVELOPED WEAPON SHOOTS A POISON DART?
A FROZEN DART, SENATOR--DELIVERS A TOXIN THAT FAKES A HEART ATTACK, YEAH.

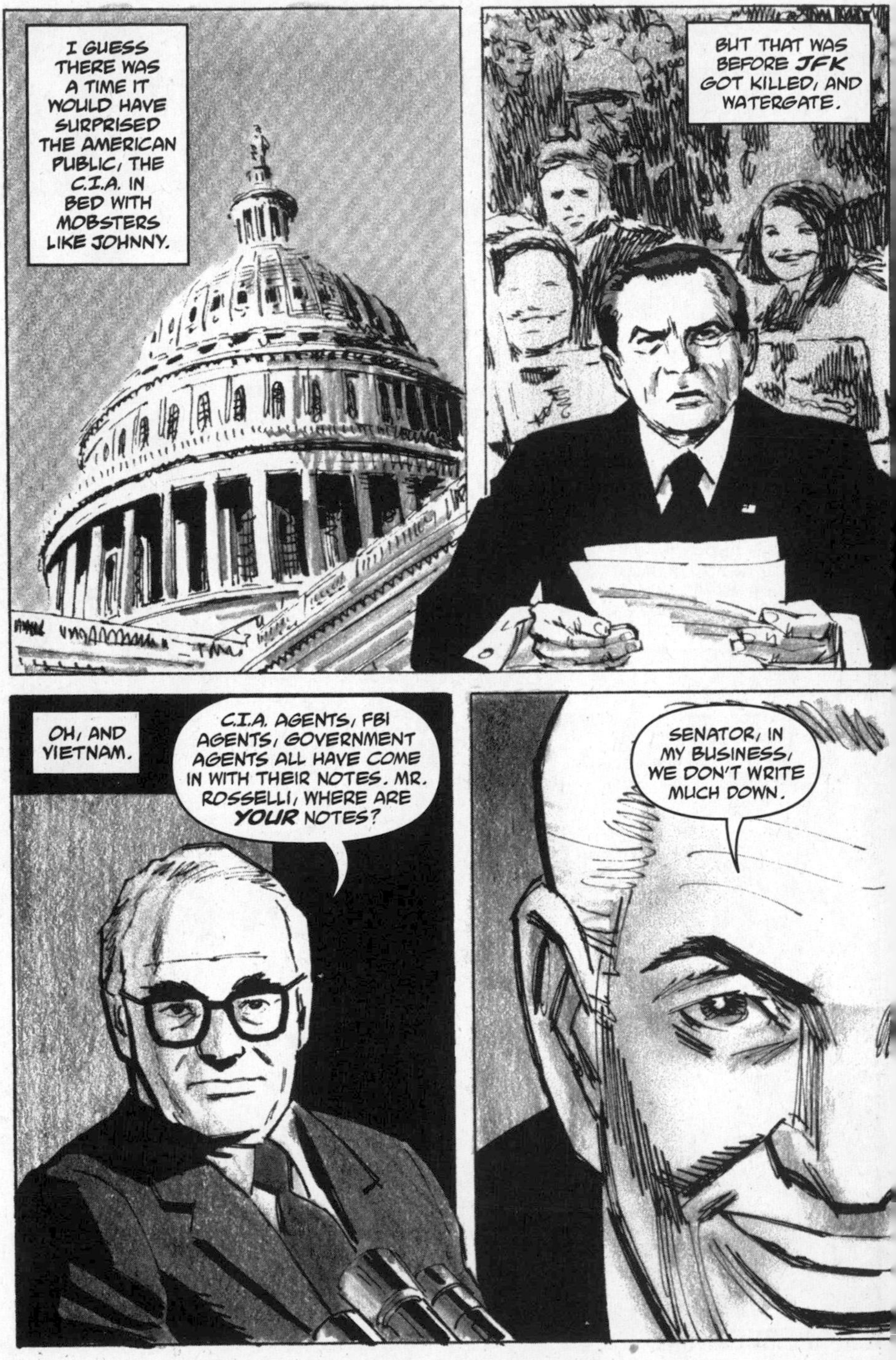

I GUESS THERE WAS A TIME IT WOULD HAVE SURPRISED THE AMERICAN PUBLIC, THE C.I.A. IN BED WITH MOBSTERS LIKE JOHNNY.
BUT THAT WAS BEFORE JFK GOT KILLED, AND WATERGATE.
OH, AND VIETNAM.
C.I.A. AGENTS, FBI AGENTS, GOVERNMENT AGENTS ALL HAVE COME IN WITH THEIR NOTES. MR. ROSSELLI, WHERE ARE YOUR NOTES?
SENATOR, IN MY BUSINESS, WE DON'T WRITE MUCH DOWN.

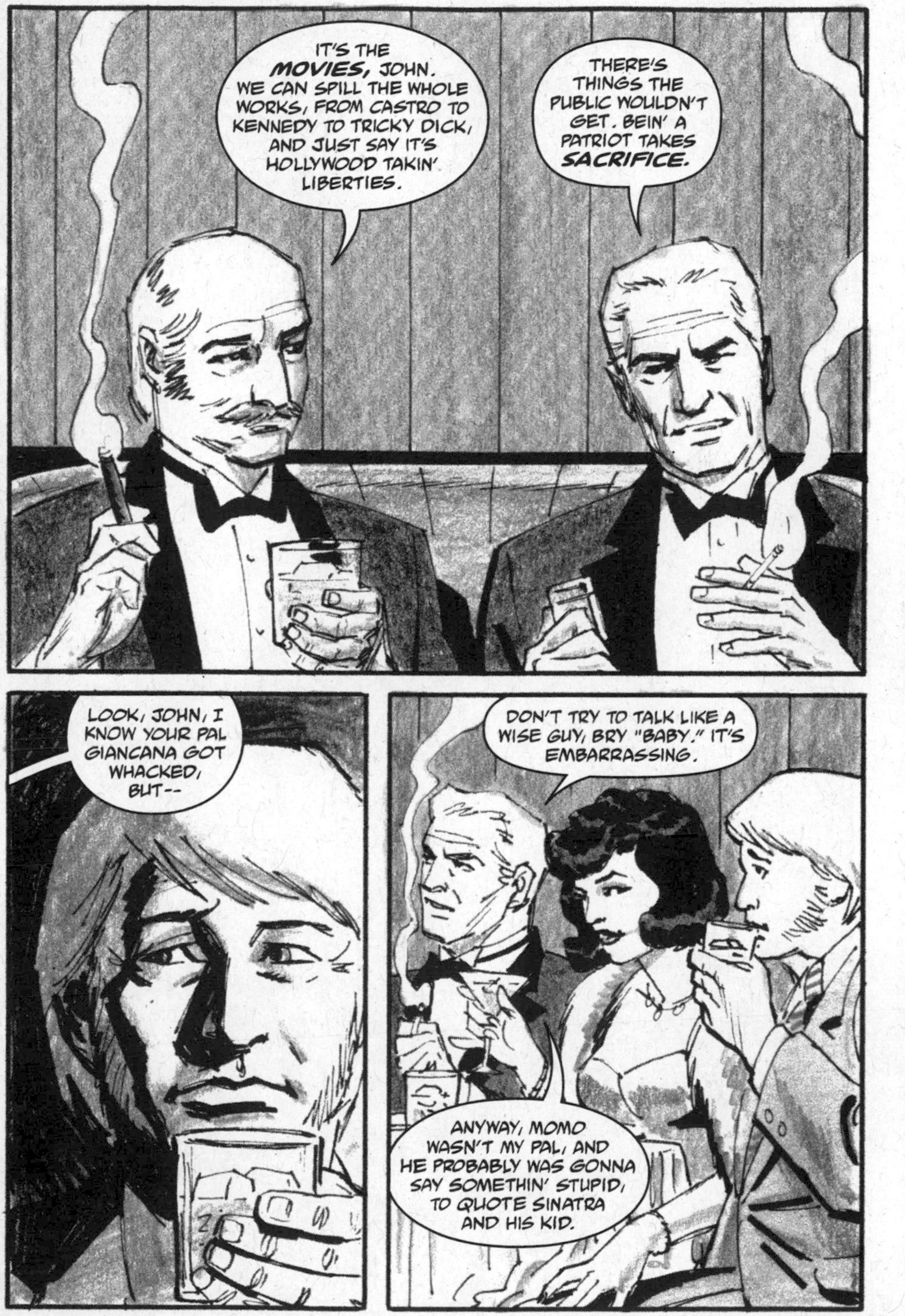
IT'S THE MOVIES, JOHN. WE CAN SPILL THE WHOLE WORKS, FROM CASTRO TO KENNEDY TO TRICKY DICK, AND JUST SAY IT'S HOLLYWOOD TAKIN' LIBERTIES.
THERE'S THINGS THE PUBLIC WOULDN'T GET. BEIN' A PATRIOT TAKES SACRIFICE.
LOOK, JOHN, I KNOW YOUR PAL GIANCANA GOT WHACKED, BUT--
DON'T TRY TO TALK LIKE A WISE GUY, BRY "BABY." IT'S EMBARRASSING.
ANYWAY, MOMO WASN'T MY PAL, AND HE PROBABLY WAS GONNA SAY SOMETHIN' STUPID, TO QUOTE SINATRA AND HIS KID.

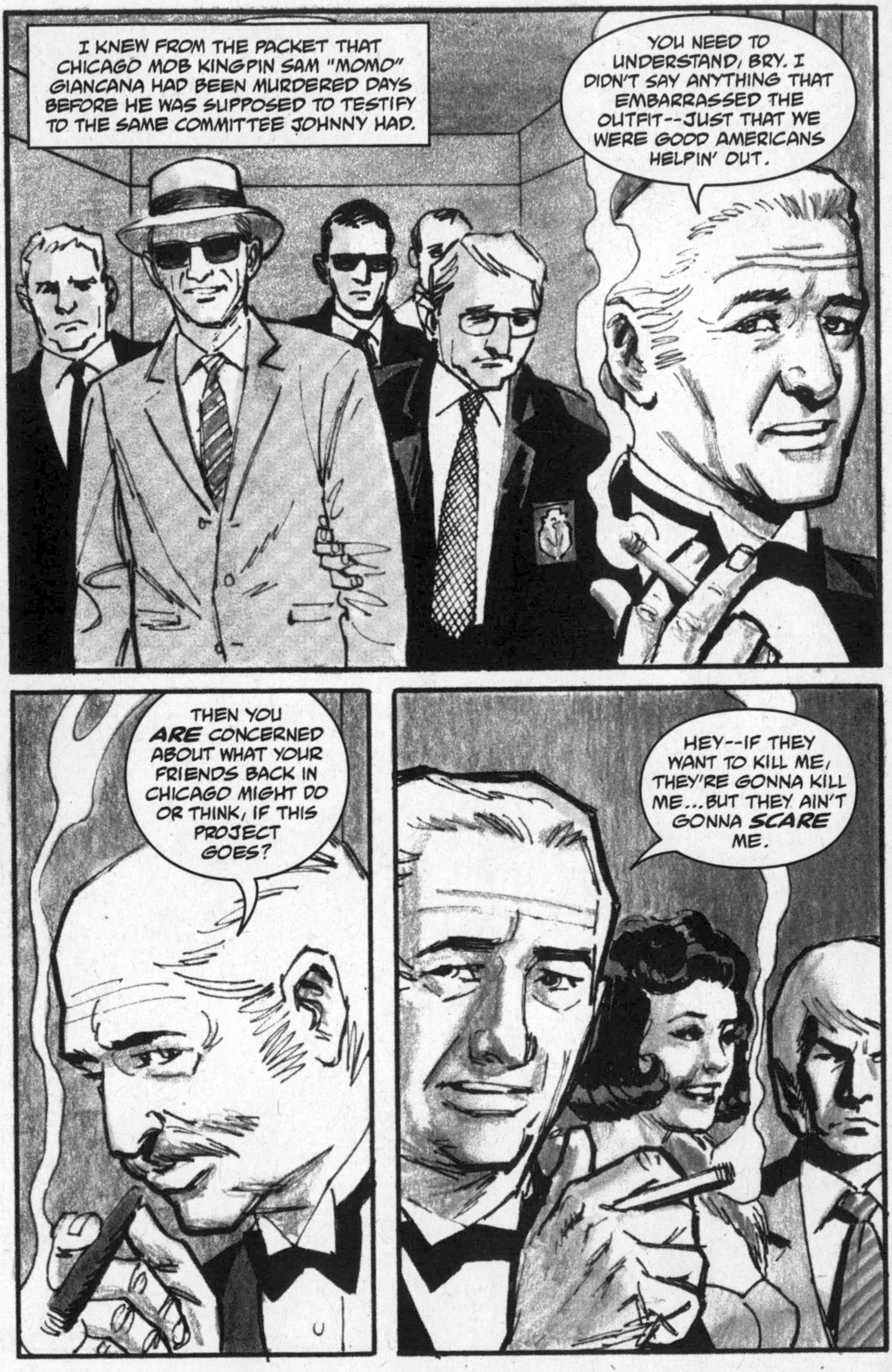
I KNEW FROM THE PACKET THAT CHICAGO MOB KINGPIN SAM "MOMO" GIANCANA HAD BEEN MURDERED DAYS BEFORE HE WAS SUPPOSED TO TESTIFY TO THE SAME COMMITTEE JOHNNY HAD.
YOU NEED TO UNDERSTAND, BRY. I DIDN'T SAY ANYTHING THAT EMBARRASSED THE OUTFIT--JUST THAT WE WERE GOOD AMERICANS HELPIN' OUT.
THEN YOU ARE CONCERNED ABOUT WHAT YOUR FRIENDS BACK IN CHICAGO MIGHT DO OR THINK, IF THIS PROJECT GOES?
HEY--IF THEY WANT TO KILL ME, THEY'RE GONNA KILL ME...BUT THEY AIN'T GONNA SCARE ME.

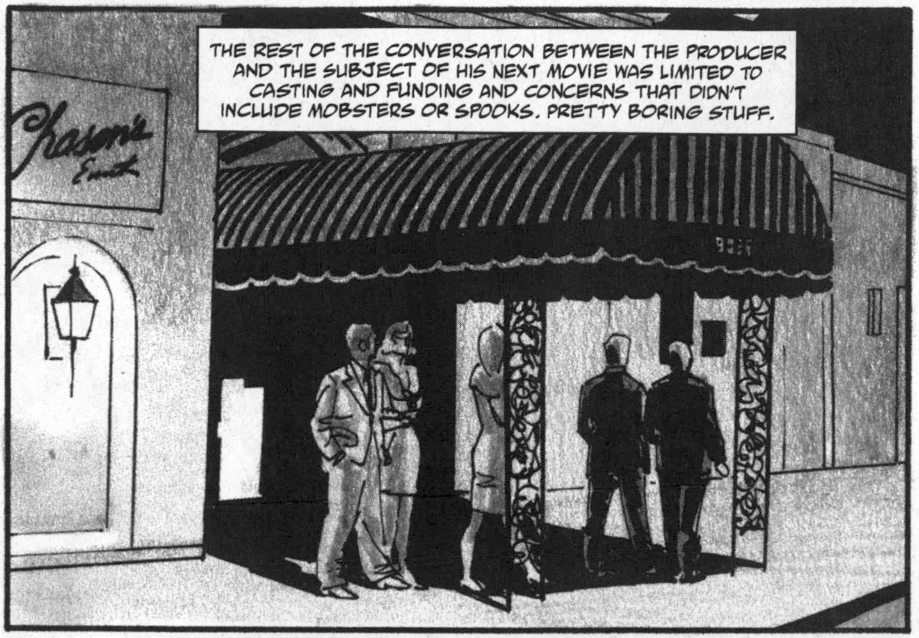
THE REST OF THE CONVERSATION BETWEEN THE PRODUCER AND THE SUBJECT OF HIS NEXT MOVIE WAS LIMITED TO CASTING AND FUNDING AND CONCERNS THAT DIDN'T INCLUDE MOBSTERS OR SPOOKS. PRETTY BORING STUFF.
Chasen's

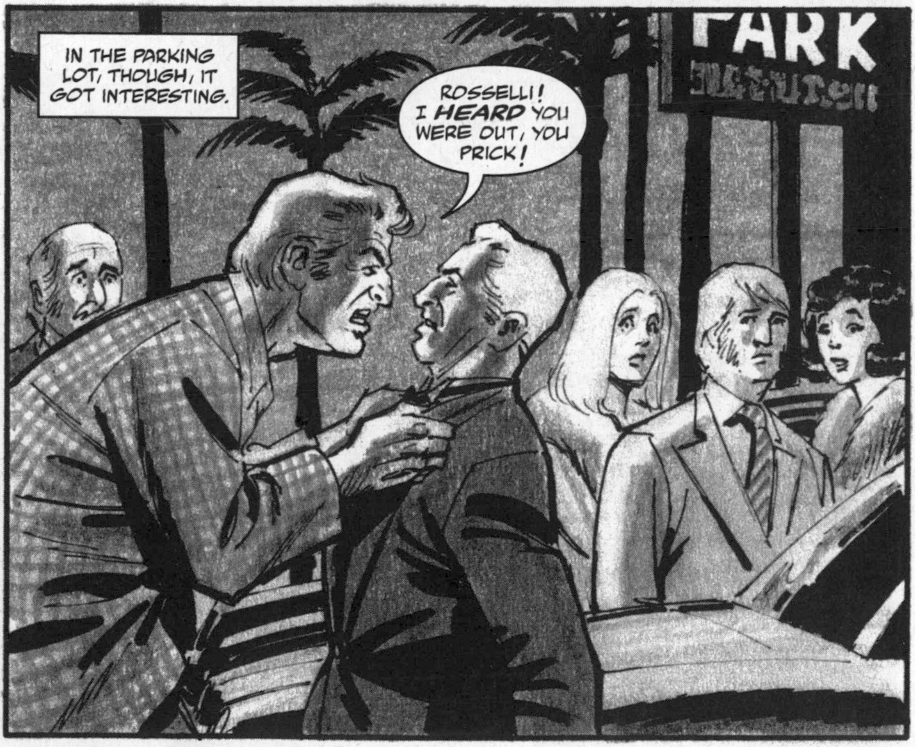
PARK
IN THE PARKING LOT, THOUGH, IT GOT INTERESTING.
ROSSELLI! I **HEARD** YOU WERE OUT, YOU PRICK!

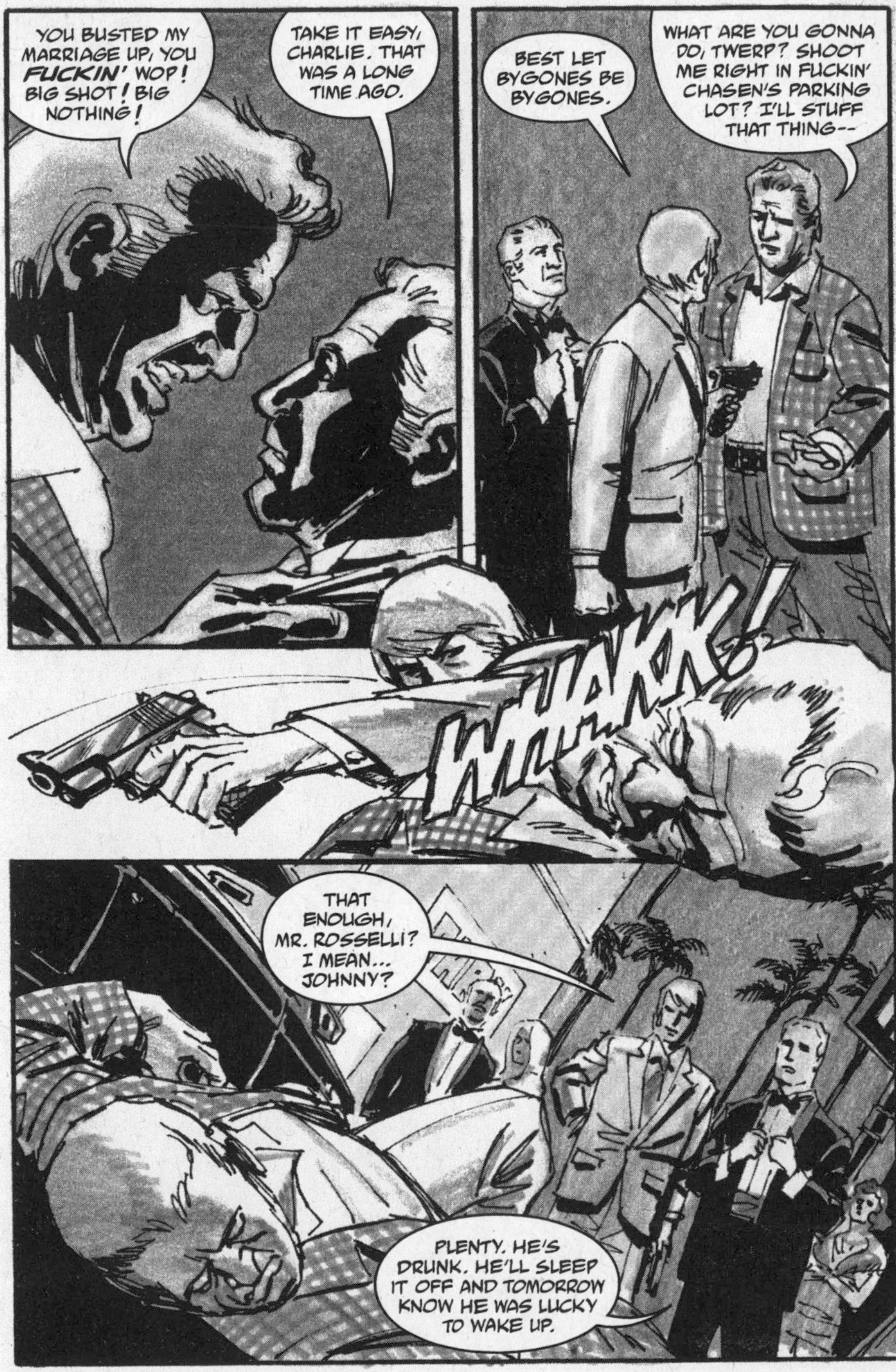
YOU BUSTED MY MARRIAGE UP, YOU FUCKIN' WOP! BIG SHOT! BIG NOTHING!
TAKE IT EASY, CHARLIE. THAT WAS A LONG TIME AGO.
BEST LET BYGONES BE BYGONES.
WHAT ARE YOU GONNA DO, TWERP? SHOOT ME RIGHT IN FUCKIN' CHASEN'S PARKING LOT? I'LL STUFF THAT THING--
WHAKK!
THAT ENOUGH, MR. ROSSELLI? I MEAN... JOHNNY?
PLENTY. HE'S DRUNK. HE'LL SLEEP IT OFF AND TOMORROW KNOW HE WAS LUCKY TO WAKE UP.

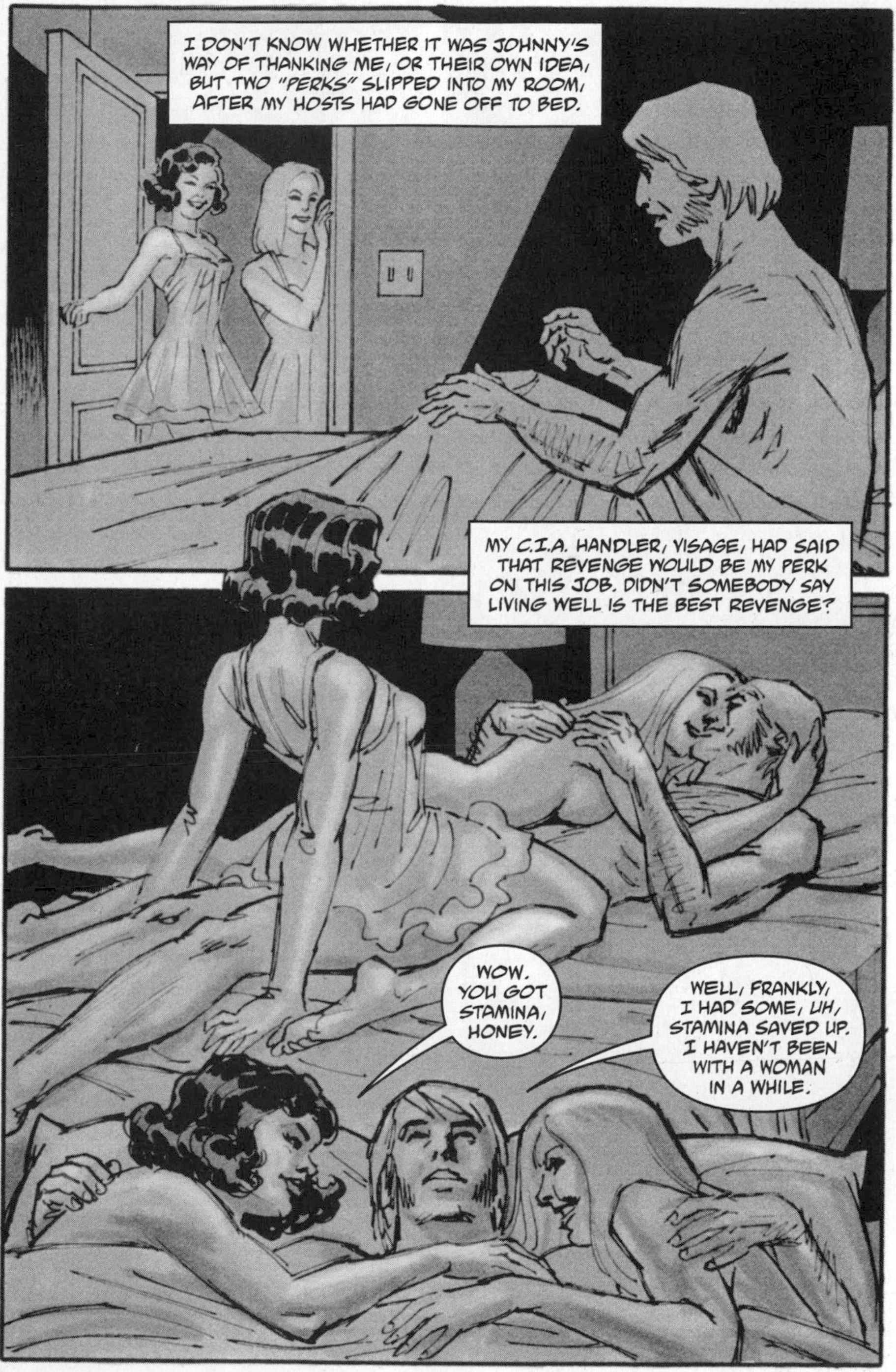
I DON'T KNOW WHETHER IT WAS JOHNNY'S WAY OF THANKING ME, OR THEIR OWN IDEA, BUT TWO "PERKS" SLIPPED INTO MY ROOM, AFTER MY HOSTS HAD GONE OFF TO BED.
MY C.I.A. HANDLER, VISAGE, HAD SAID THAT REVENGE WOULD BE MY PERK ON THIS JOB. DIDN'T SOMEBODY SAY LIVING WELL IS THE BEST REVENGE?
WOW. YOU GOT STAMINA, HONEY.
WELL, FRANKLY, I HAD SOME, UH, STAMINA SAVED UP. I HAVEN'T BEEN WITH A WOMAN IN A WHILE.

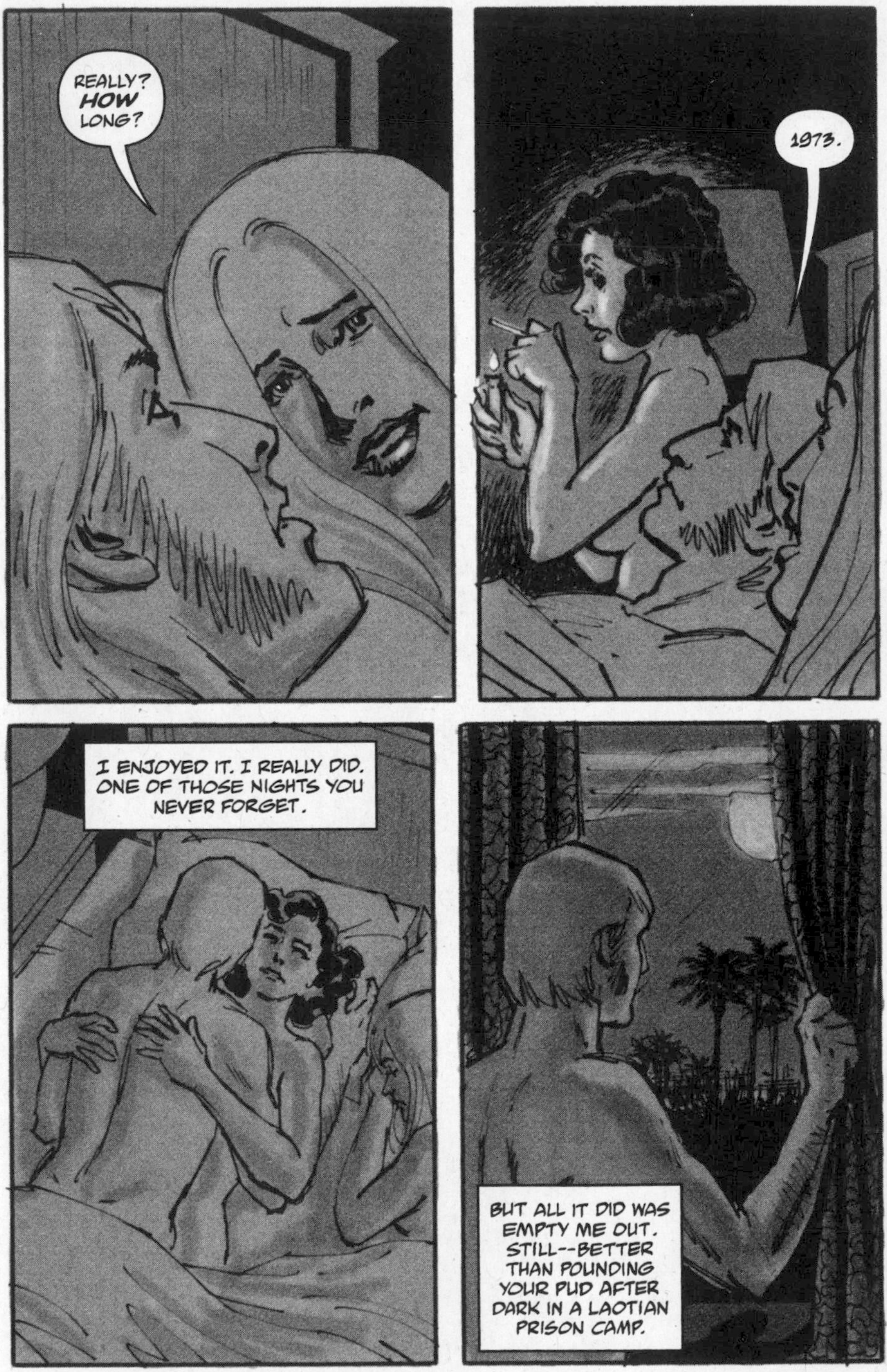
REALLY? HOW LONG?
1973.
I ENJOYED IT. I REALLY DID. ONE OF THOSE NIGHTS YOU NEVER FORGET.
BUT ALL IT DID WAS EMPTY ME OUT. STILL--BETTER THAN POUNDING YOUR PUD AFTER DARK IN A LAOTIAN PRISON CAMP.

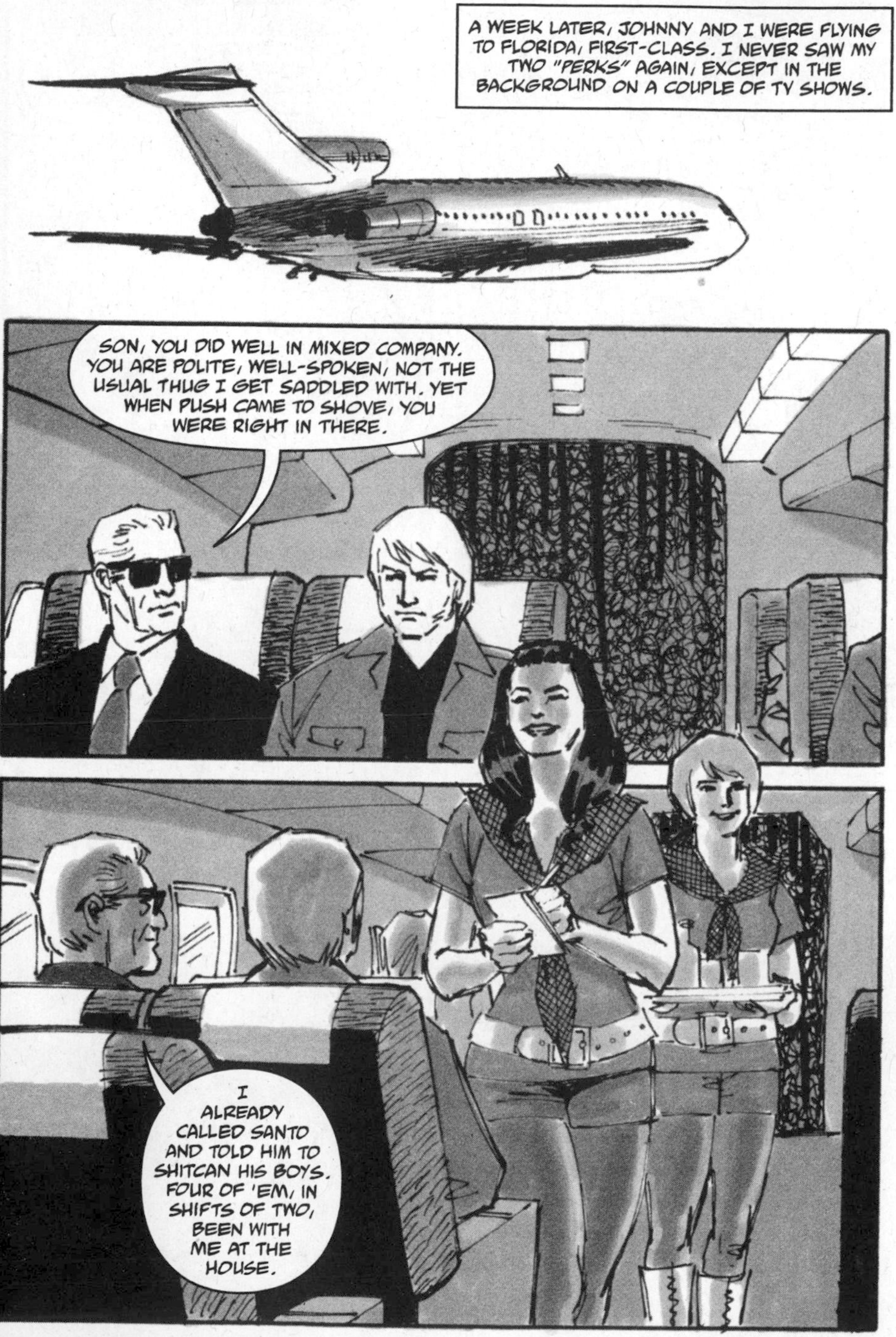
A WEEK LATER, JOHNNY AND I WERE FLYING TO FLORIDA, FIRST-CLASS. I NEVER SAW MY TWO "PERKS" AGAIN, EXCEPT IN THE BACKGROUND ON A COUPLE OF TV SHOWS.
SON, YOU DID WELL IN MIXED COMPANY. YOU ARE POLITE, WELL-SPOKEN, NOT THE USUAL THUG I GET SADDLED WITH. YET WHEN PUSH CAME TO SHOVE, YOU WERE RIGHT IN THERE.
I ALREADY CALLED SANTO AND TOLD HIM TO SHITCAN HIS BOYS. FOUR OF 'EM, IN SHIFTS OF TWO, BEEN WITH ME AT THE HOUSE.

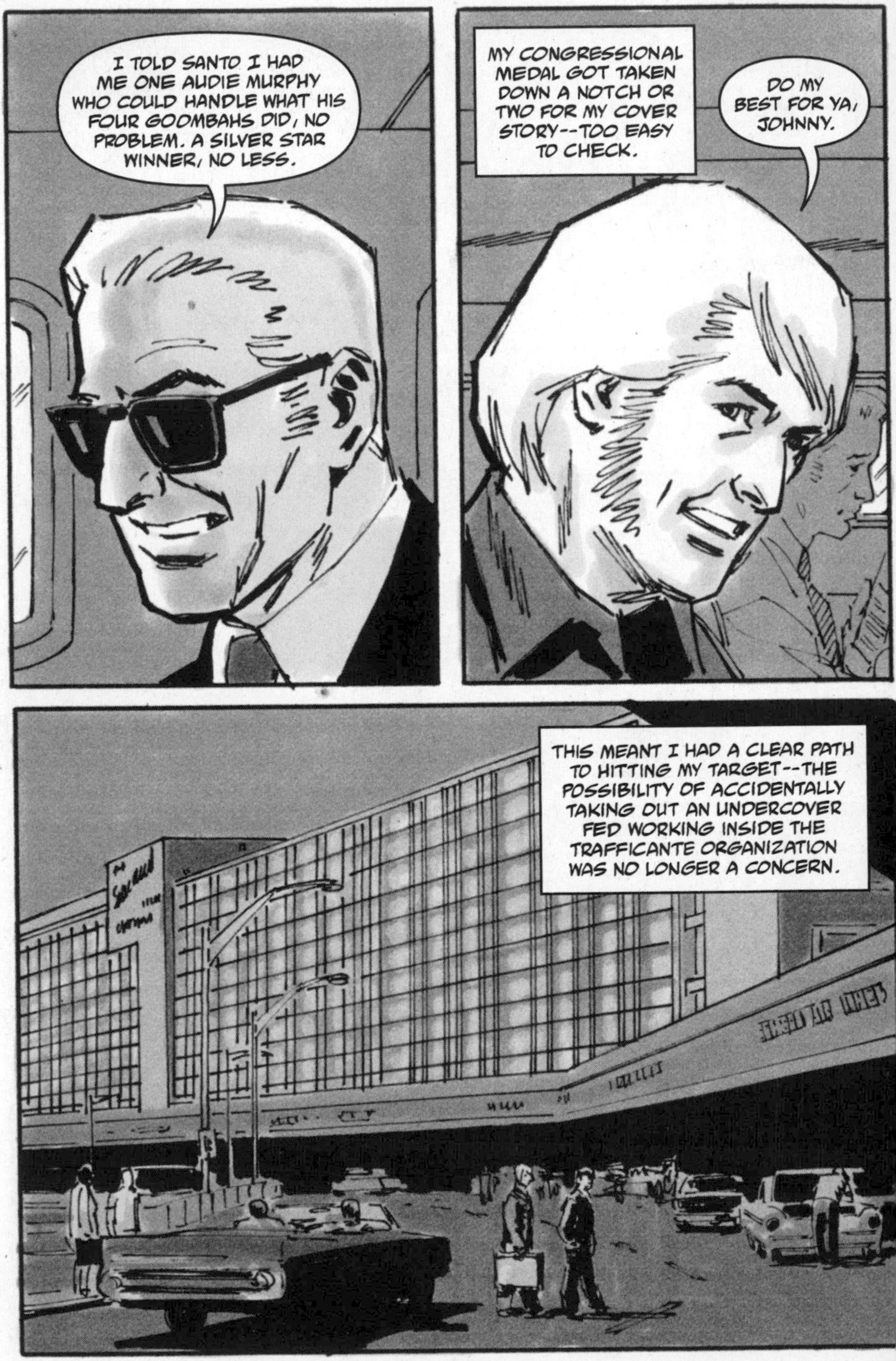
I TOLD SANTO I HAD ME ONE AUDIE MURPHY WHO COULD HANDLE WHAT HIS FOUR GOOMBAHS DID, NO PROBLEM. A SILVER STAR WINNER, NO LESS.
MY CONGRESSIONAL MEDAL GOT TAKEN DOWN A NOTCH OR TWO FOR MY COVER STORY--TOO EASY TO CHECK.
DO MY BEST FOR YA, JOHNNY.
THIS MEANT I HAD A CLEAR PATH TO HITTING MY TARGET--THE POSSIBILITY OF ACCIDENTALLY TAKING OUT AN UNDERCOVER FED WORKING INSIDE THE TRAFFICANTE ORGANIZATION WAS NO LONGER A CONCERN.

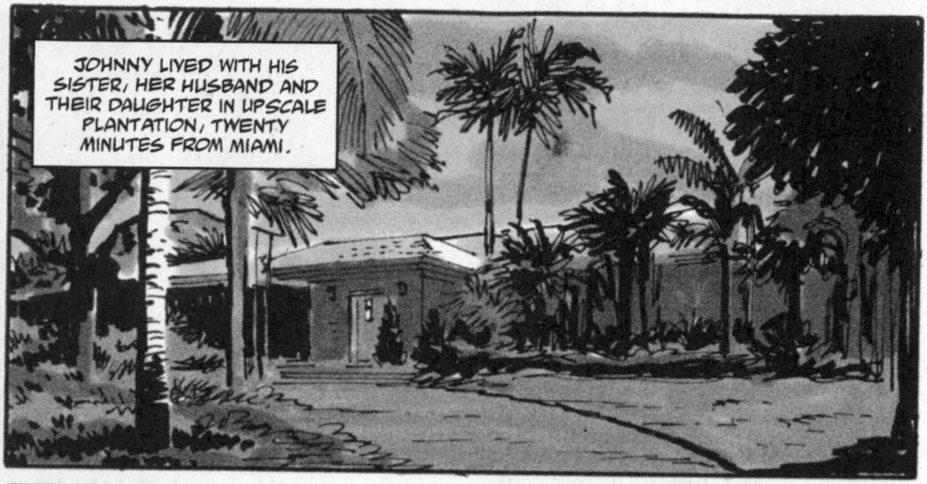
JOHNNY LIVED WITH HIS SISTER, HER HUSBAND AND THEIR DAUGHTER IN UPSCALE PLANTATION, TWENTY MINUTES FROM MIAMI.

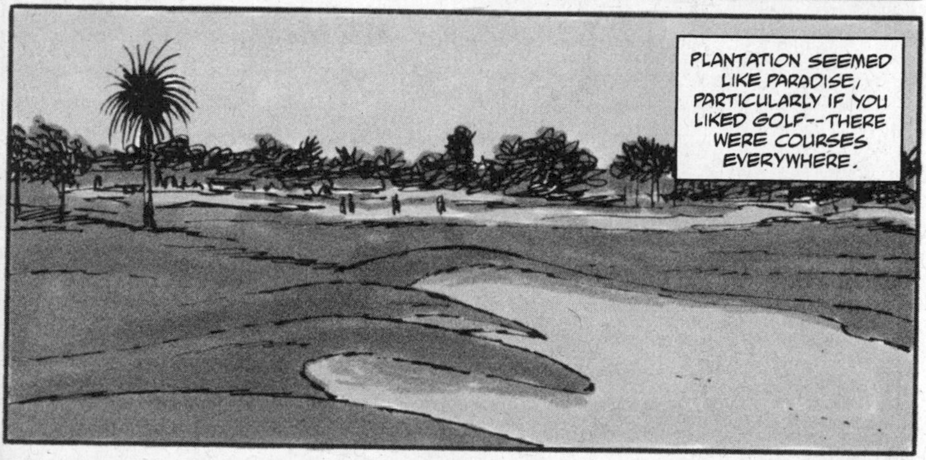
PLANTATION SEEMED LIKE PARADISE, PARTICULARLY IF YOU LIKED GOLF--THERE WERE COURSES EVERYWHERE.

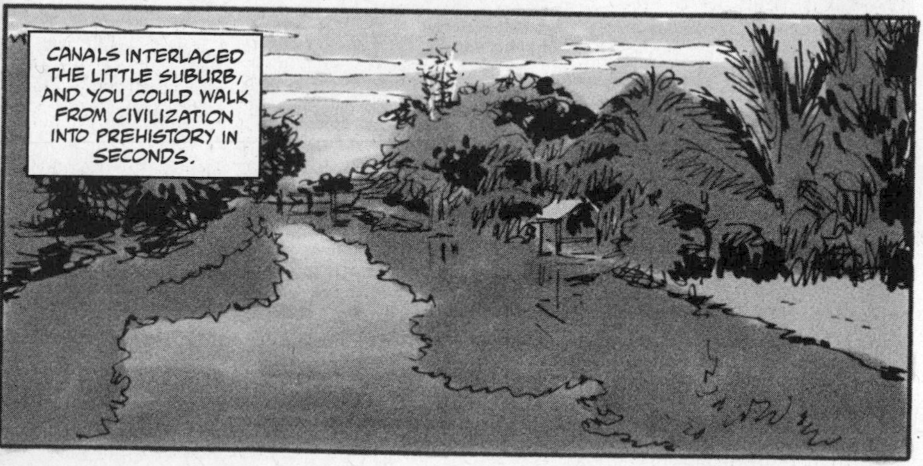
CANALS INTERLACED THE LITTLE SUBURB, AND YOU COULD WALK FROM CIVILIZATION INTO PREHISTORY IN SECONDS.

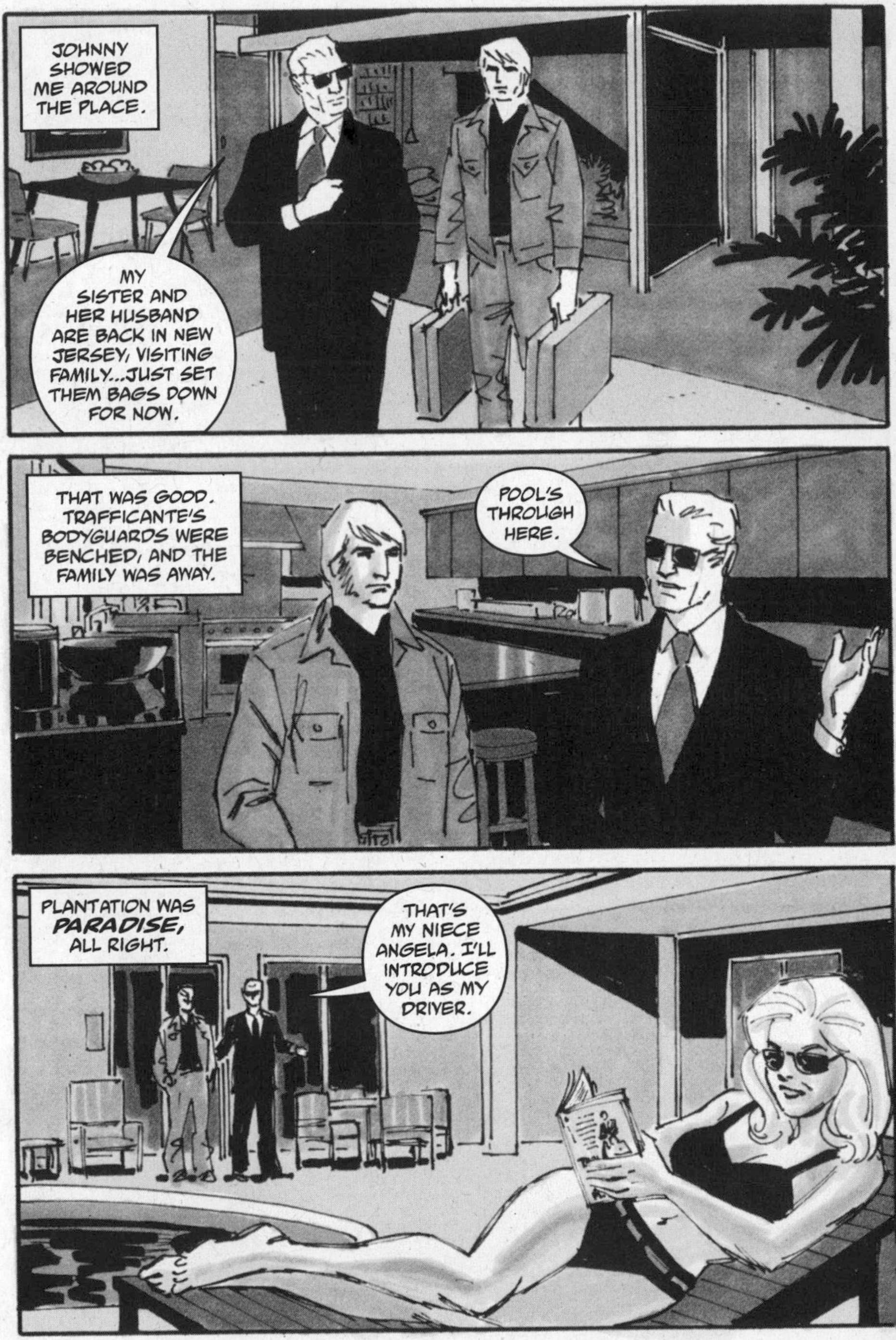
JOHNNY SHOWED ME AROUND THE PLACE.
MY SISTER AND HER HUSBAND ARE BACK IN NEW JERSEY, VISITING FAMILY...JUST SET THEM BAGS DOWN FOR NOW.
THAT WAS GOOD. TRAFFICANTE'S BODYGUARDS WERE BENCHED, AND THE FAMILY WAS AWAY.
POOL'S THROUGH HERE.
PLANTATION WAS *PARADISE,* ALL RIGHT.
THAT'S MY NIECE ANGELA. I'LL INTRODUCE YOU AS MY DRIVER.

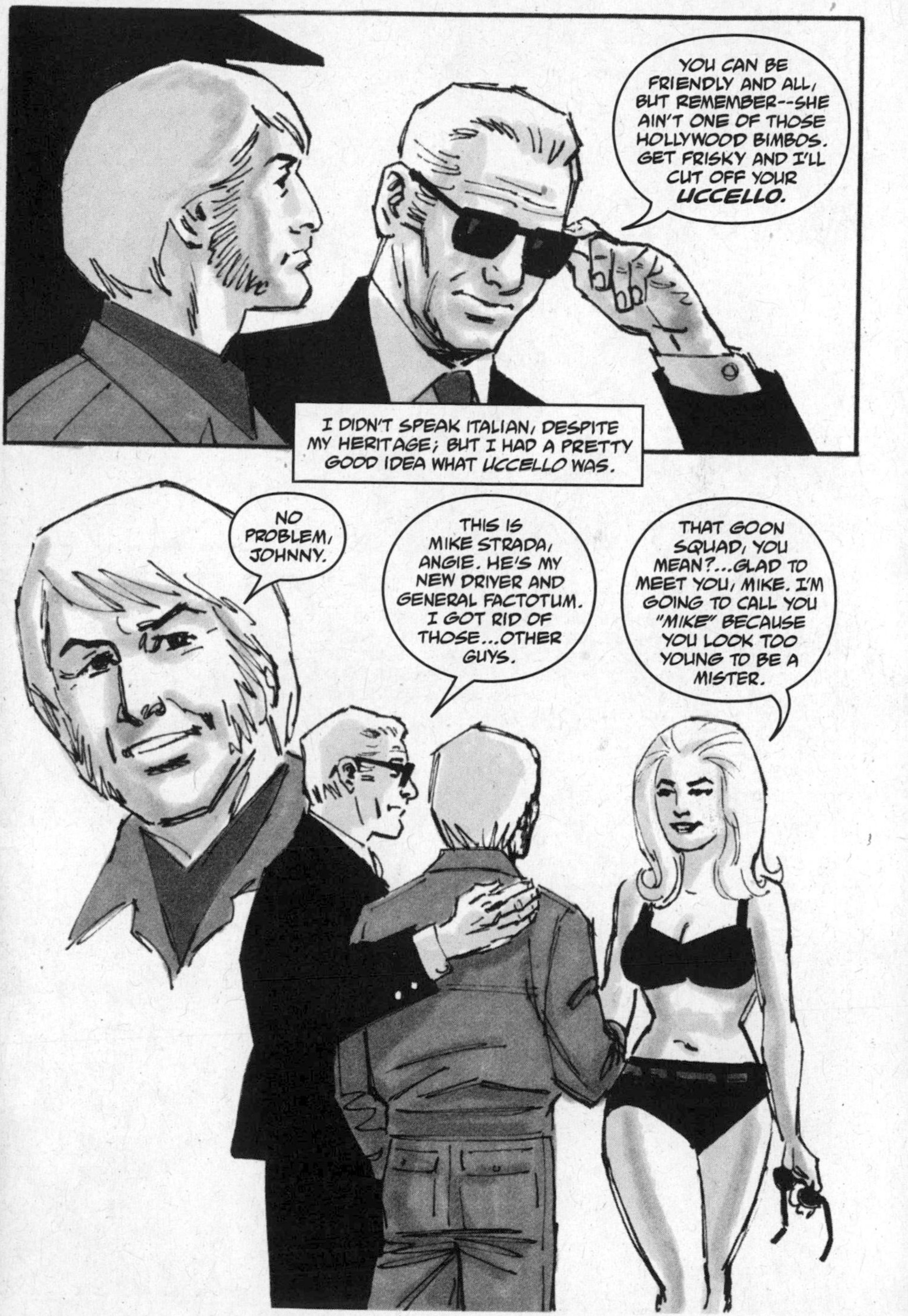
YOU CAN BE FRIENDLY AND ALL, BUT REMEMBER--SHE AIN'T ONE OF THOSE HOLLYWOOD BIMBOS. GET FRISKY AND I'LL CUT OFF YOUR *UCCELLO.*
I DIDN'T SPEAK ITALIAN, DESPITE MY HERITAGE; BUT I HAD A PRETTY GOOD IDEA WHAT *UCCELLO* WAS.
NO PROBLEM, JOHNNY.
THIS IS MIKE STRADA, ANGIE. HE'S MY NEW DRIVER AND GENERAL FACTOTUM. I GOT RID OF THOSE...OTHER GUYS.
THAT GOON SQUAD, YOU MEAN?...GLAD TO MEET YOU, MIKE. I'M GOING TO CALL YOU "MIKE" BECAUSE YOU LOOK TOO YOUNG TO BE A MISTER.

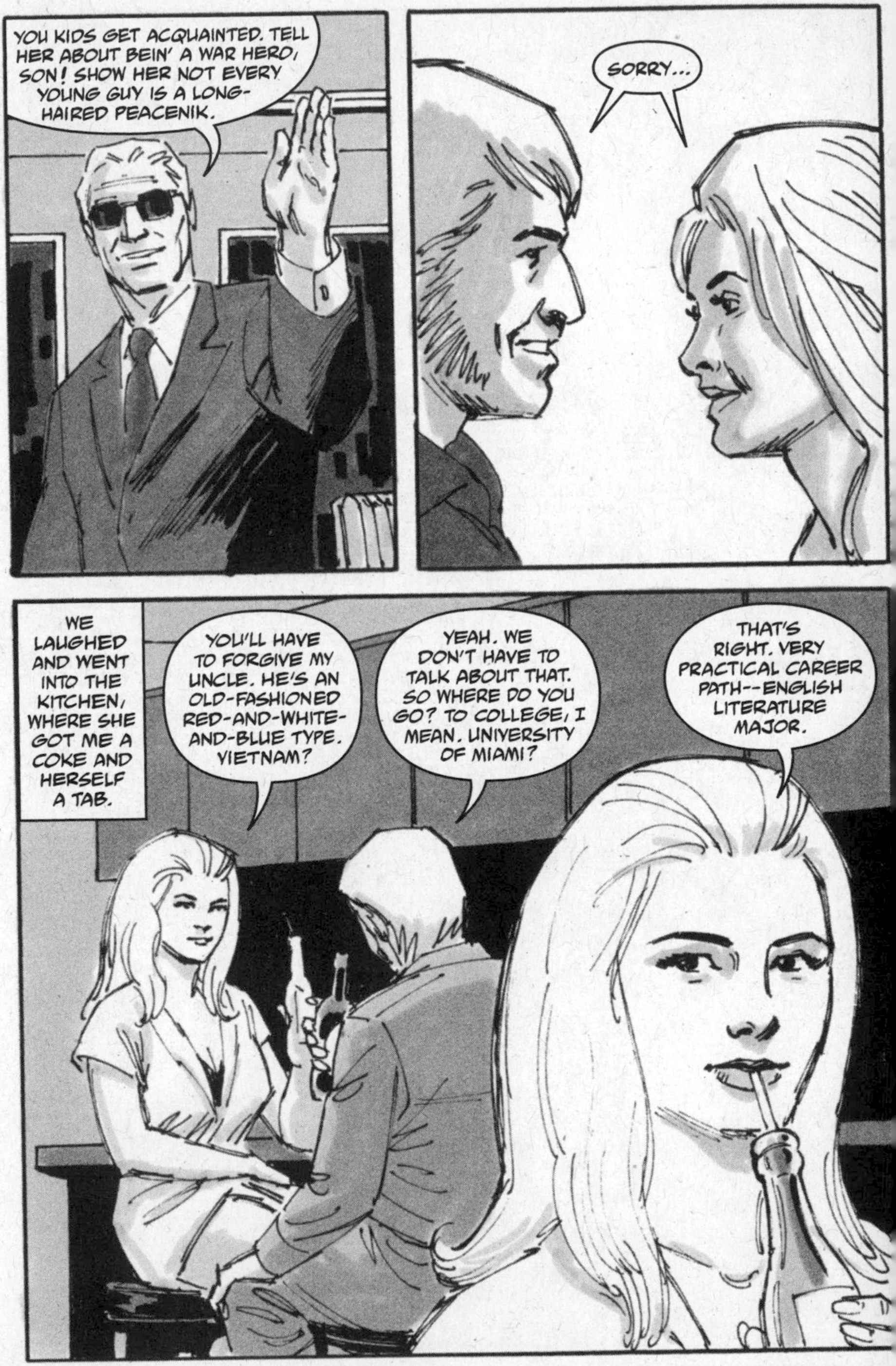
YOU KIDS GET ACQUAINTED. TELL HER ABOUT BEIN' A WAR HERO, SON! SHOW HER NOT EVERY YOUNG GUY IS A LONG-HAIRED PEACENIK.
SORRY...
WE LAUGHED AND WENT INTO THE KITCHEN, WHERE SHE GOT ME A COKE AND HERSELF A TAB.
YOU'LL HAVE TO FORGIVE MY UNCLE. HE'S AN OLD-FASHIONED RED-AND-WHITE-AND-BLUE TYPE. VIETNAM?
YEAH. WE DON'T HAVE TO TALK ABOUT THAT. SO WHERE DO YOU GO? TO COLLEGE, I MEAN. UNIVERSITY OF MIAMI?
THAT'S RIGHT. VERY PRACTICAL CAREER PATH--ENGLISH LITERATURE MAJOR.

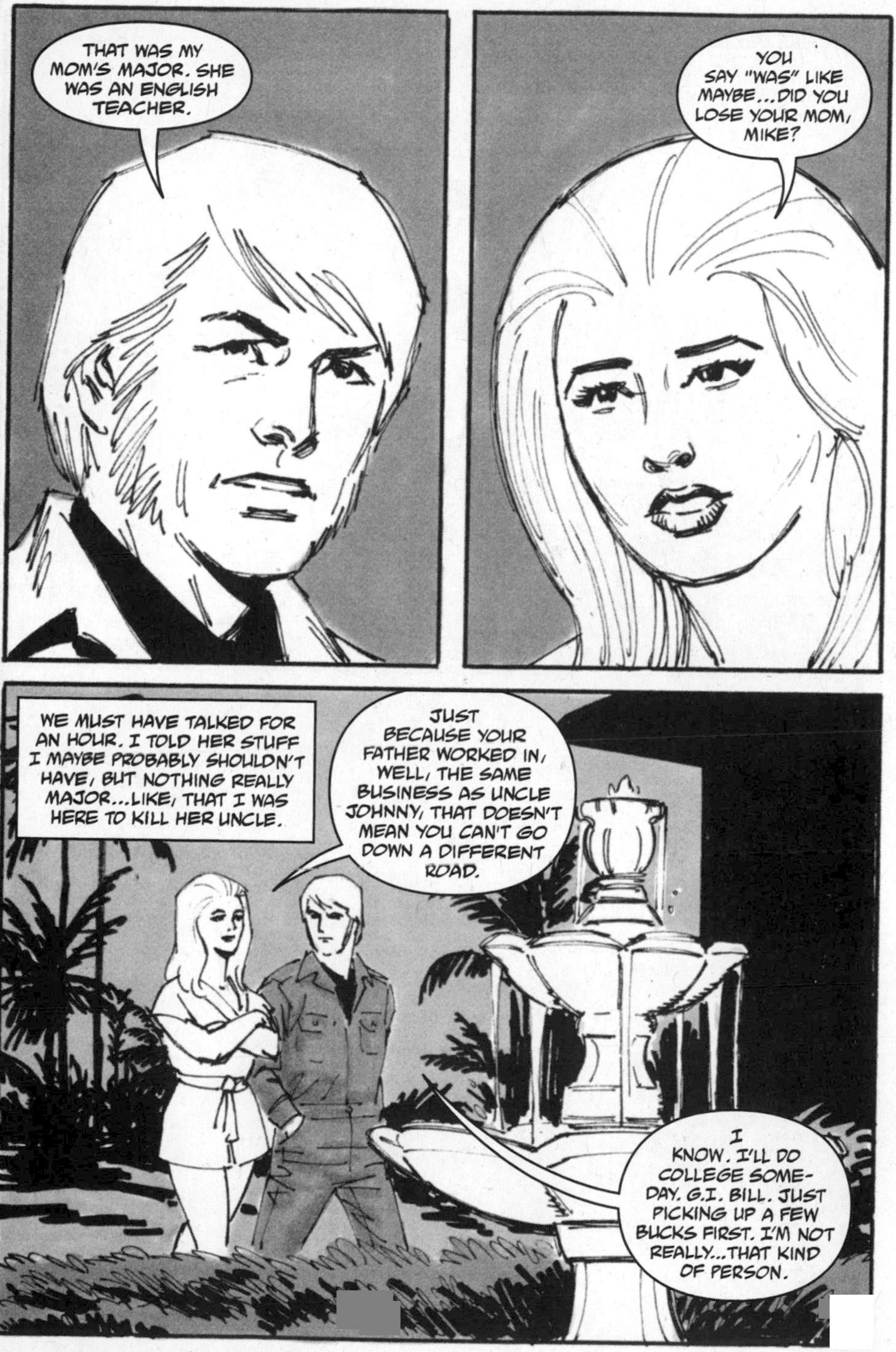
THAT WAS MY MOM'S MAJOR. SHE WAS AN ENGLISH TEACHER.
YOU SAY "WAS" LIKE MAYBE...DID YOU LOSE YOUR MOM, MIKE?
WE MUST HAVE TALKED FOR AN HOUR. I TOLD HER STUFF I MAYBE PROBABLY SHOULDN'T HAVE, BUT NOTHING REALLY MAJOR...LIKE, THAT I WAS HERE TO KILL HER UNCLE.
JUST BECAUSE YOUR FATHER WORKED IN, WELL, THE SAME BUSINESS AS UNCLE JOHNNY, THAT DOESN'T MEAN YOU CAN'T GO DOWN A DIFFERENT ROAD.
I KNOW. I'LL DO COLLEGE SOMEDAY. G.I. BILL. JUST PICKING UP A FEW BUCKS FIRST. I'M NOT REALLY...THAT KIND OF PERSON.

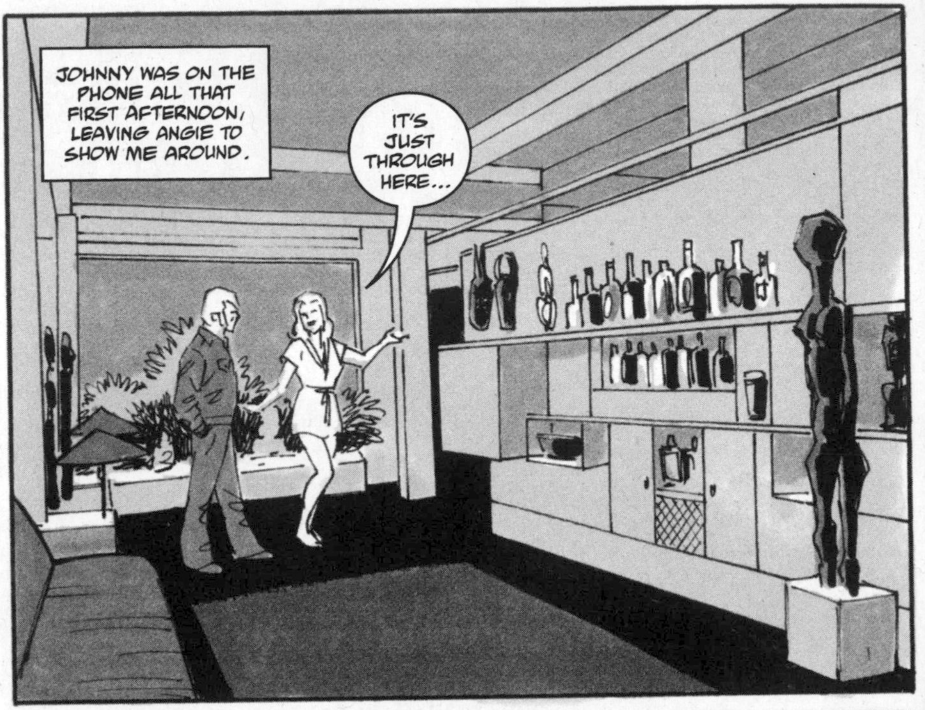
JOHNNY WAS ON THE PHONE ALL THAT FIRST AFTERNOON, LEAVING ANGIE TO SHOW ME AROUND.
IT'S JUST THROUGH HERE...

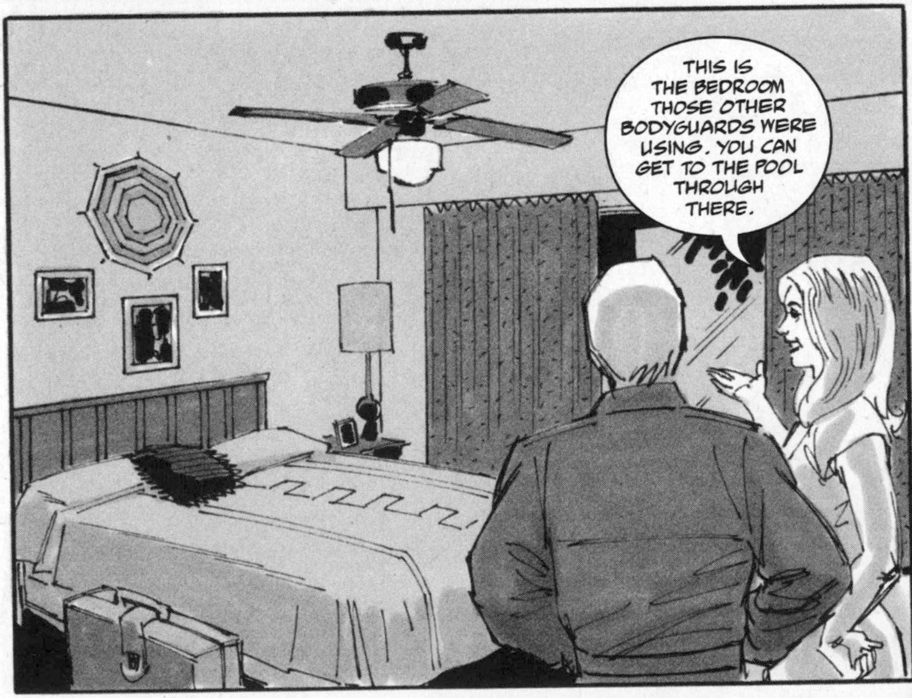
THIS IS THE BEDROOM THOSE OTHER BODYGUARDS WERE USING. YOU CAN GET TO THE POOL THROUGH THERE.

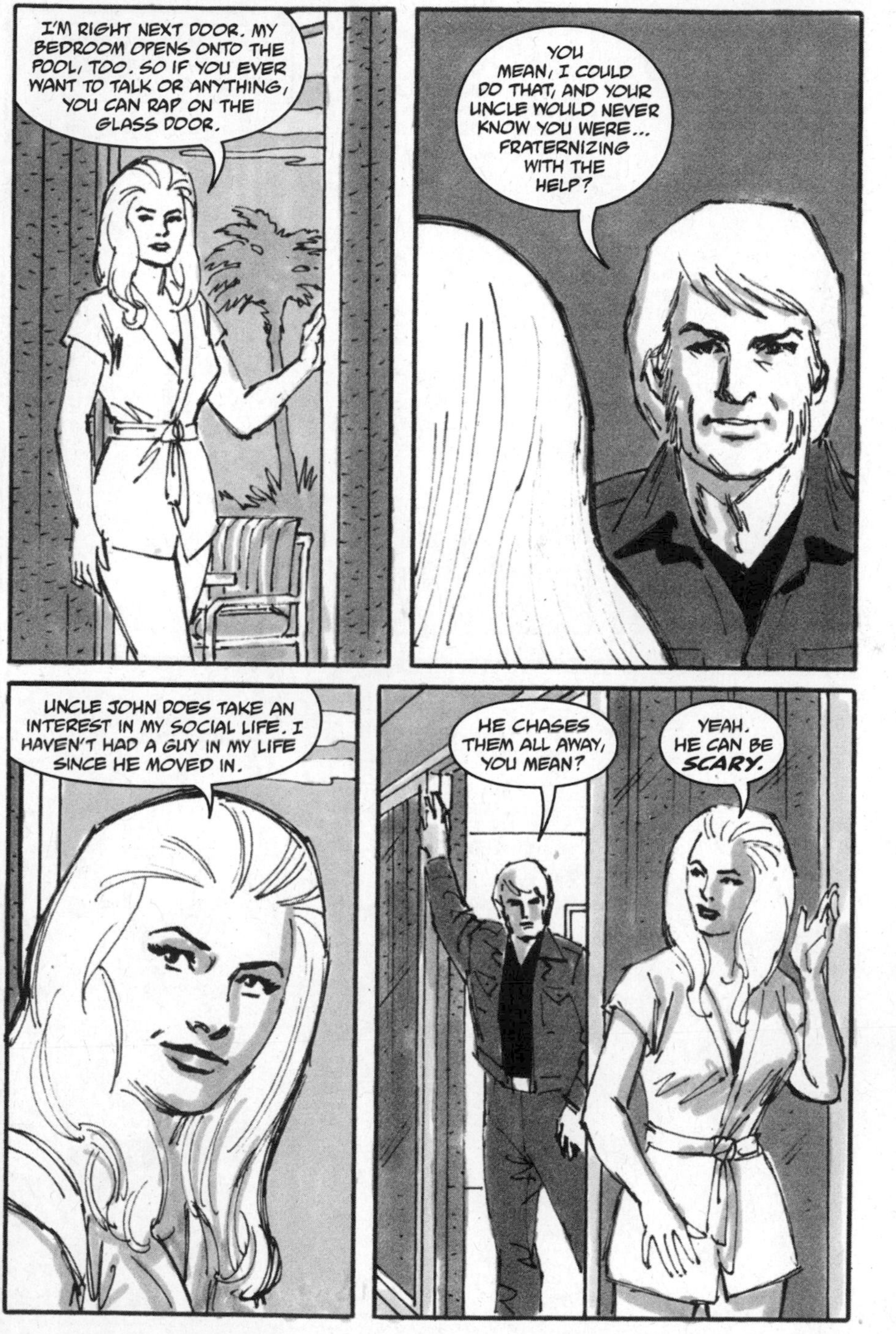
I'M RIGHT NEXT DOOR. MY BEDROOM OPENS ONTO THE POOL, TOO. SO IF YOU EVER WANT TO TALK OR ANYTHING, YOU CAN RAP ON THE GLASS DOOR.
YOU MEAN, I COULD DO THAT, AND YOUR UNCLE WOULD NEVER KNOW YOU WERE... FRATERNIZING WITH THE HELP?
UNCLE JOHN DOES TAKE AN INTEREST IN MY SOCIAL LIFE. I HAVEN'T HAD A GUY IN MY LIFE SINCE HE MOVED IN.
HE CHASES THEM ALL AWAY, YOU MEAN?
YEAH. HE CAN BE SCARY.

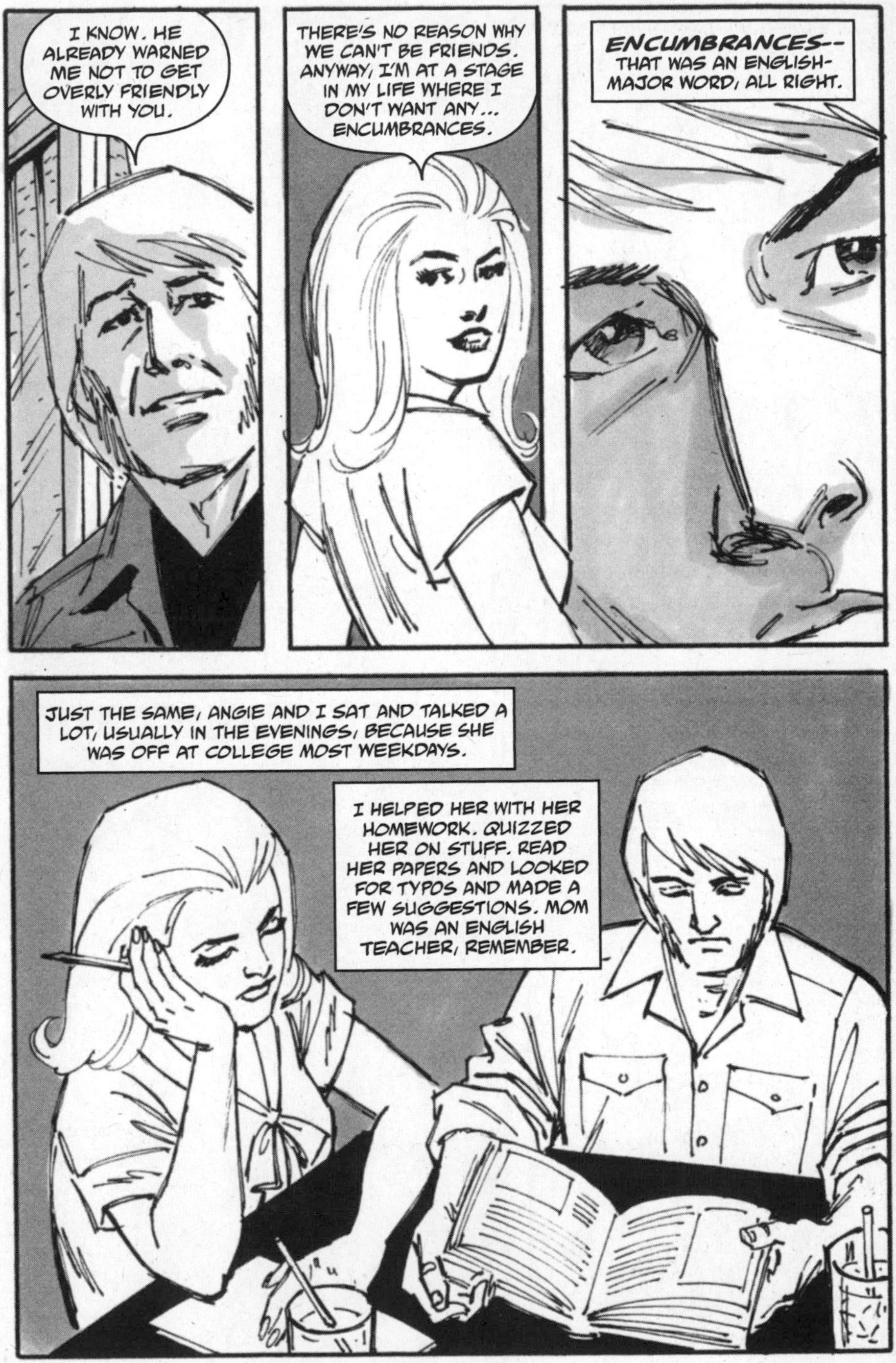
I KNOW. HE ALREADY WARNED ME NOT TO GET OVERLY FRIENDLY WITH YOU.
THERE'S NO REASON WHY WE CAN'T BE FRIENDS. ANYWAY, I'M AT A STAGE IN MY LIFE WHERE I DON'T WANT ANY... ENCUMBRANCES.
ENCUMBRANCES-- THAT WAS AN ENGLISH-MAJOR WORD, ALL RIGHT.
JUST THE SAME, ANGIE AND I SAT AND TALKED A LOT, USUALLY IN THE EVENINGS, BECAUSE SHE WAS OFF AT COLLEGE MOST WEEKDAYS.
I HELPED HER WITH HER HOMEWORK. QUIZZED HER ON STUFF. READ HER PAPERS AND LOOKED FOR TYPOS AND MADE A FEW SUGGESTIONS. MOM WAS AN ENGLISH TEACHER, REMEMBER.

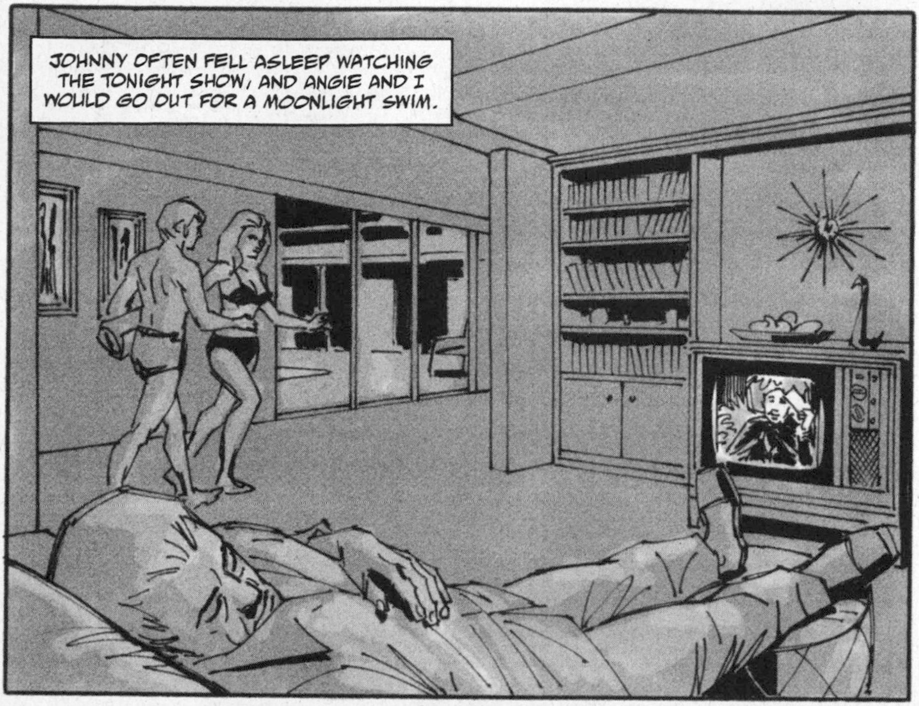
JOHNNY OFTEN FELL ASLEEP WATCHING THE TONIGHT SHOW, AND ANGIE AND I WOULD GO OUT FOR A MOONLIGHT SWIM.

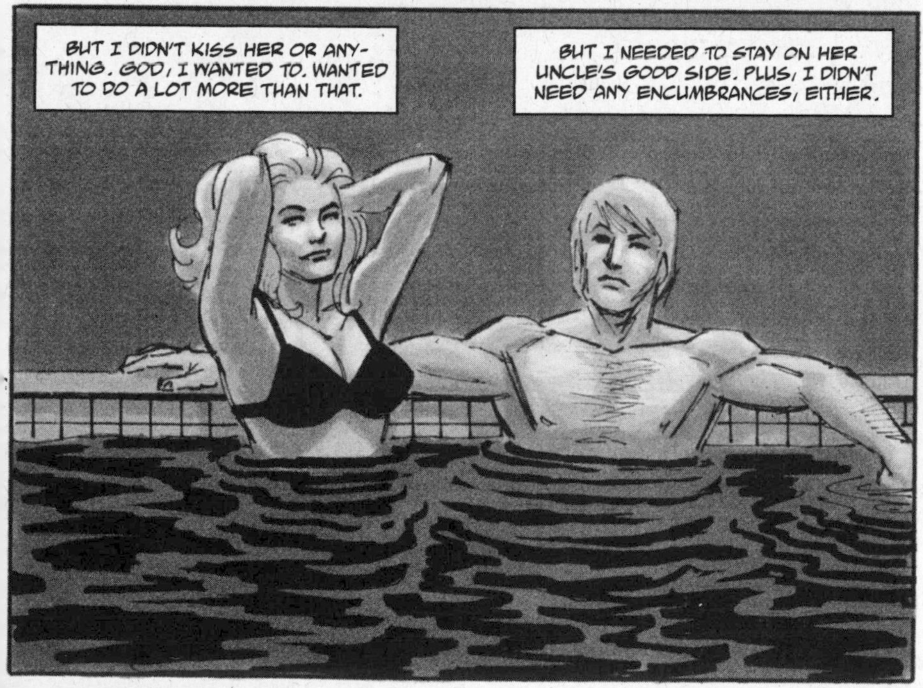
BUT I DIDN'T KISS HER OR ANY-THING. GOD, I WANTED TO. WANTED TO DO A LOT MORE THAN THAT.
BUT I NEEDED TO STAY ON HER UNCLE'S GOOD SIDE. PLUS, I DIDN'T NEED ANY ENCUMBRANCES, EITHER.

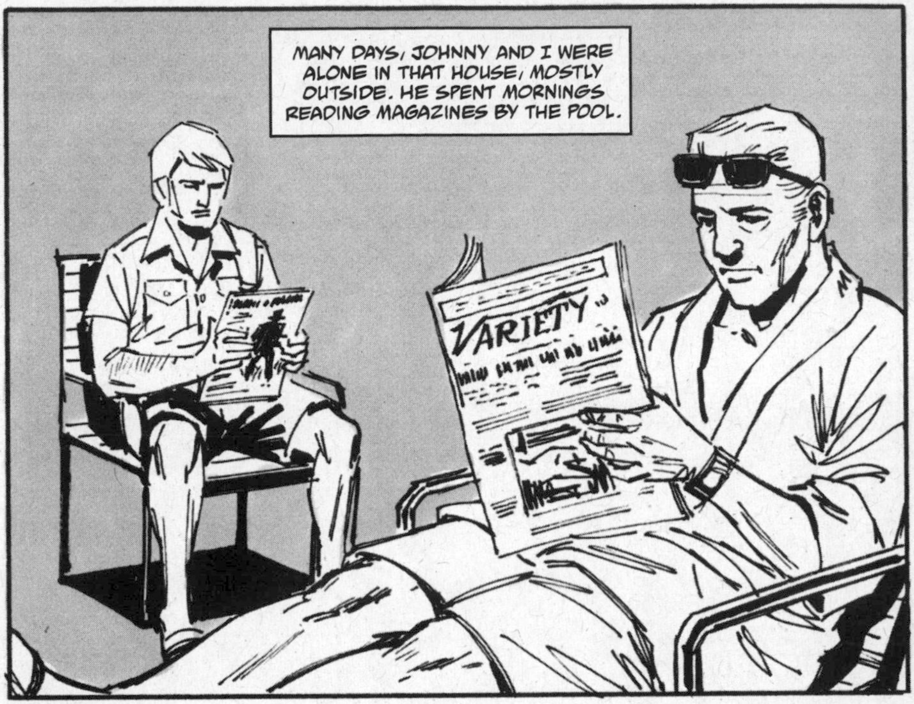
MANY DAYS, JOHNNY AND I WERE ALONE IN THAT HOUSE, MOSTLY OUTSIDE. HE SPENT MORNINGS READING MAGAZINES BY THE POOL.
VARIETY

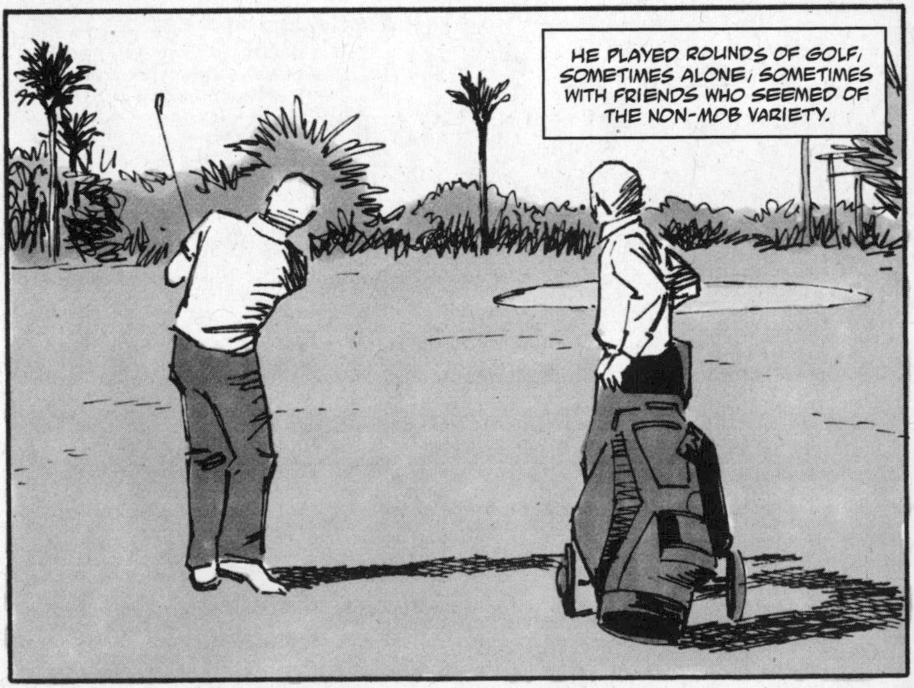
HE PLAYED ROUNDS OF GOLF, SOMETIMES ALONE, SOMETIMES WITH FRIENDS WHO SEEMED OF THE NON-MOB VARIETY.

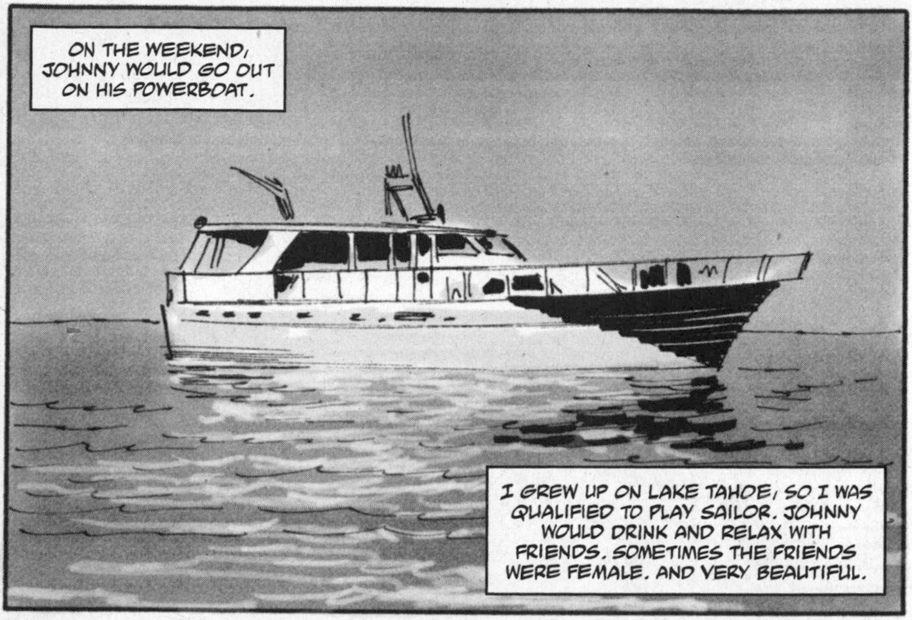
ON THE WEEKEND, JOHNNY WOULD GO OUT ON HIS POWERBOAT.
I GREW UP ON LAKE TAHOE, SO I WAS QUALIFIED TO PLAY SAILOR. JOHNNY WOULD DRINK AND RELAX WITH FRIENDS. SOMETIMES THE FRIENDS WERE FEMALE. AND VERY BEAUTIFUL.

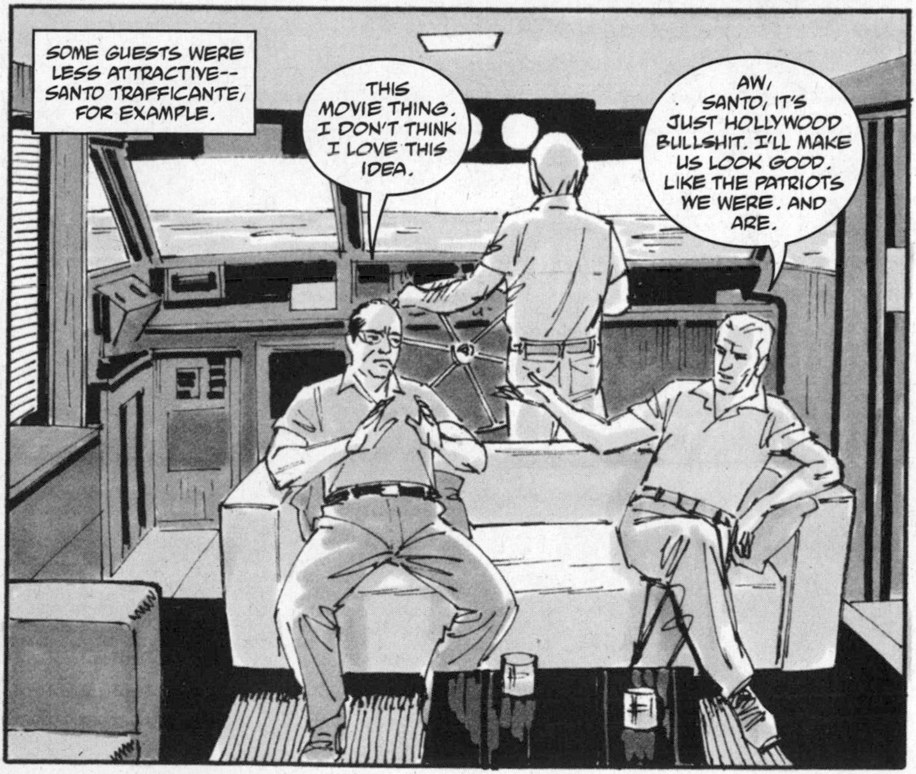
SOME GUESTS WERE LESS ATTRACTIVE-- SANTO TRAFFICANTE, FOR EXAMPLE.
THIS MOVIE THING. I DON'T THINK I LOVE THIS IDEA.
AW, SANTO, IT'S JUST HOLLYWOOD BULLSHIT. I'LL MAKE US LOOK GOOD. LIKE THE PATRIOTS WE WERE. AND ARE.

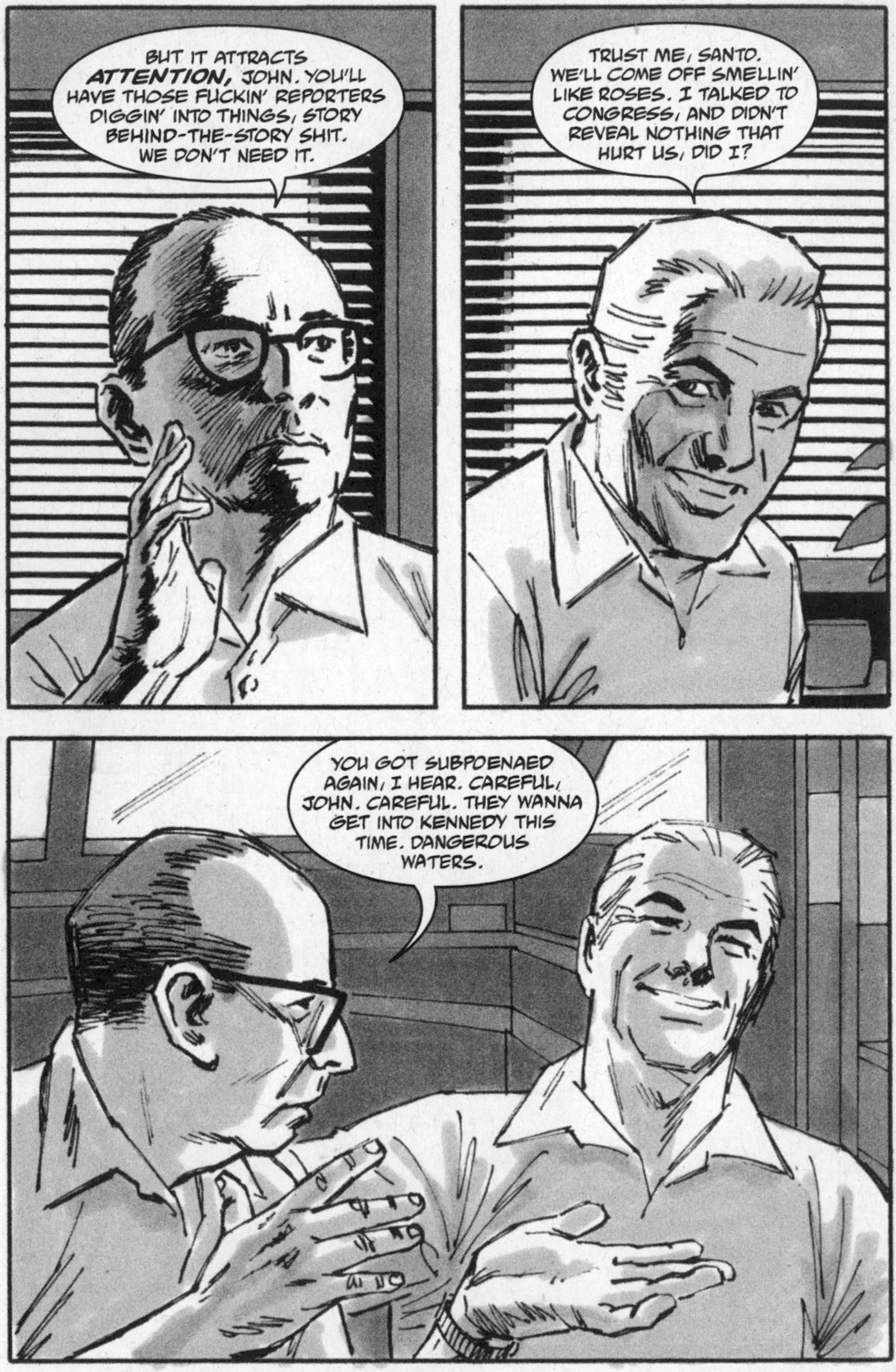
BUT IT ATTRACTS ATTENTION, JOHN. YOU'LL HAVE THOSE FUCKIN' REPORTERS DIGGIN' INTO THINGS, STORY BEHIND-THE-STORY SHIT. WE DON'T NEED IT.
TRUST ME, SANTO. WE'LL COME OFF SMELLIN' LIKE ROSES. I TALKED TO CONGRESS, AND DIDN'T REVEAL NOTHING THAT HURT US, DID I?
YOU GOT SUBPOENAED AGAIN, I HEAR. CAREFUL, JOHN. CAREFUL. THEY WANNA GET INTO KENNEDY THIS TIME. DANGEROUS WATERS.

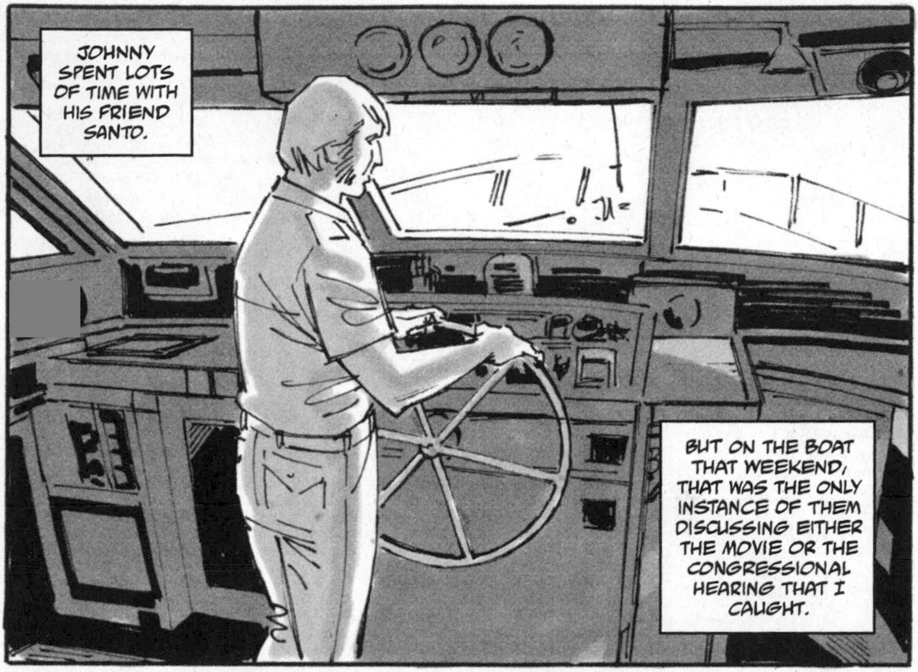
JOHNNY SPENT LOTS OF TIME WITH HIS FRIEND SANTO.
BUT ON THE BOAT THAT WEEKEND, THAT WAS THE ONLY INSTANCE OF THEM DISCUSSING EITHER THE MOVIE OR THE CONGRESSIONAL HEARING THAT I CAUGHT.

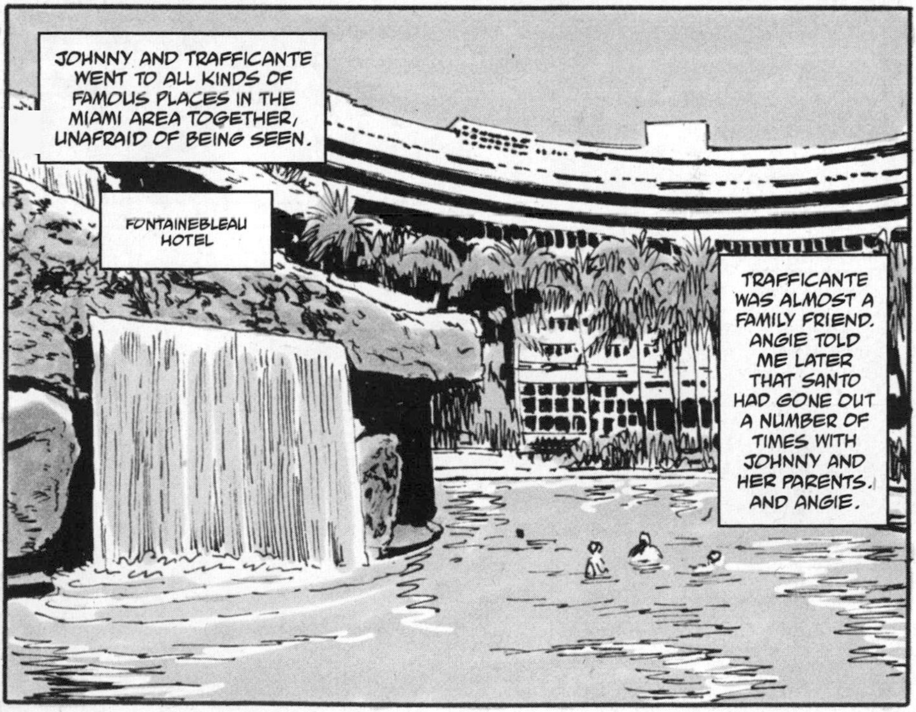
JOHNNY AND TRAFFICANTE WENT TO ALL KINDS OF FAMOUS PLACES IN THE MIAMI AREA TOGETHER, UNAFRAID OF BEING SEEN.
FONTAINEBLEAU HOTEL
TRAFFICANTE WAS ALMOST A FAMILY FRIEND. ANGIE TOLD ME LATER THAT SANTO HAD GONE OUT A NUMBER OF TIMES WITH JOHNNY AND HER PARENTS. AND ANGIE.

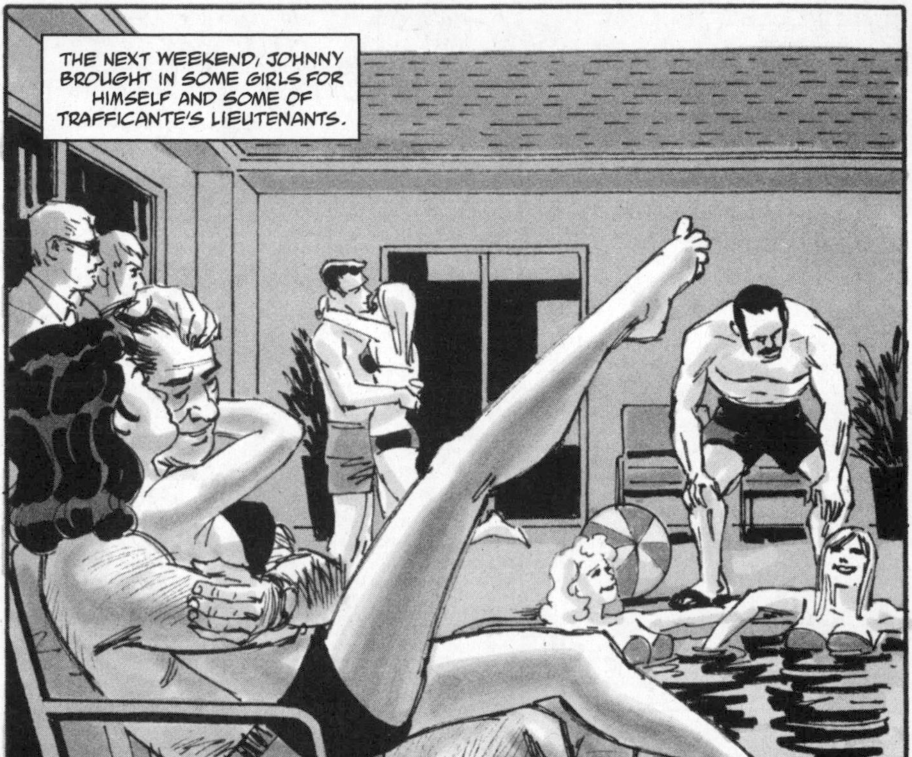
THE NEXT WEEKEND, JOHNNY BROUGHT IN SOME GIRLS FOR HIMSELF AND SOME OF TRAFFICANTE'S LIEUTENANTS.

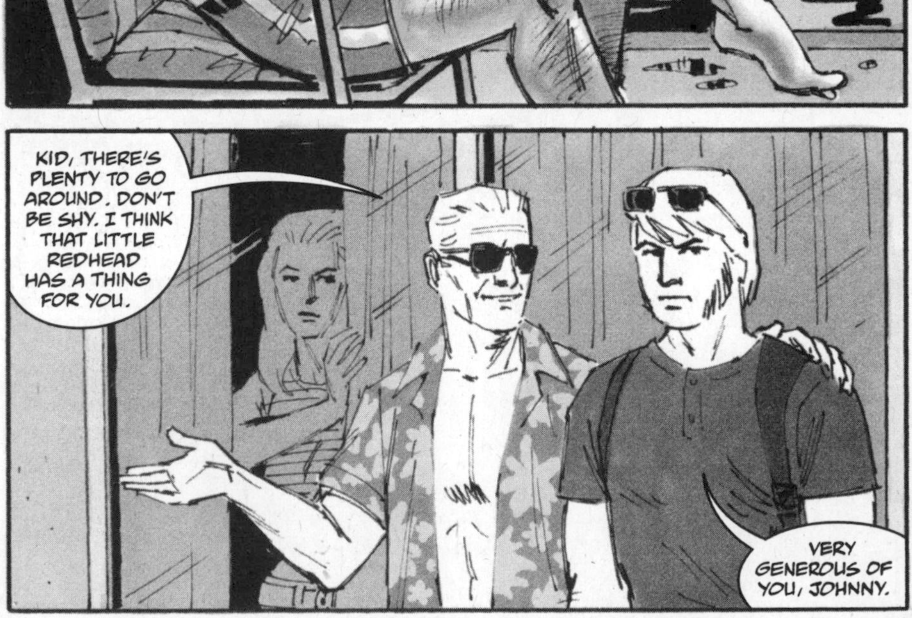
KID, THERE'S PLENTY TO GO AROUND. DON'T BE SHY. I THINK THAT LITTLE REDHEAD HAS A THING FOR YOU.
VERY GENEROUS OF YOU, JOHNNY.

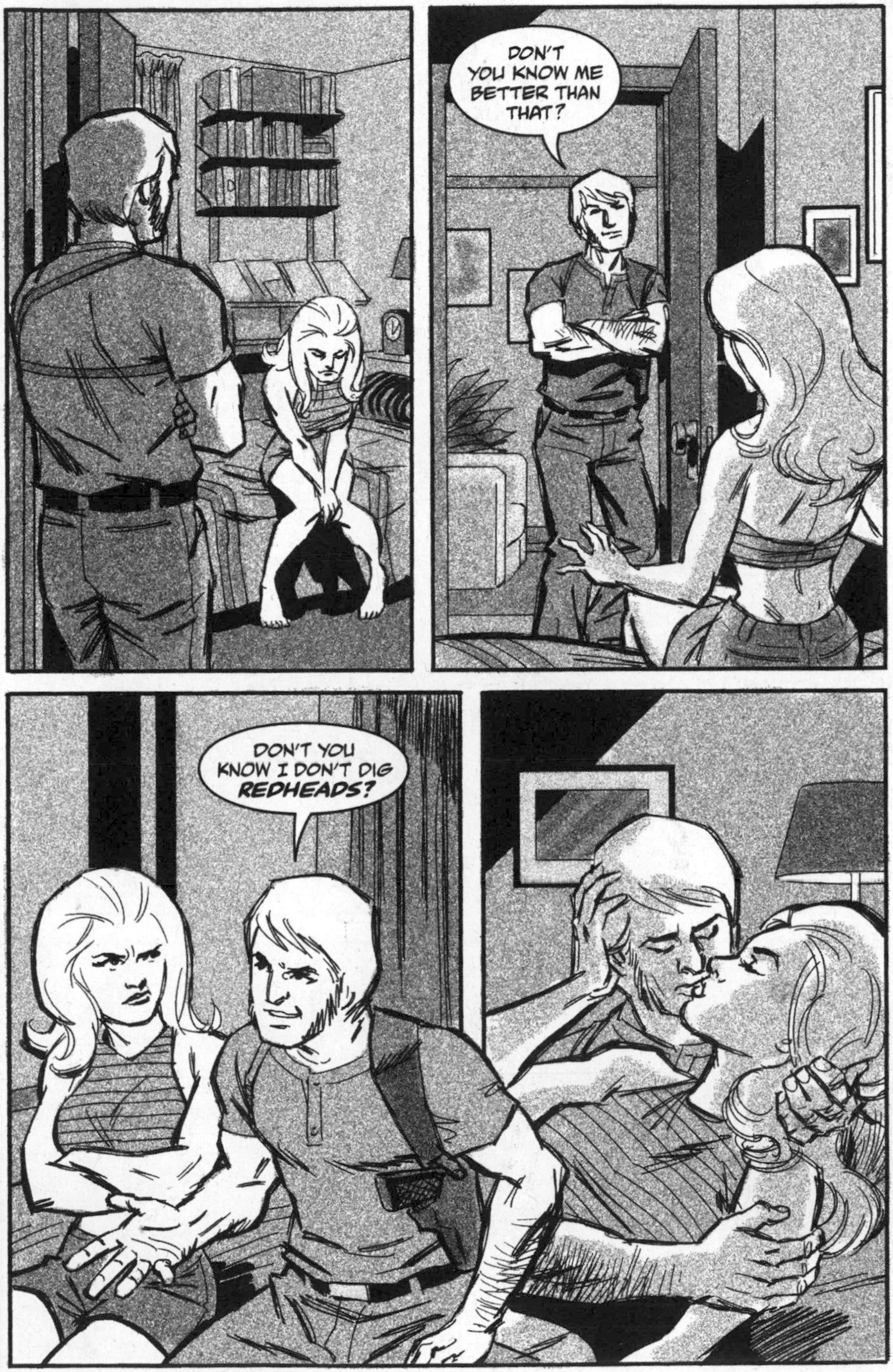
DON'T YOU KNOW ME BETTER THAN THAT?
DON'T YOU KNOW I DON'T DIG REDHEADS?

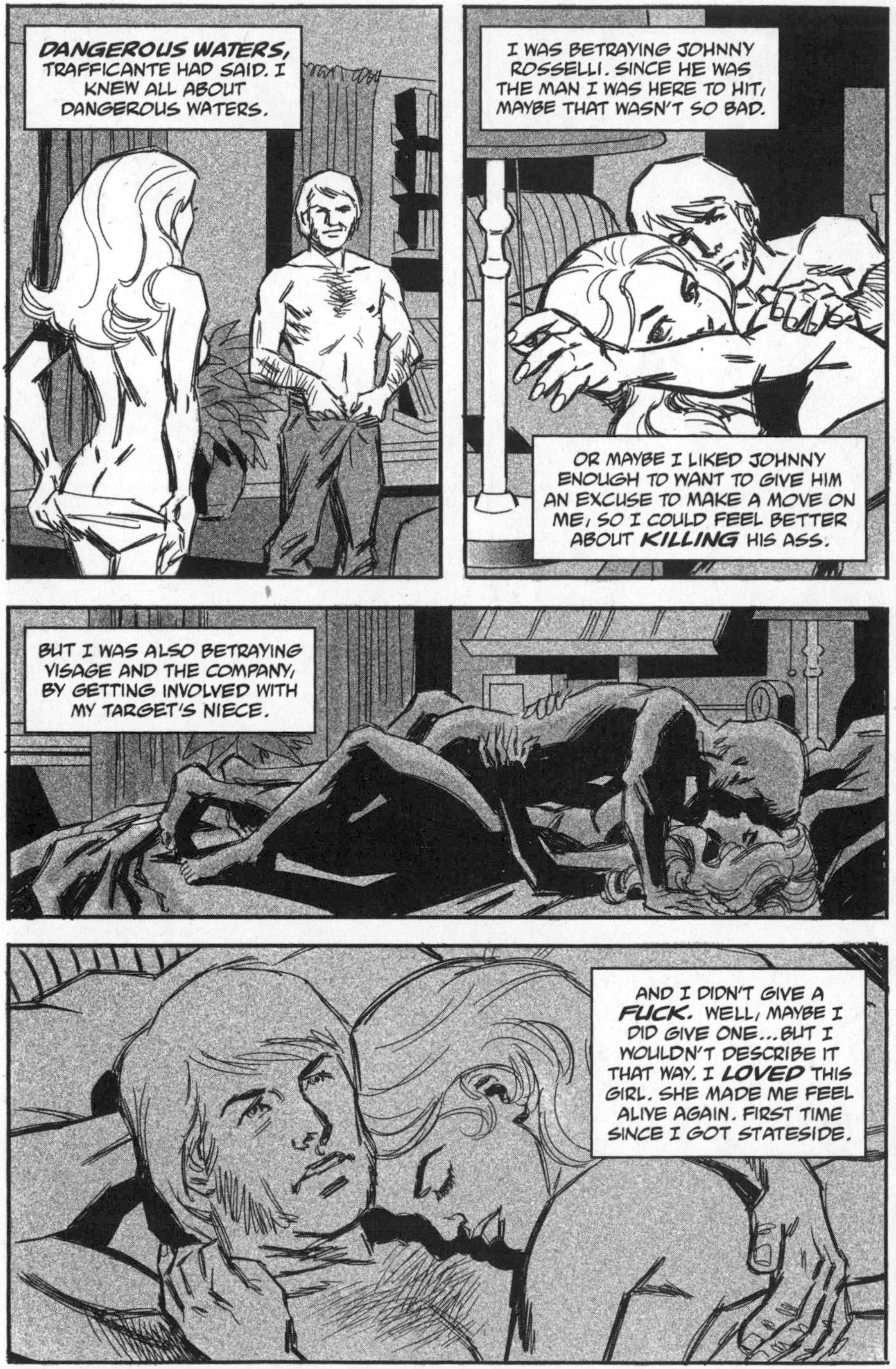
DANGEROUS WATERS, TRAFFICANTE HAD SAID. I KNEW ALL ABOUT DANGEROUS WATERS.
I WAS BETRAYING JOHNNY ROSSELLI. SINCE HE WAS THE MAN I WAS HERE TO HIT, MAYBE THAT WASN'T SO BAD.
OR MAYBE I LIKED JOHNNY ENOUGH TO WANT TO GIVE HIM AN EXCUSE TO MAKE A MOVE ON ME, SO I COULD FEEL BETTER ABOUT KILLING HIS ASS.
BUT I WAS ALSO BETRAYING VISAGE AND THE COMPANY, BY GETTING INVOLVED WITH MY TARGET'S NIECE.
AND I DIDN'T GIVE A FUCK. WELL, MAYBE I DID GIVE ONE... BUT I WOULDN'T DESCRIBE IT THAT WAY. I LOVED THIS GIRL. SHE MADE ME FEEL ALIVE AGAIN. FIRST TIME SINCE I GOT STATESIDE.

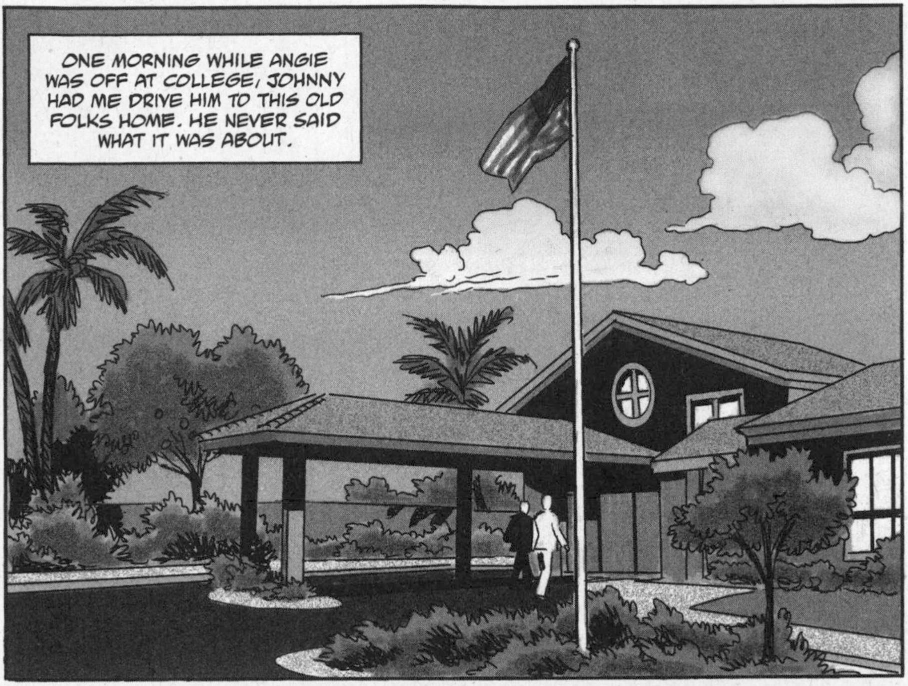
ONE MORNING WHILE ANGIE WAS OFF AT COLLEGE, JOHNNY HAD ME DRIVE HIM TO THIS OLD FOLKS HOME. HE NEVER SAID WHAT IT WAS ABOUT.

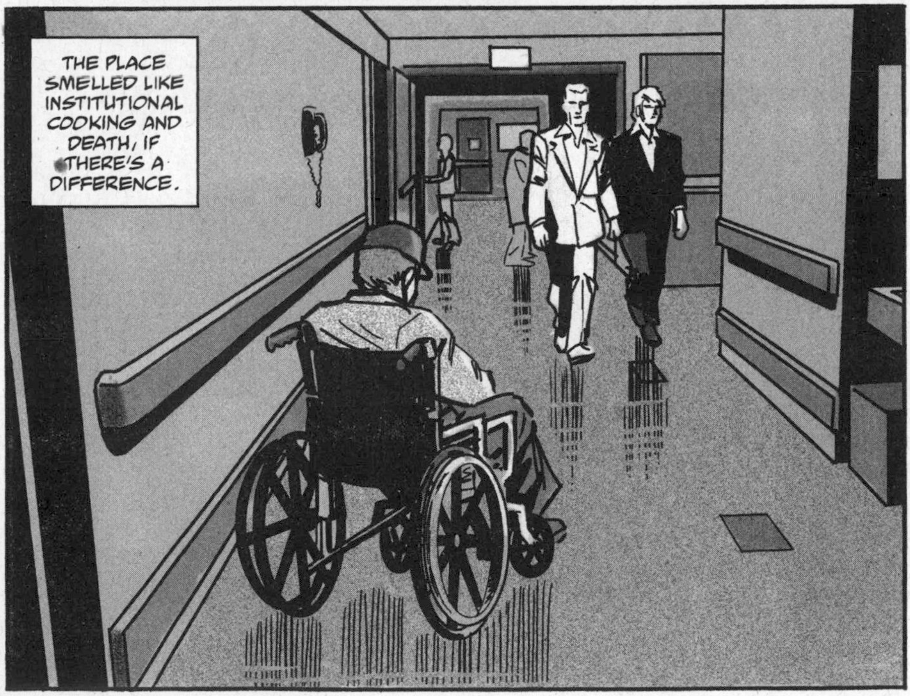
THE PLACE SMELLED LIKE INSTITUTIONAL COOKING AND DEATH, IF THERE'S A DIFFERENCE.

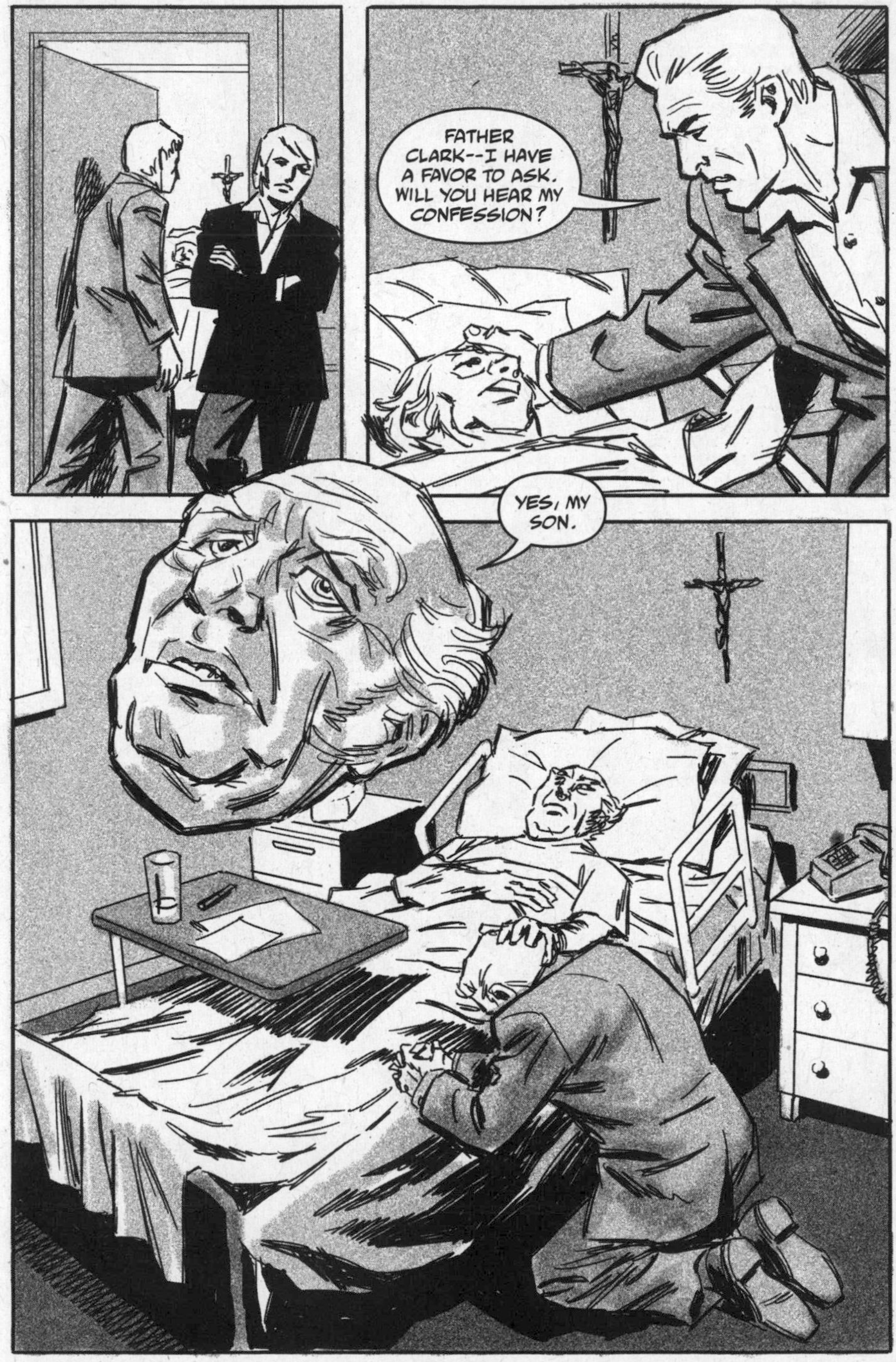
FATHER CLARK--I HAVE A FAVOR TO ASK. WILL YOU HEAR MY CONFESSION?
YES, MY SON.

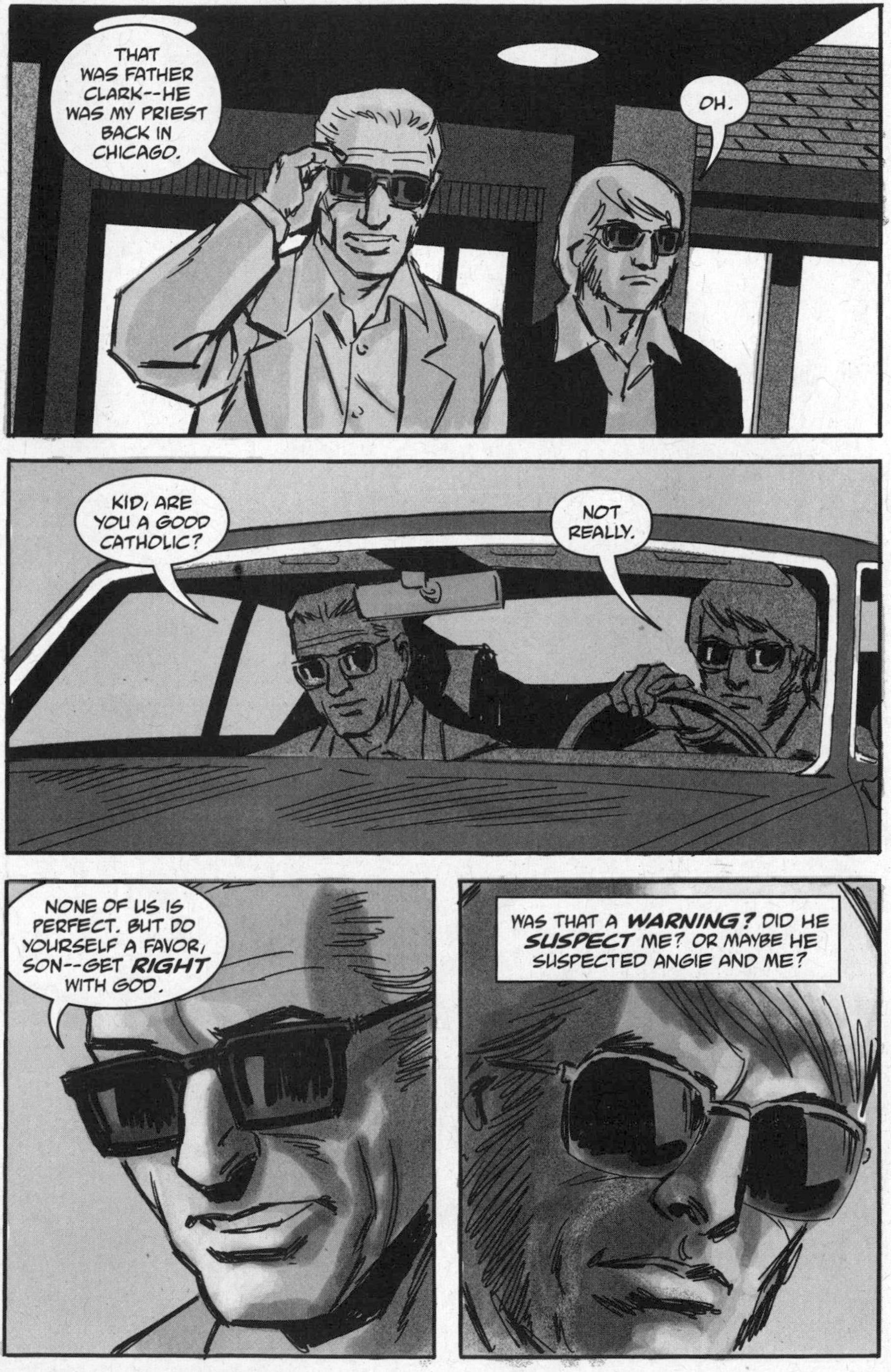
THAT WAS FATHER CLARK--HE WAS MY PRIEST BACK IN CHICAGO.
OH.
KID, ARE YOU A GOOD CATHOLIC?
NOT REALLY.
NONE OF US IS PERFECT. BUT DO YOURSELF A FAVOR, SON--GET **RIGHT** WITH GOD.
WAS THAT A **WARNING?** DID HE **SUSPECT** ME? OR MAYBE HE SUSPECTED ANGIE AND ME?

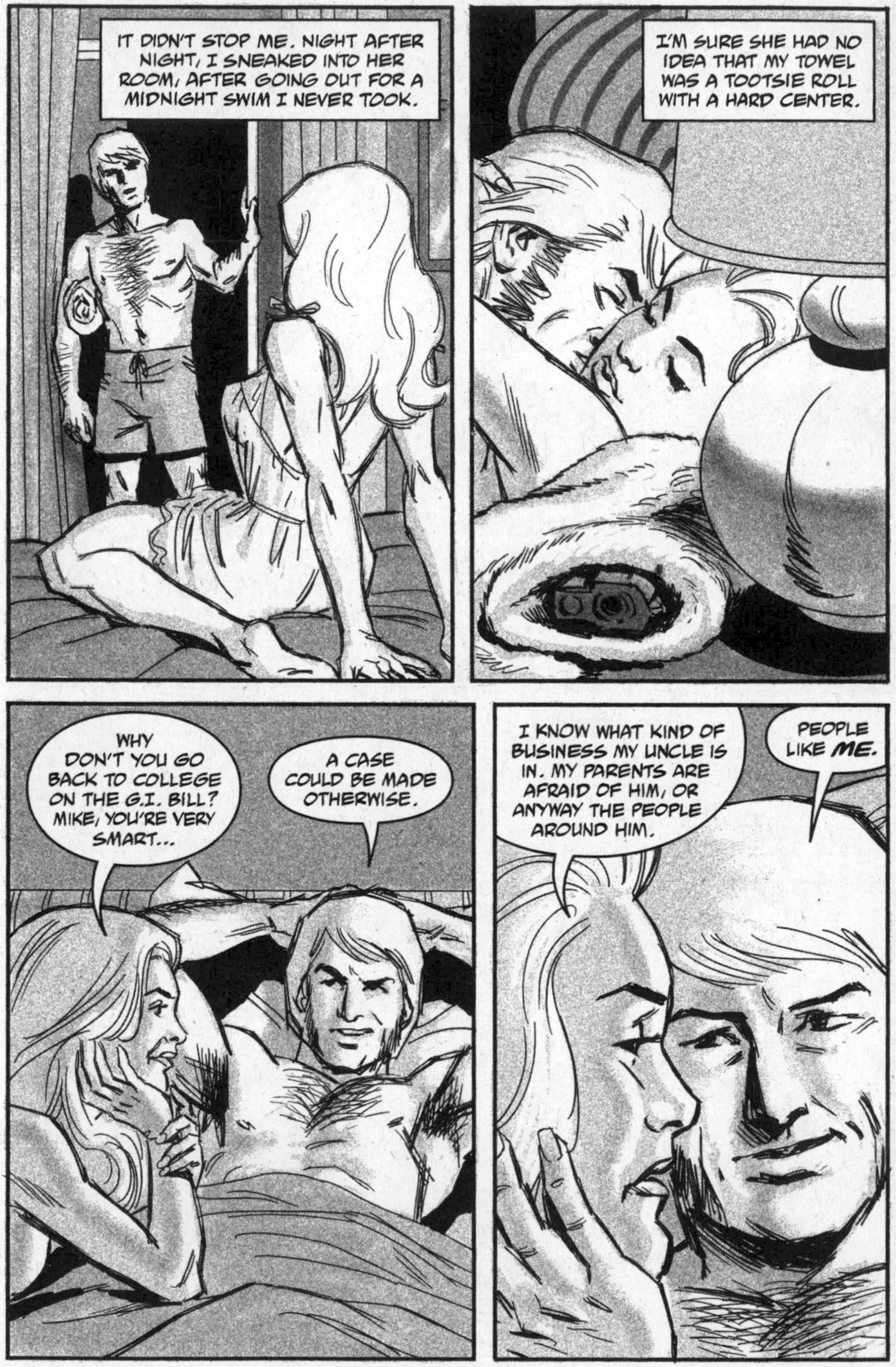
IT DIDN'T STOP ME. NIGHT AFTER NIGHT, I SNEAKED INTO HER ROOM, AFTER GOING OUT FOR A MIDNIGHT SWIM I NEVER TOOK.
I'M SURE SHE HAD NO IDEA THAT MY TOWEL WAS A TOOTSIE ROLL WITH A HARD CENTER.
WHY DON'T YOU GO BACK TO COLLEGE ON THE G.I. BILL? MIKE, YOU'RE VERY SMART...
A CASE COULD BE MADE OTHERWISE.
I KNOW WHAT KIND OF BUSINESS MY UNCLE IS IN. MY PARENTS ARE AFRAID OF HIM, OR ANYWAY THE PEOPLE AROUND HIM.
PEOPLE LIKE *ME*.

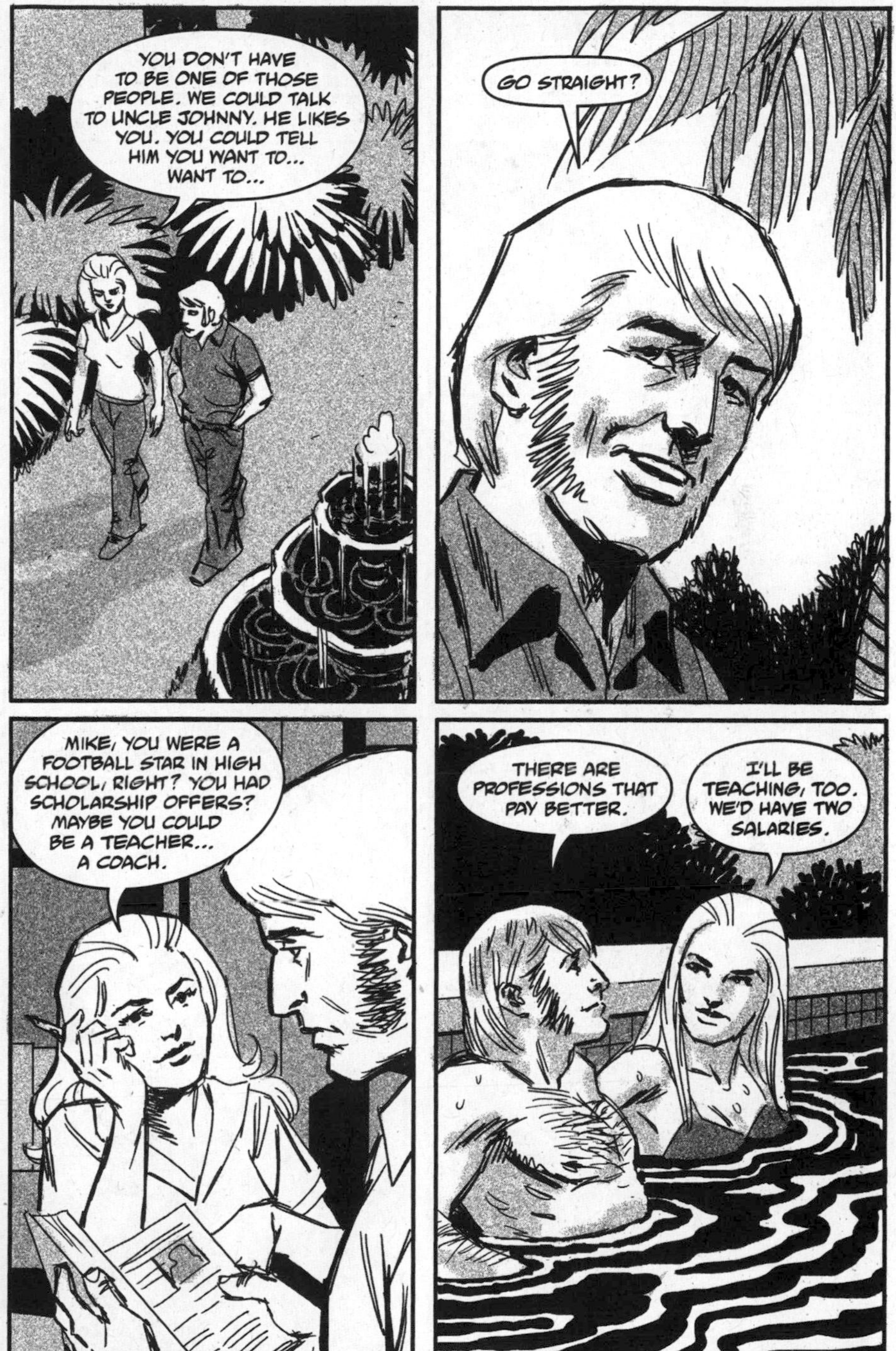
YOU DON'T HAVE TO BE ONE OF THOSE PEOPLE. WE COULD TALK TO UNCLE JOHNNY. HE LIKES YOU. YOU COULD TELL HIM YOU WANT TO... WANT TO...
GO STRAIGHT?
MIKE, YOU WERE A FOOTBALL STAR IN HIGH SCHOOL, RIGHT? YOU HAD SCHOLARSHIP OFFERS? MAYBE YOU COULD BE A TEACHER... A COACH.
THERE ARE PROFESSIONS THAT PAY BETTER.
I'LL BE TEACHING, TOO. WE'D HAVE TWO SALARIES.

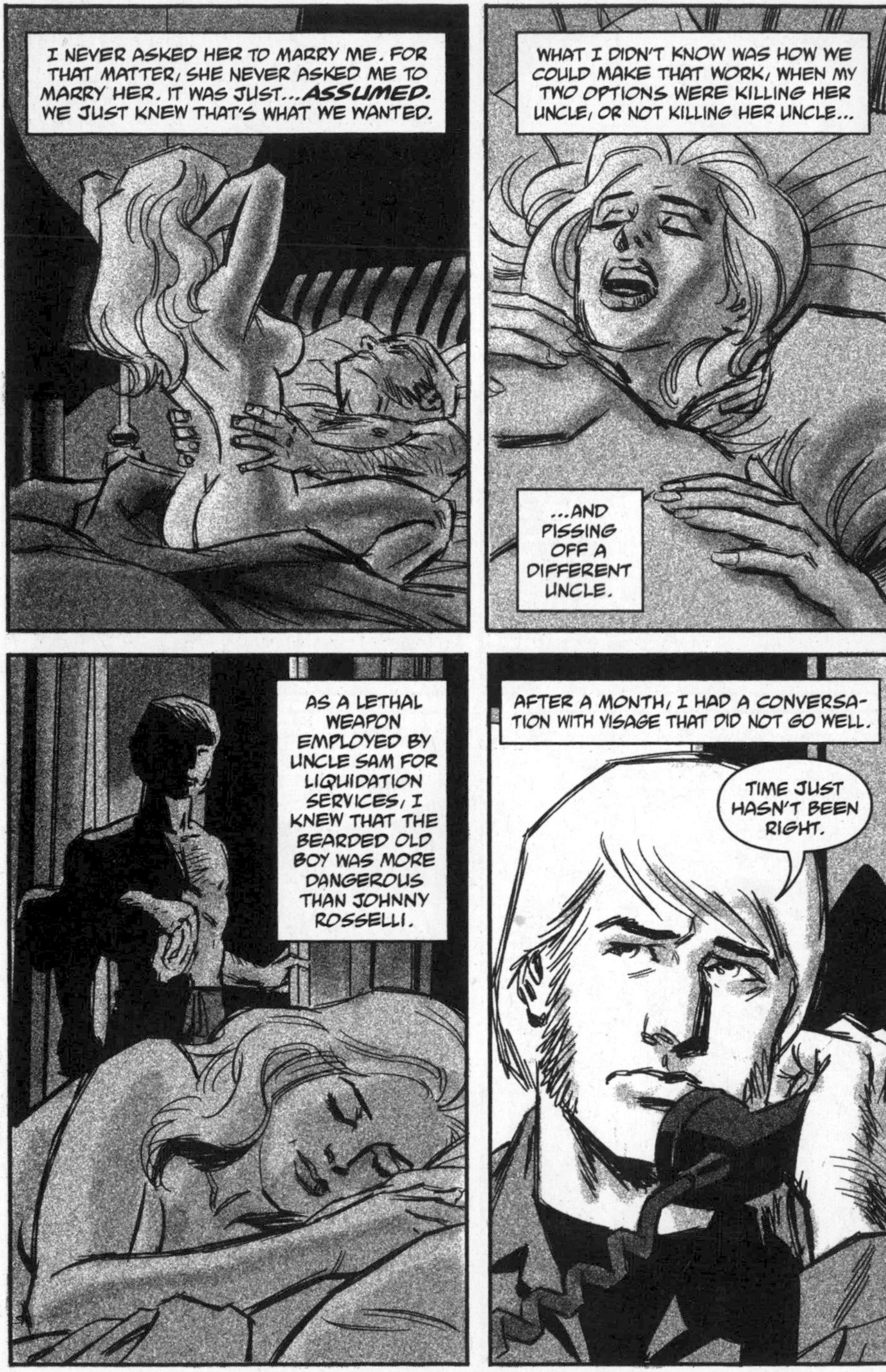
I NEVER ASKED HER TO MARRY ME. FOR THAT MATTER, SHE NEVER ASKED ME TO MARRY HER. IT WAS JUST... ASSUMED. WE JUST KNEW THAT'S WHAT WE WANTED.
WHAT I DIDN'T KNOW WAS HOW WE COULD MAKE THAT WORK, WHEN MY TWO OPTIONS WERE KILLING HER UNCLE, OR NOT KILLING HER UNCLE...
...AND PISSING OFF A DIFFERENT UNCLE.
AS A LETHAL WEAPON EMPLOYED BY UNCLE SAM FOR LIQUIDATION SERVICES, I KNEW THAT THE BEARDED OLD BOY WAS MORE DANGEROUS THAN JOHNNY ROSSELLI.
AFTER A MONTH, I HAD A CONVERSATION WITH VISAGE THAT DID NOT GO WELL.
TIME JUST HASN'T BEEN RIGHT.

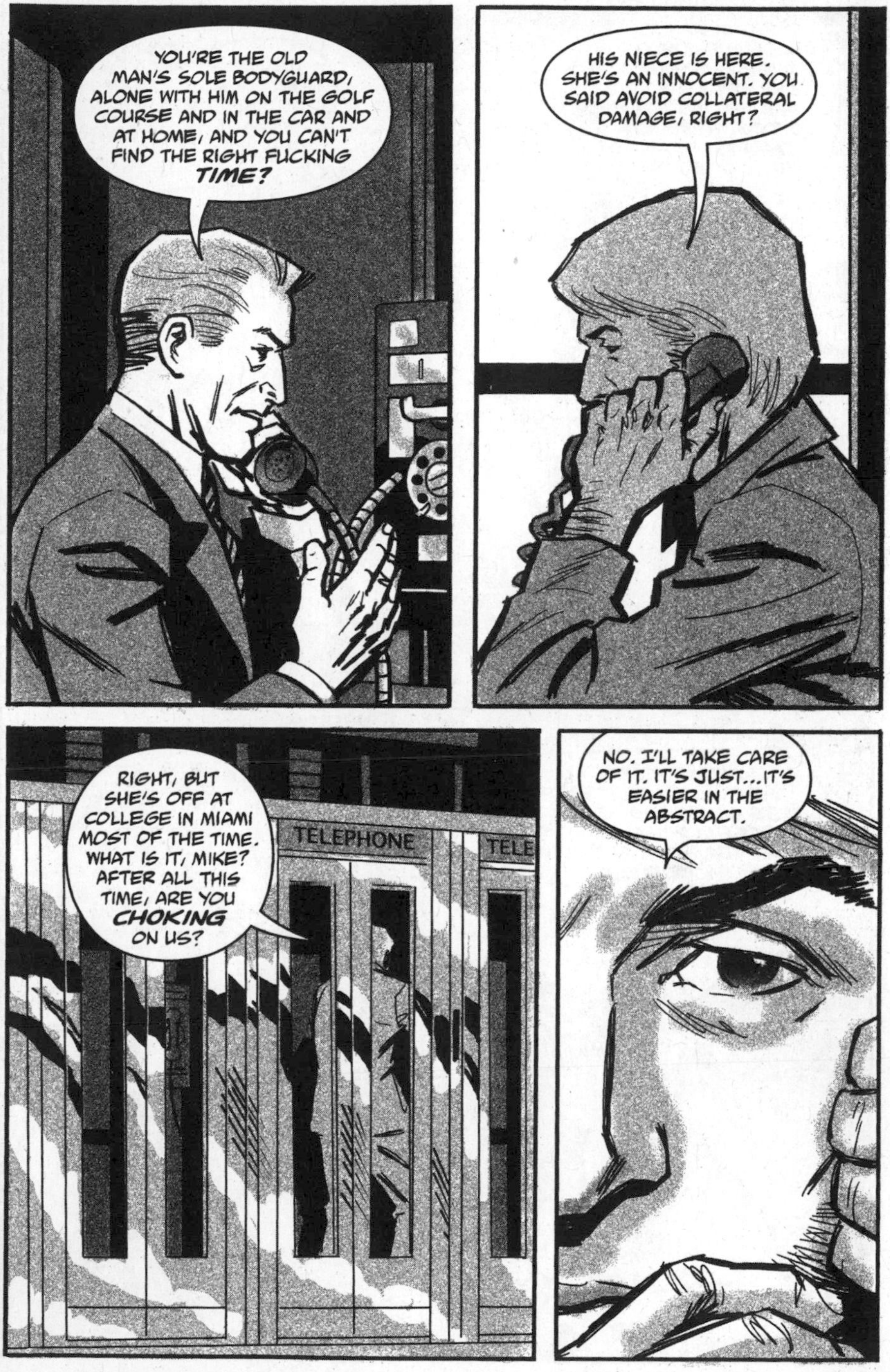
YOU'RE THE OLD MAN'S SOLE BODYGUARD, ALONE WITH HIM ON THE GOLF COURSE AND IN THE CAR AND AT HOME, AND YOU CAN'T FIND THE RIGHT FUCKING *TIME?*
HIS NIECE IS HERE. SHE'S AN INNOCENT. YOU SAID AVOID COLLATERAL DAMAGE, RIGHT?
RIGHT, BUT SHE'S OFF AT COLLEGE IN MIAMI MOST OF THE TIME. WHAT IS IT, MIKE? AFTER ALL THIS TIME, ARE YOU *CHOKING* ON US?
TELEPHONE
TELE
NO. I'LL TAKE CARE OF IT. IT'S JUST...IT'S EASIER IN THE ABSTRACT.

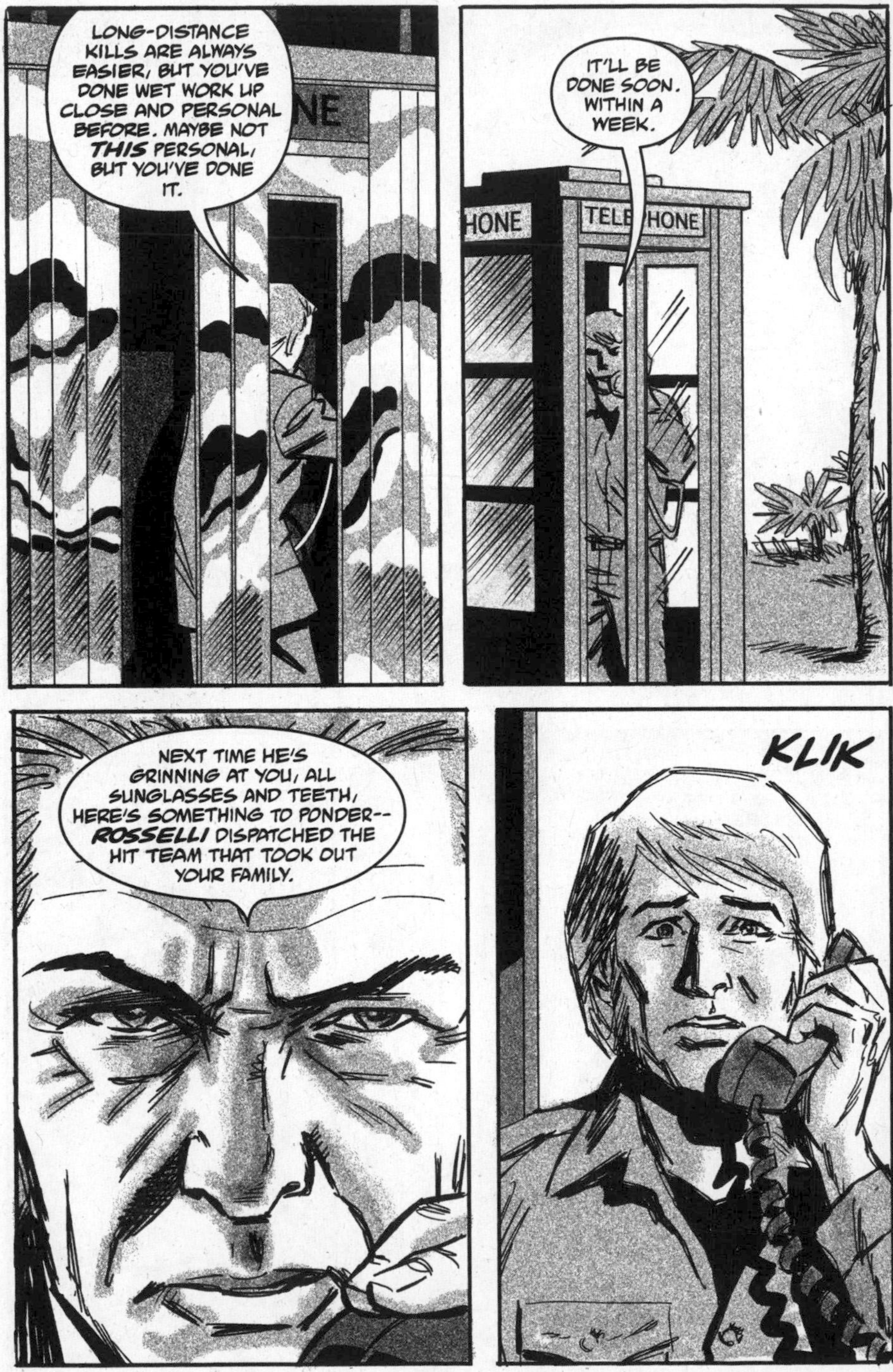
LONG-DISTANCE KILLS ARE ALWAYS EASIER, BUT YOU'VE DONE WET WORK UP CLOSE AND PERSONAL BEFORE. MAYBE NOT THIS PERSONAL, BUT YOU'VE DONE IT.
NE
HONE
TELEPHONE
IT'LL BE DONE SOON. WITHIN A WEEK.
NEXT TIME HE'S GRINNING AT YOU, ALL SUNGLASSES AND TEETH, HERE'S SOMETHING TO PONDER-- ROSSELLI DISPATCHED THE HIT TEAM THAT TOOK OUT YOUR FAMILY.
KLIK

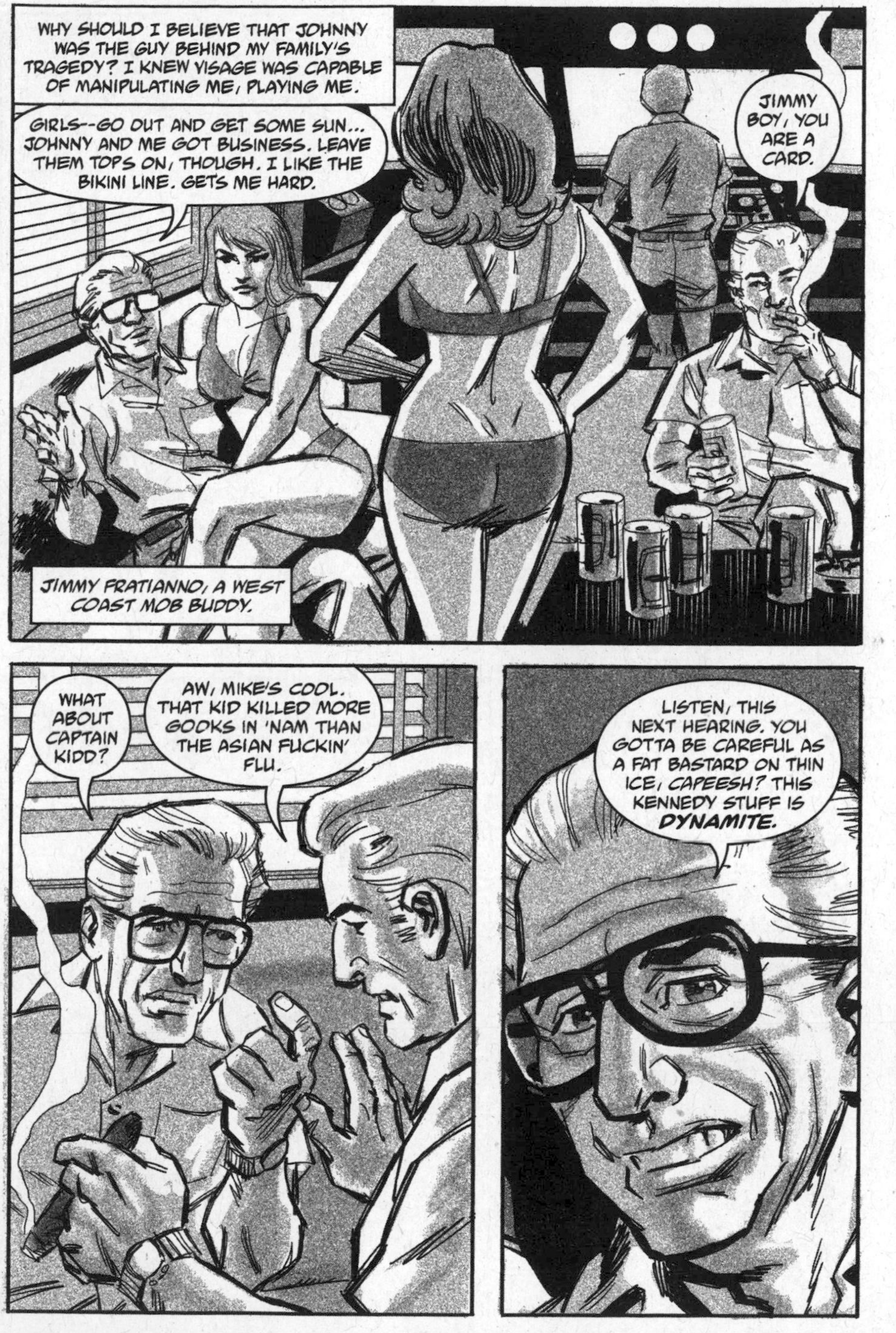
WHY SHOULD I BELIEVE THAT JOHNNY WAS THE GUY BEHIND MY FAMILY'S TRAGEDY? I KNEW VISAGE WAS CAPABLE OF MANIPULATING ME, PLAYING ME.
GIRLS--GO OUT AND GET SOME SUN... JOHNNY AND ME GOT BUSINESS. LEAVE THEM TOPS ON, THOUGH. I LIKE THE BIKINI LINE. GETS ME HARD.
JIMMY BOY, YOU ARE A CARD.
JIMMY FRATIANNO, A WEST COAST MOB BUDDY.
WHAT ABOUT CAPTAIN KIDD?
AW, MIKE'S COOL. THAT KID KILLED MORE GOOKS IN 'NAM THAN THE ASIAN FUCKIN' FLU.
LISTEN, THIS NEXT HEARING. YOU GOTTA BE CAREFUL AS A FAT BASTARD ON THIN ICE, CAPEESH? THIS KENNEDY STUFF IS **DYNAMITE.**

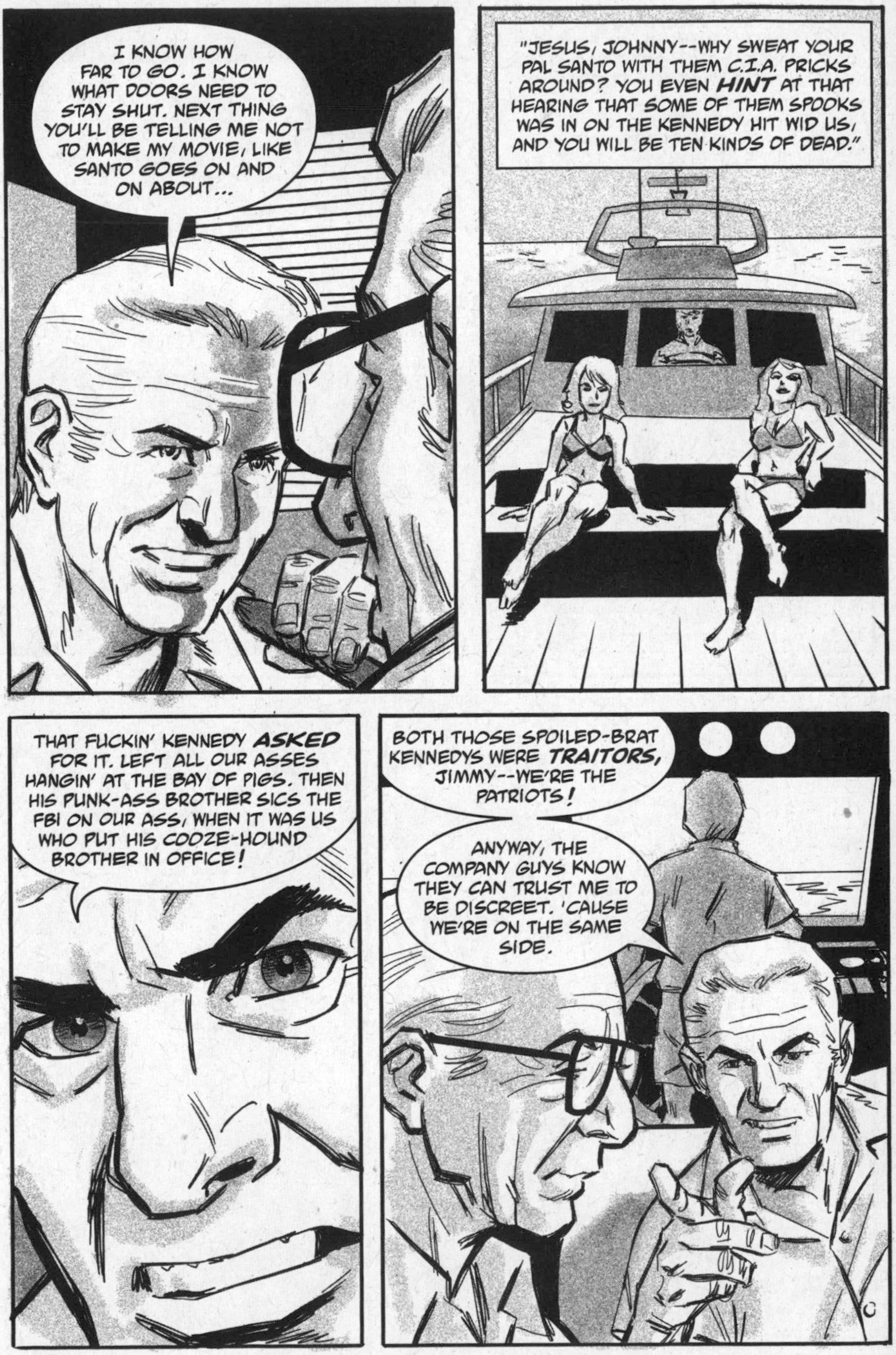
I KNOW HOW FAR TO GO. I KNOW WHAT DOORS NEED TO STAY SHUT. NEXT THING YOU'LL BE TELLING ME NOT TO MAKE MY MOVIE, LIKE SANTO GOES ON AND ON ABOUT...
"JESUS, JOHNNY--WHY SWEAT YOUR PAL SANTO WITH THEM C.I.A. PRICKS AROUND? YOU EVEN HINT AT THAT HEARING THAT SOME OF THEM SPOOKS WAS IN ON THE KENNEDY HIT WID US, AND YOU WILL BE TEN KINDS OF DEAD."
THAT FUCKIN' KENNEDY ASKED FOR IT. LEFT ALL OUR ASSES HANGIN' AT THE BAY OF PIGS. THEN HIS PUNK-ASS BROTHER SICS THE FBI ON OUR ASS, WHEN IT WAS US WHO PUT HIS COOZE-HOUND BROTHER IN OFFICE!
BOTH THOSE SPOILED-BRAT KENNEDYS WERE TRAITORS, JIMMY--WE'RE THE PATRIOTS!
ANYWAY, THE COMPANY GUYS KNOW THEY CAN TRUST ME TO BE DISCREET. 'CAUSE WE'RE ON THE SAME SIDE.

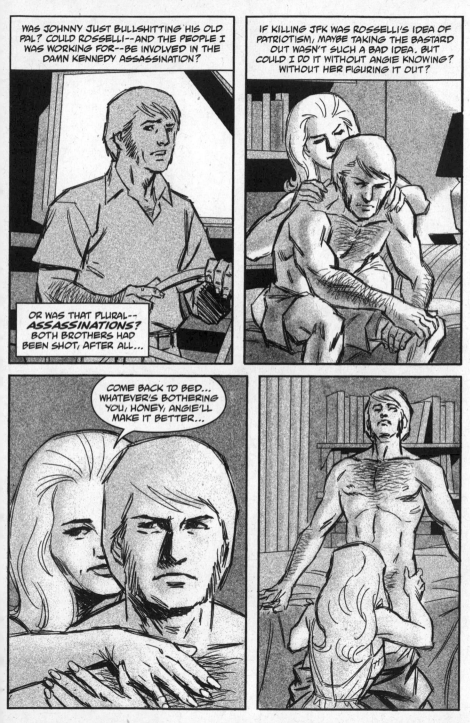

WAS JOHNNY JUST BULLSHITTING HIS OLD PAL? COULD ROSSELLI--AND THE PEOPLE I WAS WORKING FOR--BE INVOLVED IN THE DAMN KENNEDY ASSASSINATION?

IF KILLING JFK WAS ROSSELLI'S IDEA OF PATRIOTISM, MAYBE TAKING THE BASTARD OUT WASN'T SUCH A BAD IDEA. BUT COULD I DO IT WITHOUT ANGIE KNOWING? WITHOUT HER FIGURING IT OUT?

OR WAS THAT PLURAL-- **ASSASSINATIONS?** BOTH BROTHERS HAD BEEN SHOT, AFTER ALL...

COME BACK TO BED... WHATEVER'S BOTHERING YOU, HONEY, ANGIE'LL MAKE IT BETTER...

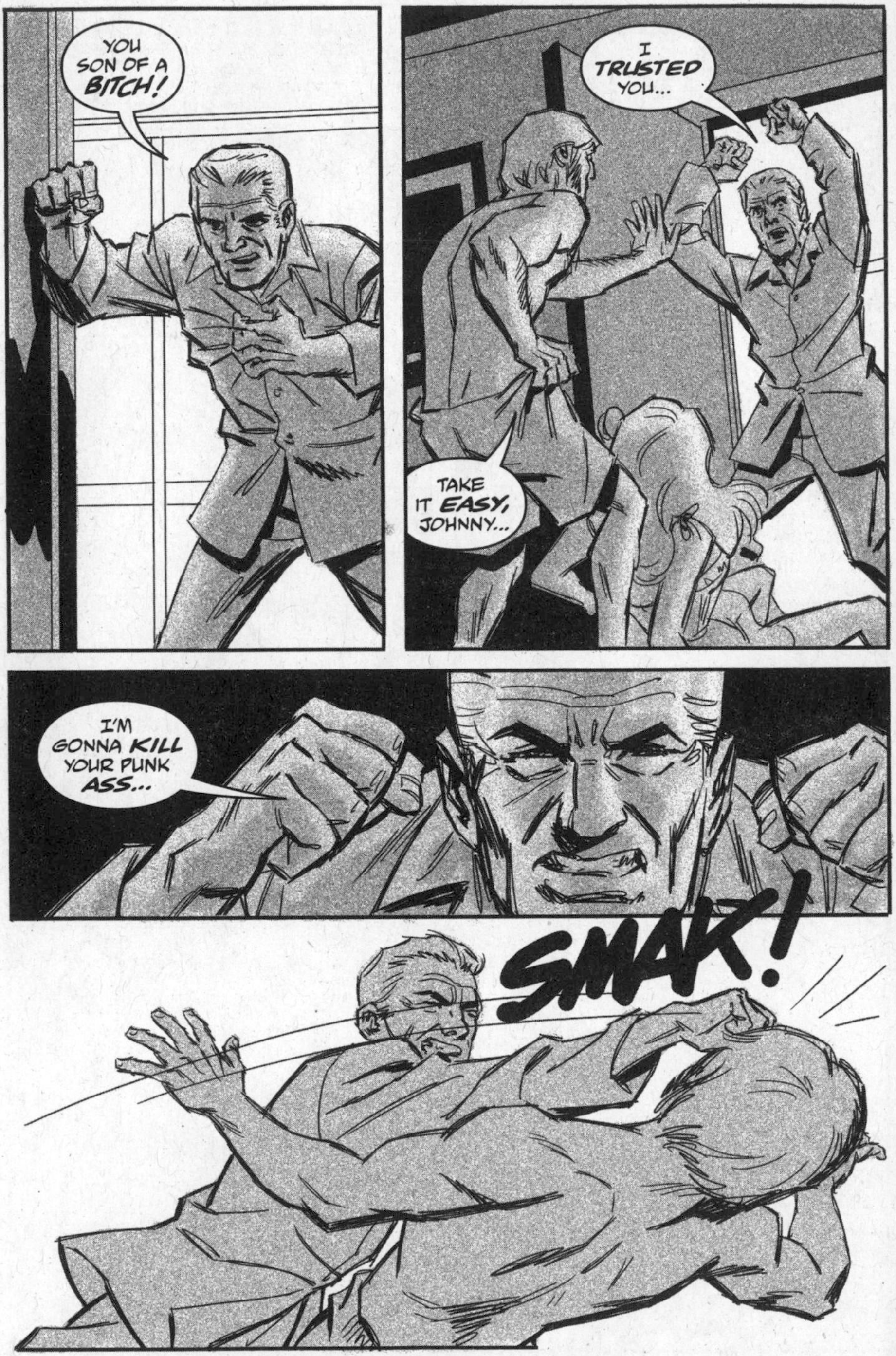
YOU SON OF A BITCH!
I TRUSTED YOU...
TAKE IT EASY, JOHNNY...
I'M GONNA KILL YOUR PUNK ASS...
SMAK!

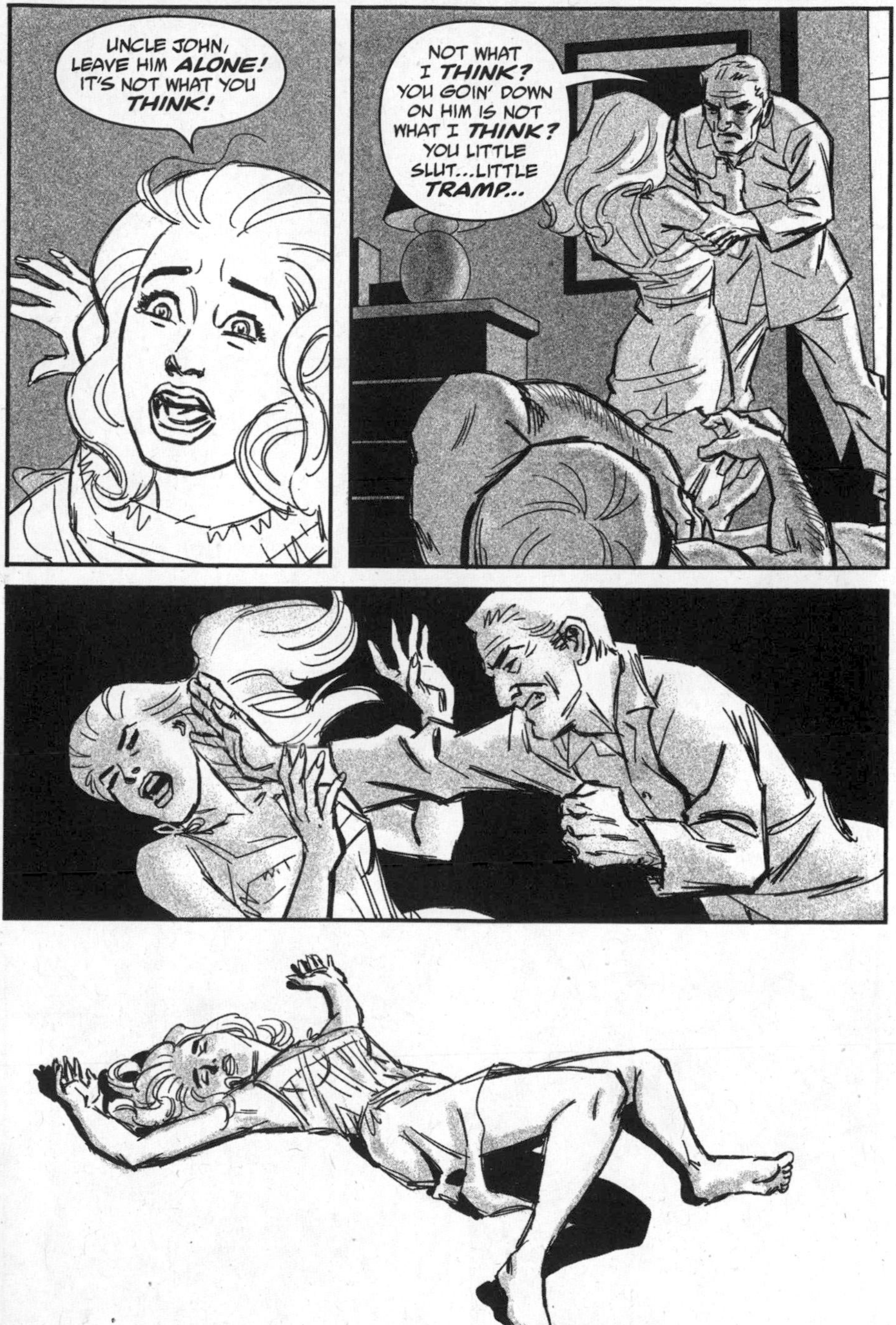
UNCLE JOHN, LEAVE HIM ALONE! IT'S NOT WHAT YOU THINK!
NOT WHAT I THINK? YOU GOIN' DOWN ON HIM IS NOT WHAT I THINK? YOU LITTLE SLUT...LITTLE TRAMP...

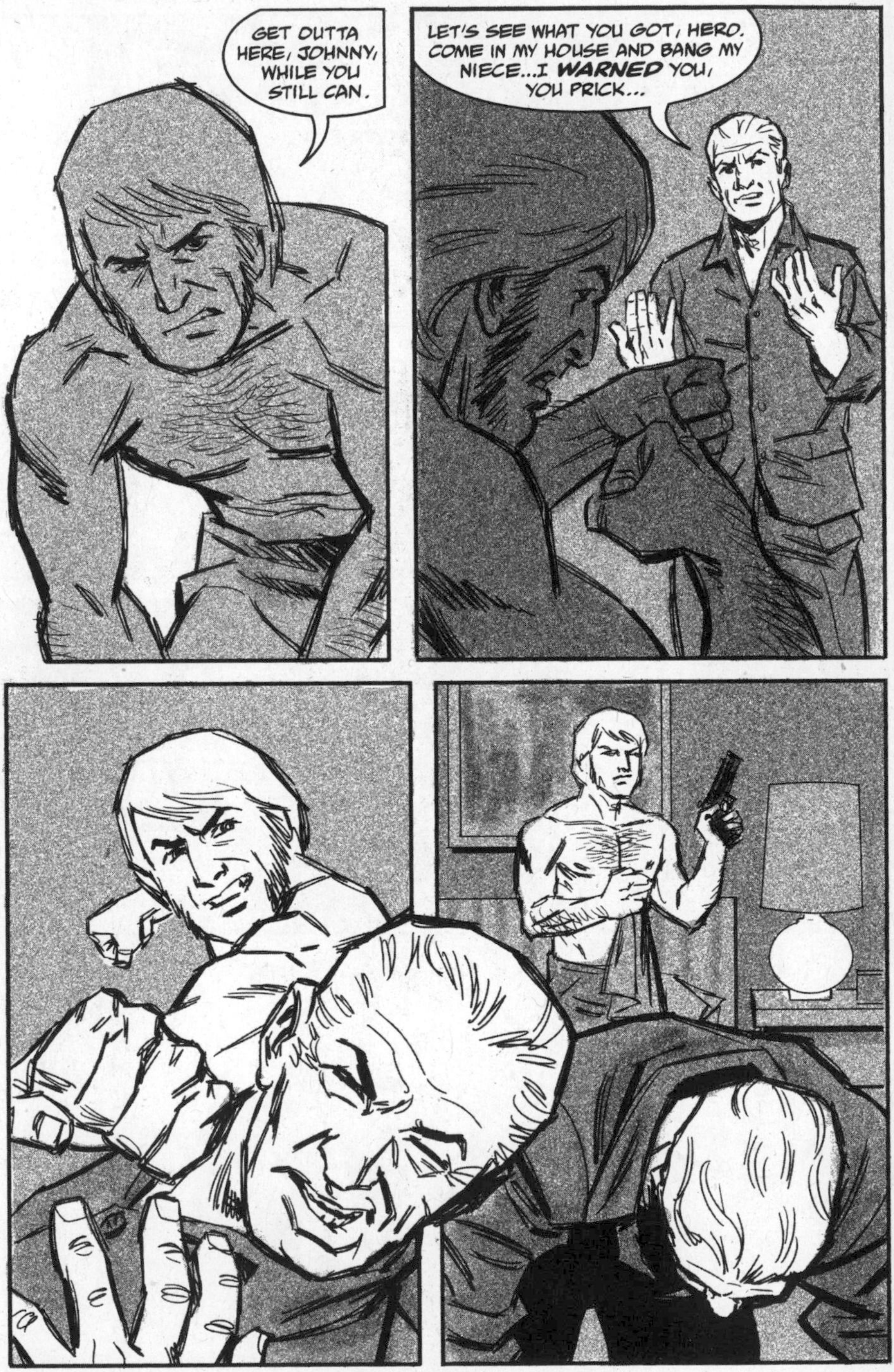
GET OUTTA HERE, JOHNNY, WHILE YOU STILL CAN.
LET'S SEE WHAT YOU GOT, HERO. COME IN MY HOUSE AND BANG MY NIECE...I **WARNED** YOU, YOU PRICK...

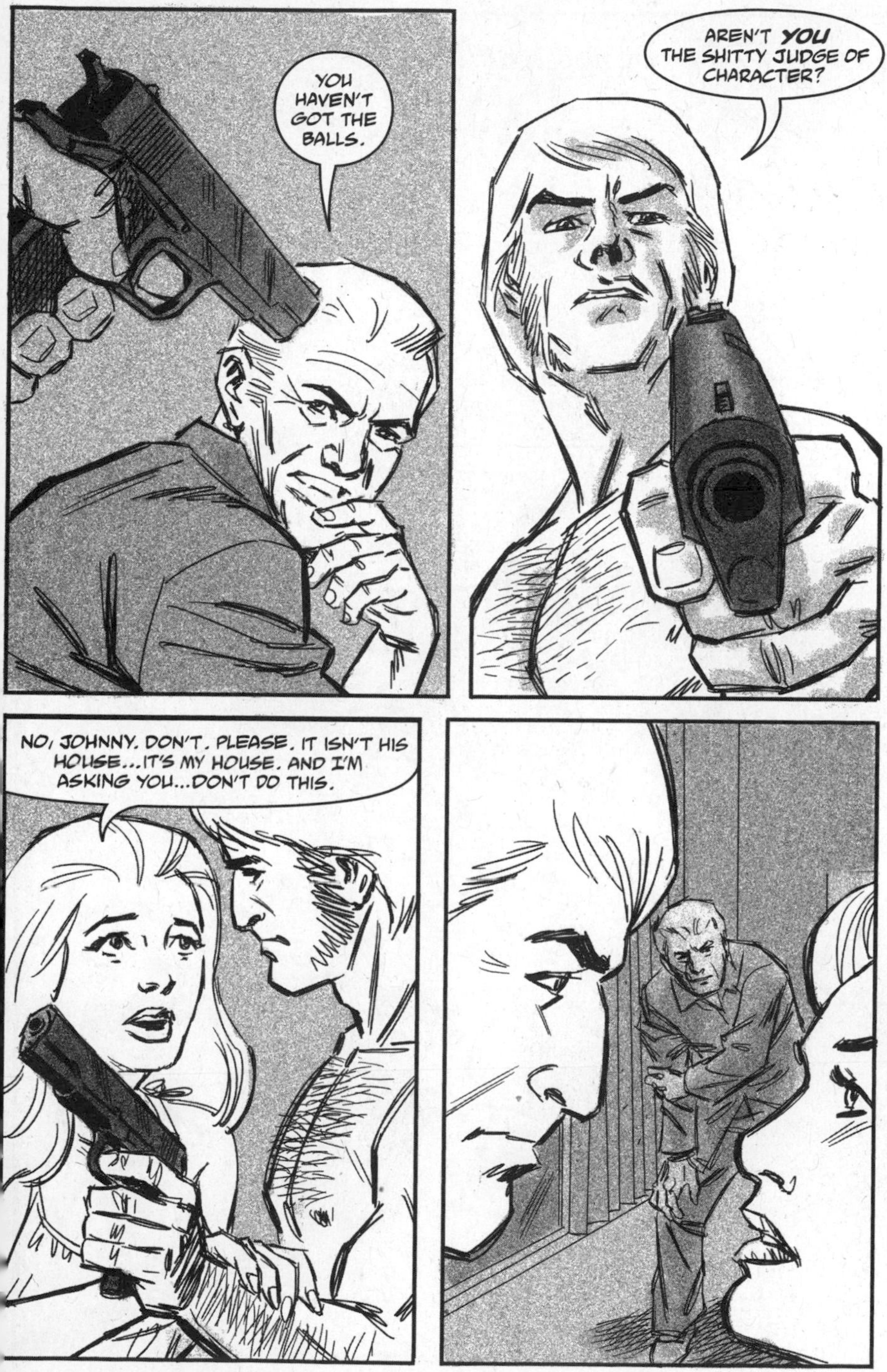
YOU HAVEN'T GOT THE BALLS.
AREN'T YOU THE SHITTY JUDGE OF CHARACTER?
NO, JOHNNY. DON'T. PLEASE. IT ISN'T HIS HOUSE...IT'S MY HOUSE. AND I'M ASKING YOU...DON'T DO THIS.

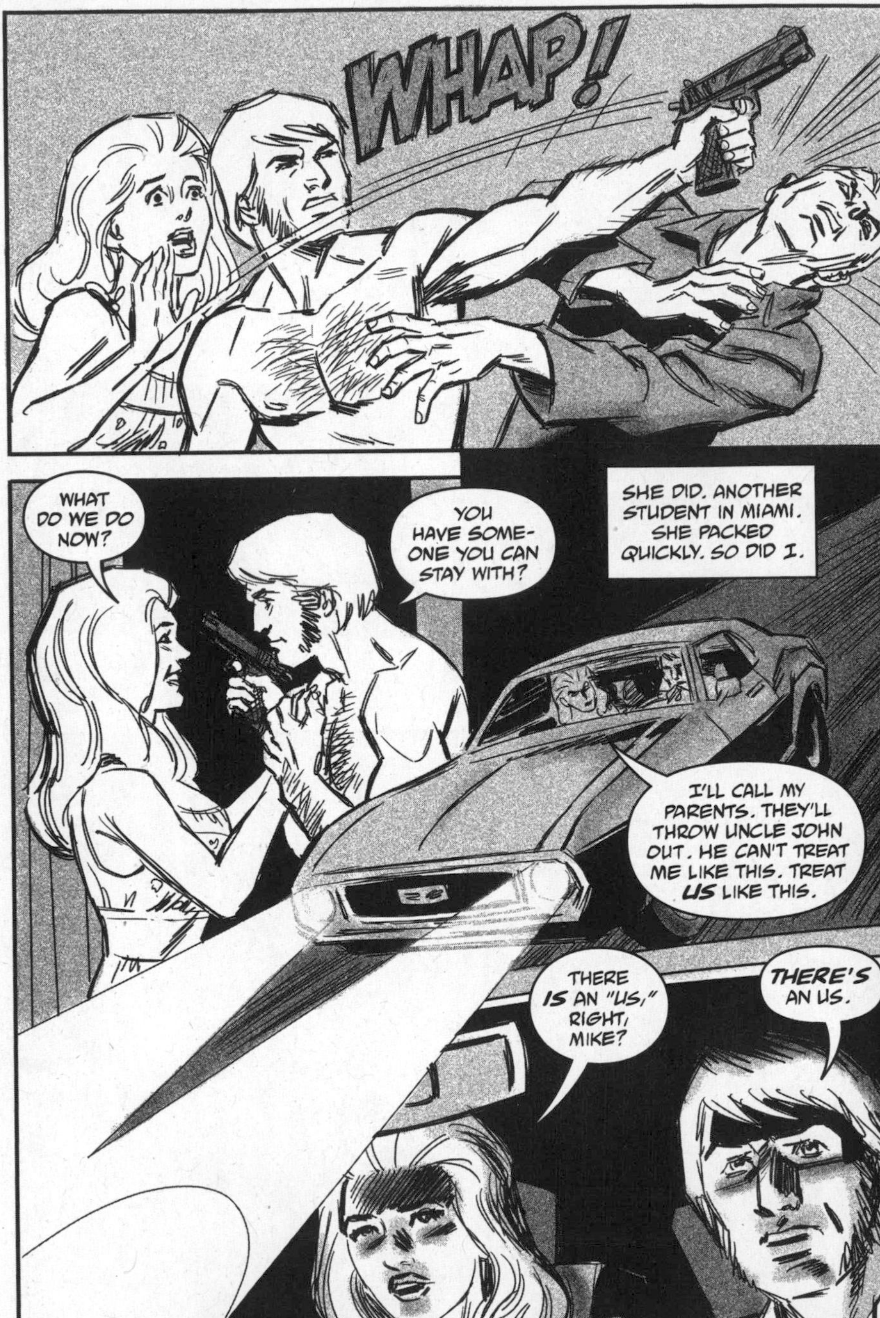
WHAP!
WHAT DO WE DO NOW?
YOU HAVE SOME-ONE YOU CAN STAY WITH?
SHE DID. ANOTHER STUDENT IN MIAMI. SHE PACKED QUICKLY. SO DID I.
I'LL CALL MY PARENTS. THEY'LL THROW UNCLE JOHN OUT. HE CAN'T TREAT ME LIKE THIS. TREAT **US** LIKE THIS.
THERE **IS** AN "US," RIGHT, MIKE?
THERE'S AN US.

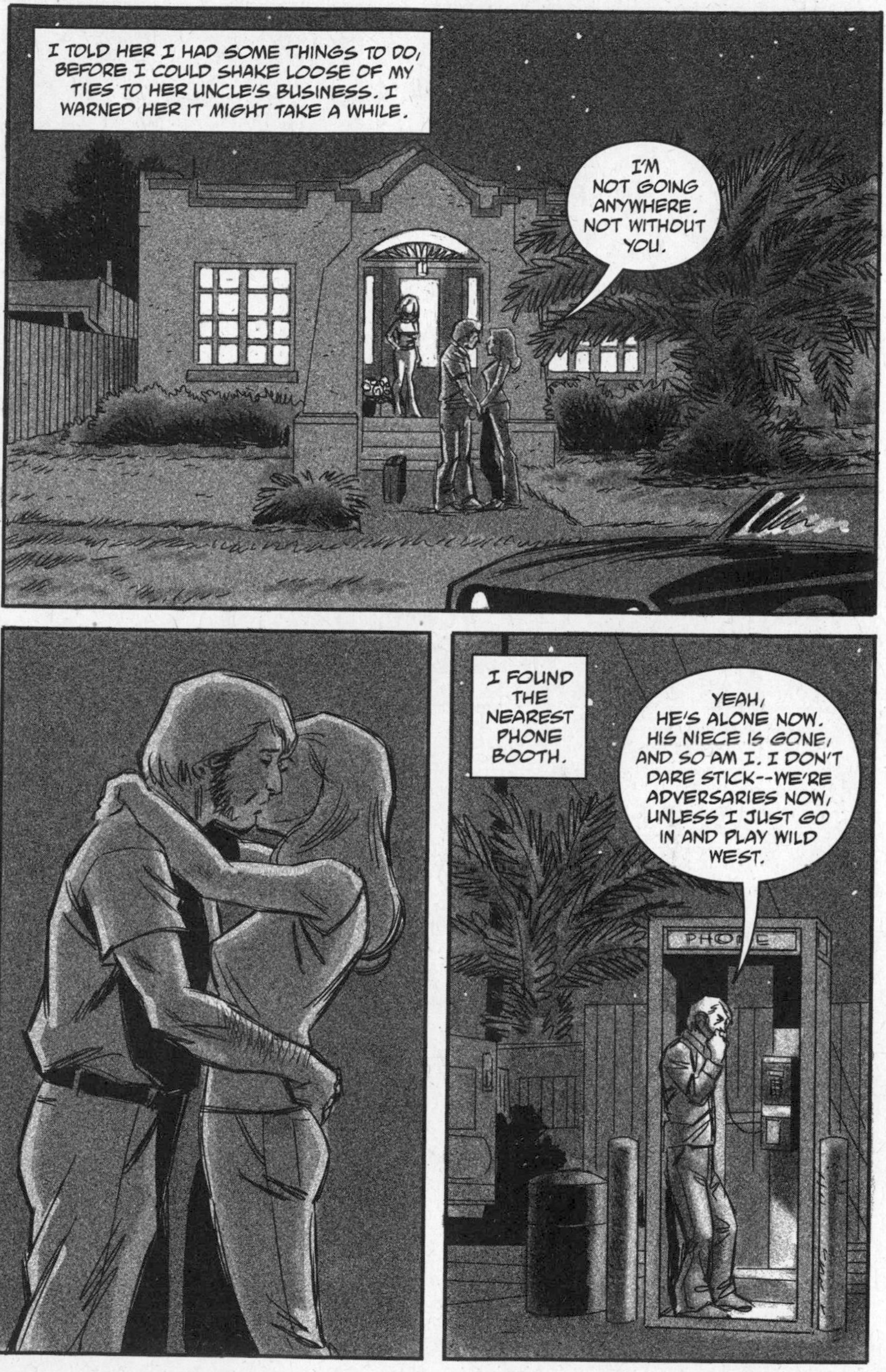
I TOLD HER I HAD SOME THINGS TO DO, BEFORE I COULD SHAKE LOOSE OF MY TIES TO HER UNCLE'S BUSINESS. I WARNED HER IT MIGHT TAKE A WHILE.
I'M NOT GOING ANYWHERE. NOT WITHOUT YOU.
I FOUND THE NEAREST PHONE BOOTH.
YEAH, HE'S ALONE NOW. HIS NIECE IS GONE, AND SO AM I. I DON'T DARE STICK--WE'RE ADVERSARIES NOW, UNLESS I JUST GO IN AND PLAY WILD WEST.

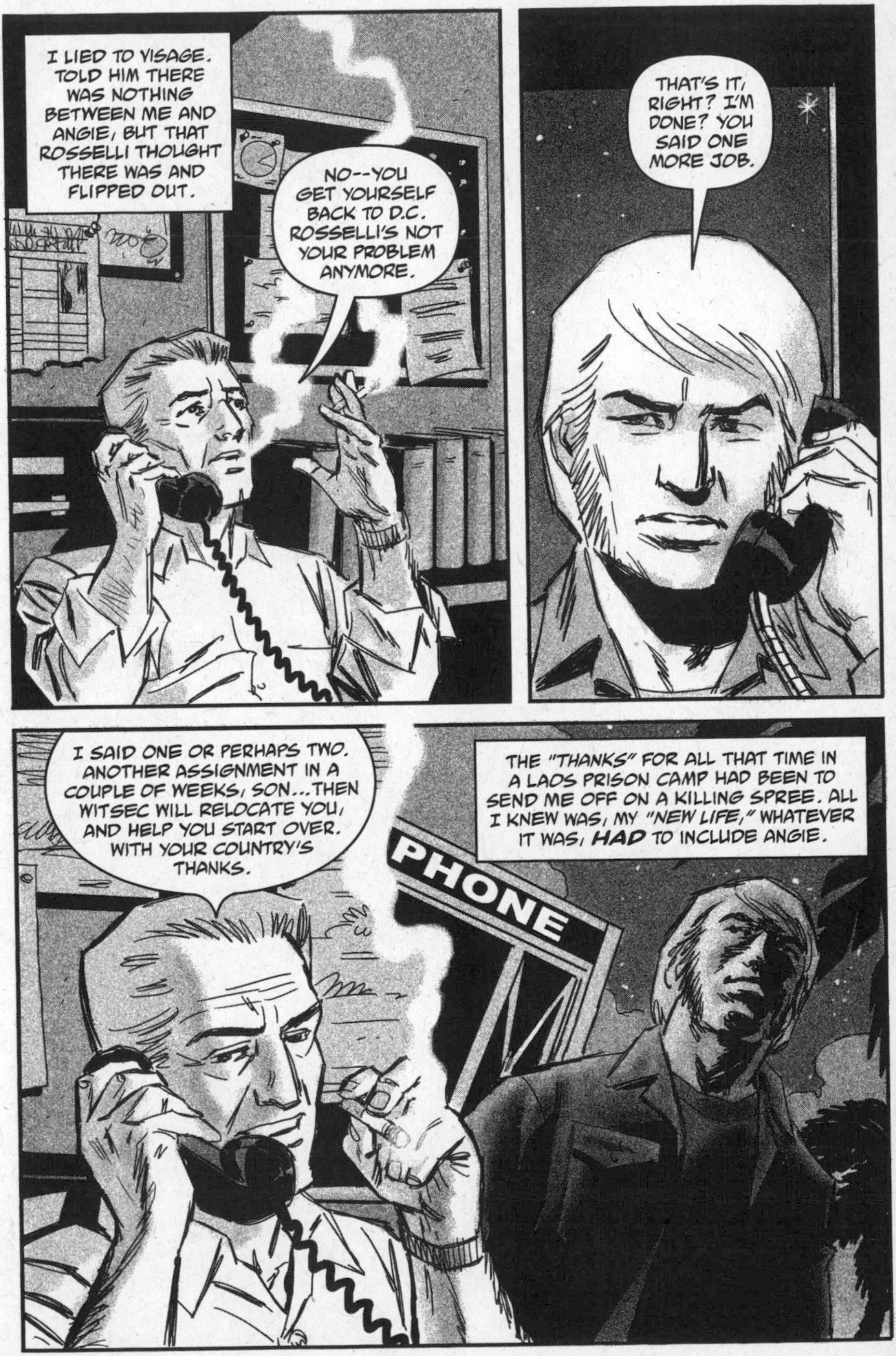
I LIED TO VISAGE. TOLD HIM THERE WAS NOTHING BETWEEN ME AND ANGIE, BUT THAT ROSSELLI THOUGHT THERE WAS AND FLIPPED OUT.
NO--YOU GET YOURSELF BACK TO D.C. ROSSELLI'S NOT YOUR PROBLEM ANYMORE.
THAT'S IT, RIGHT? I'M DONE? YOU SAID ONE MORE JOB.
I SAID ONE OR PERHAPS TWO. ANOTHER ASSIGNMENT IN A COUPLE OF WEEKS, SON...THEN WITSEC WILL RELOCATE YOU, AND HELP YOU START OVER. WITH YOUR COUNTRY'S THANKS.
PHONE
THE "THANKS" FOR ALL THAT TIME IN A LAOS PRISON CAMP HAD BEEN TO SEND ME OFF ON A KILLING SPREE. ALL I KNEW WAS, MY "NEW LIFE," WHATEVER IT WAS, HAD TO INCLUDE ANGIE.

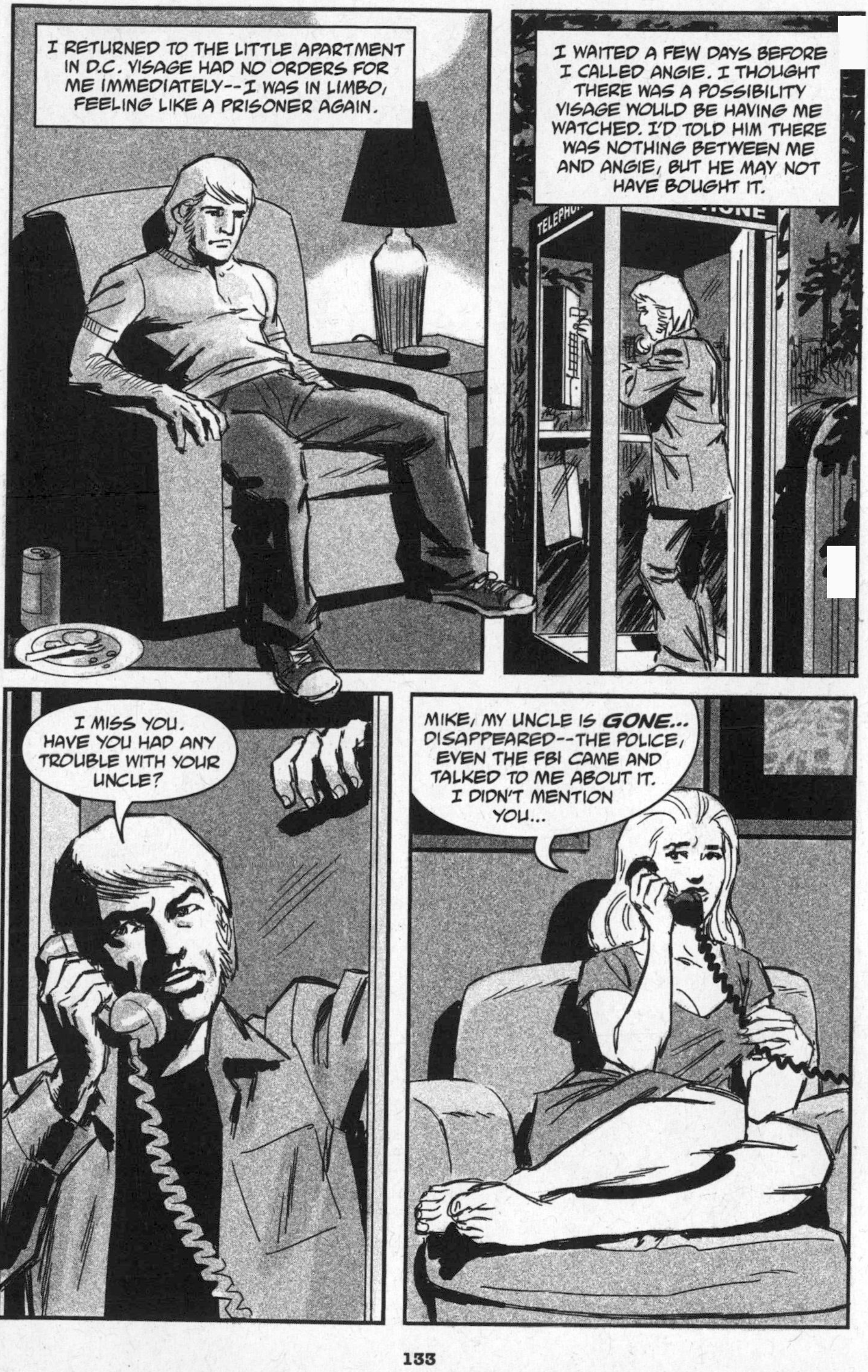
I RETURNED TO THE LITTLE APARTMENT IN D.C. VISAGE HAD NO ORDERS FOR ME IMMEDIATELY--I WAS IN LIMBO, FEELING LIKE A PRISONER AGAIN.
I WAITED A FEW DAYS BEFORE I CALLED ANGIE. I THOUGHT THERE WAS A POSSIBILITY VISAGE WOULD BE HAVING ME WATCHED. I'D TOLD HIM THERE WAS NOTHING BETWEEN ME AND ANGIE, BUT HE MAY NOT HAVE BOUGHT IT.
I MISS YOU. HAVE YOU HAD ANY TROUBLE WITH YOUR UNCLE?
MIKE, MY UNCLE IS **GONE...** DISAPPEARED--THE POLICE, EVEN THE FBI CAME AND TALKED TO ME ABOUT IT. I DIDN'T MENTION YOU...

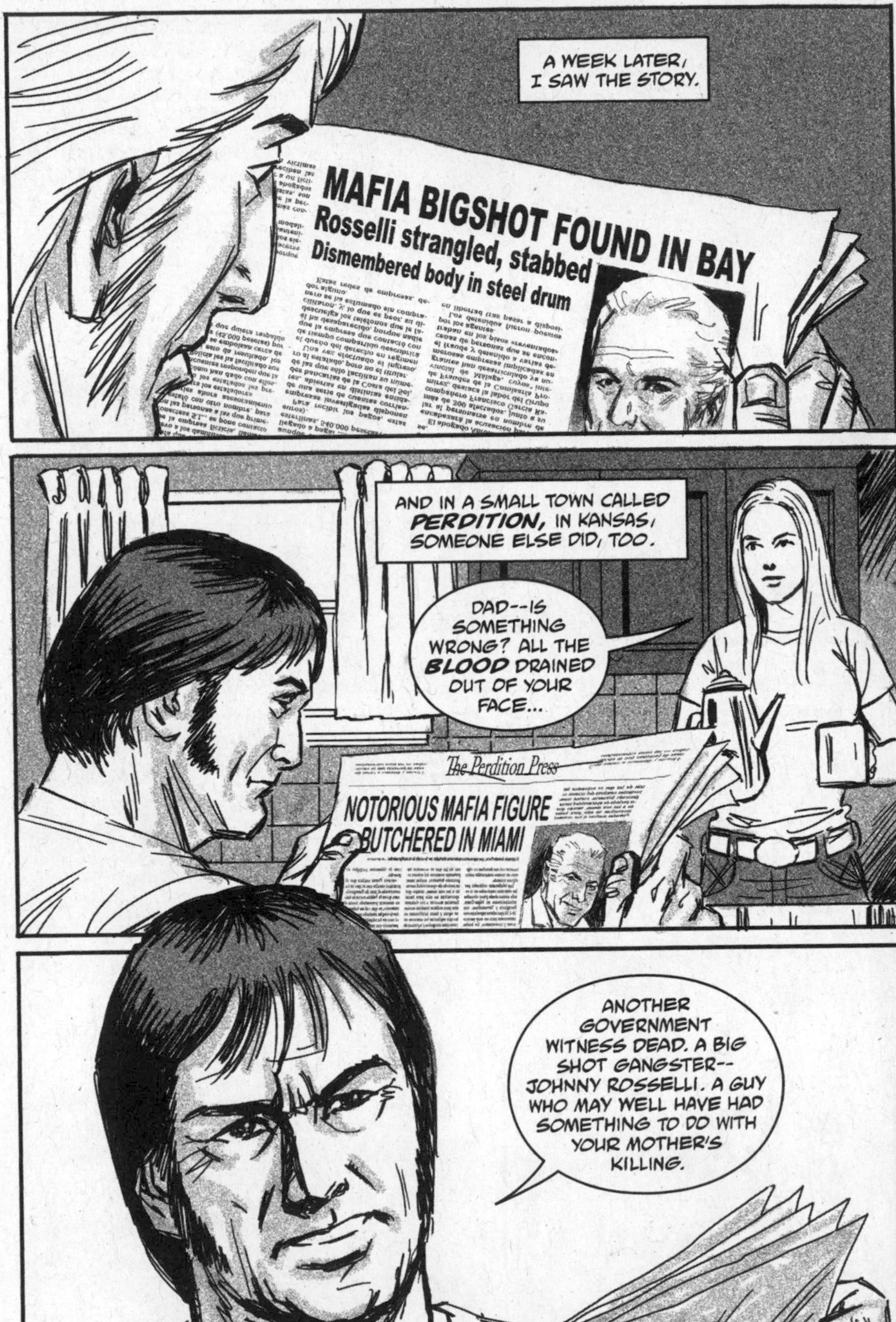
A WEEK LATER, I SAW THE STORY.
MAFIA BIGSHOT FOUND IN BAY
Rosselli strangled, stabbed
Dismembered body in steel drum
AND IN A SMALL TOWN CALLED PERDITION, IN KANSAS, SOMEONE ELSE DID, TOO.
DAD--IS SOMETHING WRONG? ALL THE BLOOD DRAINED OUT OF YOUR FACE...
The Perdition Press
NOTORIOUS MAFIA FIGURE BUTCHERED IN MIAMI
ANOTHER GOVERNMENT WITNESS DEAD. A BIG SHOT GANGSTER--JOHNNY ROSSELLI. A GUY WHO MAY WELL HAVE HAD SOMETHING TO DO WITH YOUR MOTHER'S KILLING.

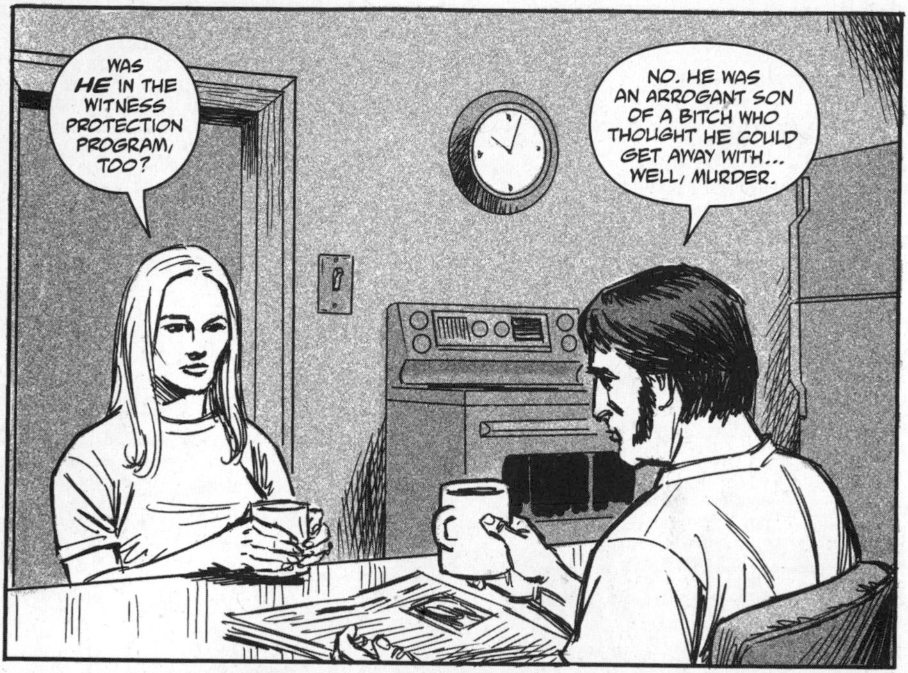
WAS HE IN THE WITNESS PROTECTION PROGRAM, TOO?
NO. HE WAS AN ARROGANT SON OF A BITCH WHO THOUGHT HE COULD GET AWAY WITH... WELL, MURDER.

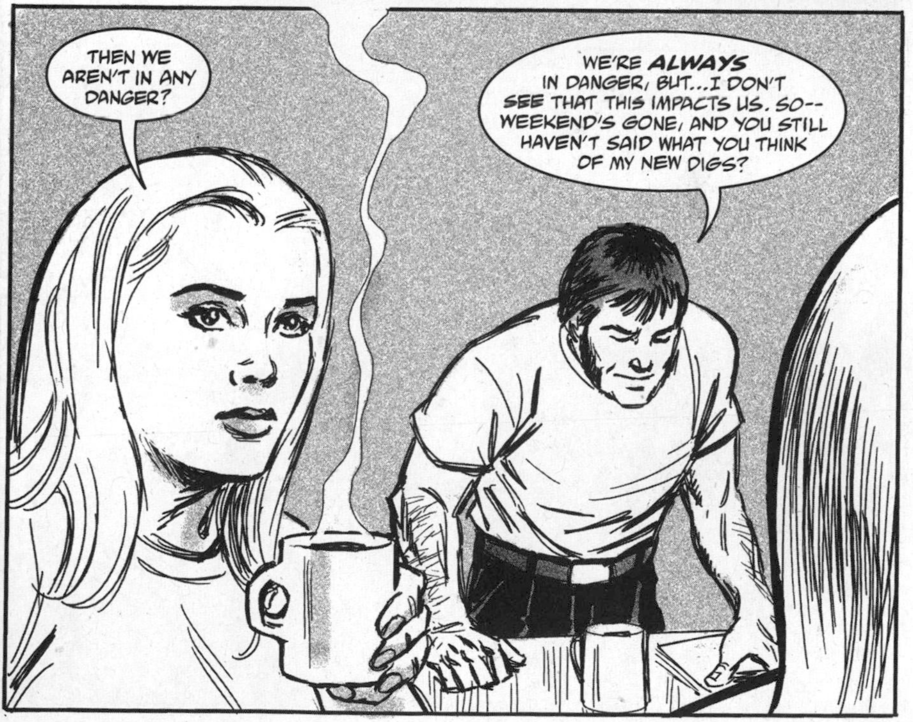
THEN WE AREN'T IN ANY DANGER?
WE'RE ALWAYS IN DANGER, BUT...I DON'T SEE THAT THIS IMPACTS US. SO--WEEKEND'S GONE, AND YOU STILL HAVEN'T SAID WHAT YOU THINK OF MY NEW DIGS?

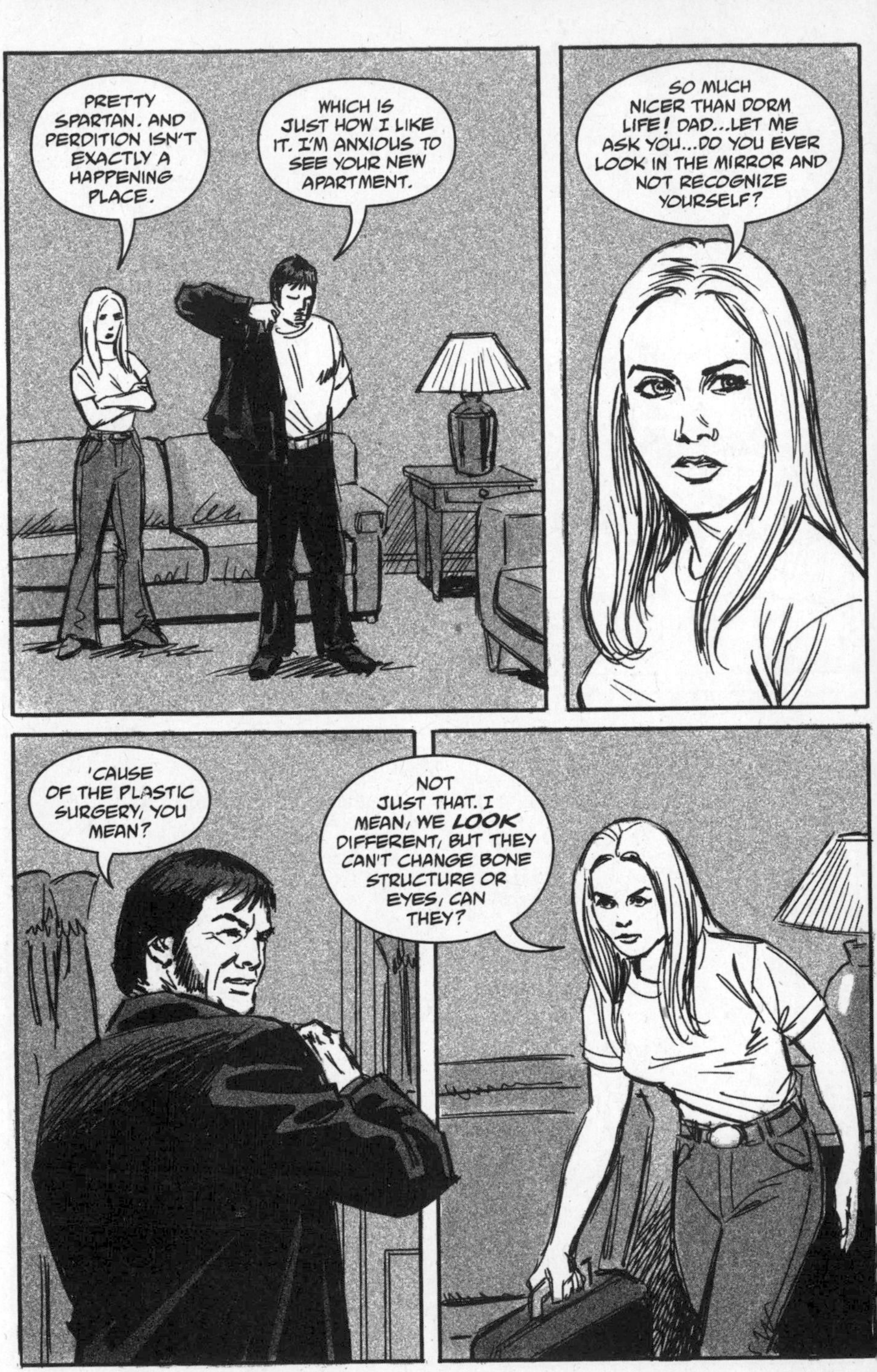
PRETTY SPARTAN. AND PERDITION ISN'T EXACTLY A HAPPENING PLACE.
WHICH IS JUST HOW I LIKE IT. I'M ANXIOUS TO SEE YOUR NEW APARTMENT.
SO MUCH NICER THAN DORM LIFE! DAD...LET ME ASK YOU...DO YOU EVER LOOK IN THE MIRROR AND NOT RECOGNIZE YOURSELF?
'CAUSE OF THE PLASTIC SURGERY, YOU MEAN?
NOT JUST THAT. I MEAN, WE LOOK DIFFERENT, BUT THEY CAN'T CHANGE BONE STRUCTURE OR EYES, CAN THEY?

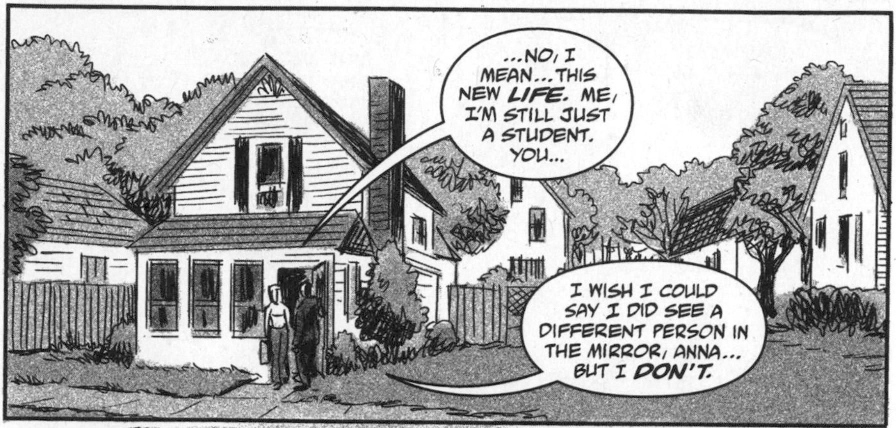
...NO, I MEAN...THIS NEW LIFE. ME, I'M STILL JUST A STUDENT. YOU...
I WISH I COULD SAY I DID SEE A DIFFERENT PERSON IN THE MIRROR, ANNA... BUT I DON'T.

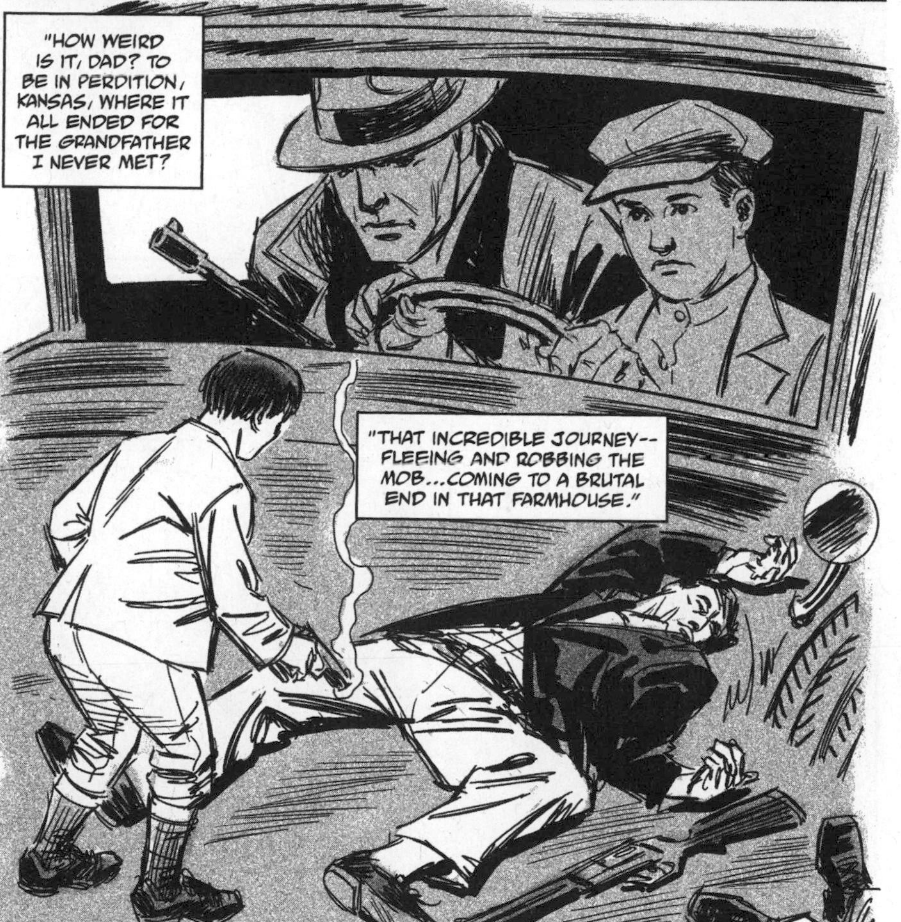
"HOW WEIRD IS IT, DAD? TO BE IN PERDITION, KANSAS, WHERE IT ALL ENDED FOR THE GRANDFATHER I NEVER MET?
"THAT INCREDIBLE JOURNEY-- FLEEING AND ROBBING THE MOB...COMING TO A BRUTAL END IN THAT FARMHOUSE."

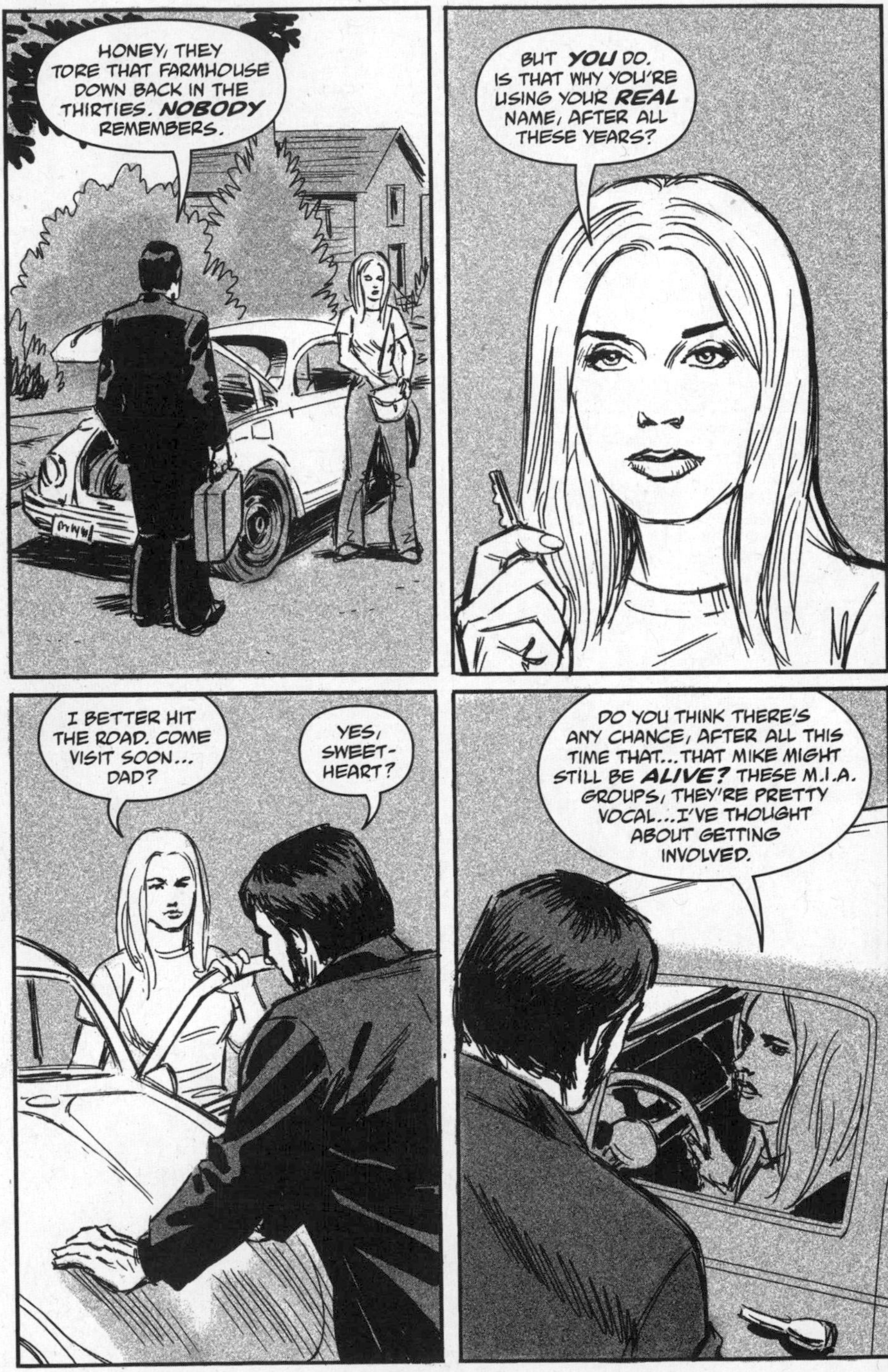
HONEY, THEY TORE THAT FARMHOUSE DOWN BACK IN THE THIRTIES. NOBODY REMEMBERS.
BUT YOU DO. IS THAT WHY YOU'RE USING YOUR REAL NAME, AFTER ALL THESE YEARS?
I BETTER HIT THE ROAD. COME VISIT SOON... DAD?
YES, SWEET-HEART?
DO YOU THINK THERE'S ANY CHANCE, AFTER ALL THIS TIME THAT...THAT MIKE MIGHT STILL BE ALIVE? THESE M.I.A. GROUPS, THEY'RE PRETTY VOCAL...I'VE THOUGHT ABOUT GETTING INVOLVED.

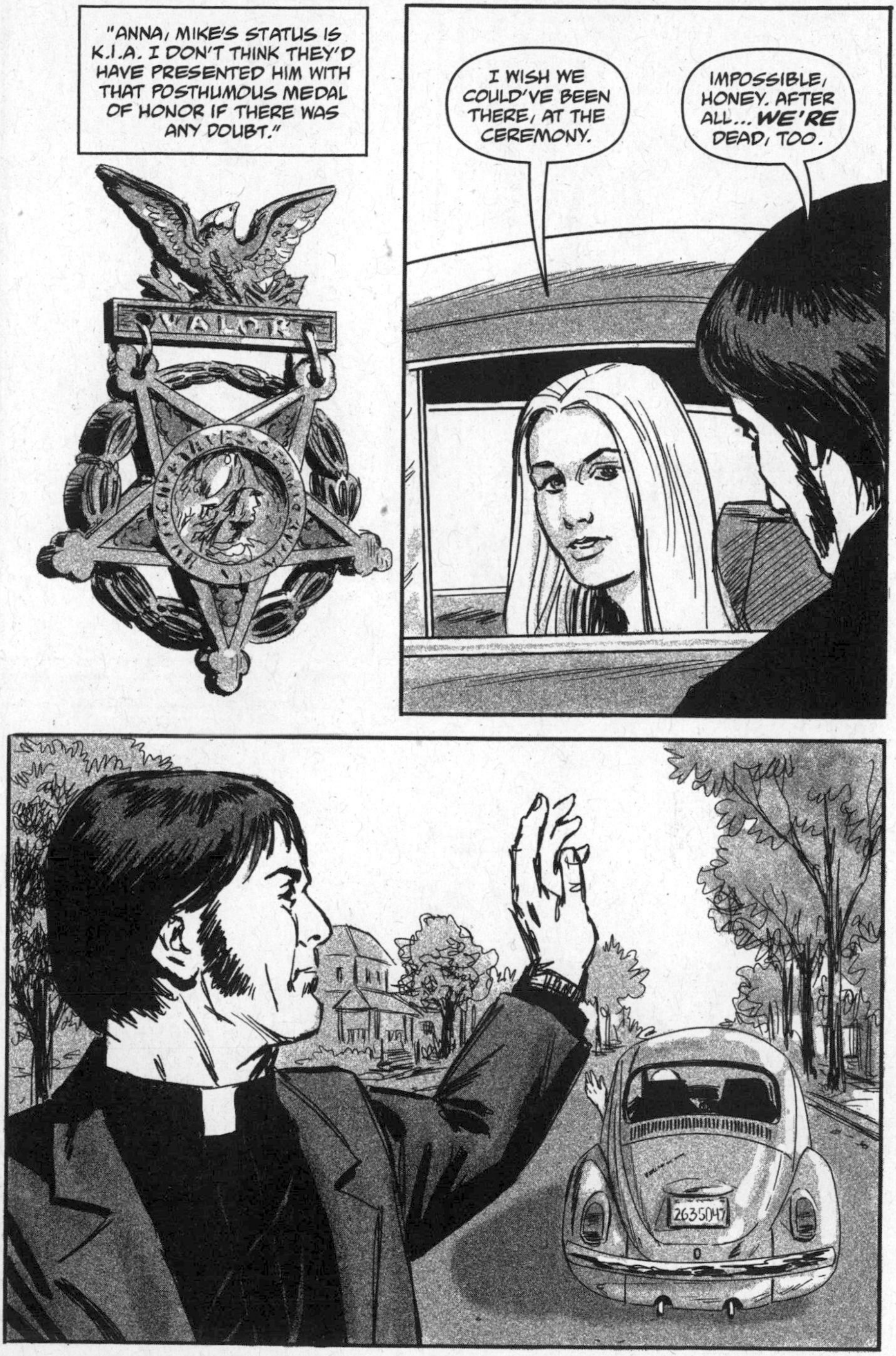
"ANNA, MIKE'S STATUS IS K.I.A. I DON'T THINK THEY'D HAVE PRESENTED HIM WITH THAT POSTHUMOUS MEDAL OF HONOR IF THERE WAS ANY DOUBT."
VALOR
I WISH WE COULD'VE BEEN THERE, AT THE CEREMONY.
IMPOSSIBLE, HONEY. AFTER ALL... **WE'RE** DEAD, TOO.
2635047

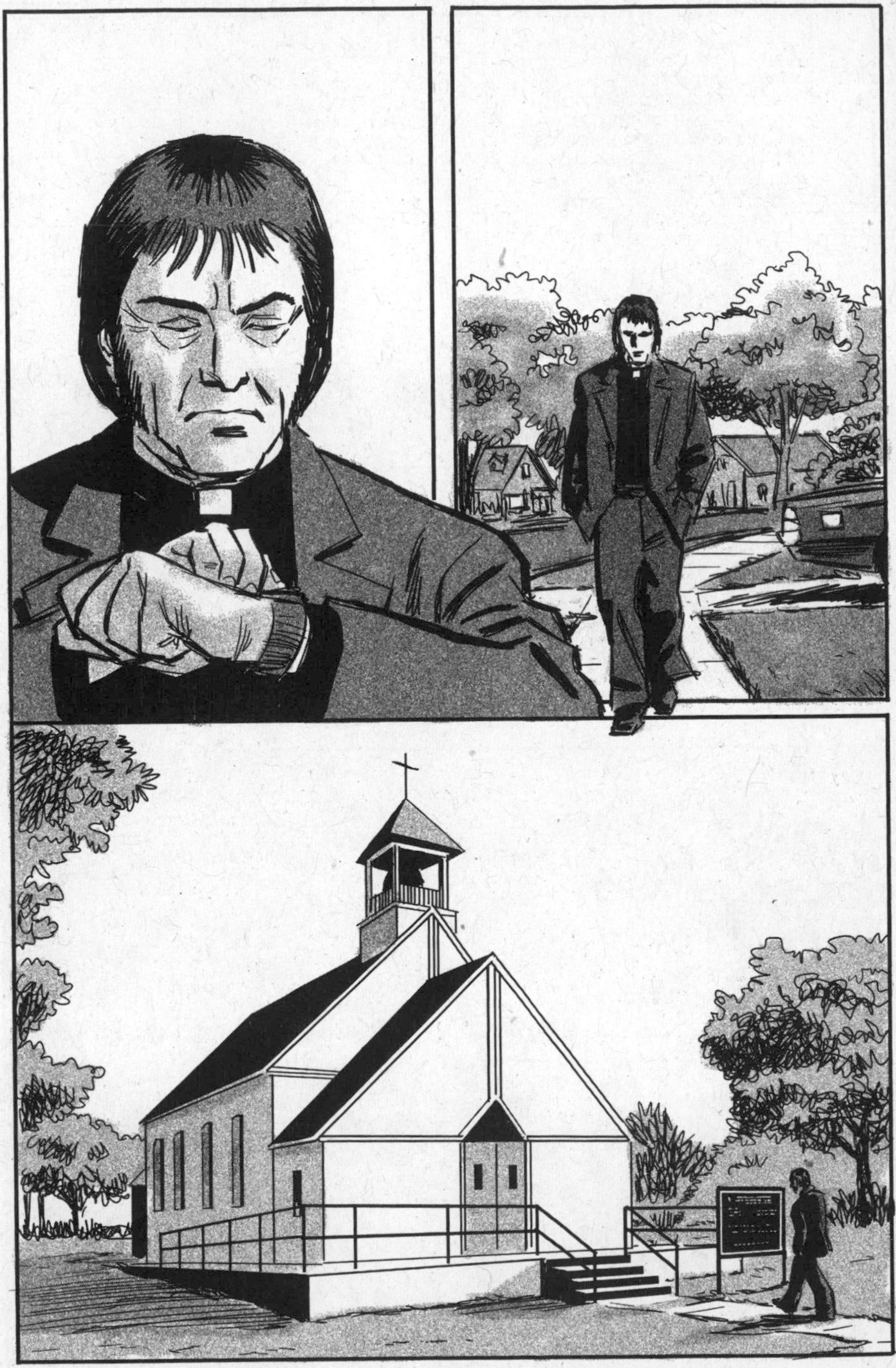

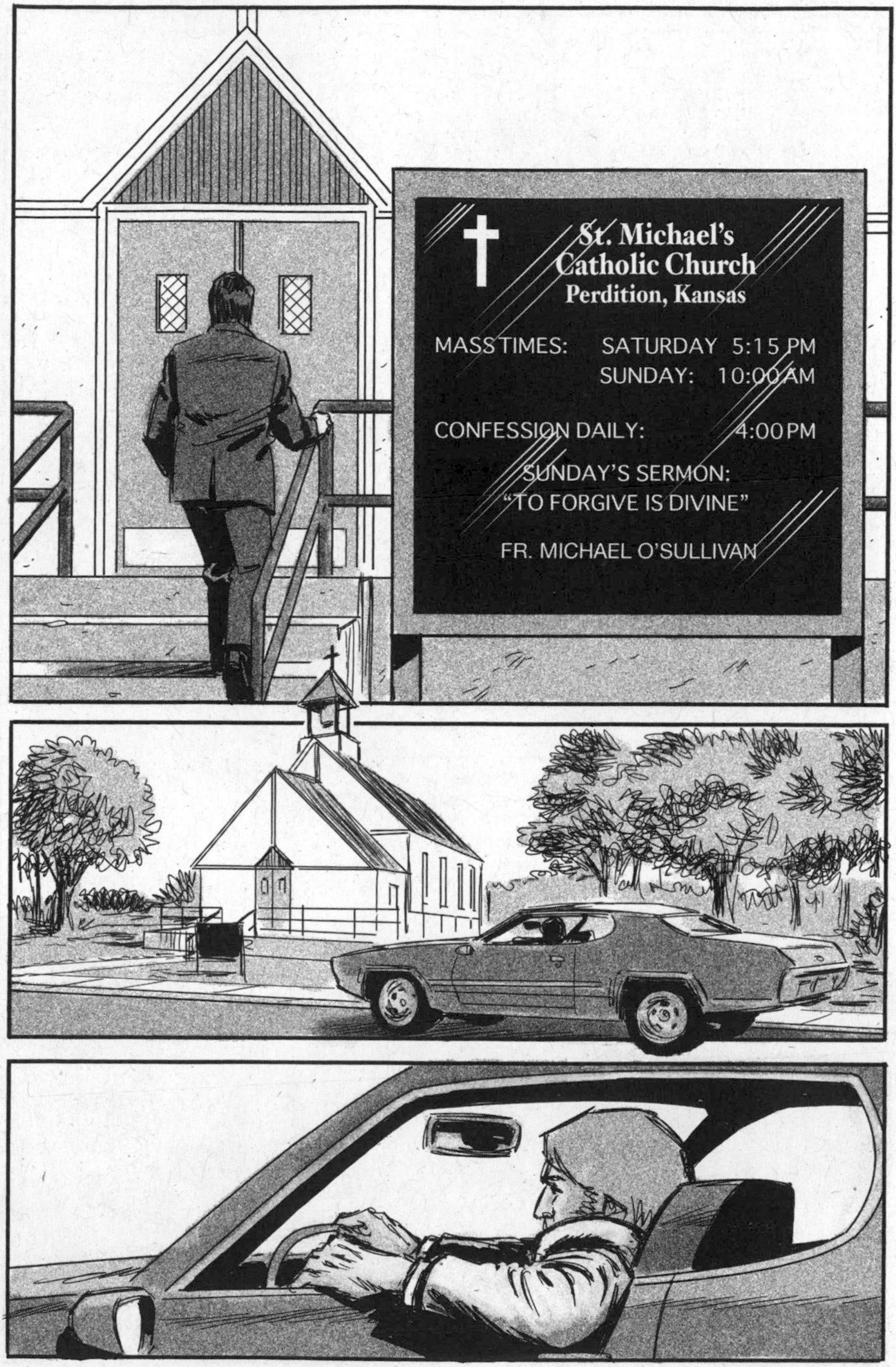
St. Michael's
Catholic Church
Perdition, Kansas
MASS TIMES: SATURDAY 5:15 PM
SUNDAY: 10:00 AM
CONFESSION DAILY: 4:00 PM
SUNDAY'S SERMON:
"TO FORGIVE IS DIVINE"
FR. MICHAEL O'SULLIVAN

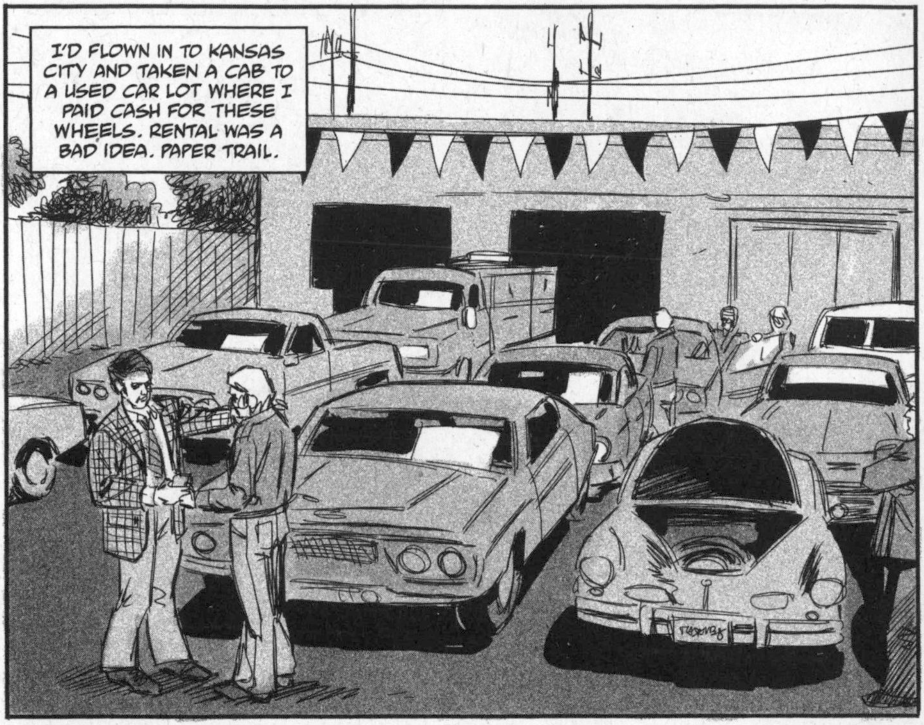
I'D FLOWN IN TO KANSAS CITY AND TAKEN A CAB TO A USED CAR LOT WHERE I PAID CASH FOR THESE WHEELS. RENTAL WAS A BAD IDEA. PAPER TRAIL.

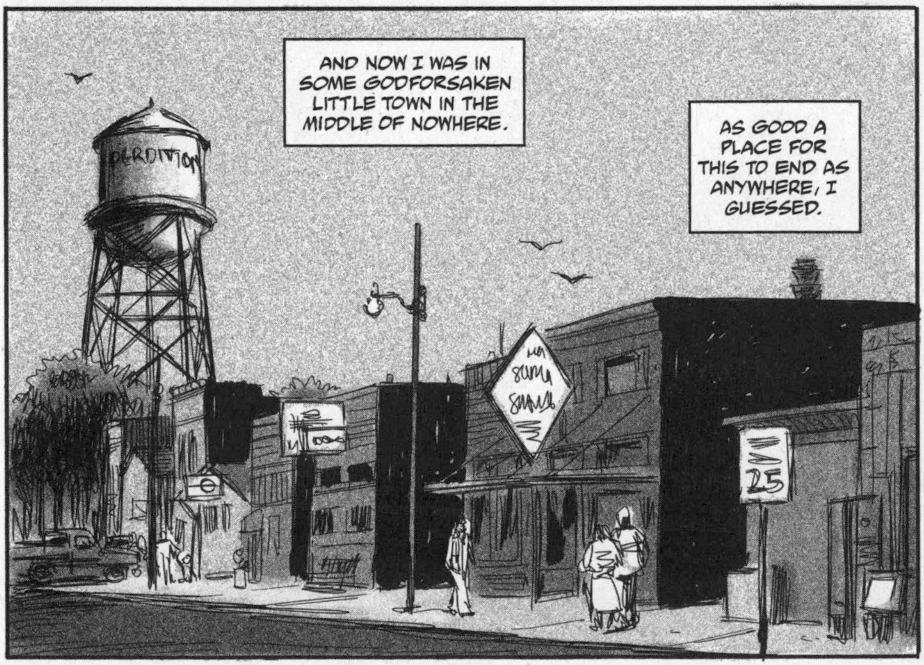
AND NOW I WAS IN SOME GODFORSAKEN LITTLE TOWN IN THE MIDDLE OF NOWHERE.
AS GOOD A PLACE FOR THIS TO END AS ANYWHERE, I GUESSED.

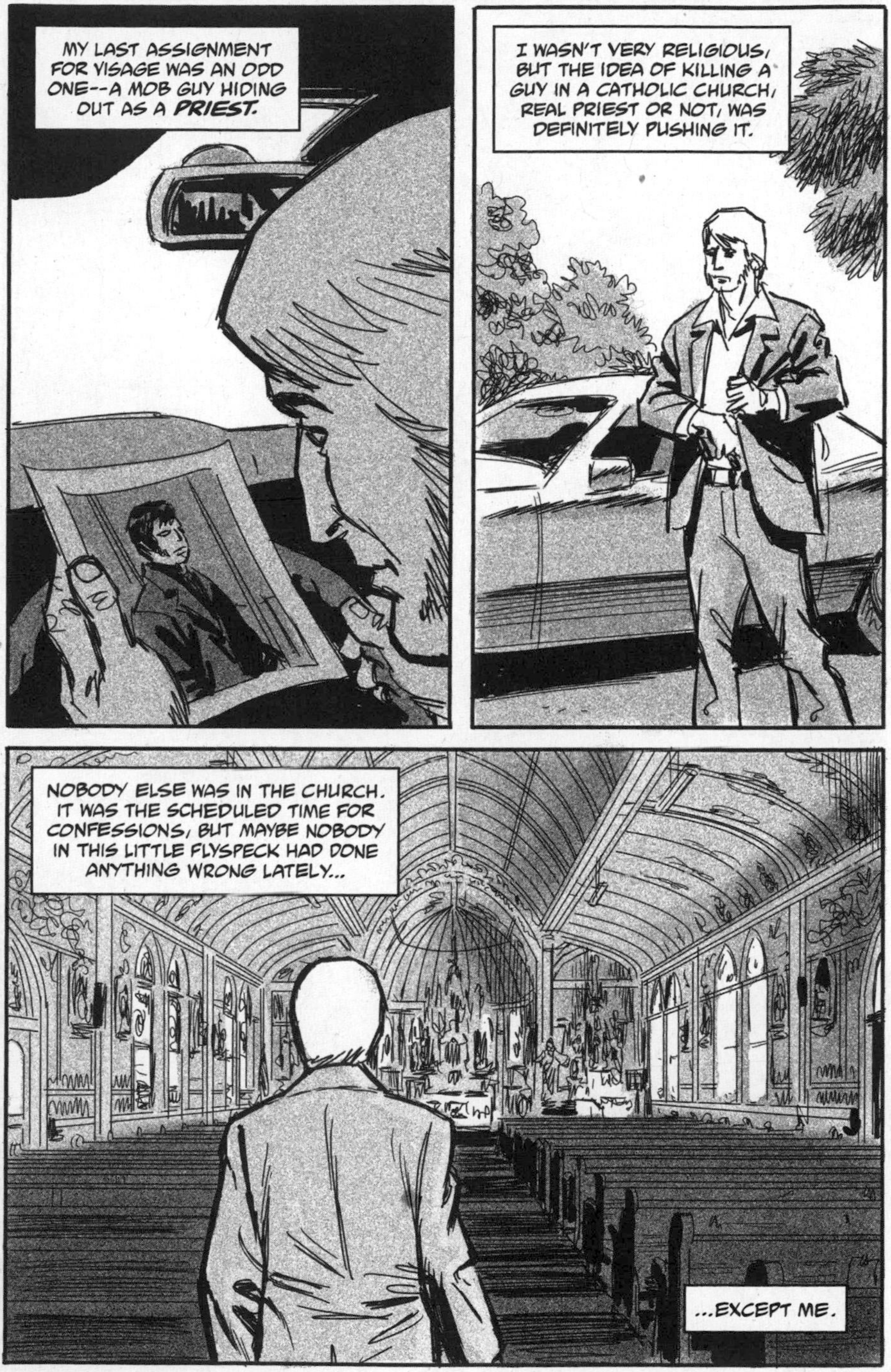
MY LAST ASSIGNMENT FOR VISAGE WAS AN ODD ONE--A MOB GUY HIDING OUT AS A PRIEST.
I WASN'T VERY RELIGIOUS, BUT THE IDEA OF KILLING A GUY IN A CATHOLIC CHURCH, REAL PRIEST OR NOT, WAS DEFINITELY PUSHING IT.
NOBODY ELSE WAS IN THE CHURCH. IT WAS THE SCHEDULED TIME FOR CONFESSIONS, BUT MAYBE NOBODY IN THIS LITTLE FLYSPECK HAD DONE ANYTHING WRONG LATELY...
...EXCEPT ME.

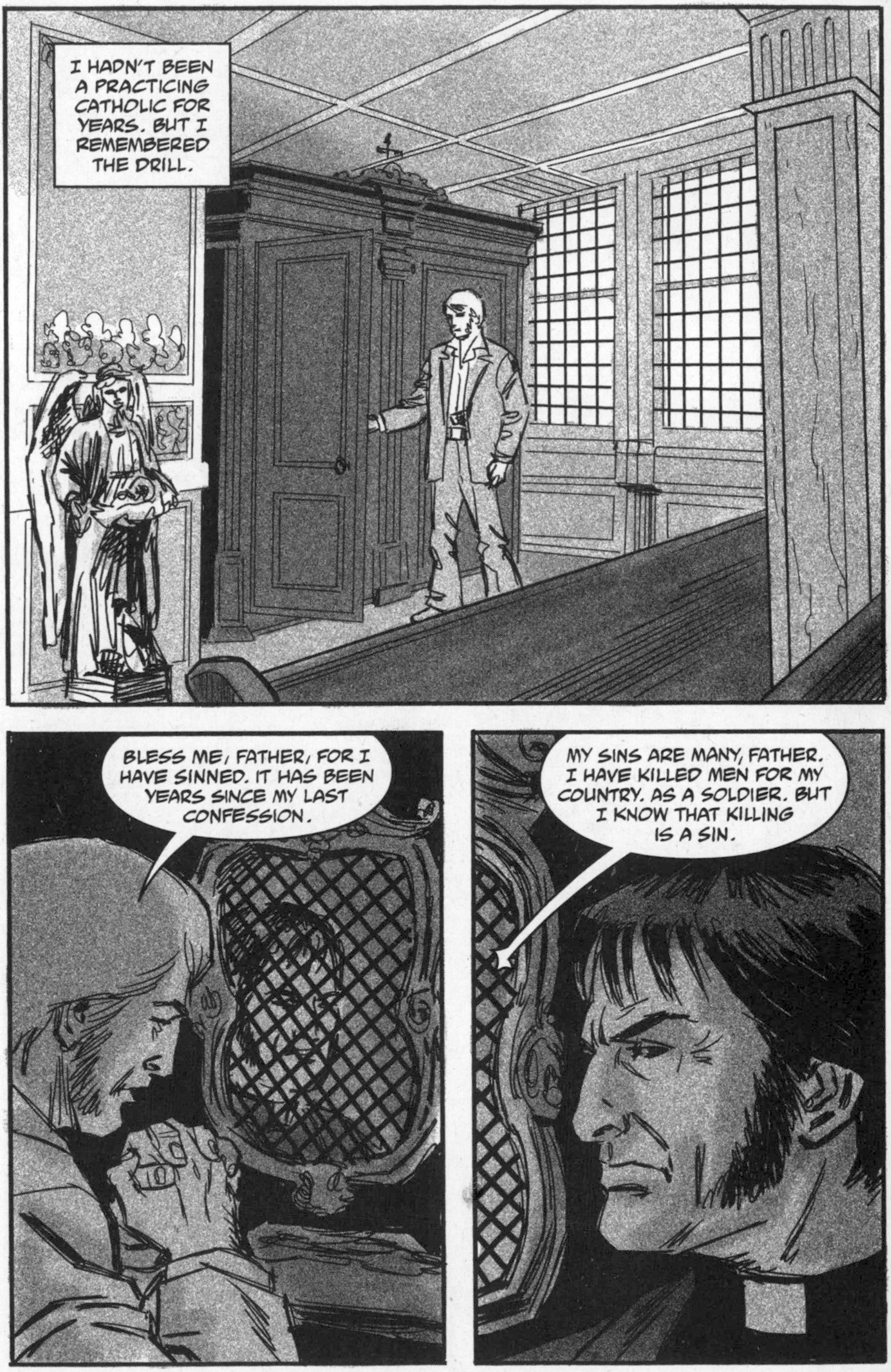
I HADN'T BEEN A PRACTICING CATHOLIC FOR YEARS. BUT I REMEMBERED THE DRILL.
BLESS ME, FATHER, FOR I HAVE SINNED. IT HAS BEEN YEARS SINCE MY LAST CONFESSION.
MY SINS ARE MANY, FATHER. I HAVE KILLED MEN FOR MY COUNTRY. AS A SOLDIER. BUT I KNOW THAT KILLING IS A SIN.

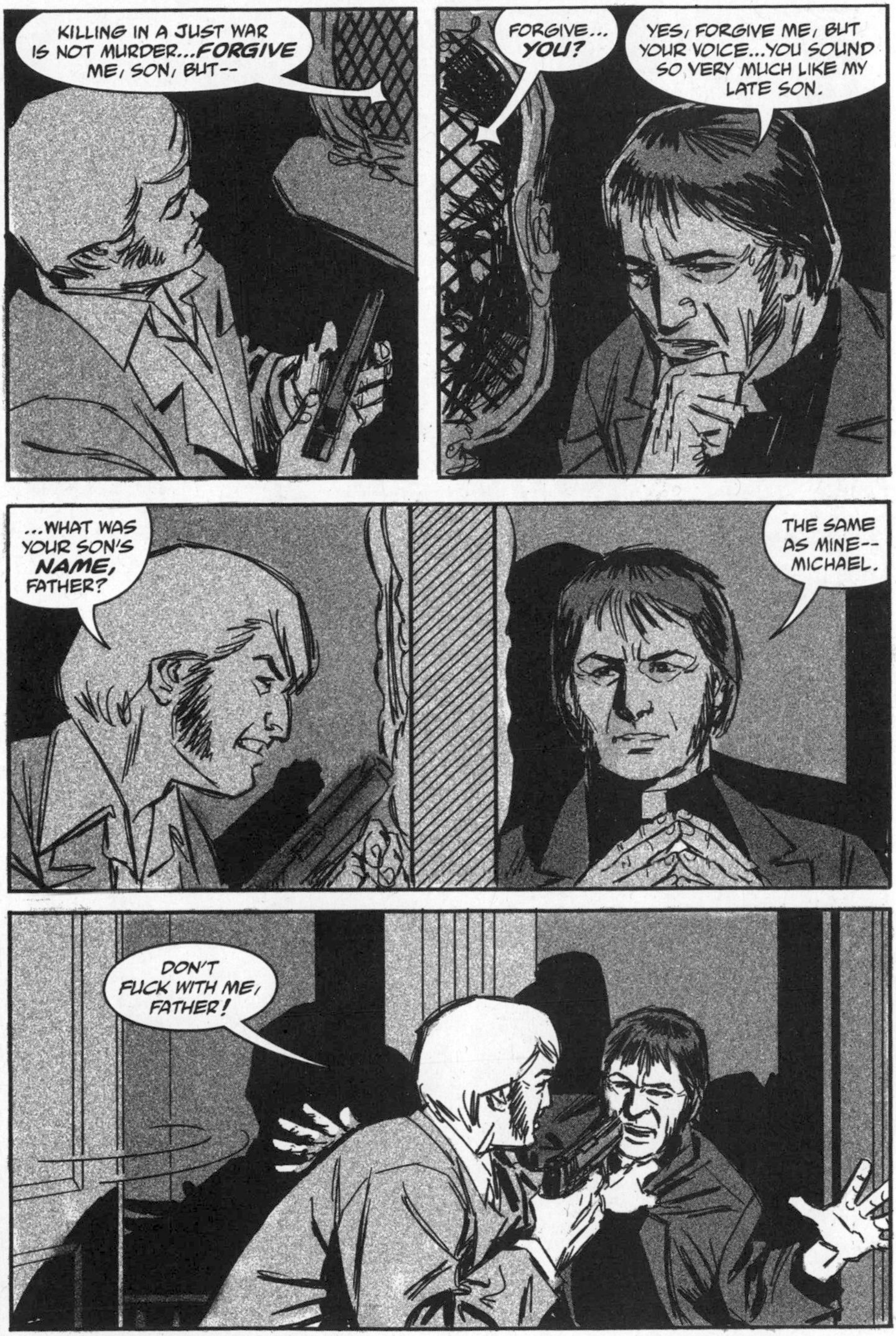
KILLING IN A JUST WAR IS NOT MURDER...FORGIVE ME, SON, BUT--
FORGIVE... YOU?
YES, FORGIVE ME, BUT YOUR VOICE...YOU SOUND SO VERY MUCH LIKE MY LATE SON.
...WHAT WAS YOUR SON'S NAME, FATHER?
THE SAME AS MINE-- MICHAEL.
DON'T FUCK WITH ME, FATHER!

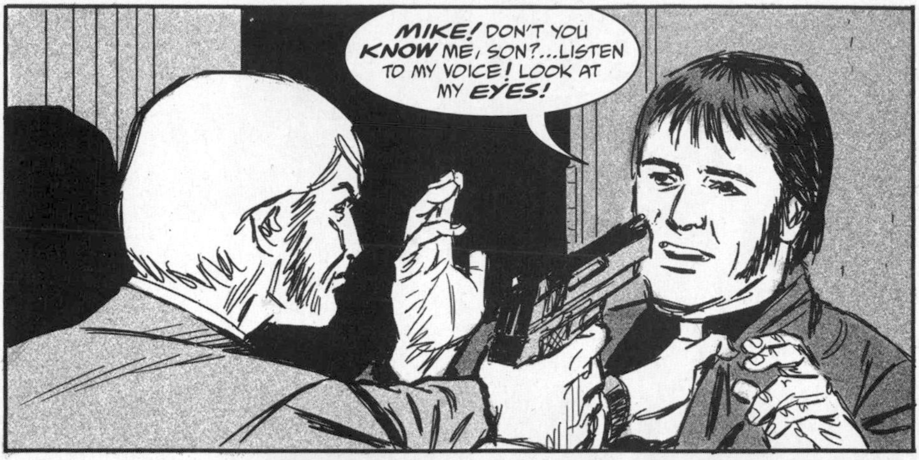
MIKE! DON'T YOU KNOW ME, SON?...LISTEN TO MY VOICE! LOOK AT MY EYES!
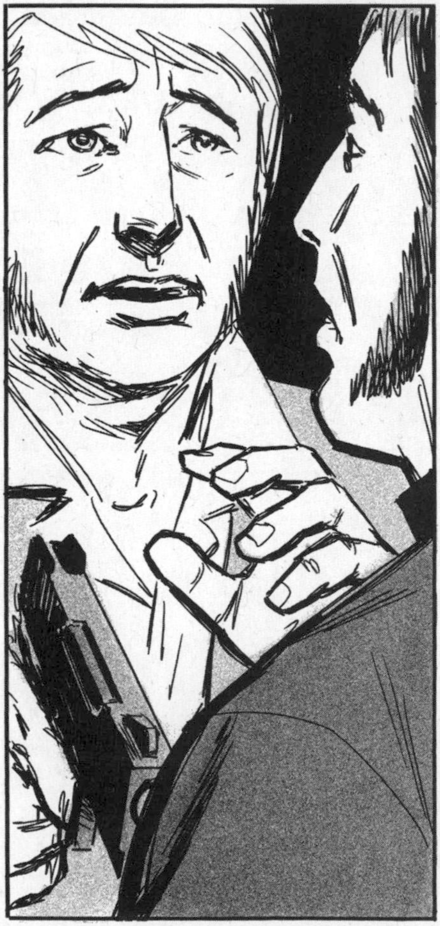
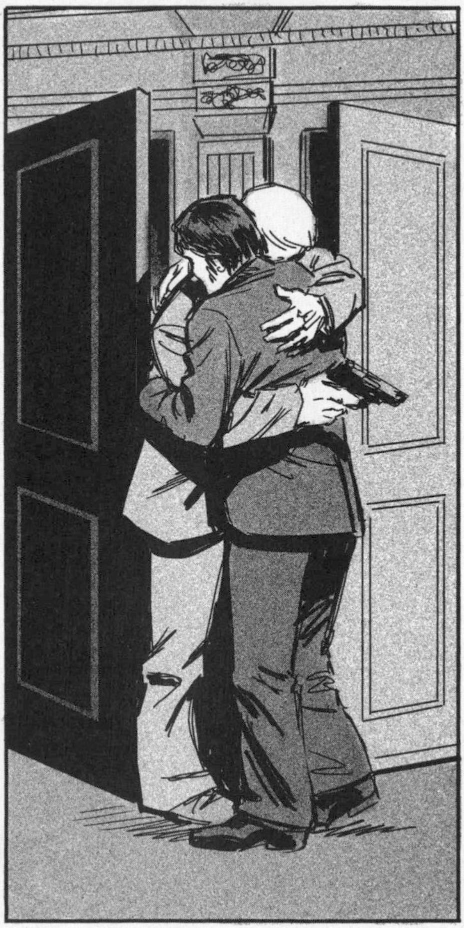

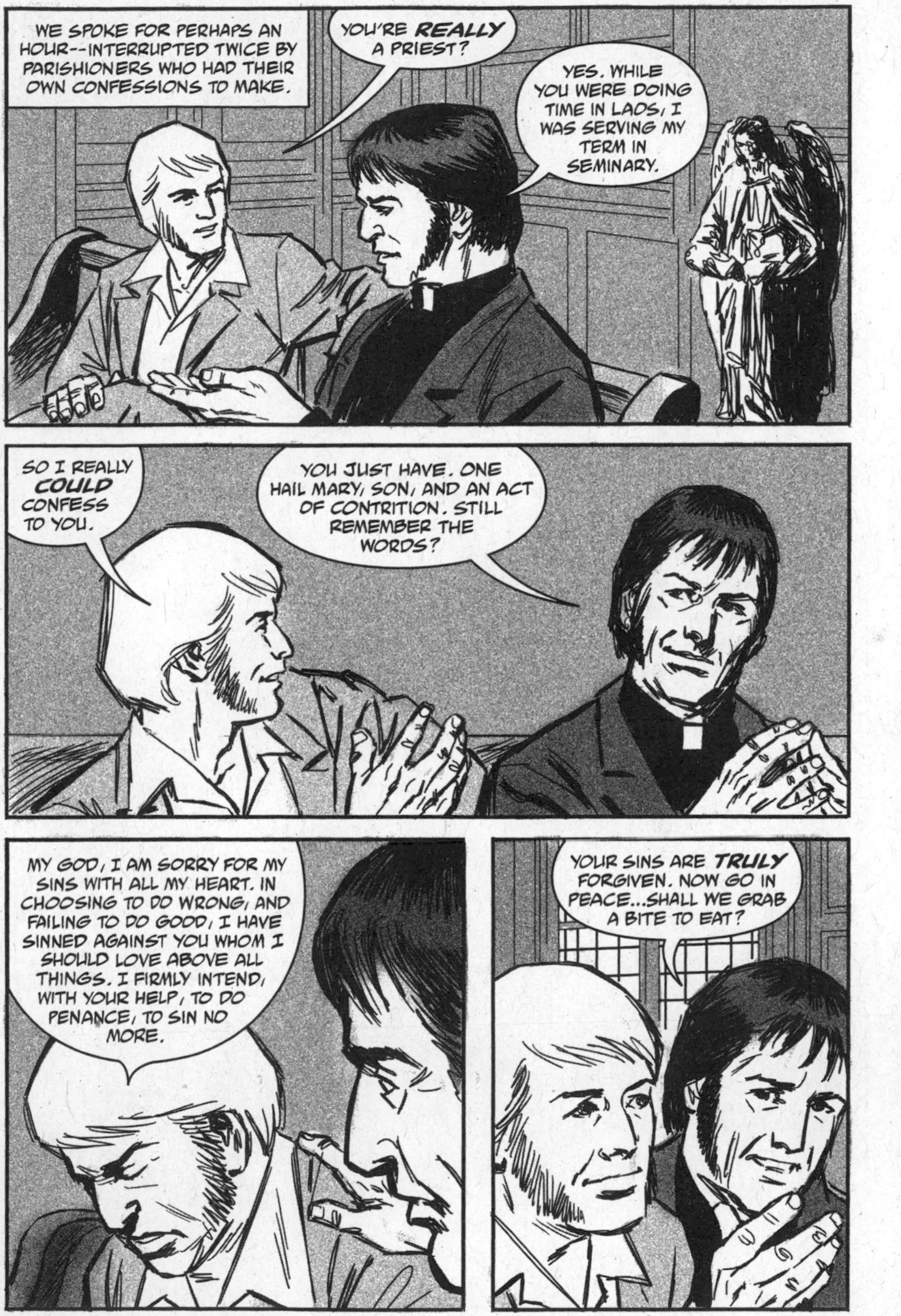
WE SPOKE FOR PERHAPS AN HOUR--INTERRUPTED TWICE BY PARISHIONERS WHO HAD THEIR OWN CONFESSIONS TO MAKE.
YOU'RE REALLY A PRIEST?
YES. WHILE YOU WERE DOING TIME IN LAOS, I WAS SERVING MY TERM IN SEMINARY.
SO I REALLY COULD CONFESS TO YOU.
YOU JUST HAVE. ONE HAIL MARY, SON, AND AN ACT OF CONTRITION. STILL REMEMBER THE WORDS?
MY GOD, I AM SORRY FOR MY SINS WITH ALL MY HEART. IN CHOOSING TO DO WRONG, AND FAILING TO DO GOOD, I HAVE SINNED AGAINST YOU WHOM I SHOULD LOVE ABOVE ALL THINGS. I FIRMLY INTEND, WITH YOUR HELP, TO DO PENANCE, TO SIN NO MORE.
YOUR SINS ARE TRULY FORGIVEN. NOW GO IN PEACE...SHALL WE GRAB A BITE TO EAT?

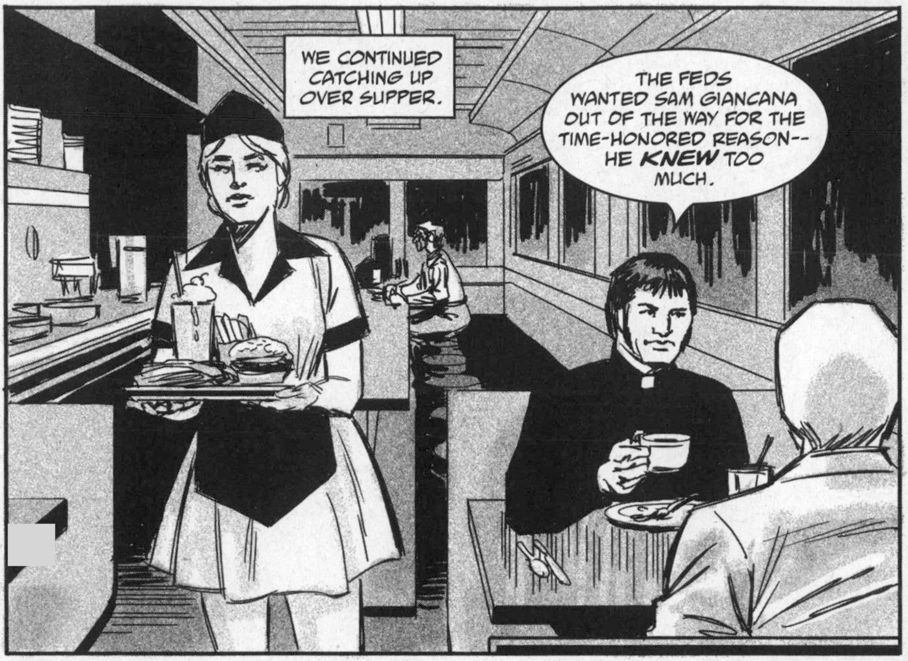
WE CONTINUED CATCHING UP OVER SUPPER.
THE FEDS WANTED SAM GIANCANA OUT OF THE WAY FOR THE TIME-HONORED REASON-- HE **KNEW** TOO MUCH.

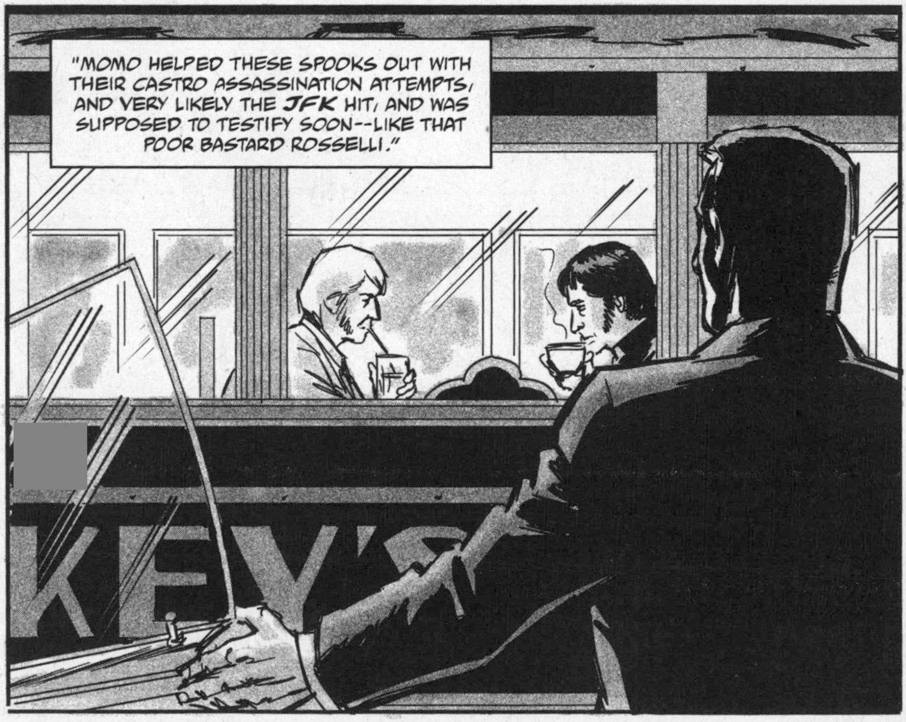
"MOMO HELPED THESE SPOOKS OUT WITH THEIR CASTRO ASSASSINATION ATTEMPTS, AND VERY LIKELY THE **JFK** HIT, AND WAS SUPPOSED TO TESTIFY SOON--LIKE THAT POOR BASTARD ROSSELLI."
KEY'S

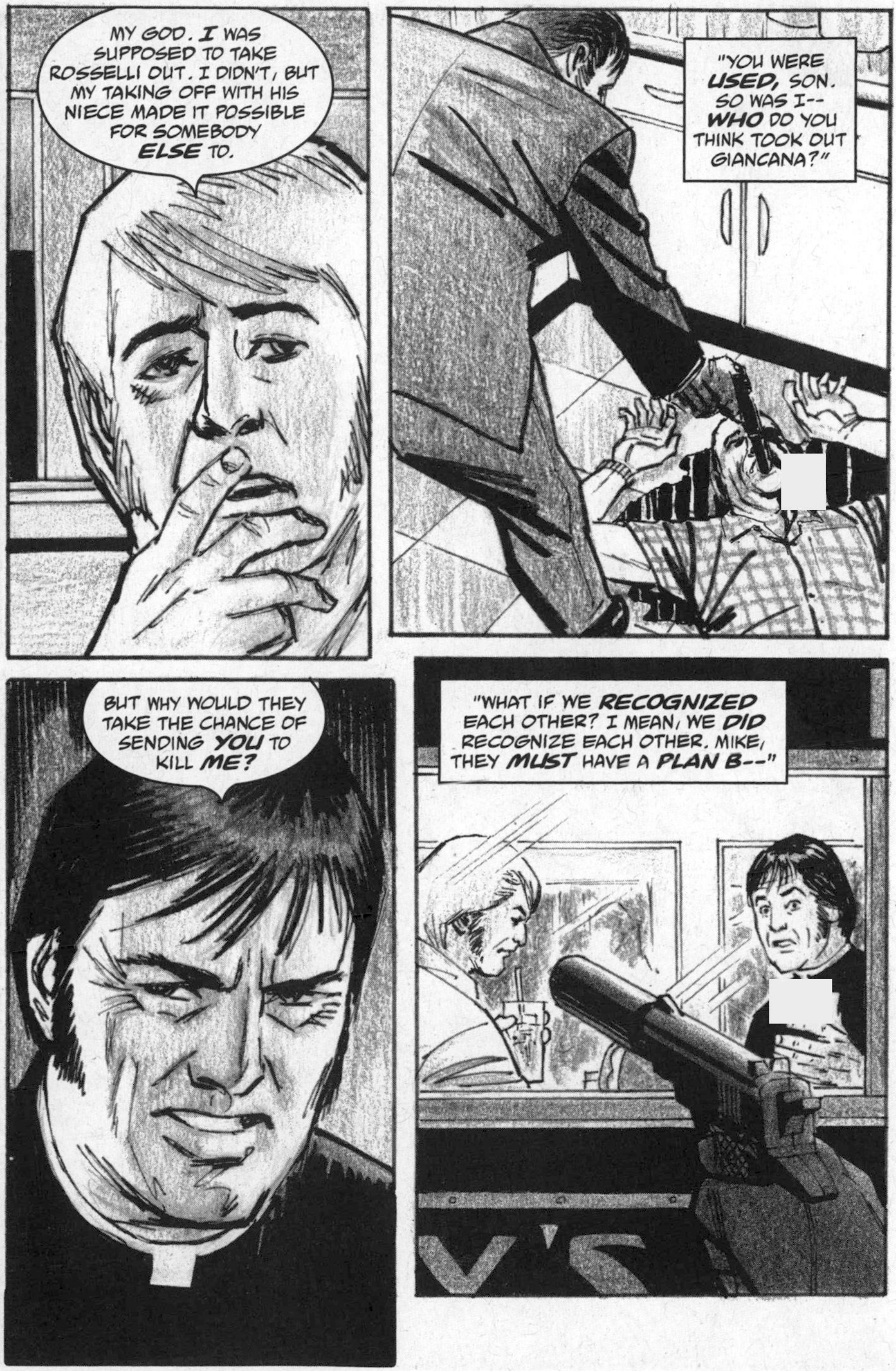
MY GOD. I WAS SUPPOSED TO TAKE ROSSELLI OUT. I DIDN'T, BUT MY TAKING OFF WITH HIS NIECE MADE IT POSSIBLE FOR SOMEBODY ELSE TO.
"YOU WERE USED, SON. SO WAS I-- WHO DO YOU THINK TOOK OUT GIANCANA?"
BUT WHY WOULD THEY TAKE THE CHANCE OF SENDING YOU TO KILL ME?
"WHAT IF WE RECOGNIZED EACH OTHER? I MEAN, WE DID RECOGNIZE EACH OTHER. MIKE, THEY MUST HAVE A PLAN B--"
V'S

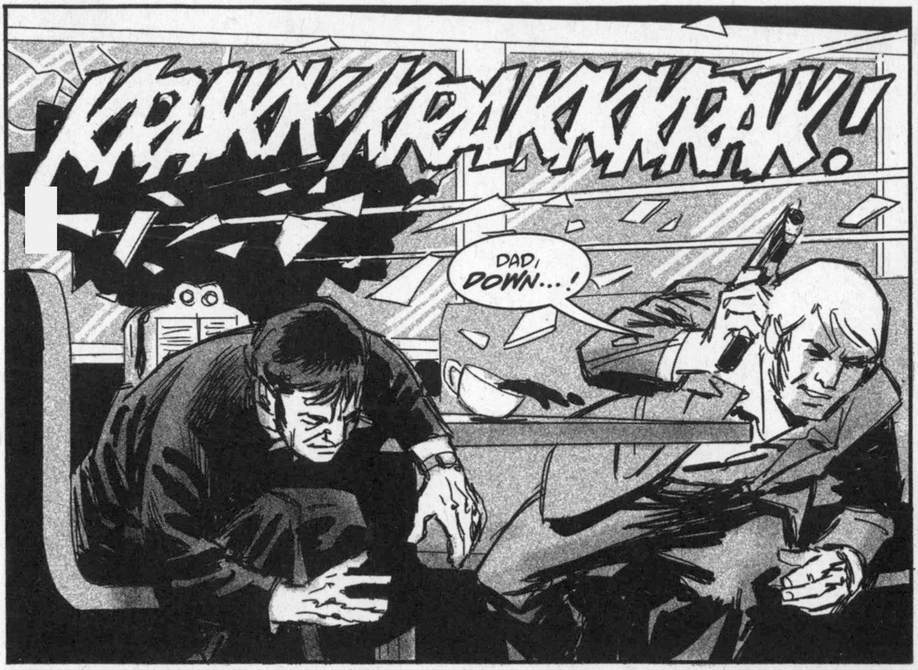
KRAKK KRAKAKKRAK!
DAD, DOWN...!

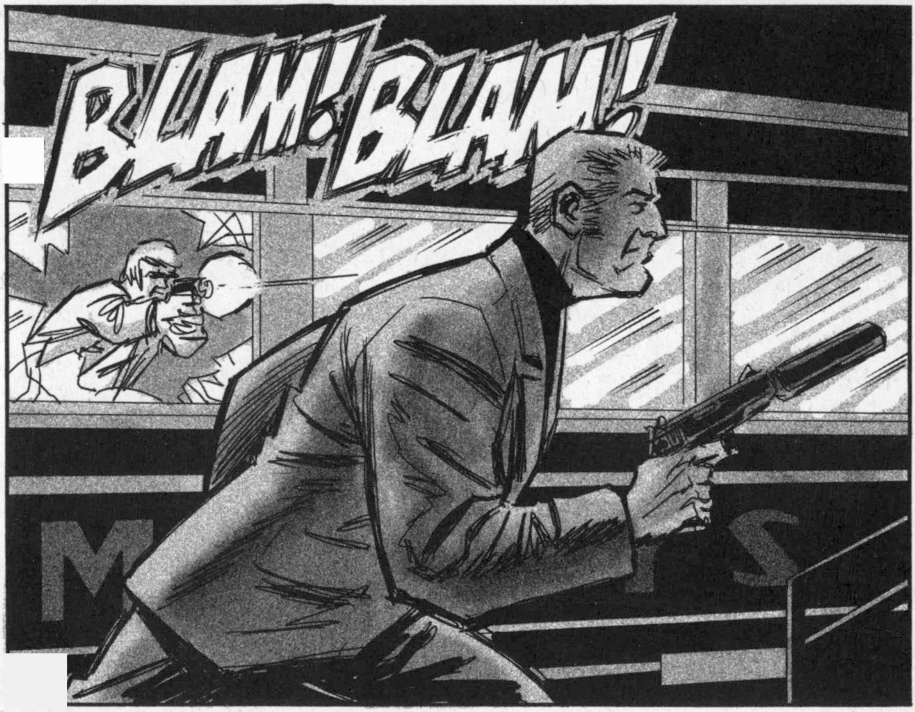
BLAM! BLAM!

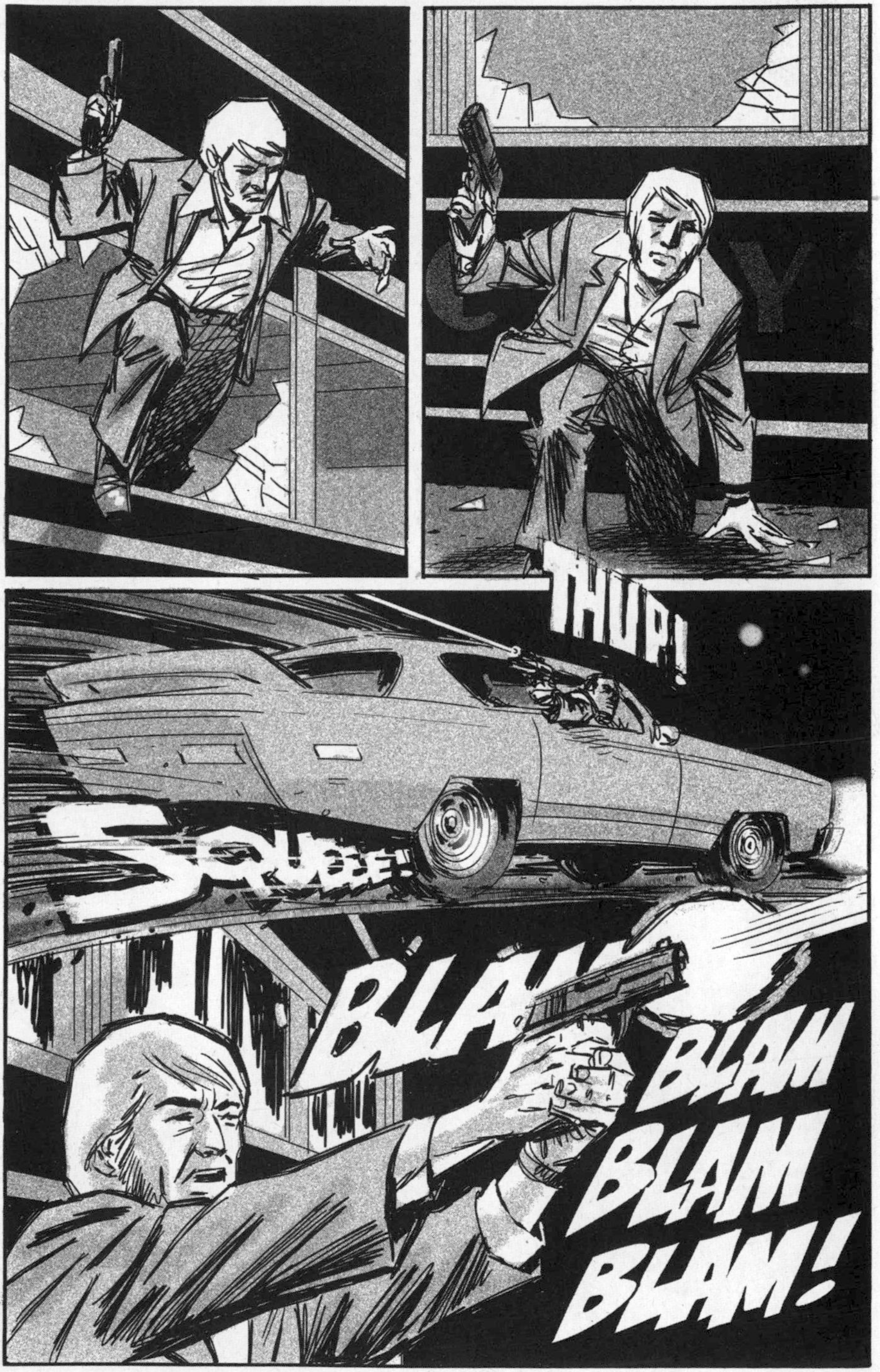
THUP!
SQUEEE!
BLAM
BLAM
BLAM
BLAM!

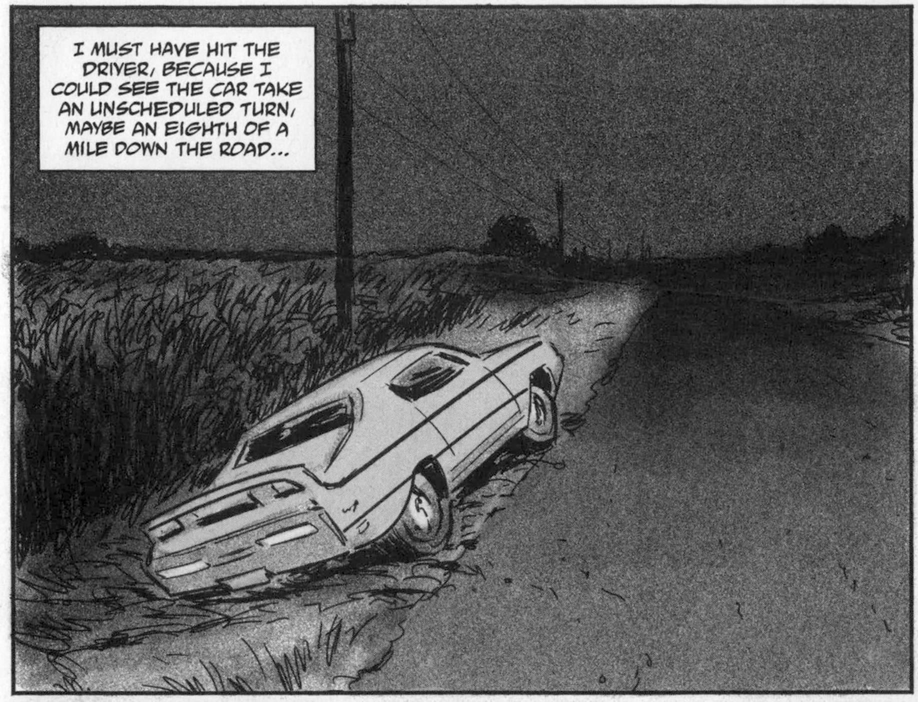
I MUST HAVE HIT THE DRIVER, BECAUSE I COULD SEE THE CAR TAKE AN UNSCHEDULED TURN, MAYBE AN EIGHTH OF A MILE DOWN THE ROAD...

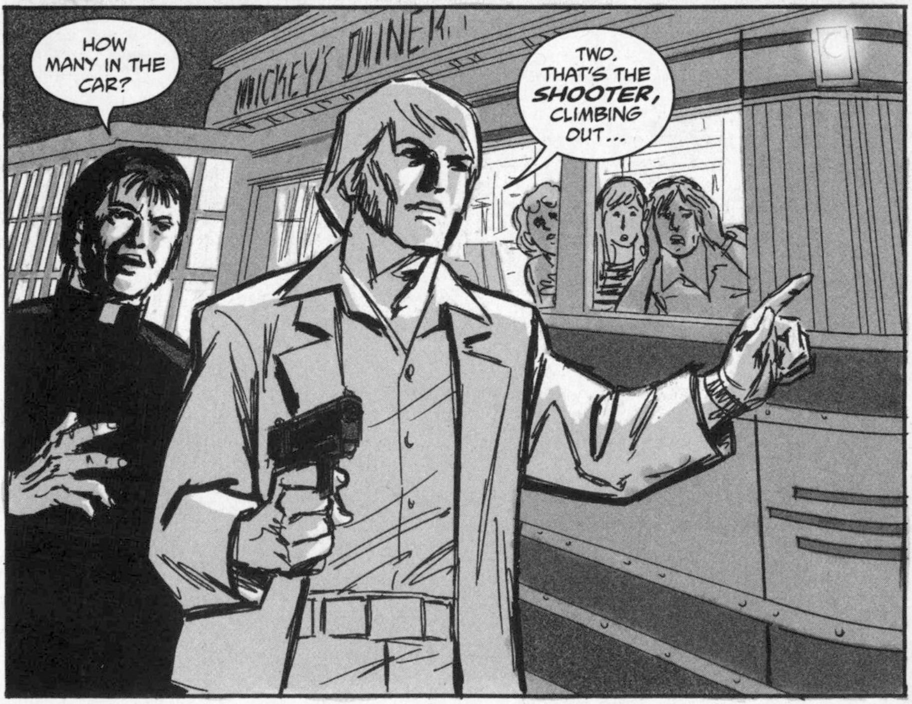
HOW MANY IN THE CAR?
MICKEY'S DINER
TWO. THAT'S THE *SHOOTER*, CLIMBING OUT...

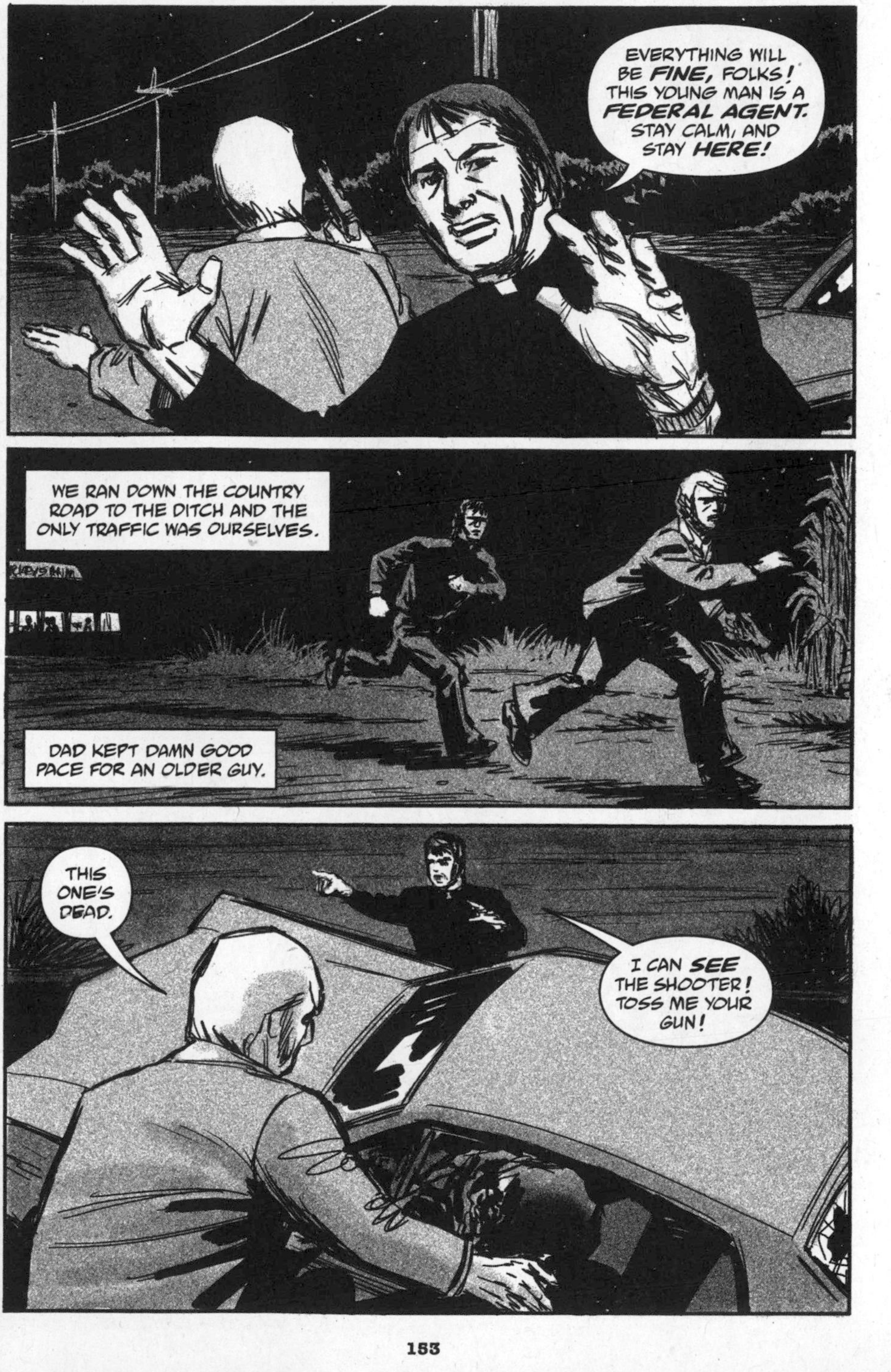
EVERYTHING WILL BE FINE, FOLKS! THIS YOUNG MAN IS A FEDERAL AGENT. STAY CALM, AND STAY HERE!
WE RAN DOWN THE COUNTRY ROAD TO THE DITCH AND THE ONLY TRAFFIC WAS OURSELVES.
DAD KEPT DAMN GOOD PACE FOR AN OLDER GUY.
THIS ONE'S DEAD.
I CAN SEE THE SHOOTER! TOSS ME YOUR GUN!

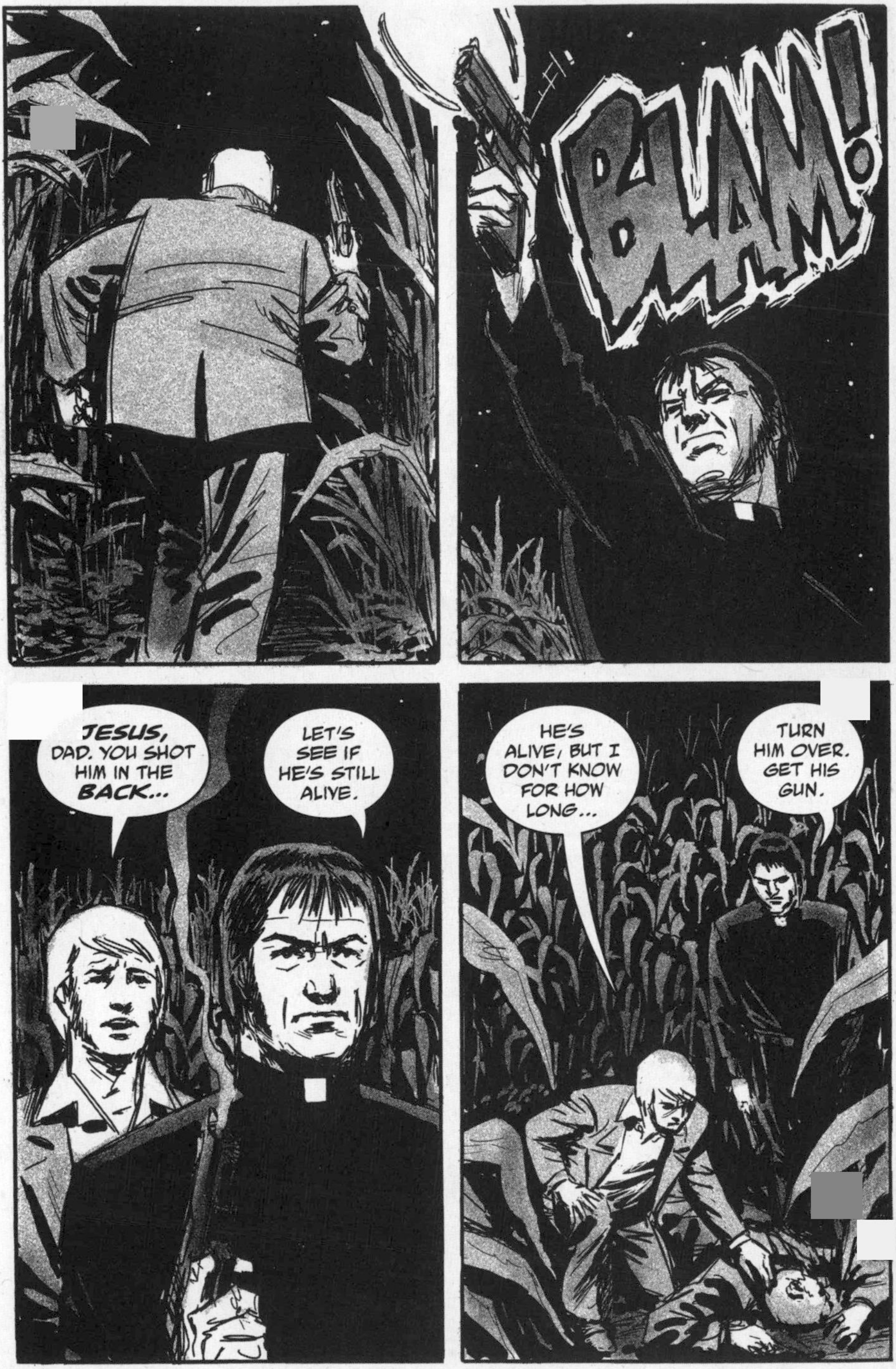
BLAM!
JESUS, DAD. YOU SHOT HIM IN THE BACK...
LET'S SEE IF HE'S STILL ALIVE.
HE'S ALIVE, BUT I DON'T KNOW FOR HOW LONG...
TURN HIM OVER. GET HIS GUN.

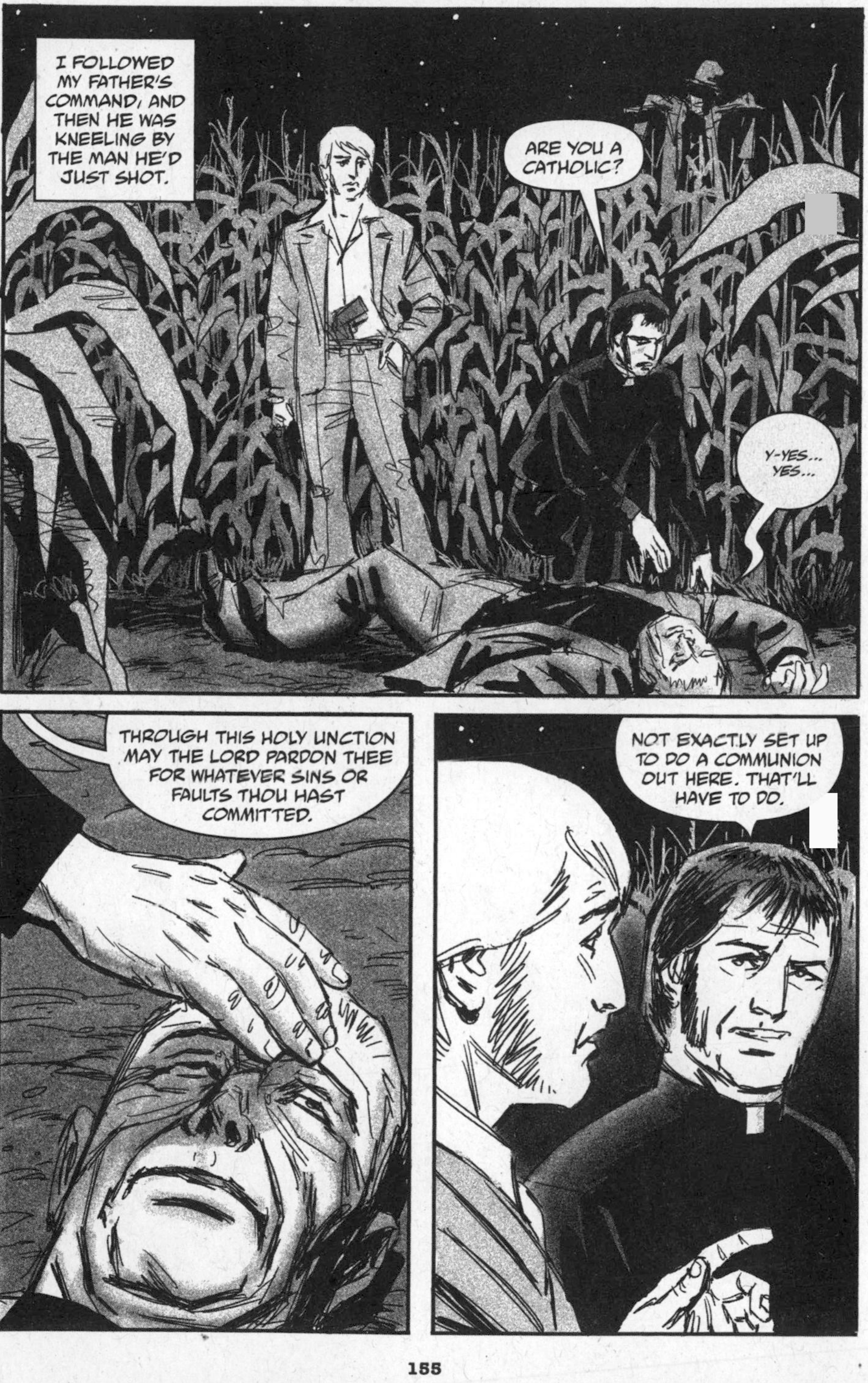
I FOLLOWED MY FATHER'S COMMAND, AND THEN HE WAS KNEELING BY THE MAN HE'D JUST SHOT.
ARE YOU A CATHOLIC?
Y-YES... YES...
THROUGH THIS HOLY UNCTION MAY THE LORD PARDON THEE FOR WHATEVER SINS OR FAULTS THOU HAST COMMITTED.
NOT EXACTLY SET UP TO DO A COMMUNION OUT HERE. THAT'LL HAVE TO DO.

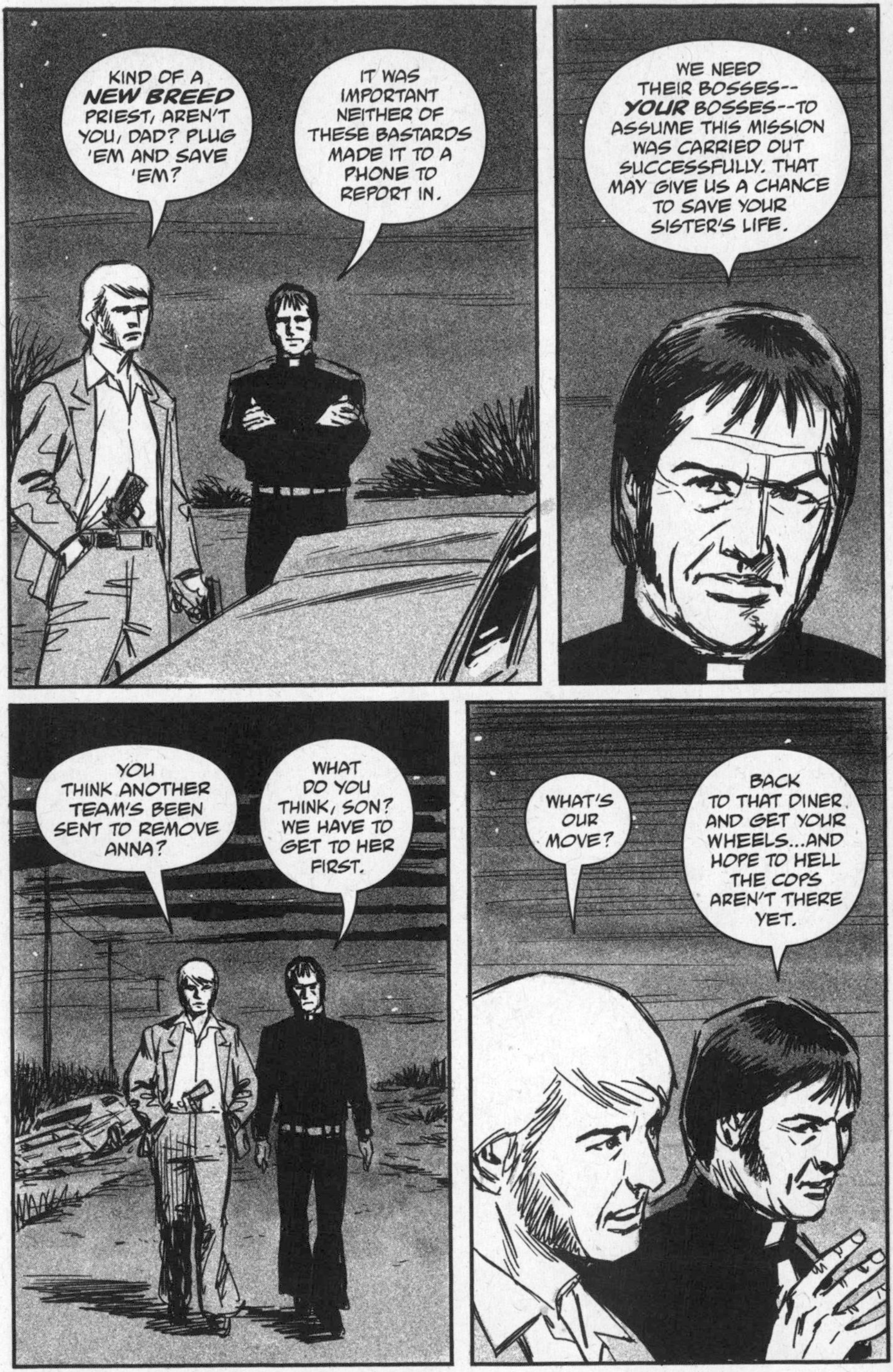
KIND OF A NEW BREED PRIEST, AREN'T YOU, DAD? PLUG 'EM AND SAVE 'EM?
IT WAS IMPORTANT NEITHER OF THESE BASTARDS MADE IT TO A PHONE TO REPORT IN.
WE NEED THEIR BOSSES-- YOUR BOSSES--TO ASSUME THIS MISSION WAS CARRIED OUT SUCCESSFULLY. THAT MAY GIVE US A CHANCE TO SAVE YOUR SISTER'S LIFE.
YOU THINK ANOTHER TEAM'S BEEN SENT TO REMOVE ANNA?
WHAT DO YOU THINK, SON? WE HAVE TO GET TO HER FIRST.
WHAT'S OUR MOVE?
BACK TO THAT DINER AND GET YOUR WHEELS...AND HOPE TO HELL THE COPS AREN'T THERE YET.

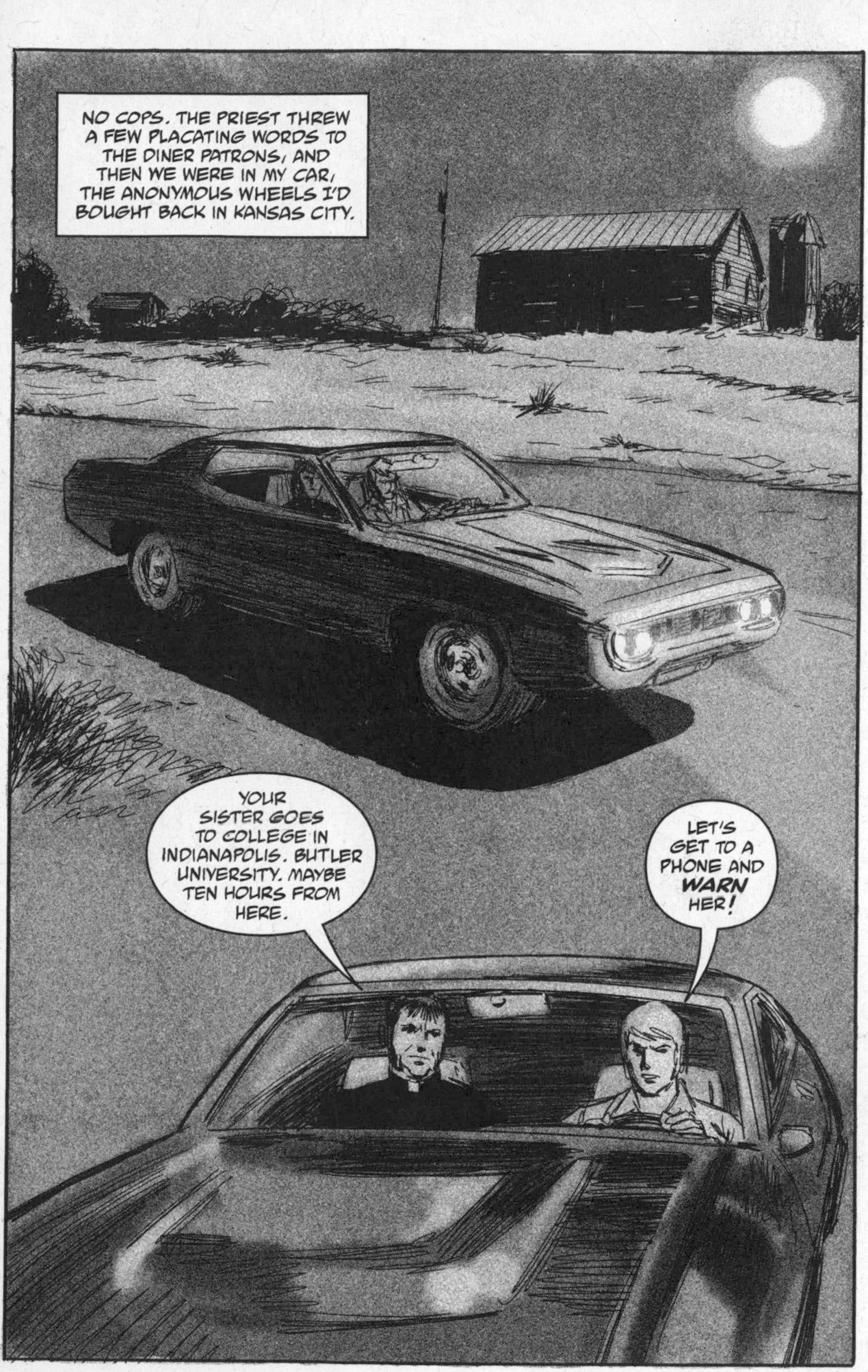
NO COPS. THE PRIEST THREW A FEW PLACATING WORDS TO THE DINER PATRONS, AND THEN WE WERE IN MY CAR, THE ANONYMOUS WHEELS I'D BOUGHT BACK IN KANSAS CITY.
YOUR SISTER GOES TO COLLEGE IN INDIANAPOLIS. BUTLER UNIVERSITY. MAYBE TEN HOURS FROM HERE.
LET'S GET TO A PHONE AND **WARN** HER!

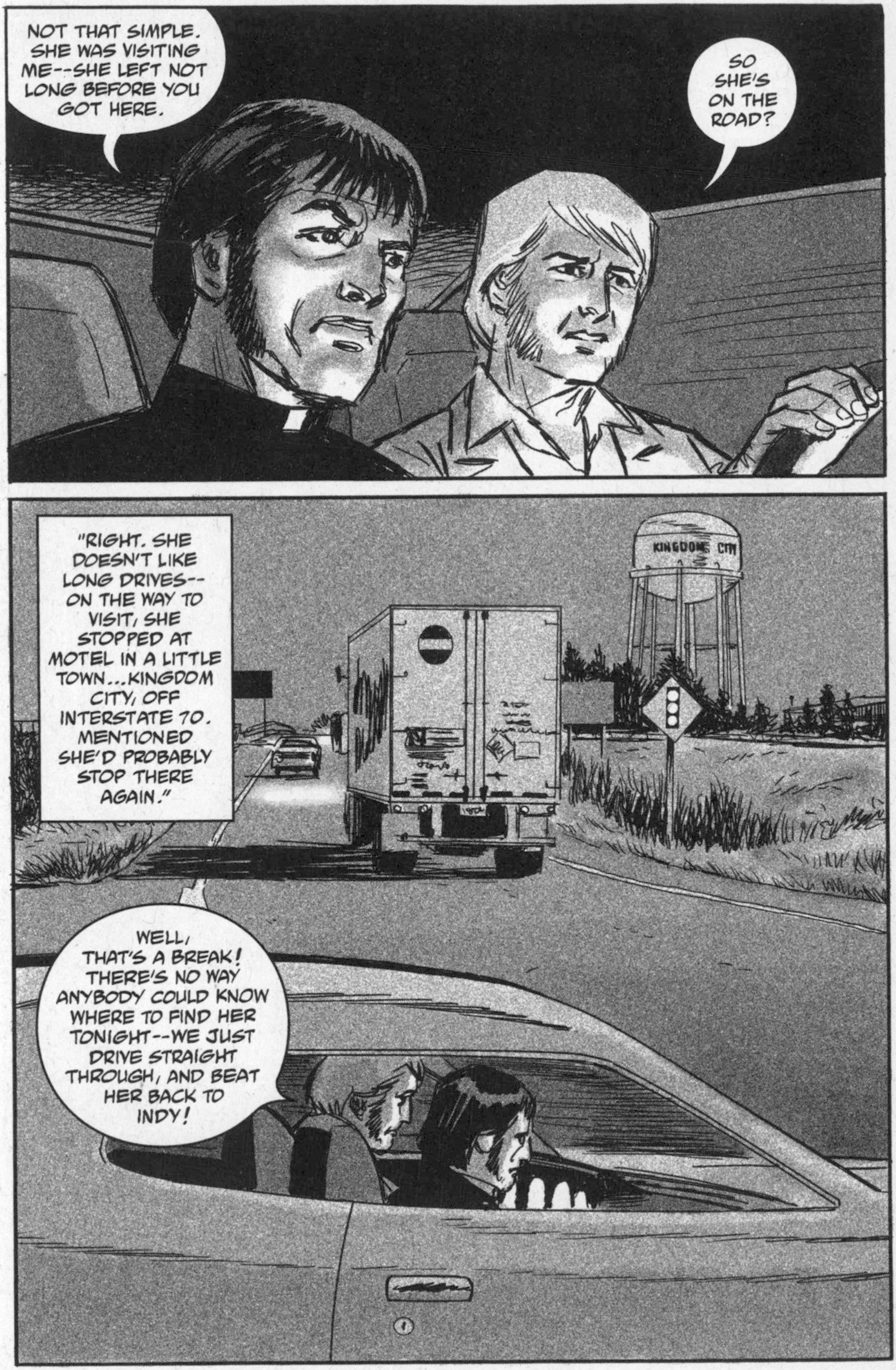
NOT THAT SIMPLE. SHE WAS VISITING ME--SHE LEFT NOT LONG BEFORE YOU GOT HERE.
SO SHE'S ON THE ROAD?
"RIGHT. SHE DOESN'T LIKE LONG DRIVES--ON THE WAY TO VISIT, SHE STOPPED AT MOTEL IN A LITTLE TOWN...KINGDOM CITY, OFF INTERSTATE 70. MENTIONED SHE'D PROBABLY STOP THERE AGAIN."
KINGDOM CITY
WELL, THAT'S A BREAK! THERE'S NO WAY ANYBODY COULD KNOW WHERE TO FIND HER TONIGHT--WE JUST DRIVE STRAIGHT THROUGH, AND BEAT HER BACK TO INDY!

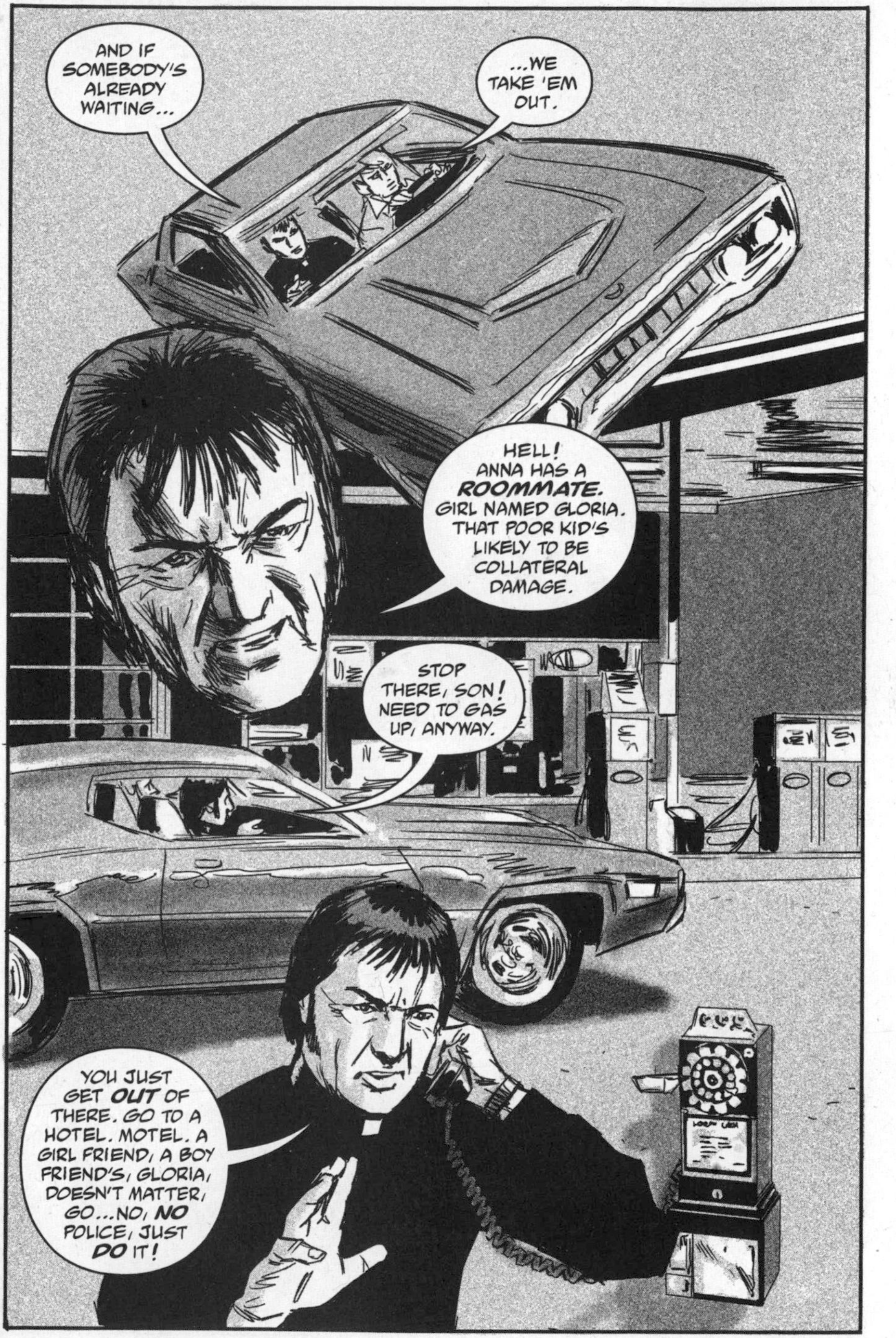
AND IF SOMEBODY'S ALREADY WAITING...
...WE TAKE 'EM OUT.
HELL! ANNA HAS A ROOMMATE. GIRL NAMED GLORIA. THAT POOR KID'S LIKELY TO BE COLLATERAL DAMAGE.
STOP THERE, SON! NEED TO GAS UP, ANYWAY.
YOU JUST GET OUT OF THERE. GO TO A HOTEL. MOTEL. A GIRL FRIEND, A BOY FRIEND'S, GLORIA, DOESN'T MATTER, GO...NO, NO POLICE, JUST DO IT!

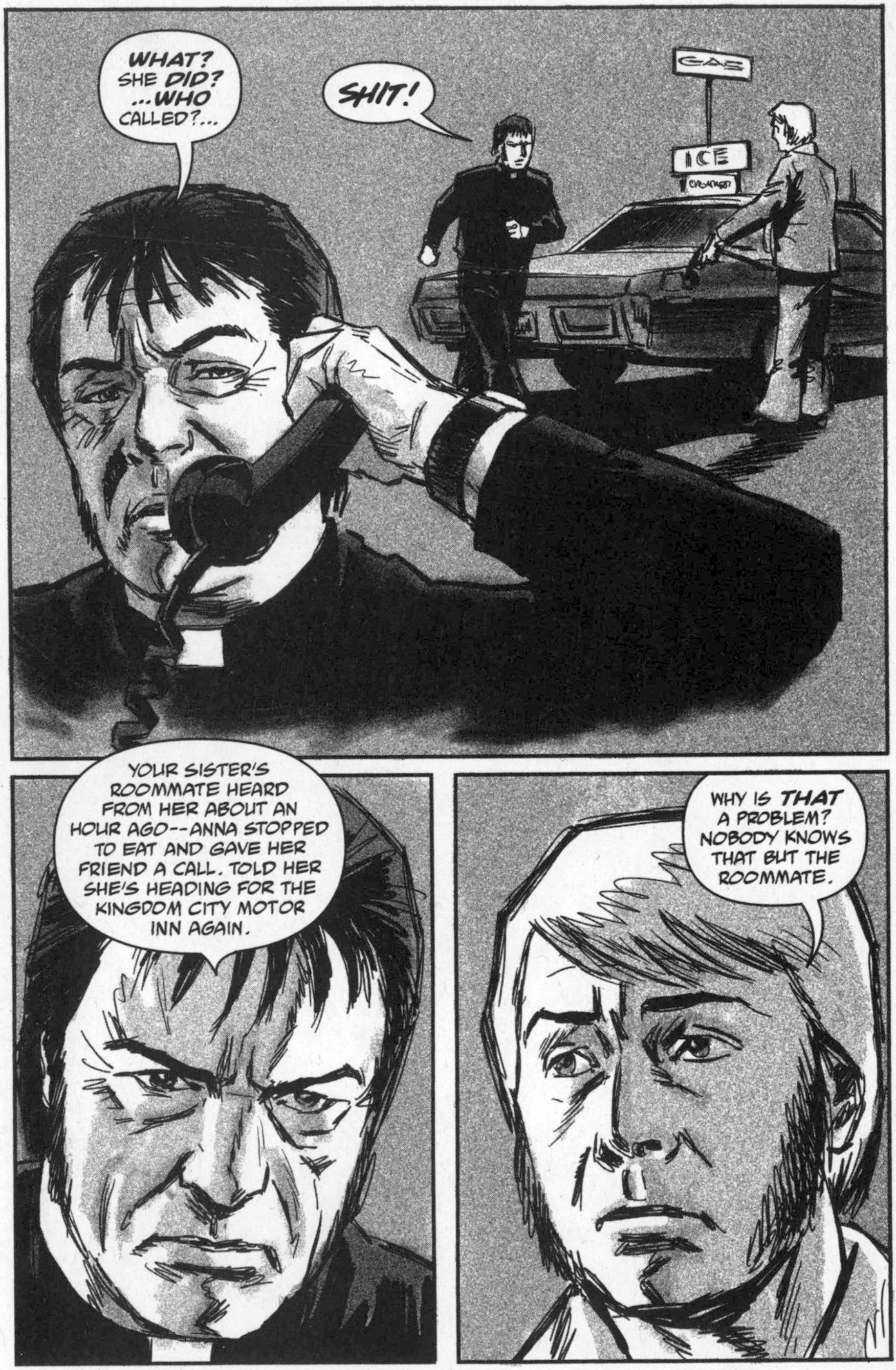
WHAT? SHE DID? ...WHO CALLED?...
SHIT!
GAS
ICE
YOUR SISTER'S ROOMMATE HEARD FROM HER ABOUT AN HOUR AGO--ANNA STOPPED TO EAT AND GAVE HER FRIEND A CALL. TOLD HER SHE'S HEADING FOR THE KINGDOM CITY MOTOR INN AGAIN.
WHY IS THAT A PROBLEM? NOBODY KNOWS THAT BUT THE ROOMMATE.

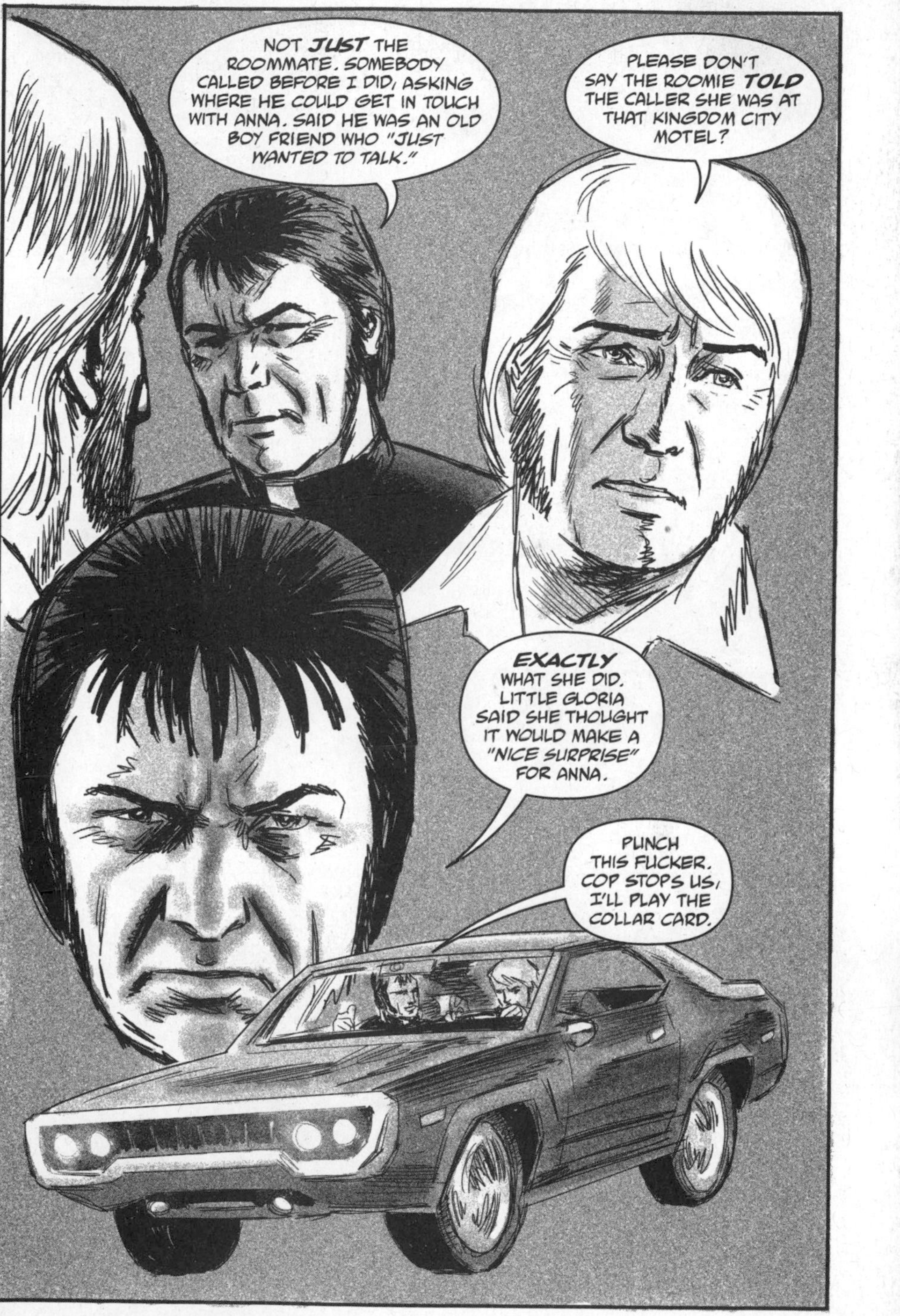
NOT JUST THE ROOMMATE. SOMEBODY CALLED BEFORE I DID, ASKING WHERE HE COULD GET IN TOUCH WITH ANNA. SAID HE WAS AN OLD BOY FRIEND WHO "JUST WANTED TO TALK."
PLEASE DON'T SAY THE ROOMIE TOLD THE CALLER SHE WAS AT THAT KINGDOM CITY MOTEL?
EXACTLY WHAT SHE DID. LITTLE GLORIA SAID SHE THOUGHT IT WOULD MAKE A "NICE SURPRISE" FOR ANNA.
PUNCH THIS FUCKER. COP STOPS US, I'LL PLAY THE COLLAR CARD.

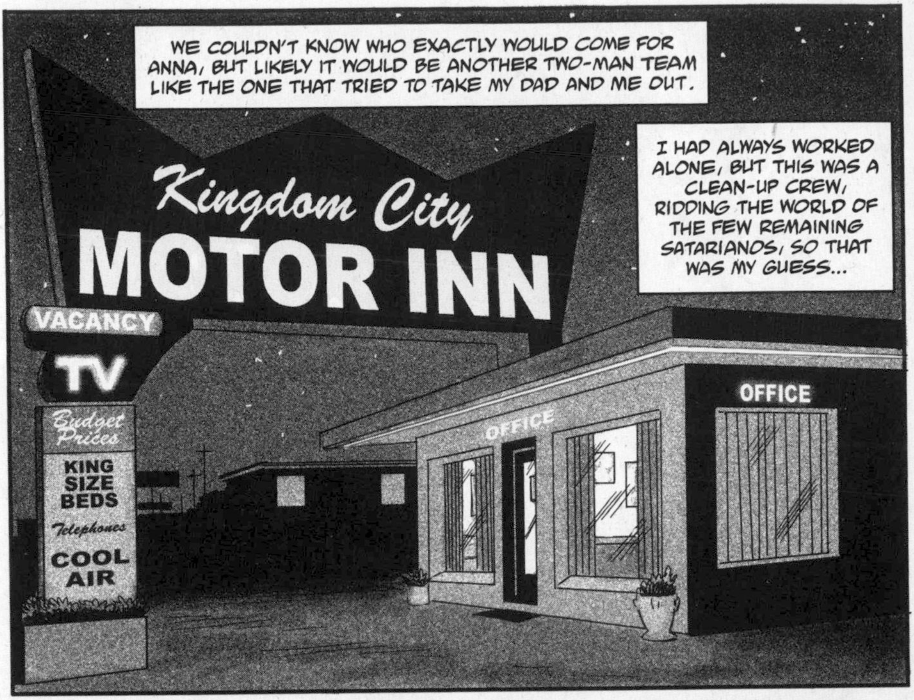
WE COULDN'T KNOW WHO EXACTLY WOULD COME FOR ANNA, BUT LIKELY IT WOULD BE ANOTHER TWO-MAN TEAM LIKE THE ONE THAT TRIED TO TAKE MY DAD AND ME OUT.
I HAD ALWAYS WORKED ALONE, BUT THIS WAS A CLEAN-UP CREW, RIDDING THE WORLD OF THE FEW REMAINING SATARIANOS, SO THAT WAS MY GUESS...
Kingdom City
MOTOR INN
VACANCY
TV
Budget Prices
KING SIZE BEDS
Telephones
COOL AIR
OFFICE
OFFICE

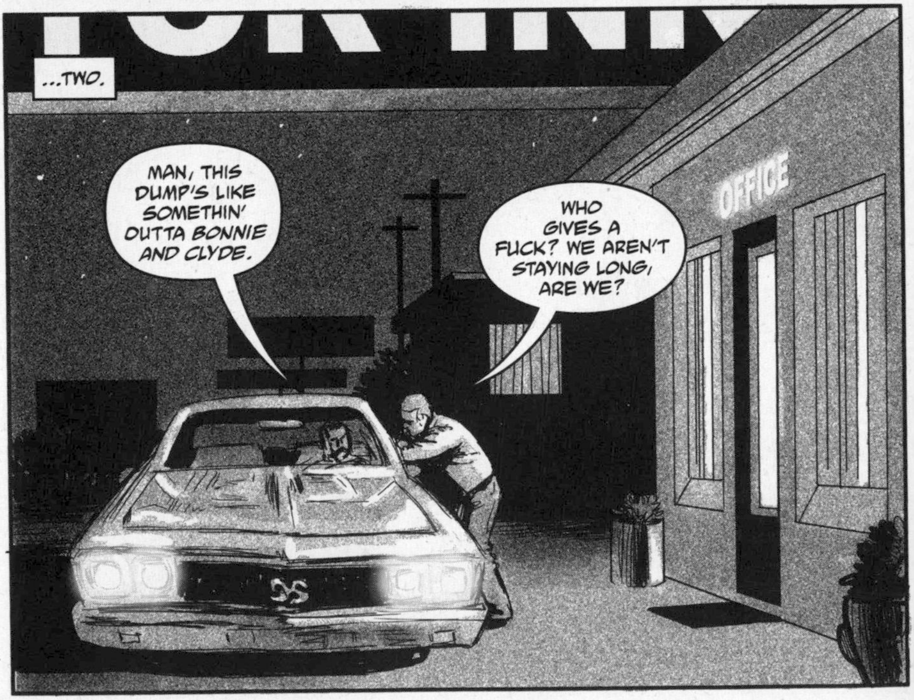
...TWO.
MAN, THIS DUMP'S LIKE SOMETHIN' OUTTA BONNIE AND CLYDE.
WHO GIVES A FUCK? WE AREN'T STAYING LONG, ARE WE?
OFFICE

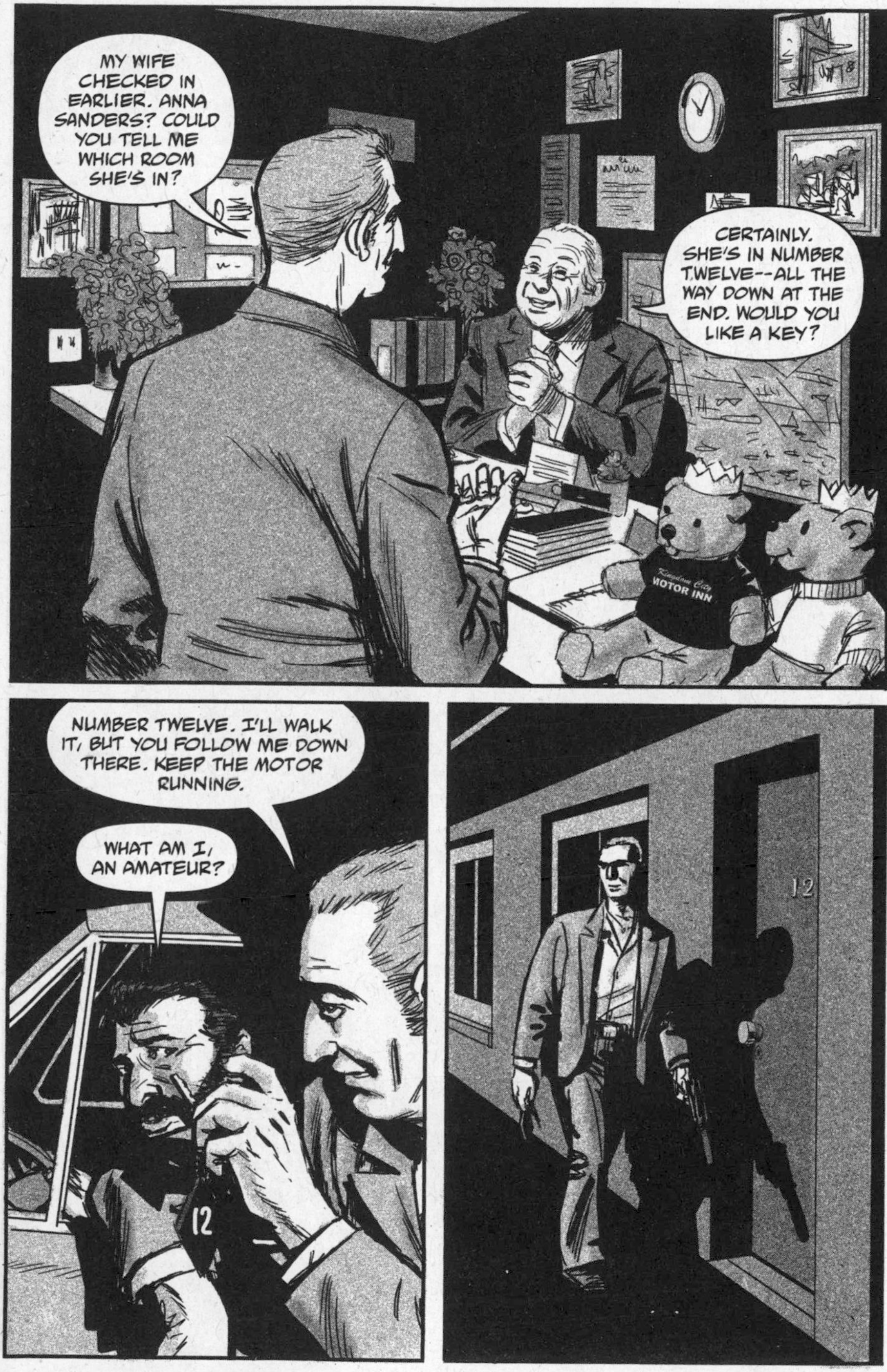
MY WIFE CHECKED IN EARLIER. ANNA SANDERS? COULD YOU TELL ME WHICH ROOM SHE'S IN?
CERTAINLY. SHE'S IN NUMBER TWELVE--ALL THE WAY DOWN AT THE END. WOULD YOU LIKE A KEY?
Kingdom City
MOTOR INN
NUMBER TWELVE. I'LL WALK IT, BUT YOU FOLLOW ME DOWN THERE. KEEP THE MOTOR RUNNING.
WHAT AM I, AN AMATEUR?
12
12

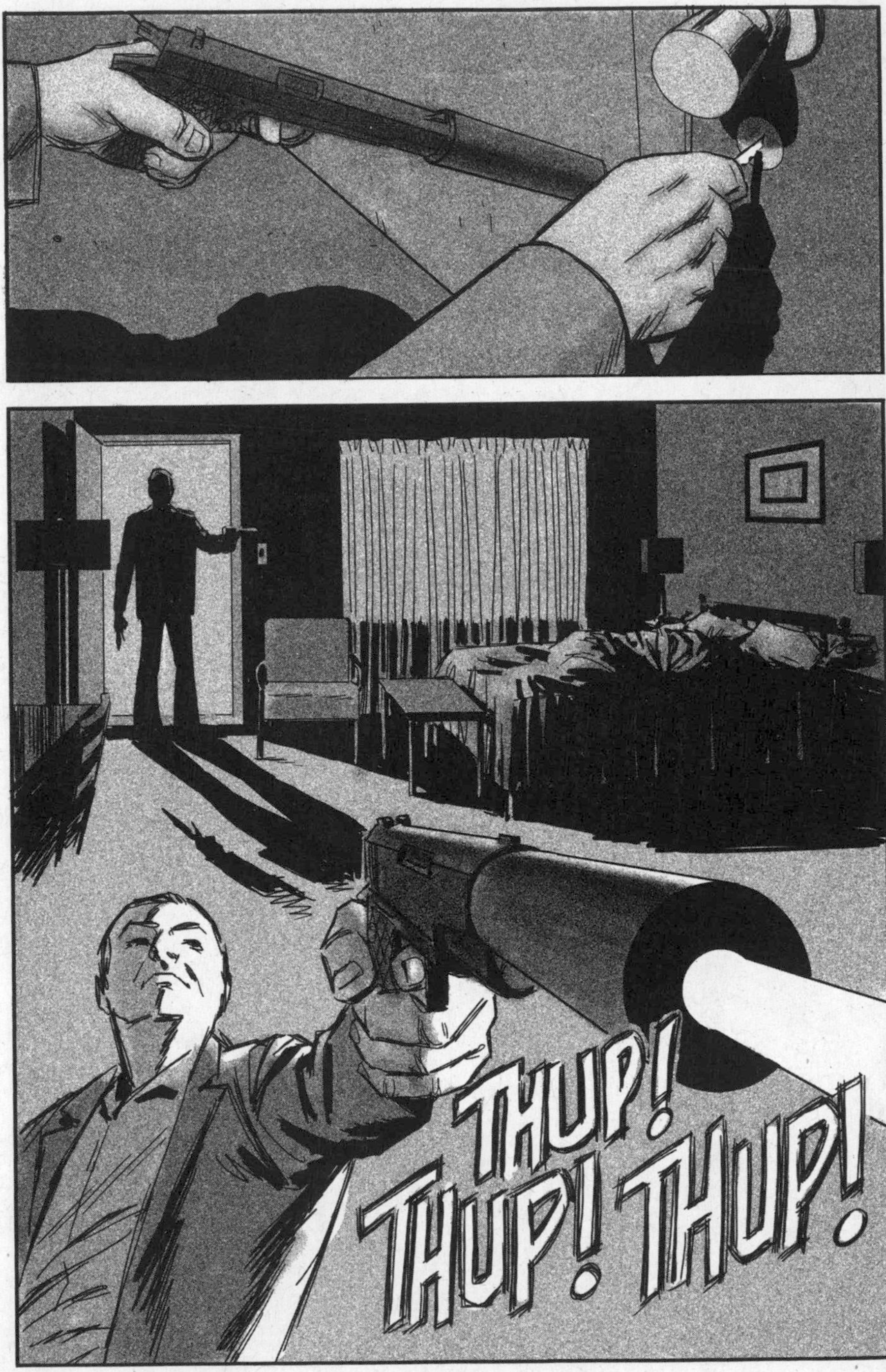
THUP!
THUP! THUP!

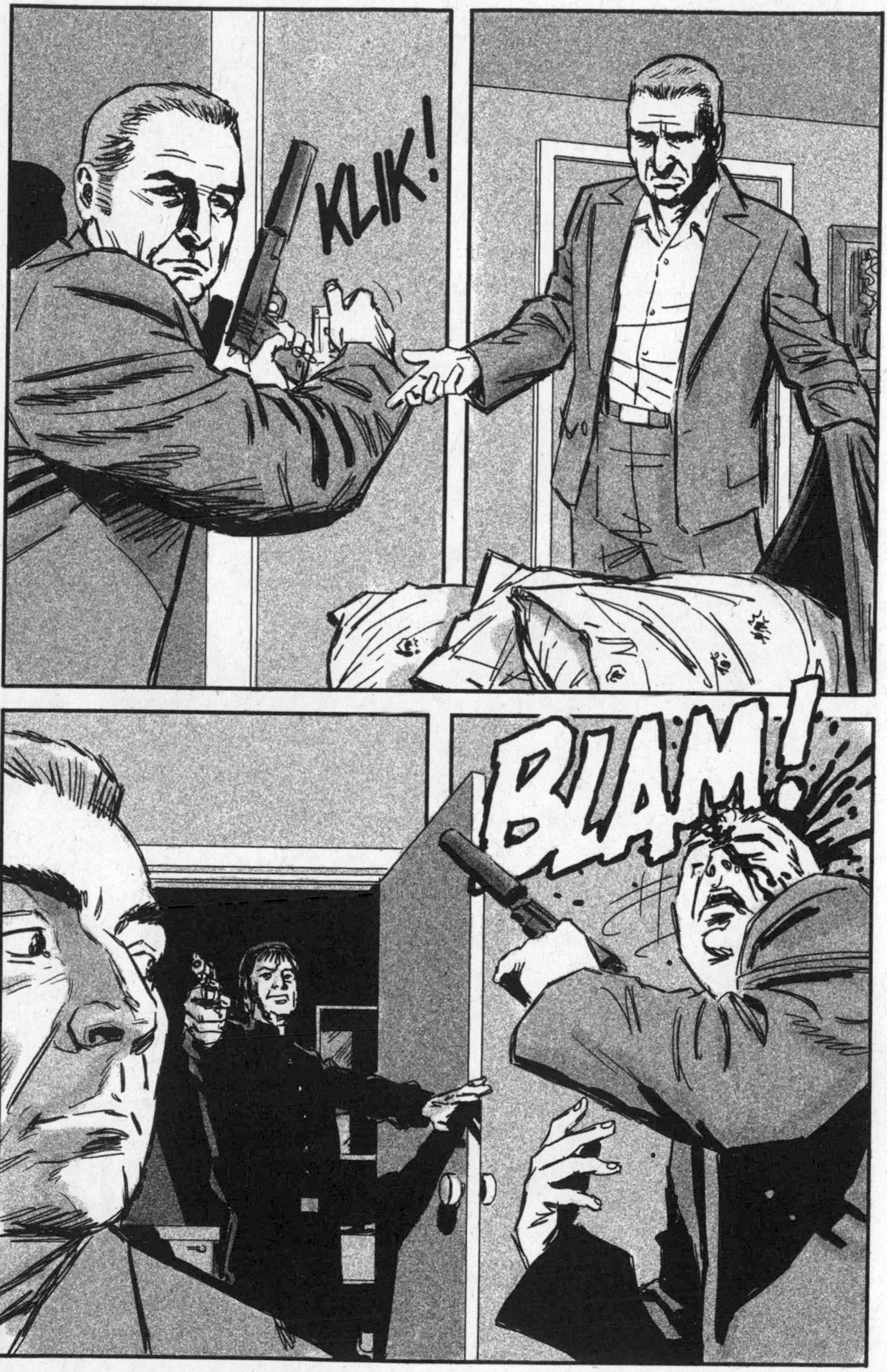
KLIK!
BLAM!

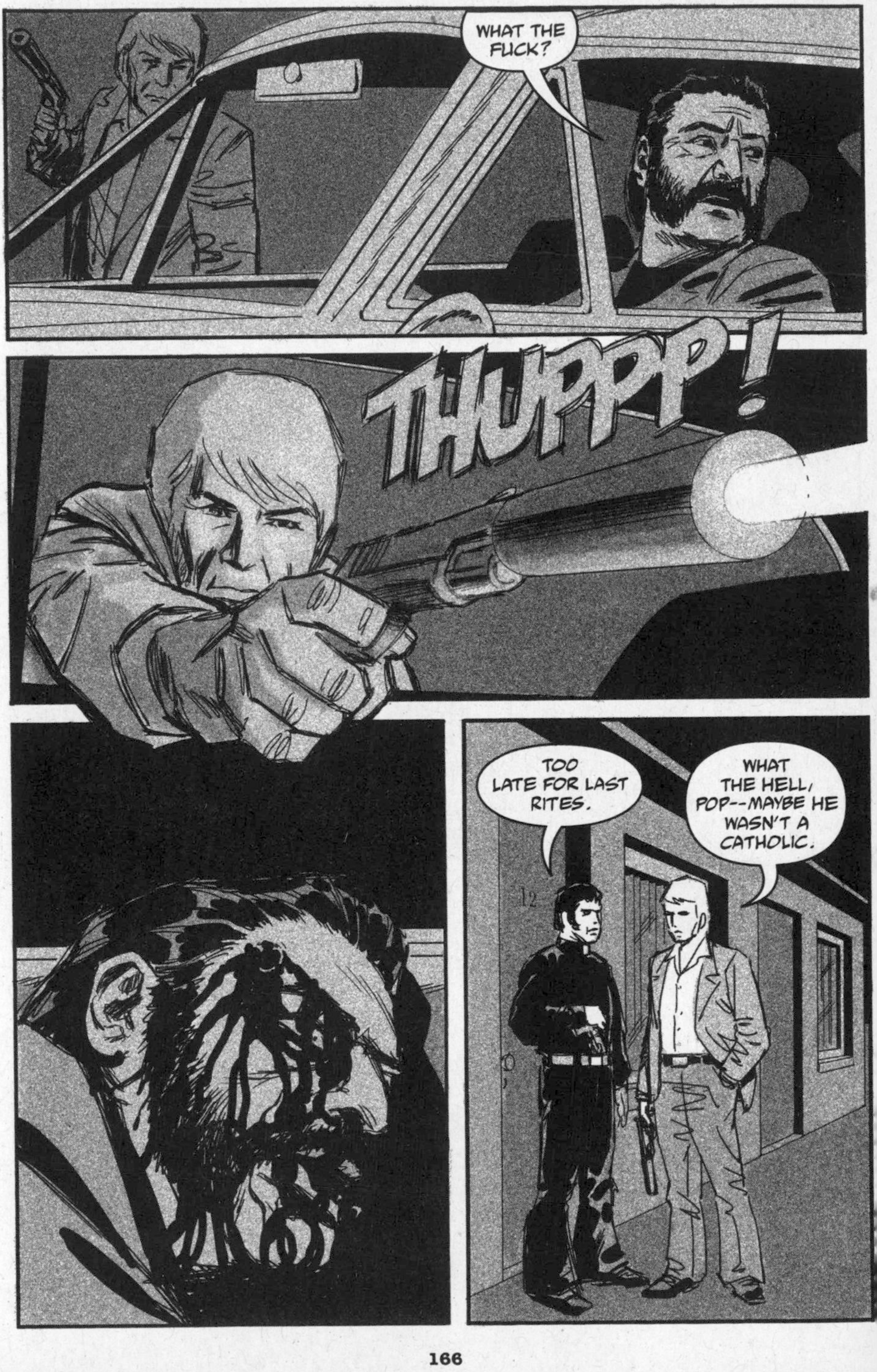
WHAT THE FUCK?
THUPPP!
TOO LATE FOR LAST RITES.
WHAT THE HELL, POP--MAYBE HE WASN'T A CATHOLIC.

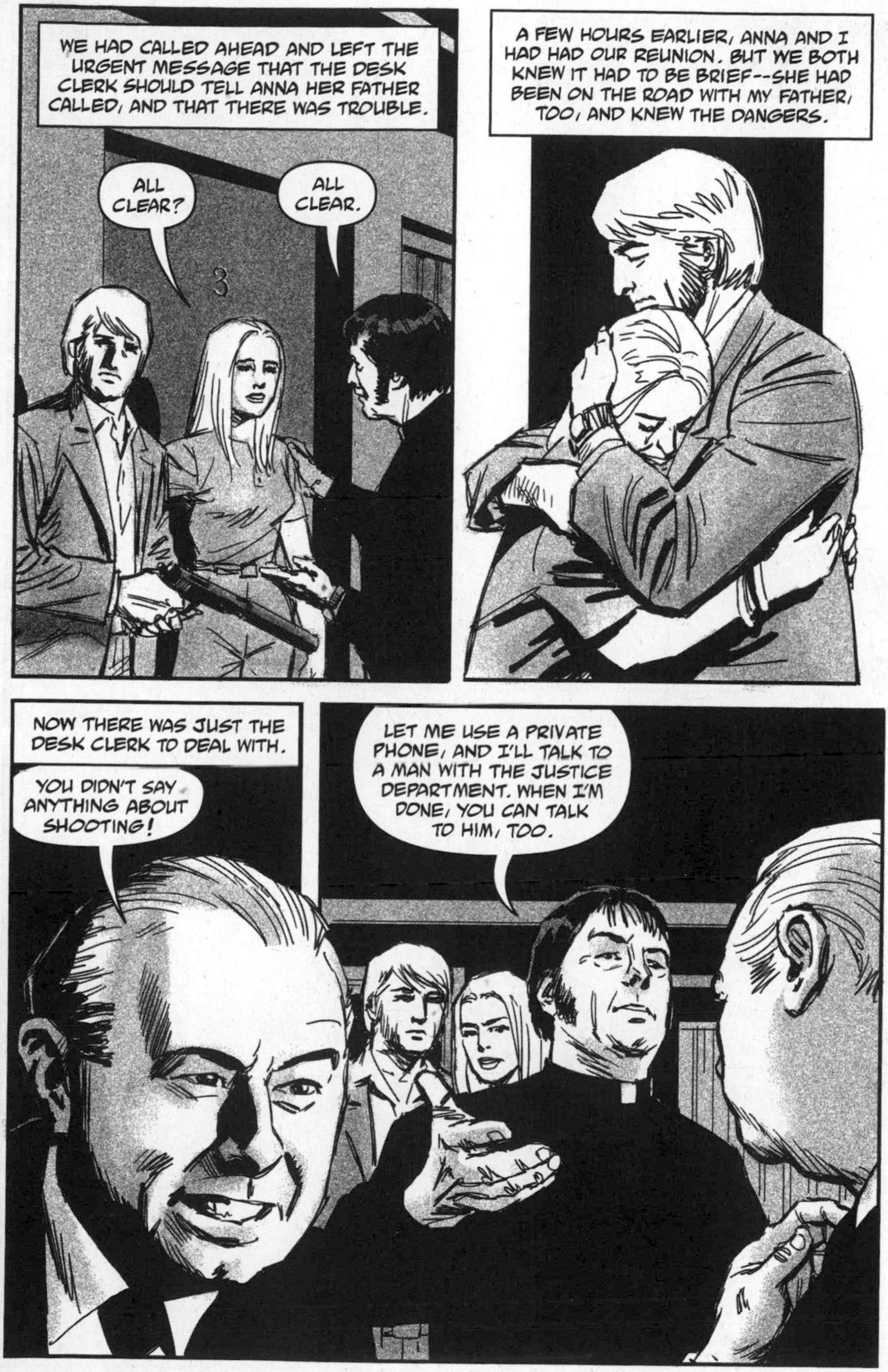
WE HAD CALLED AHEAD AND LEFT THE URGENT MESSAGE THAT THE DESK CLERK SHOULD TELL ANNA HER FATHER CALLED, AND THAT THERE WAS TROUBLE.
ALL CLEAR?
ALL CLEAR.
3
A FEW HOURS EARLIER, ANNA AND I HAD HAD OUR REUNION. BUT WE BOTH KNEW IT HAD TO BE BRIEF--SHE HAD BEEN ON THE ROAD WITH MY FATHER, TOO, AND KNEW THE DANGERS.
NOW THERE WAS JUST THE DESK CLERK TO DEAL WITH.
YOU DIDN'T SAY ANYTHING ABOUT SHOOTING!
LET ME USE A PRIVATE PHONE, AND I'LL TALK TO A MAN WITH THE JUSTICE DEPARTMENT. WHEN I'M DONE, YOU CAN TALK TO HIM, TOO.

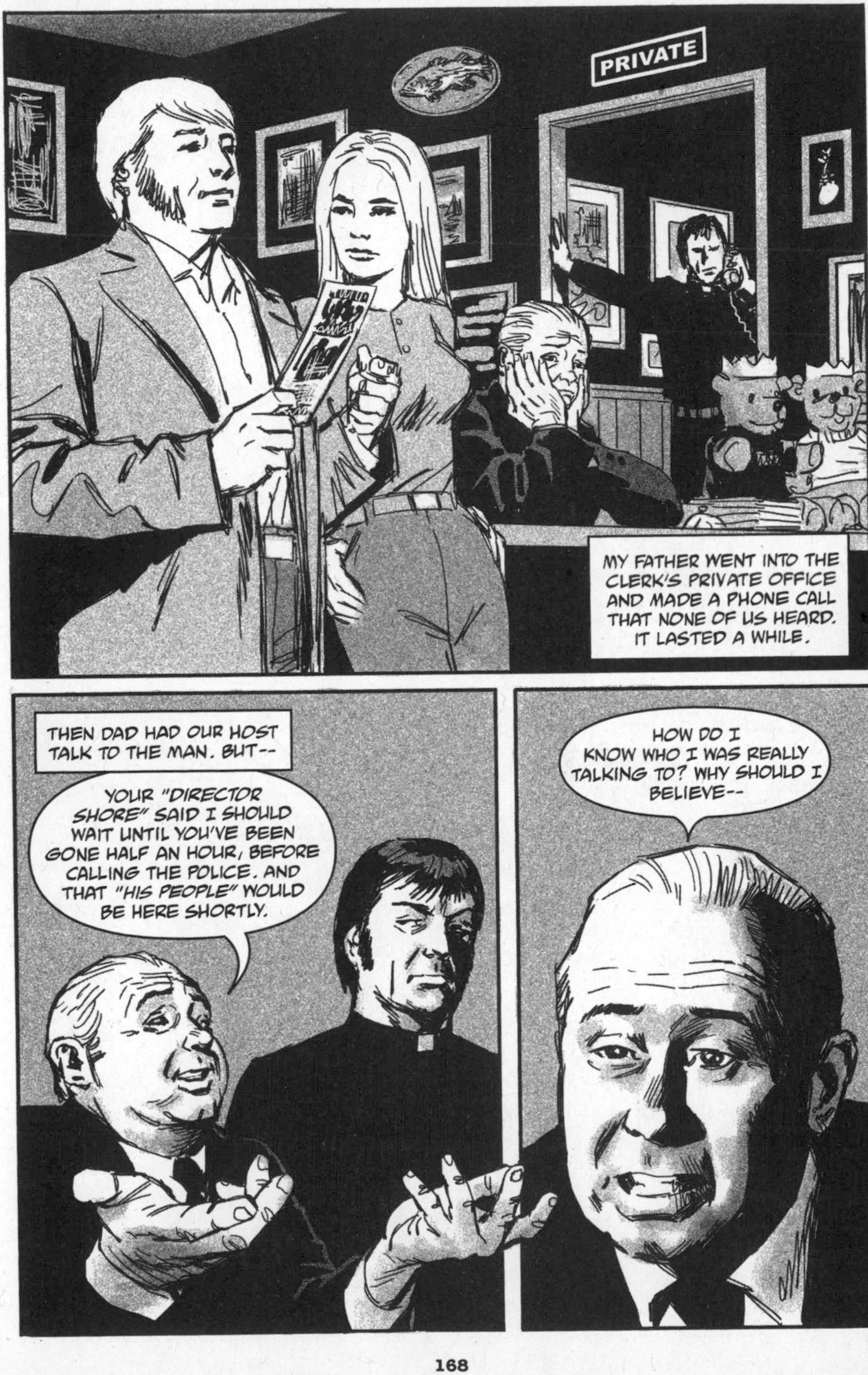
PRIVATE
MY FATHER WENT INTO THE CLERK'S PRIVATE OFFICE AND MADE A PHONE CALL THAT NONE OF US HEARD. IT LASTED A WHILE.
THEN DAD HAD OUR HOST TALK TO THE MAN. BUT--
YOUR "DIRECTOR SHORE" SAID I SHOULD WAIT UNTIL YOU'VE BEEN GONE HALF AN HOUR, BEFORE CALLING THE POLICE. AND THAT "HIS PEOPLE" WOULD BE HERE SHORTLY.
HOW DO I KNOW WHO I WAS REALLY TALKING TO? WHY SHOULD I BELIEVE--

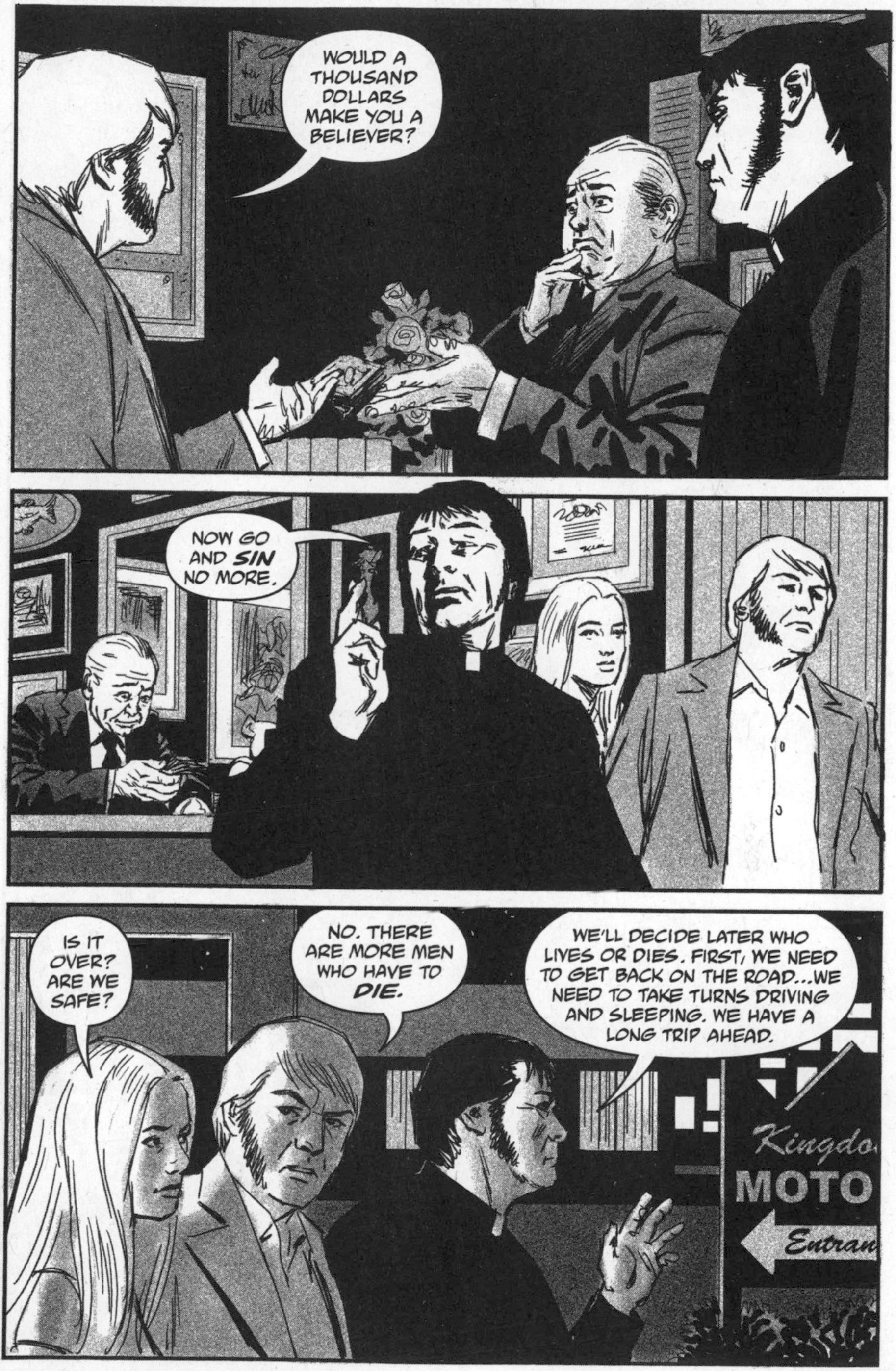
WOULD A THOUSAND DOLLARS MAKE YOU A BELIEVER?
NOW GO AND **SIN** NO MORE.
IS IT OVER? ARE WE SAFE?
NO. THERE ARE MORE MEN WHO HAVE TO **DIE.**
WE'LL DECIDE LATER WHO LIVES OR DIES. FIRST, WE NEED TO GET BACK ON THE ROAD...WE NEED TO TAKE TURNS DRIVING AND SLEEPING. WE HAVE A LONG TRIP AHEAD.
MOTO

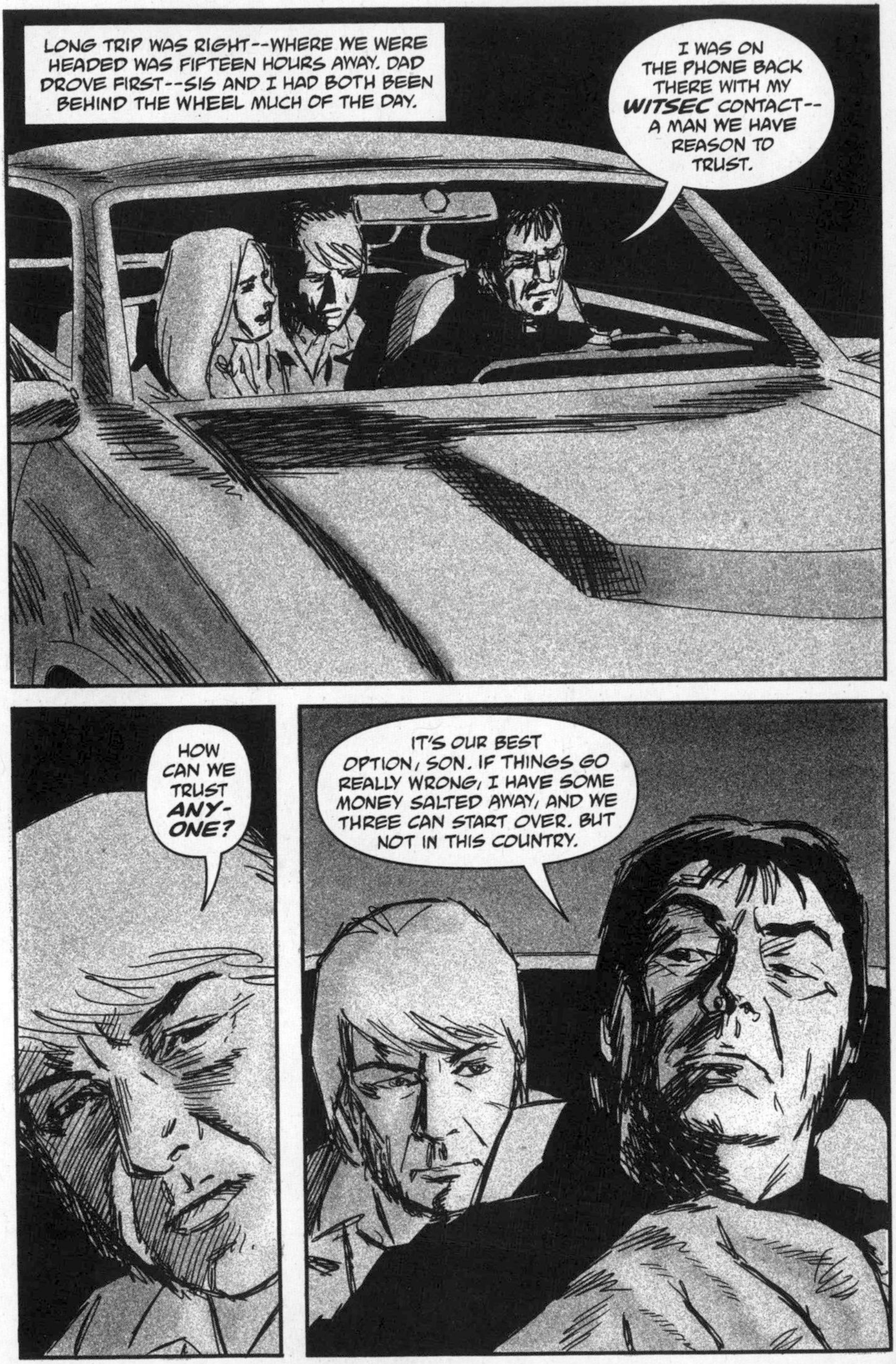
LONG TRIP WAS RIGHT--WHERE WE WERE HEADED WAS FIFTEEN HOURS AWAY. DAD DROVE FIRST--SIS AND I HAD BOTH BEEN BEHIND THE WHEEL MUCH OF THE DAY.
I WAS ON THE PHONE BACK THERE WITH MY WITSEC CONTACT--A MAN WE HAVE REASON TO TRUST.
HOW CAN WE TRUST ANY-ONE?
IT'S OUR BEST OPTION, SON. IF THINGS GO REALLY WRONG, I HAVE SOME MONEY SALTED AWAY, AND WE THREE CAN START OVER. BUT NOT IN THIS COUNTRY.

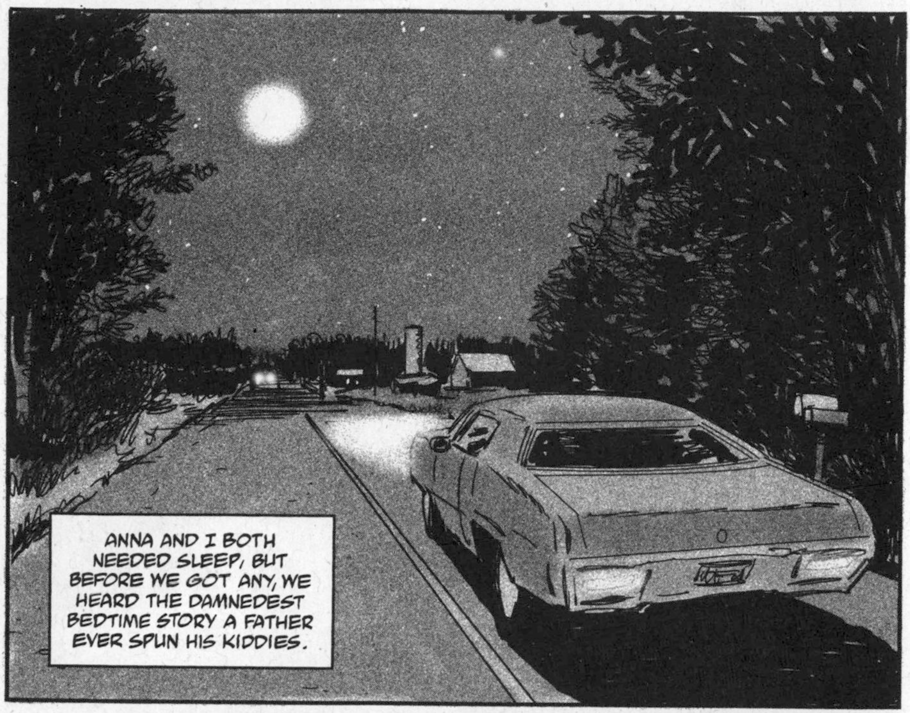
ANNA AND I BOTH NEEDED SLEEP, BUT BEFORE WE GOT ANY, WE HEARD THE DAMNEDEST BEDTIME STORY A FATHER EVER SPUN HIS KIDDIES.

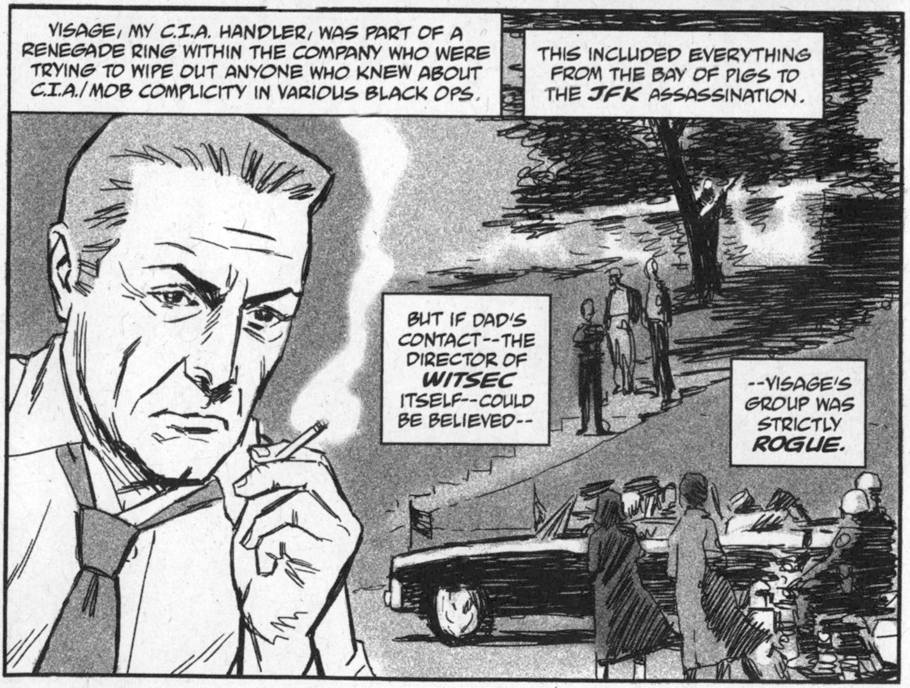
VISAGE, MY C.I.A. HANDLER, WAS PART OF A RENEGADE RING WITHIN THE COMPANY WHO WERE TRYING TO WIPE OUT ANYONE WHO KNEW ABOUT C.I.A./MOB COMPLICITY IN VARIOUS BLACK OPS.
THIS INCLUDED EVERYTHING FROM THE BAY OF PIGS TO THE JFK ASSASSINATION.
BUT IF DAD'S CONTACT--THE DIRECTOR OF WITSEC ITSELF--COULD BE BELIEVED--
--VISAGE'S GROUP WAS STRICTLY ROGUE.

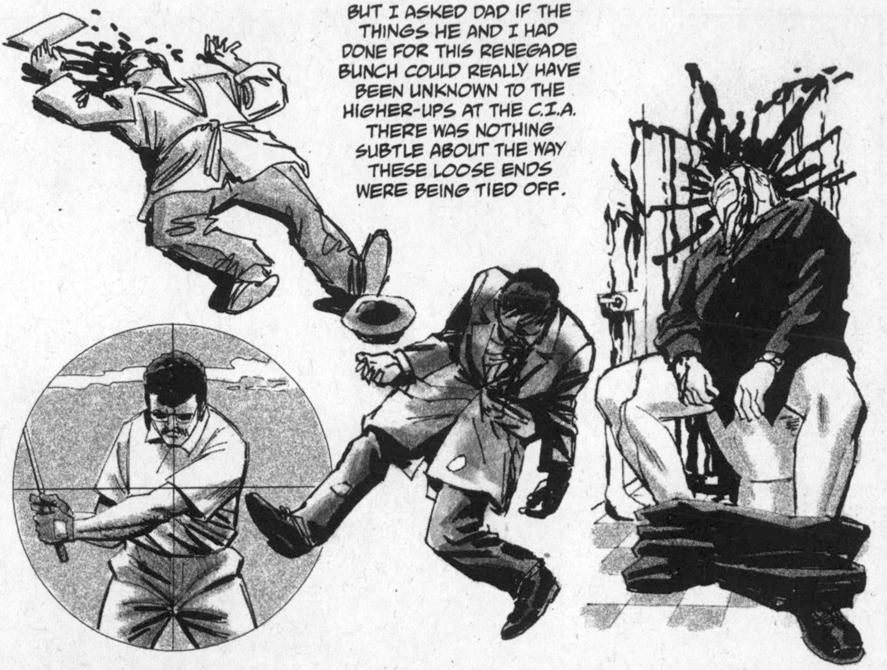
BUT I ASKED DAD IF THE THINGS HE AND I HAD DONE FOR THIS RENEGADE BUNCH COULD REALLY HAVE BEEN UNKNOWN TO THE HIGHER-UPS AT THE C.I.A. THERE WAS NOTHING SUBTLE ABOUT THE WAY THESE LOOSE ENDS WERE BEING TIED OFF.

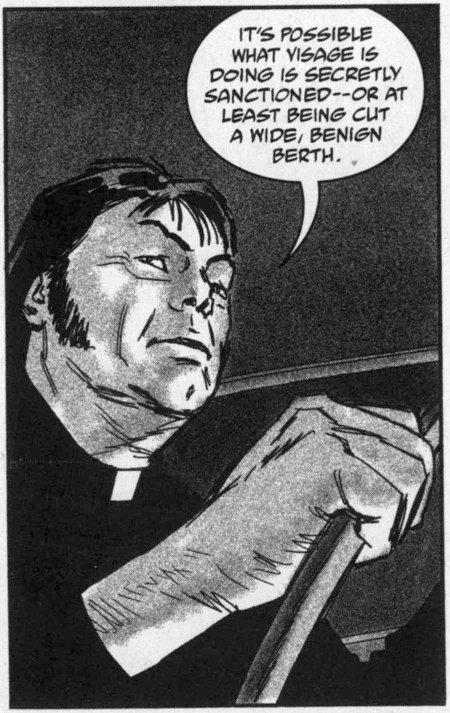
IT'S POSSIBLE WHAT VISAGE IS DOING IS SECRETLY SANCTIONED--OR AT LEAST BEING CUT A WIDE, BENIGN BERTH.

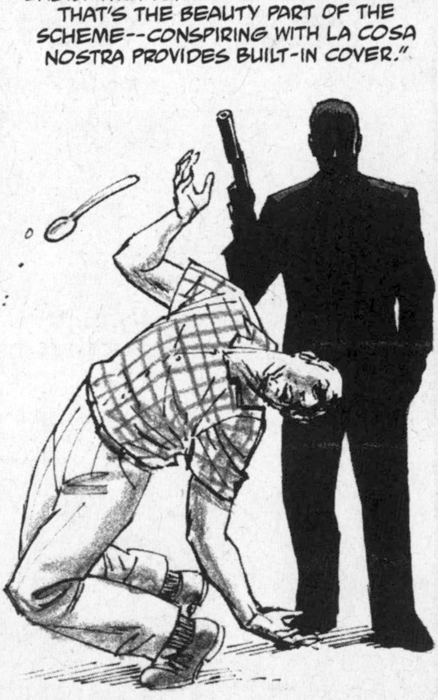
"BUT THE JOBS WE DID, SON--THEY ARE EASILY WRITTEN OFF AS MOB KILLINGS. THAT'S THE BEAUTY PART OF THE SCHEME--CONSPIRING WITH LA COSA NOSTRA PROVIDES BUILT-IN COVER."

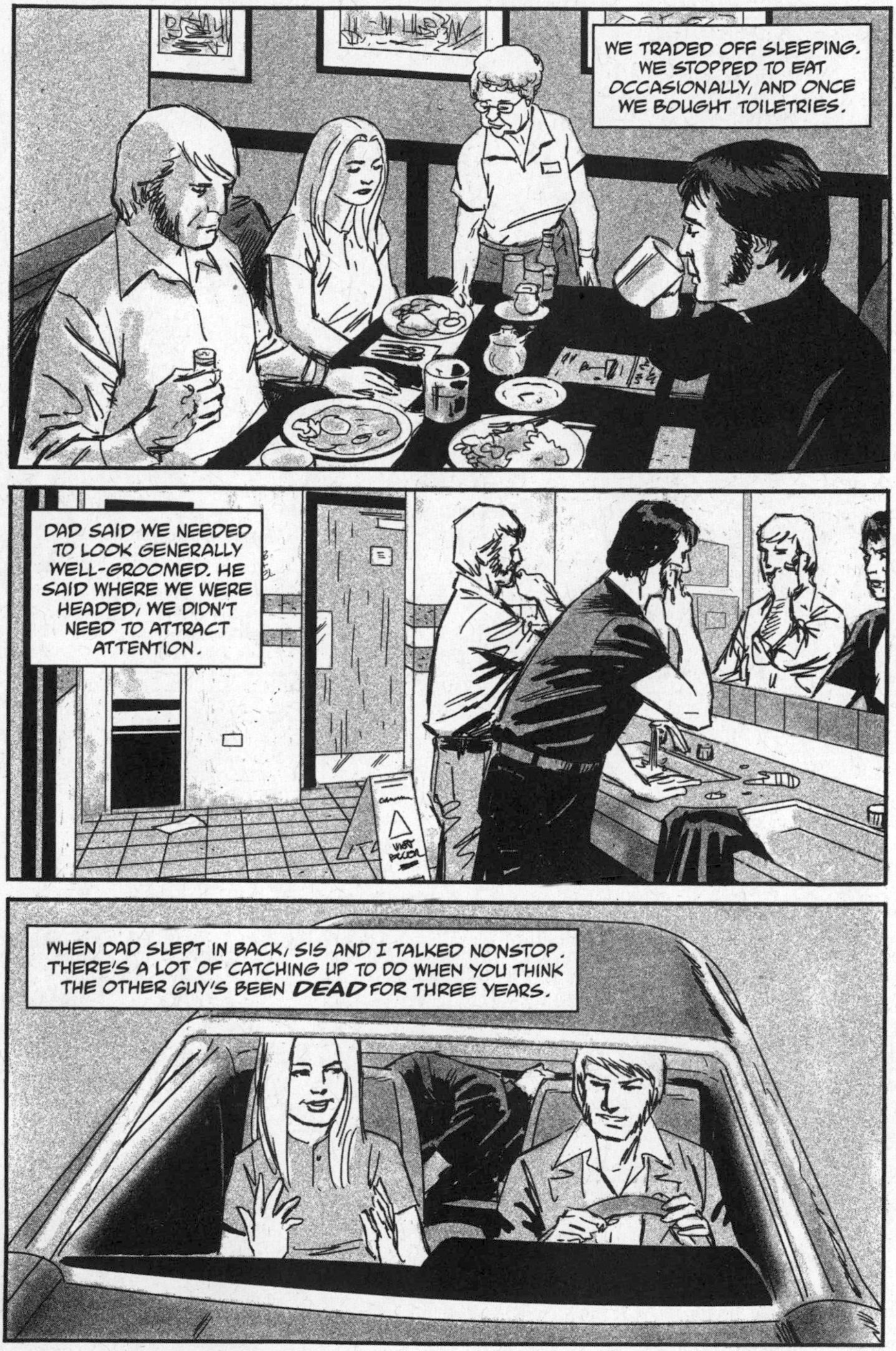
WE TRADED OFF SLEEPING. WE STOPPED TO EAT OCCASIONALLY, AND ONCE WE BOUGHT TOILETRIES.
DAD SAID WE NEEDED TO LOOK GENERALLY WELL-GROOMED. HE SAID WHERE WE WERE HEADED, WE DIDN'T NEED TO ATTRACT ATTENTION.
WHEN DAD SLEPT IN BACK, SIS AND I TALKED NONSTOP. THERE'S A LOT OF CATCHING UP TO DO WHEN YOU THINK THE OTHER GUY'S BEEN **DEAD** FOR THREE YEARS.

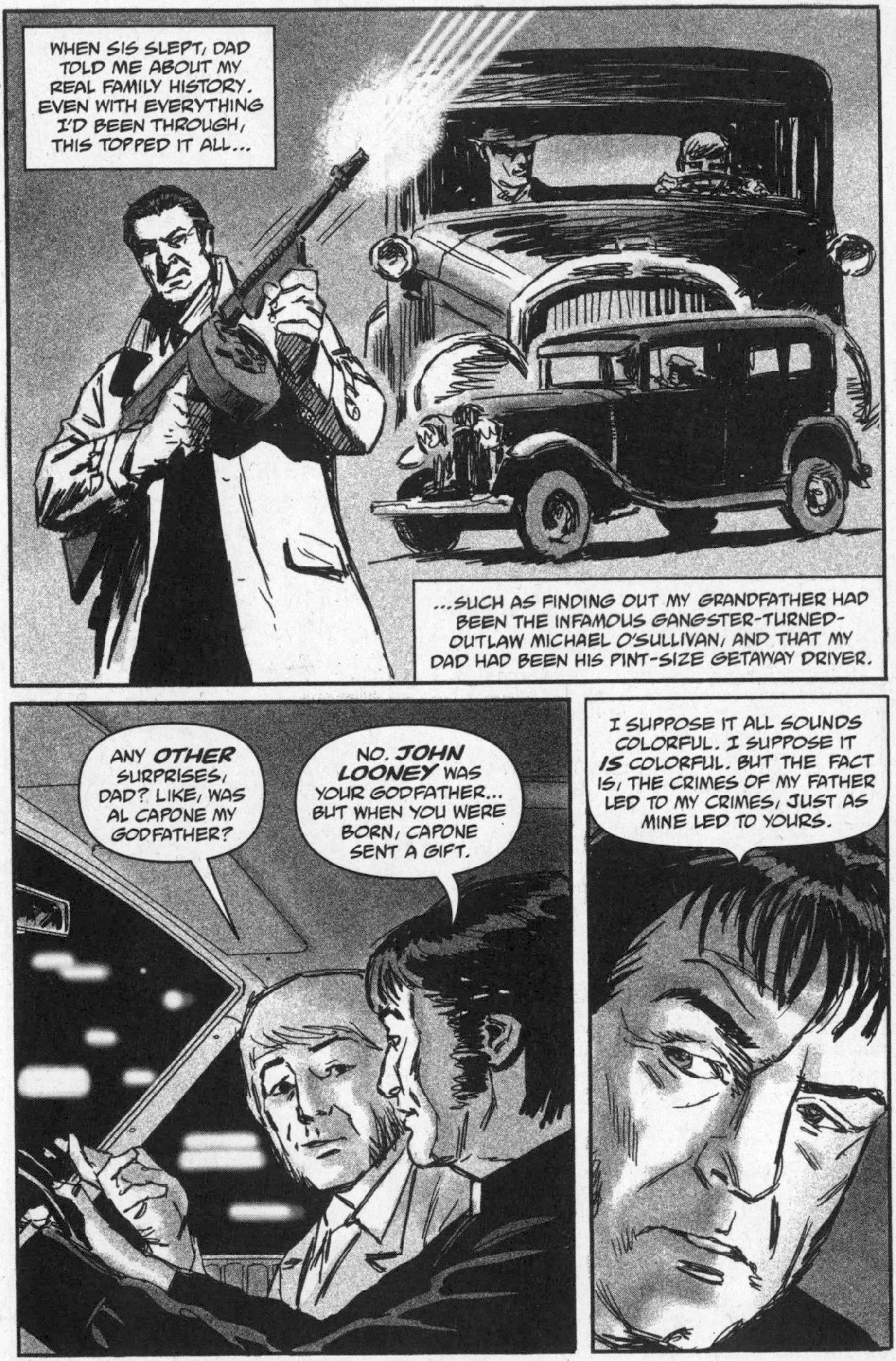
WHEN SIS SLEPT, DAD TOLD ME ABOUT MY REAL FAMILY HISTORY. EVEN WITH EVERYTHING I'D BEEN THROUGH, THIS TOPPED IT ALL...
...SUCH AS FINDING OUT MY GRANDFATHER HAD BEEN THE INFAMOUS GANGSTER-TURNED-OUTLAW MICHAEL O'SULLIVAN, AND THAT MY DAD HAD BEEN HIS PINT-SIZE GETAWAY DRIVER.
ANY **OTHER** SURPRISES, DAD? LIKE, WAS AL CAPONE MY GODFATHER?
NO. **JOHN LOONEY** WAS YOUR GODFATHER... BUT WHEN YOU WERE BORN, CAPONE SENT A GIFT.
I SUPPOSE IT ALL SOUNDS COLORFUL. I SUPPOSE IT **IS** COLORFUL. BUT THE FACT IS, THE CRIMES OF MY FATHER LED TO MY CRIMES, JUST AS MINE LED TO YOURS.

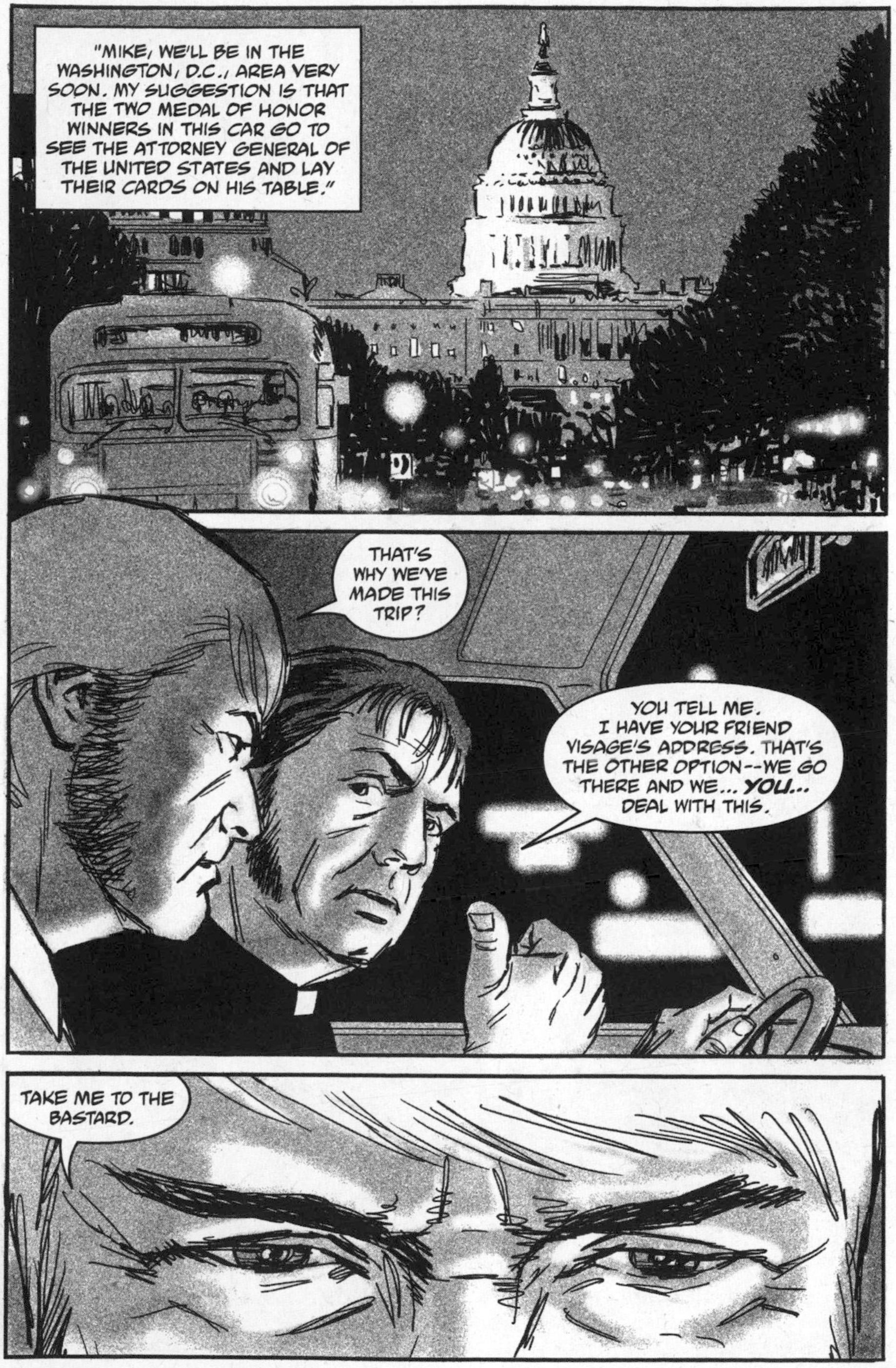
"MIKE, WE'LL BE IN THE WASHINGTON, D.C., AREA VERY SOON. MY SUGGESTION IS THAT THE TWO MEDAL OF HONOR WINNERS IN THIS CAR GO TO SEE THE ATTORNEY GENERAL OF THE UNITED STATES AND LAY THEIR CARDS ON HIS TABLE."
THAT'S WHY WE'VE MADE THIS TRIP?
YOU TELL ME. I HAVE YOUR FRIEND VISAGE'S ADDRESS. THAT'S THE OTHER OPTION--WE GO THERE AND WE... YOU... DEAL WITH THIS.
TAKE ME TO THE BASTARD.

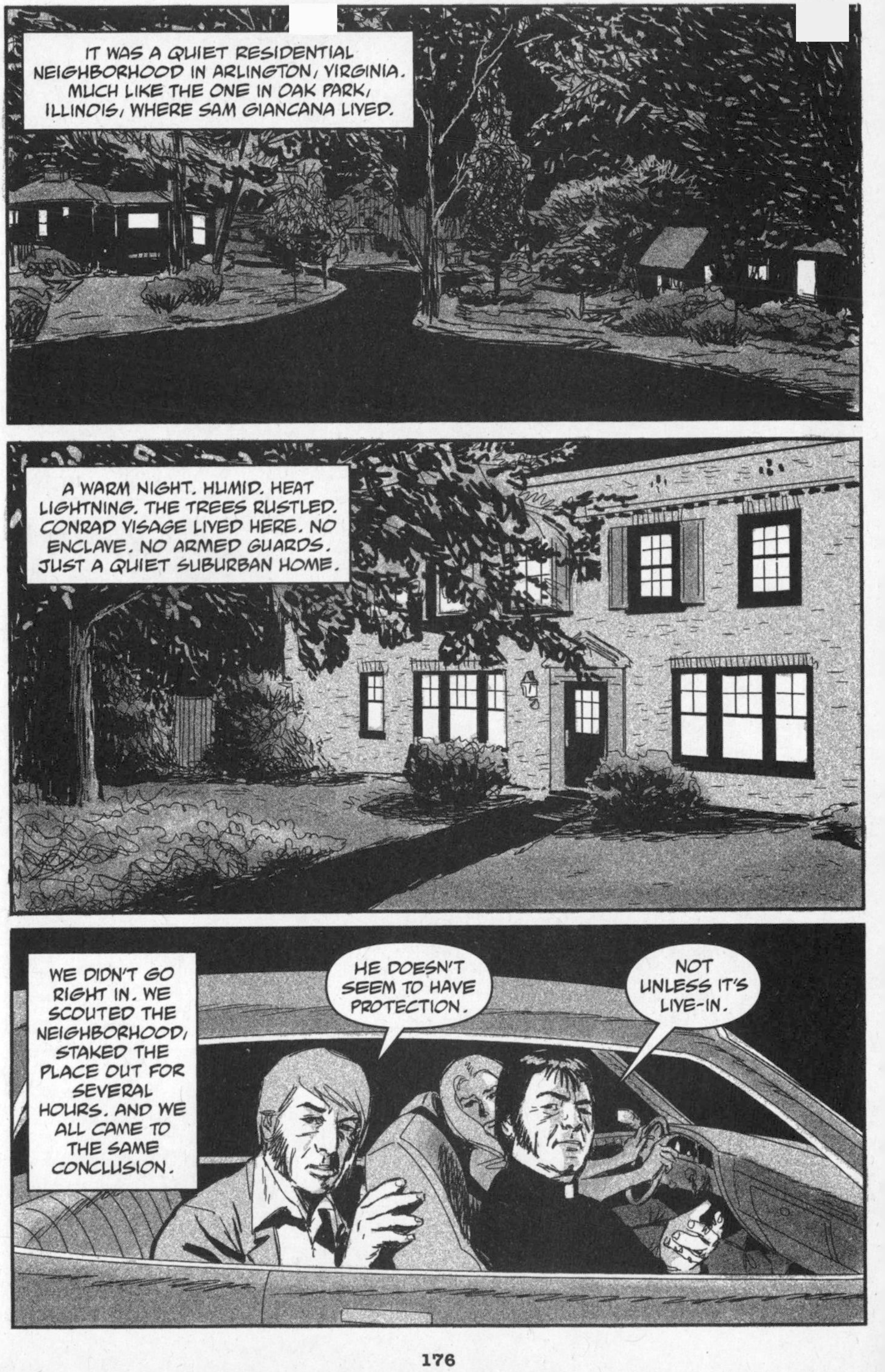
IT WAS A QUIET RESIDENTIAL NEIGHBORHOOD IN ARLINGTON, VIRGINIA. MUCH LIKE THE ONE IN OAK PARK, ILLINOIS, WHERE SAM GIANCANA LIVED.
A WARM NIGHT. HUMID. HEAT LIGHTNING. THE TREES RUSTLED. CONRAD VISAGE LIVED HERE. NO ENCLAVE. NO ARMED GUARDS. JUST A QUIET SUBURBAN HOME.
WE DIDN'T GO RIGHT IN. WE SCOUTED THE NEIGHBORHOOD, STAKED THE PLACE OUT FOR SEVERAL HOURS. AND WE ALL CAME TO THE SAME CONCLUSION.
HE DOESN'T SEEM TO HAVE PROTECTION.
NOT UNLESS IT'S LIVE-IN.

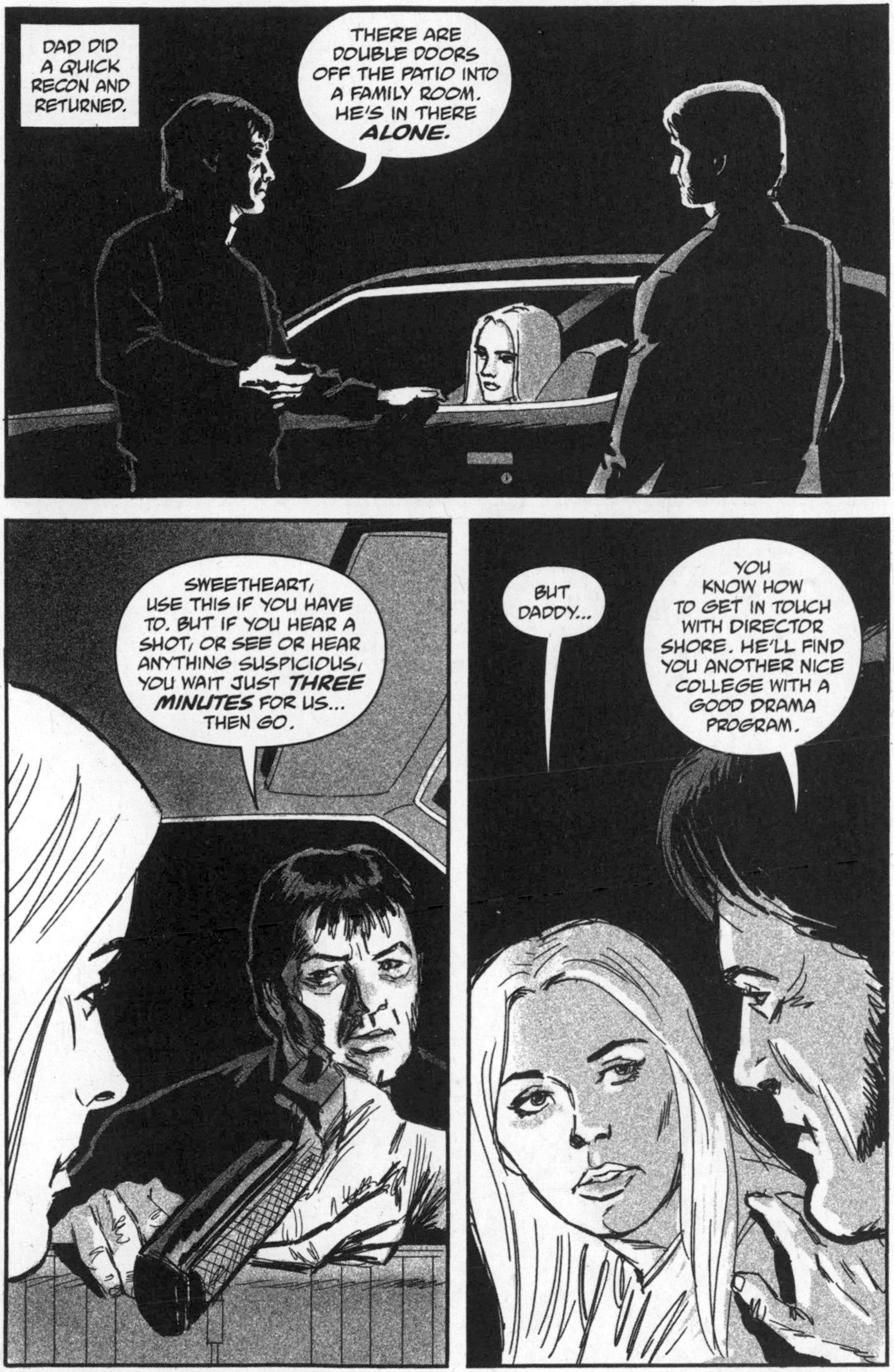
DAD DID A QUICK RECON AND RETURNED.
THERE ARE DOUBLE DOORS OFF THE PATIO INTO A FAMILY ROOM. HE'S IN THERE ***ALONE.***
SWEETHEART, USE THIS IF YOU HAVE TO. BUT IF YOU HEAR A SHOT, OR SEE OR HEAR ANYTHING SUSPICIOUS, YOU WAIT JUST ***THREE MINUTES*** FOR US... THEN GO.
BUT DADDY...
YOU KNOW HOW TO GET IN TOUCH WITH DIRECTOR SHORE. HE'LL FIND YOU ANOTHER NICE COLLEGE WITH A GOOD DRAMA PROGRAM.

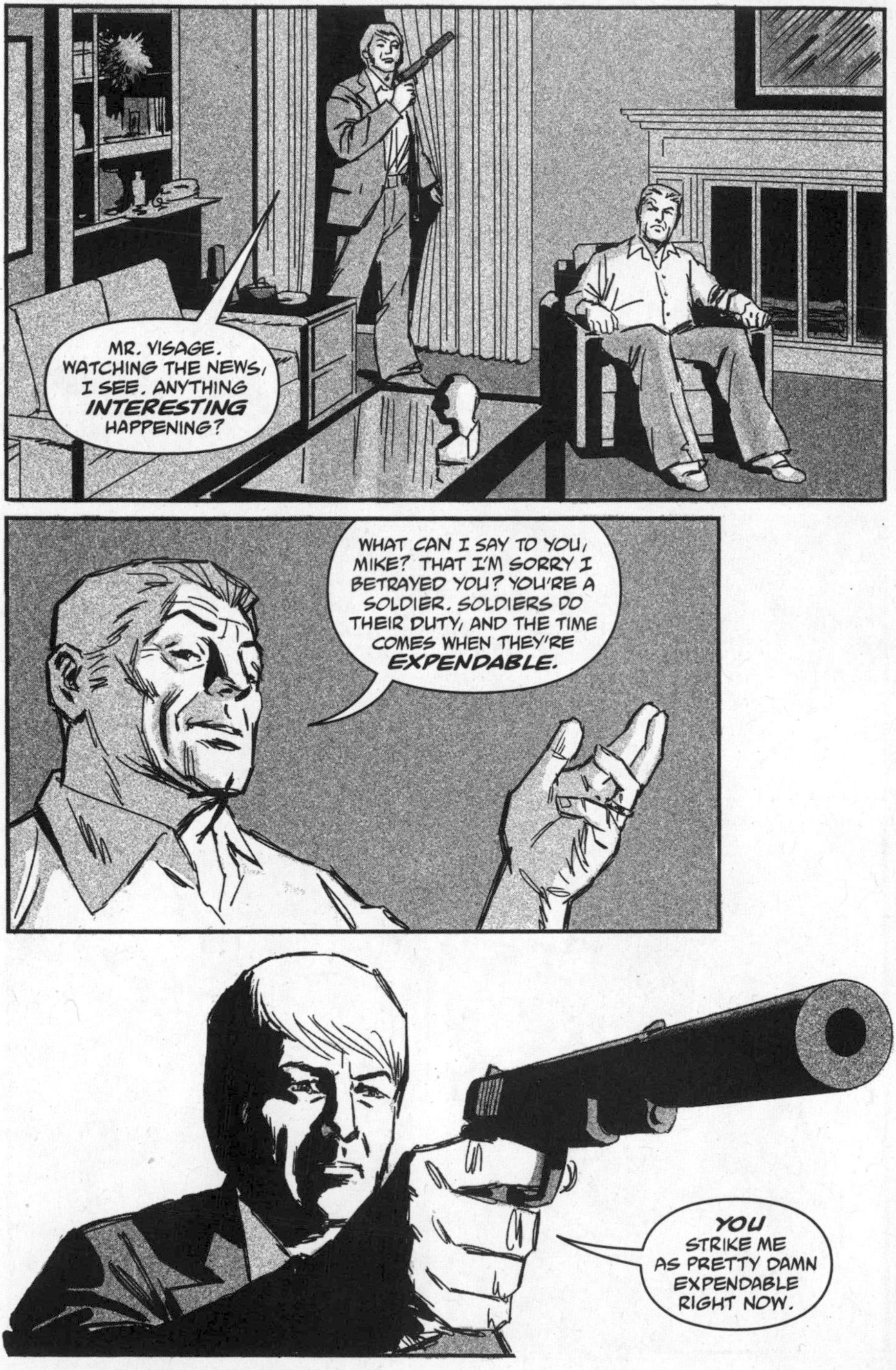
MR. VISAGE. WATCHING THE NEWS, I SEE. ANYTHING INTERESTING HAPPENING?
WHAT CAN I SAY TO YOU, MIKE? THAT I'M SORRY I BETRAYED YOU? YOU'RE A SOLDIER. SOLDIERS DO THEIR DUTY, AND THE TIME COMES WHEN THEY'RE EXPENDABLE.
YOU STRIKE ME AS PRETTY DAMN EXPENDABLE RIGHT NOW.

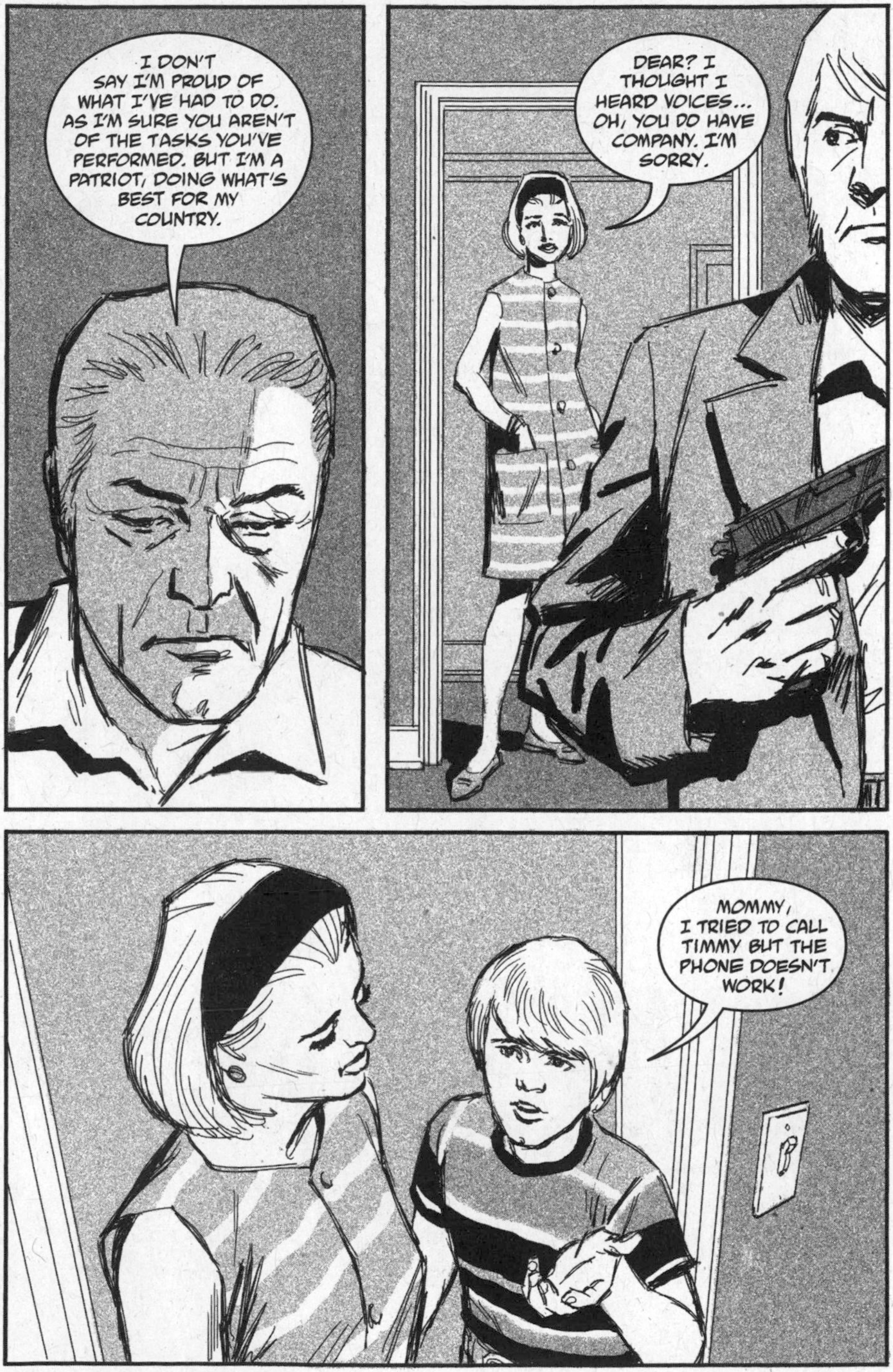
I DON'T SAY I'M PROUD OF WHAT I'VE HAD TO DO. AS I'M SURE YOU AREN'T OF THE TASKS YOU'VE PERFORMED. BUT I'M A PATRIOT, DOING WHAT'S BEST FOR MY COUNTRY.
DEAR? I THOUGHT I HEARD VOICES... OH, YOU DO HAVE COMPANY. I'M SORRY.
MOMMY, I TRIED TO CALL TIMMY BUT THE PHONE DOESN'T WORK!

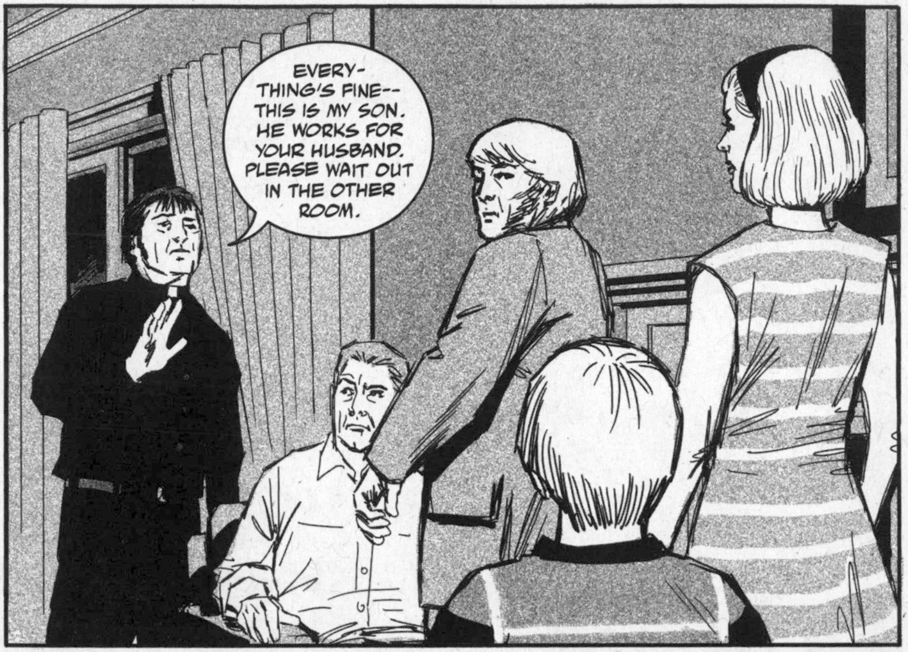
EVERY-THING'S FINE--THIS IS MY SON. HE WORKS FOR YOUR HUSBAND. PLEASE WAIT OUT IN THE OTHER ROOM.

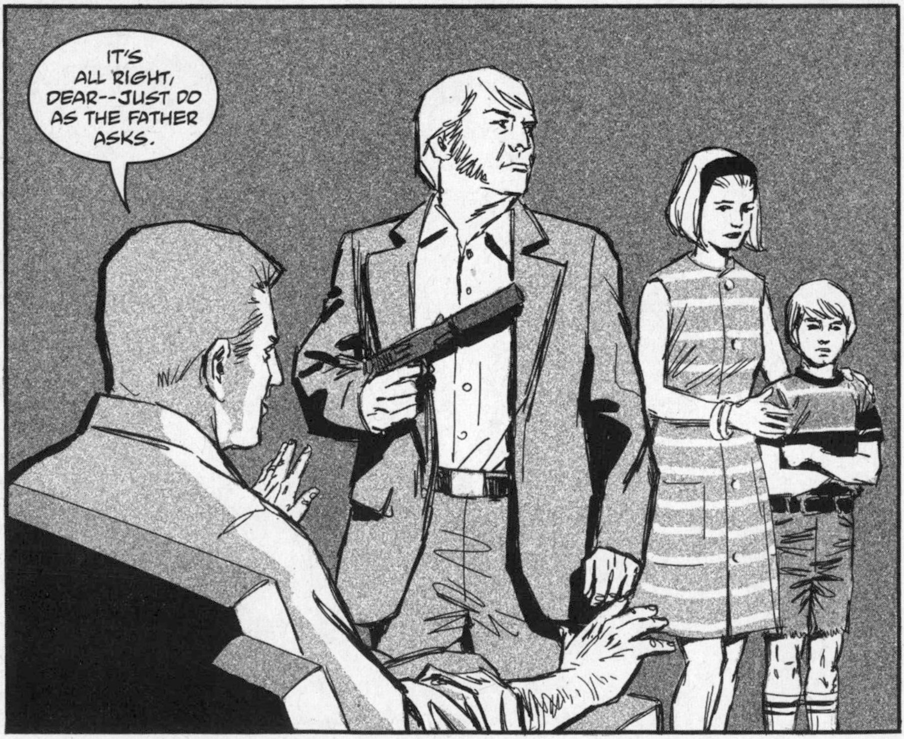
IT'S ALL RIGHT, DEAR--JUST DO AS THE FATHER ASKS.

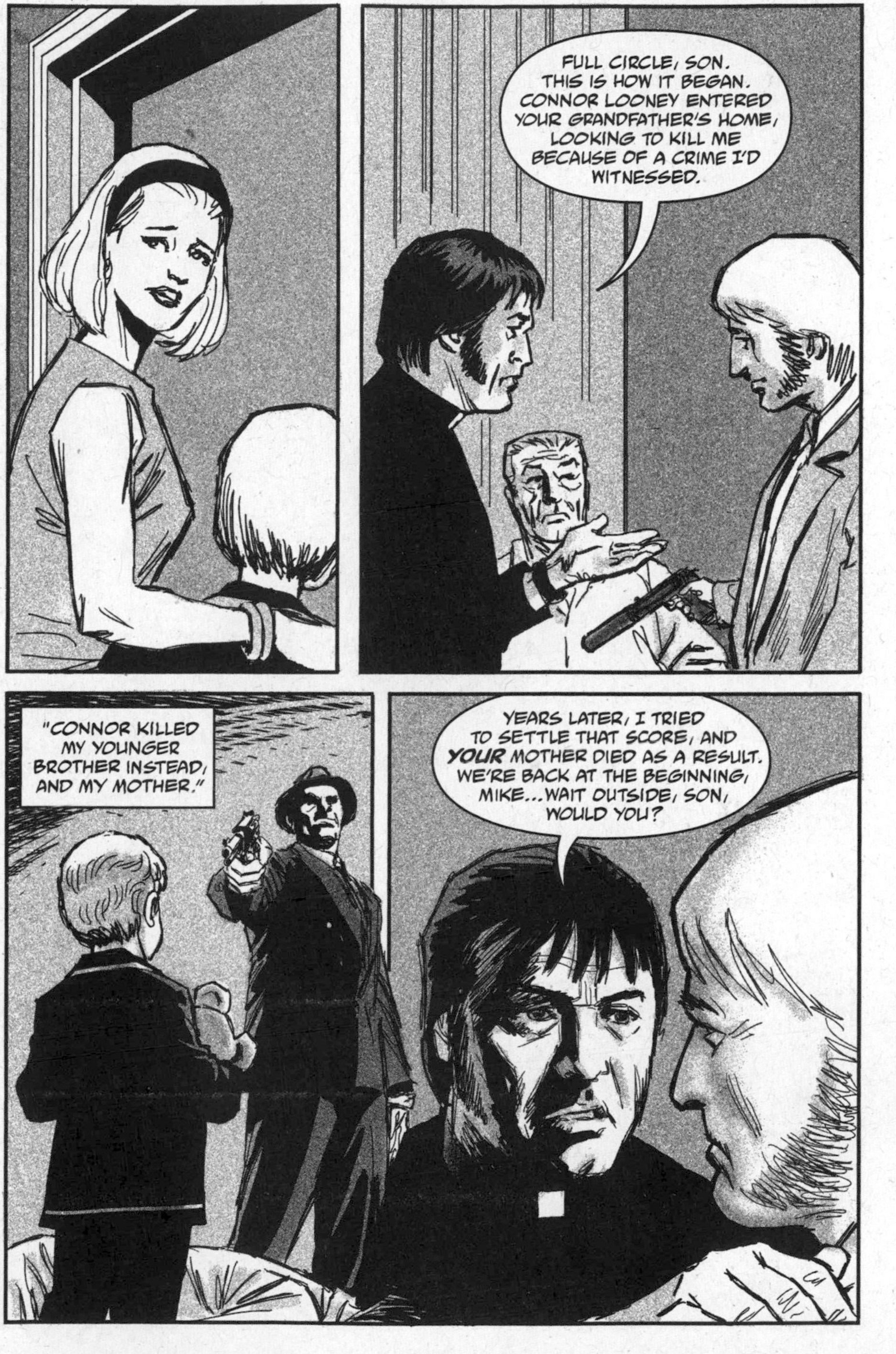
FULL CIRCLE, SON. THIS IS HOW IT BEGAN. CONNOR LOONEY ENTERED YOUR GRANDFATHER'S HOME, LOOKING TO KILL ME BECAUSE OF A CRIME I'D WITNESSED.
"CONNOR KILLED MY YOUNGER BROTHER INSTEAD, AND MY MOTHER."
YEARS LATER, I TRIED TO SETTLE THAT SCORE, AND *YOUR* MOTHER DIED AS A RESULT. WE'RE BACK AT THE BEGINNING, MIKE...WAIT OUTSIDE, SON, WOULD YOU?

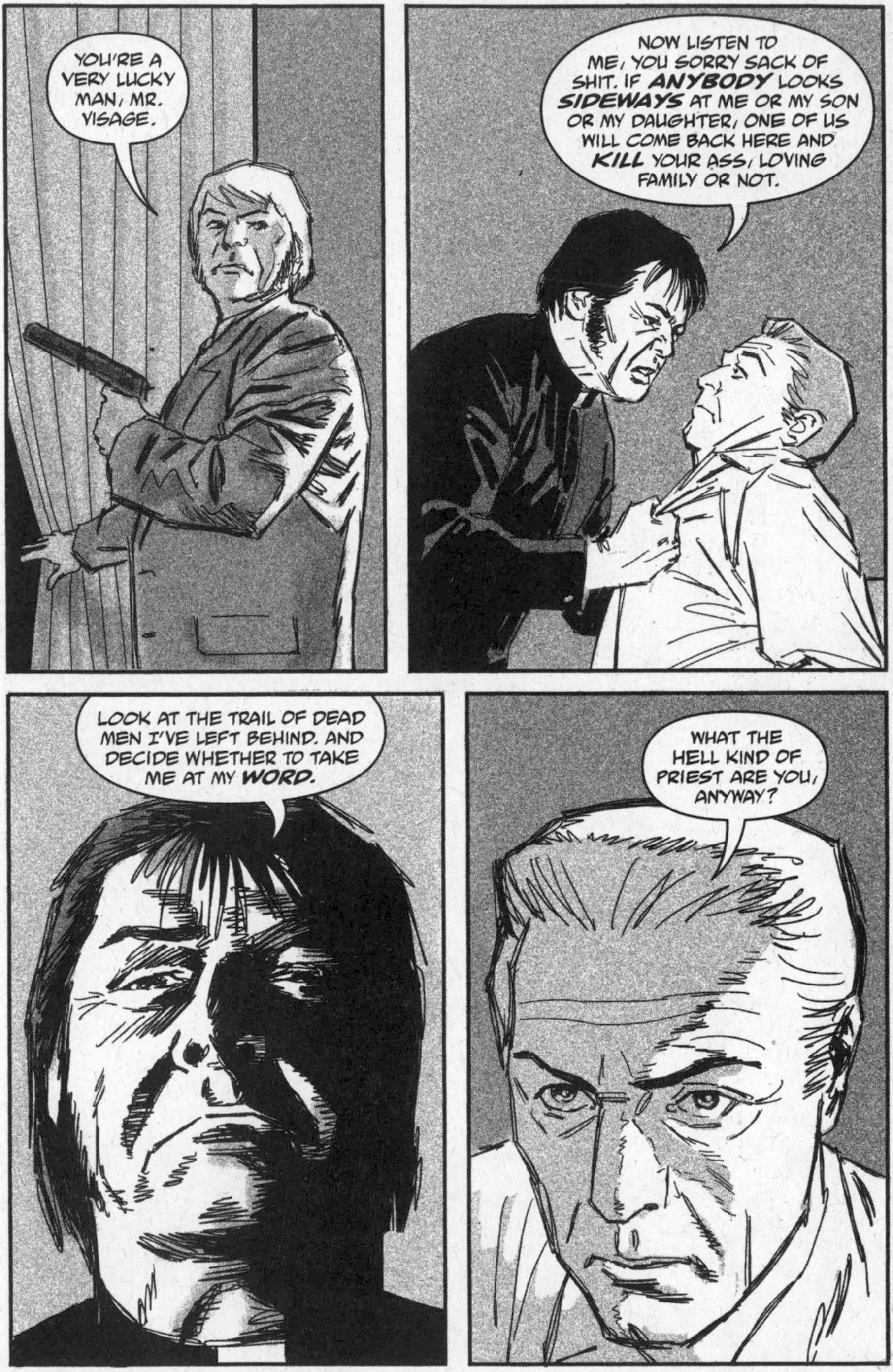
YOU'RE A VERY LUCKY MAN, MR. VISAGE.
NOW LISTEN TO ME, YOU SORRY SACK OF SHIT. IF ANYBODY LOOKS SIDEWAYS AT ME OR MY SON OR MY DAUGHTER, ONE OF US WILL COME BACK HERE AND KILL YOUR ASS, LOVING FAMILY OR NOT.
LOOK AT THE TRAIL OF DEAD MEN I'VE LEFT BEHIND. AND DECIDE WHETHER TO TAKE ME AT MY WORD.
WHAT THE HELL KIND OF PRIEST ARE YOU, ANYWAY?

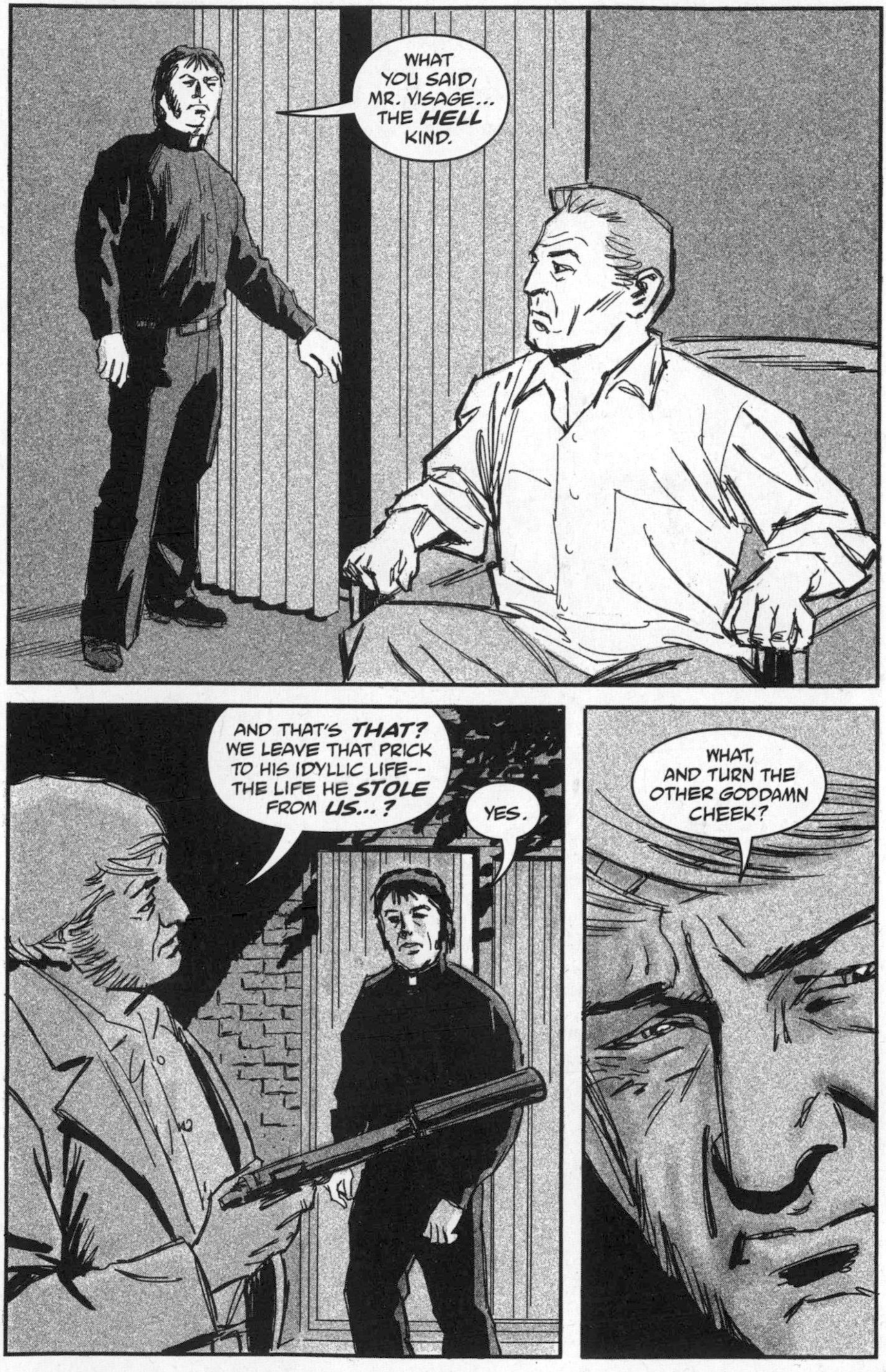
WHAT YOU SAID, MR. VISAGE... THE HELL KIND.
AND THAT'S THAT? WE LEAVE THAT PRICK TO HIS IDYLLIC LIFE-- THE LIFE HE STOLE FROM US...?
YES.
WHAT, AND TURN THE OTHER GODDAMN CHEEK?

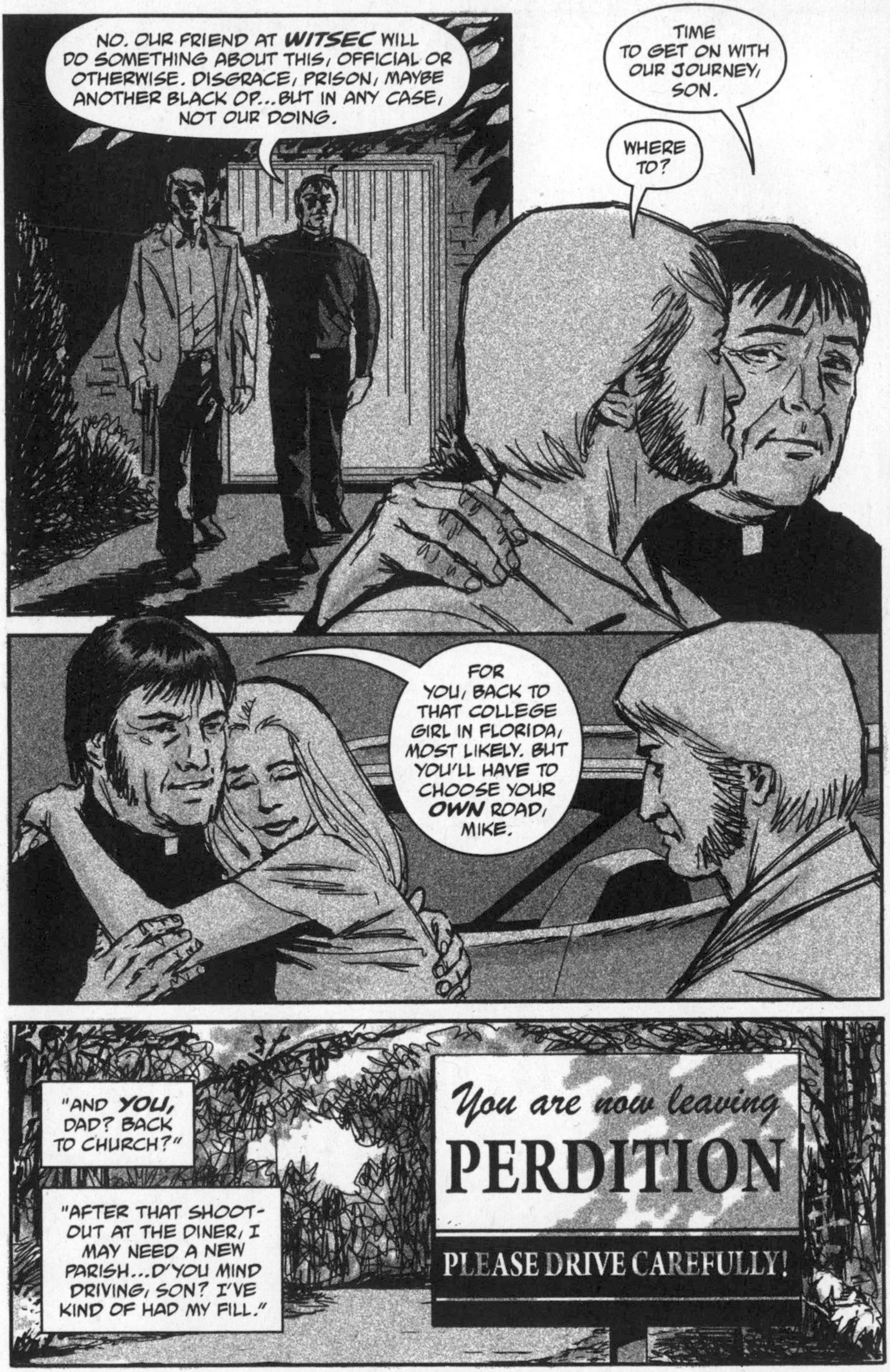
NO. OUR FRIEND AT WITSEC WILL DO SOMETHING ABOUT THIS, OFFICIAL OR OTHERWISE. DISGRACE, PRISON, MAYBE ANOTHER BLACK OP...BUT IN ANY CASE, NOT OUR DOING.
TIME TO GET ON WITH OUR JOURNEY, SON.
WHERE TO?
FOR YOU, BACK TO THAT COLLEGE GIRL IN FLORIDA, MOST LIKELY. BUT YOU'LL HAVE TO CHOOSE YOUR OWN ROAD, MIKE.
"AND YOU, DAD? BACK TO CHURCH?"
"AFTER THAT SHOOT-OUT AT THE DINER, I MAY NEED A NEW PARISH...D'YOU MIND DRIVING, SON? I'VE KIND OF HAD MY FILL."
You are now leaving
PERDITION
PLEASE DRIVE CAREFULLY!

TIP OF THE FEDORA

This saga began with the graphic novel *Road to Perdition* (1998), so beautifully illustrated by my British brother Richard Piers Rayner, and was continued in another graphic novel, *Road to Perdition 2: On the Road* (2004), drawn by José García-López, Steve Leiber and Josef Rubinstein, who so effectively took on the unenviable task of filling Richard's huge shoes.

Return to Perdition, however, is a more direct coda to my prose *Perdition* sequels, *Road to Purgatory* (2004) and *Road to Paradise* (2005). I hope one day to create graphic novels of these works as well. And while *Return to Perdition* is the end of the road, I am considering a prequel or two; so while the journey may be over, side trips remain a possibility.

While this story is a work of fiction, the historical underpinnings are real. Many nonfiction works were consulted, but I wish in particular to acknowledge *All American Mafioso: The Johnny Rosselli Story* (1991) by Charles Rappleye and Ed Becker. Although the basic depiction of Rosselli's latter days is accurate, the character of his niece, Angie, is wholly fictional.

As usual, George Hagenauer – my longtime research associate on the Nathan Heller novels – provided input, and my wife, writer Barbara Collins, provided encouragement and editorial aid. Thanks also to agent Ken Levin.

I am grateful to my longtime collaborator, Terry Beatty, for joining the distinguished list of *Perdition* artists. A big "thank you" goes to editor Will Dennis, with whom it was a genuine pleasure to work; and grateful bows to Andy Helfer, the editor who made the original graphic novel happen, and Paul Levitz, who – after the Paradox Graphic Mystery line had been shut down – decided to publish *Perdition* anyway. That was a bullet the creator of all the Michael O'Sullivans was glad to duck.

M.A.C.
November 2010

For my children, Elizabeth and Kirby, who make my road worth traveling.

— **Terry Beatty**

DON'T MISS THESE OTHER VERTIGO CRIME BOOKS

NOCHE ROJA
SIMON OLIVER
JASON LATOUR
— CHRISTOS GAGE
VERTIGO CRIME

NOCHE ROJA

Written by **SIMON OLIVER**
Art by **JASON LATOUR**

At the border, life is cheap. But death costs nothing at all.

"Deftly merges noir with a torn-from-the-headlines story. Noir is timeless, and this book proves it!"
– **Christos Gage** (AREA 10)

RAT CATCHER

Written by **ANDY DIGGLE** (THE LOSERS)
Art by **VICTOR IBAÑEZ**

A washed-up FBI agent on a desperate hunt for a notorious mob hit man finds out the hard way that he's the assassin's latest target!

"Compelling graphic storytelling, full of twists, turns and vivid characters."
– **Dave Gibbons** (WATCHMEN)

ANDY DIGGLE
ART BY VICTOR IBAÑEZ
RAT CATCHER
VERTIGO CRIME

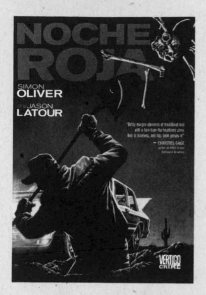

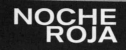

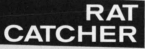

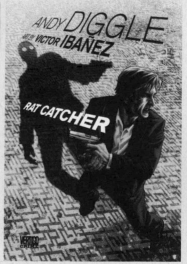

MORE FROM VERTIGO CRIME

AVAILABLE NOW

THE CHILL
Written by JASON STARR
(Best-selling author of *Panic Attack* and *The Follower*)

Art by MICK BERTILORENZI

A modern thriller steeped in Celtic mythology — a broken-down cop tracks a seductive killer who possesses the supernatural power known as "the chill." Can he stop her before her next victim dies horribly... but with a smile on his face?

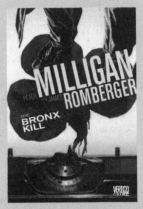

THE BRONX KILL
Written by PETER MILLIGAN
(GREEK STREET)

Art by JAMES ROMBERGER

A struggling writer is investigating his Irish cop roots for his next novel. When he returns home from a research trip, his wife is missing and finding her will lead him to a dark secret buried deep in his family's past.

AREA 10
Written by CHRISTOS N. GAGE
(*Law & Order: SVU*)

Art by CHRIS SAMNEE

When a detective — tracking a serial killer who decapitates his victims — receives a bizarre head injury himself, he suspects a connection between his own fate and the killer's fascination with Trepanation — the ancient art of skull drilling.

A HISTORY OF VIOLENCE

Written by **JOHN WAGNER**
Art by **VINCE LOCKE**

A new edition of the hard-hitting graphic novel that inspired the
Academy Award-nominated 2005 motion picture.

ROAD TO PERDITION

Written by **MAX ALLAN COLLINS**
Art by **RICHARD PIERS RAYNER**

The basis for the major motion picture,
ROAD TO PERDITION is an enthralling crime noir
about revenge, morality and family loyalty.

ROAD TO PERDITION
VOL. 2: ON THE ROAD

Written by **MAX ALLAN COLLINS**

Art by **JOSÉ LUIS GARCÍA-LÓPEZ,
STEVE LIEBER AND JOSEF RUBINSTEIN**

A collection of three crime stories set between
the pages of the original ROAD TO PERDITION.